# PRISONS AND JAILS

## A DETERRENT TO CRIME?

ISSN 1536-5190

2

# PRISONS AND JAILS
## A DETERRENT TO CRIME?

Thomas Wiloch

**INFORMATION PLUS® REFERENCE SERIES**
Formerly Published by Information Plus, Wylie, Texas

THOMSON
GALE

Detroit • New York • San Francisco • San Diego • New Haven, Conn. • Waterville, Maine • London • Munich

# THOMSON
™
## GALE

**Prisons and Jails: A Deterrent to Crime?**
Thomas Wiloch
Paula Kepos, Series Editor

**Project Editor**
John McCoy

**Permissions**
Margaret Abendroth, Edna Hedblad,
Emma Hull

**Composition and Electronic Prepress**
Evi Seoud

**Manufacturing**
Drew Kalasky

ISBN 0-7876-5103-6 (set)
ISBN 1-4144-0424-7
ISSN 1536-5190

This title is also available as an e-book.
ISBN 1-4144-0477-8 (set)
Contact your Thomson Gale sales representative for ordering information.

Printed in the United States of America
10 9 8 7 6 5 4 3 2 1

# TABLE OF CONTENTS

Prisoners do not surrender all their constitutional rights and are entitled to challenge the conditions of their imprisonment if they believe their rights have been wrongfully denied. This chapter describes key court decisions pertaining to prisoners' rights and discusses the challenges of preventing frivolous lawsuits while still ensuring that prisoners are not mistreated.

# PREFACE

*Prisons and Jails: A Deterrent to Crime?* is part of the *Information Plus Reference Series*. The purpose of each volume of the series is to present the latest facts on a topic of pressing concern in modern American life. These topics include today's most controversial and most studied social issues: abortion, capital punishment, care for the elderly, crime, the environment, health care, immigration, minorities, national security, social welfare, women, youth, and many more. Although written especially for the high school and undergraduate student, this series is an excellent resource for anyone in need of factual information on current affairs.

By presenting the facts, it is Thomson Gale's intention to provide its readers with everything they need to reach an informed opinion on current issues. To that end, there is a particular emphasis in this series on the presentation of scientific studies, surveys, and statistics. These data are generally presented in the form of tables, charts, and other graphics placed within the text of each book. Every graphic is directly referred to and carefully explained in the text. The source of each graphic is presented within the graphic itself. The data used in these graphics are drawn from the most reputable and reliable sources, in particular from the various branches of the U.S. government and from major independent polling organizations. Every effort has been made to secure the most recent information available. The reader should bear in mind that many major studies take years to conduct, and that additional years often pass before the data from these studies is made available to the public. Therefore, in many cases the most recent information available in 2005 is dated from 2002 or 2003. Older statistics are sometimes presented as well if they are of particular interest and no more recent information exists.

Although statistics are a major focus of the *Information Plus Reference Series*, they are by no means its only content. Each book also presents the widely held positions and important ideas that shape how the book's subject is discussed in the United States. These positions are explained in detail and, where possible, in the words of their proponents. Some of the other material to be found in these books includes: historical background; descriptions of major events related to the subject; relevant laws and court cases; and examples of how these issues play out in American life. Some books also feature primary documents or have pro and con debate sections giving the words and opinions of prominent Americans on both sides of a controversial topic. All material is presented in an even-handed and unbiased manner; the reader will never be encouraged to accept one view of an issue over another.

## HOW TO USE THIS BOOK

The U.S. penal system—it's prisons and jails—is an important and controversial part of the effort to control crime in the United States. Much public funding is spent on the construction of new prisons and jails and the maintenance of old ones, but many people question the effectiveness of prisons and jails as a deterrent to crime. Is the purpose of institutions such as prisons and jails to rehabilitate criminals or to punish them? Are certain races or ethnicities more prevalent in the prison population than others? Does juvenile incarceration work? What should day-to-day life be like for those in prisons and jails? What rights do prisoners give up and what rights do they retain? These and other basic questions are discussed in this volume.

*Prisons and Jails: A Deterrent to Crime?* consists of eleven chapters and three appendices. Each of the chapters is devoted to a particular aspect of prisons and jails in the United States. For a summary of the information covered in each chapter, please see the synopses provided in the Table of Contents at the front of the book. Chapters generally begin with an overview of the basic facts and background information on the chapter's topic, then proceed to examine subtopics of particular interest. For example, Chapter 7, Juvenile Confinement, begins with a discussion of exactly how America defines a "juvenile" as that term relates to criminals. It then examines changing approaches to juvenile delinquency, trends in juvenile arrests and disposition (including racial and gender differences), juveniles held in jails and prisons, and juveniles in residential placement facilities and boot camps. The chapter concludes with an examination of juveniles and the death penalty. Readers can find their way through a chapter by looking for the section and subsection headings, which are clearly set off from the text. They can also refer to the book's extensive index if they already know what they are looking for.

### Statistical Information

The tables and figures featured throughout *Prisons and Jails: A Deterrent to Crime?* will be of particular use to the reader in learning about this issue. These tables and figures represent an extensive collection of the most recent and important statistics on prisons and jails and related issues—for example, graphics in this book cover the number of people in jail or prison in the United States, characteristics of those incarcerated, and the amount of money spent on the prison system. Thomson Gale believes that making this information available to the reader is the most important way in which we fulfill the goal of this book: to help readers to understand the issues and controversies surrounding prisons and jails in the United States and to reach their own conclusions.

Each table or figure has a unique identifier appearing above it for ease of identification and reference. Titles for the tables and figures explain their purpose. At the end of each table or figure, the original source of the data is provided.

In order to help readers understand these often complicated statistics, all tables and figures are explained in the text. References in the text direct the reader to the relevant statistics. Furthermore, the contents of all tables and figures are fully indexed. Please see the opening section of the index at the back of this volume for a description of how to find tables and figures within it.

### Appendices

In addition to the main body text and images, *Prisons and Jails: A Deterrent to Crime?* has three appendices. The first is the Important Names and Addresses directory. Here the reader will find contact information for a number of government and private organizations that can provide further information on the American prison and jail system. The second appendix is the Resources section, which can also assist the reader in conducting his or her own research. In this section, the author and editors of *Prisons and Jails: A Deterrent to Crime?* describe some of the sources that were most useful during the compilation of this book. The final appendix is the detailed Index, which facilitates reader access to specific topics in this book.

### ADVISORY BOARD CONTRIBUTIONS

The staff of Information Plus would like to extend their heartfelt appreciation to the Information Plus Advisory Board. This dedicated group of media professionals provides feedback on the series on an ongoing basis. Their comments allow the editorial staff who work on the project to make the series better and more user-friendly. Our top priorities are to produce the highest-quality and most useful books possible, and the Advisory Board's contributions to this process are invaluable.

The members of the Information Plus Advisory Board are:

- Kathleen R. Bonn, Librarian, Newbury Park High School, Newbury Park, California
- Madelyn Garner, Librarian, San Jacinto College— North Campus, Houston, Texas
- Anne Oxenrider, Media Specialist, Dundee High School, Dundee, Michigan
- Charles R. Rodgers, Director of Libraries, Pasco-Hernando Community College, Dade City, Florida
- James N. Zitzelsberger, Library Media Department Chairman, Oshkosh West High School, Oshkosh, Wisconsin

### COMMENTS AND SUGGESTIONS

The editors of the *Information Plus Reference Series* welcome your feedback on *Prisons and Jails: A Deterrent to Crime?* Please direct all correspondence to:

Editors
*Information Plus Reference Series*
27500 Drake Rd.
Farmington Hills, MI 48331-3535

# CHAPTER 1
# HISTORY OF CORRECTIONS—PUNISHMENT, PREVENTION, OR REHABILITATION?

*A terrible stinking dark and dismal place situated underground into which no daylight can come. It was paved with stone; the prisoners had no beds and lay on the pavement and whereby they endured great misery and hardship.*

— Inmate at Newgate Prison, London (1724)

Public views of punishment for crimes have changed over the centuries. History has its clement and its stormy seasons, and during times of war, famine, and disorder, gains made in peace and plenty are sometimes lost. Yet generally over time most societies have moved from the extraction of personal or family justice—vengeful acts such as blood feuds or the practice of "an eye for an eye"—toward formal systems based on written codes and orderly process. Jails and prisons have changed from being holding places where prisoners awaited deportation, maiming, whippings, beatings, or execution. Confinement itself has become the punishment. In the United States today, as articulated by the U.S. Supreme Court, punishment has at least four justifications: deterrence, societal retribution, rehabilitation, and incapacitation—the last category intended to protect society by permanently incarcerating those who cannot be reformed.

## ANCIENT TIMES

Many ancient cultures allowed the victim or a member of the victim's family to deliver justice. The offender often fled to his or her family for protection. As a result, blood feuds developed in which the victim's family sought revenge against the offender's family. Sometimes the offender's family responded by striking back. Retaliation could continue until the families tired of killing or stealing from each other or until one or both families were destroyed or financially ruined.

As societies organized into tribes and villages, local communities increasingly began to assume the responsibility for punishing crimes against the community and its members. Punishments could be brutal—the condemned boiled in oil or fed to wild beasts. The development of writing led to the creation of lists of crimes and their respective punishments. The Code of Hammurabi in Babylon (circa 1750 B.C.E.) is generally considered the first such set of laws. The laws of Moses, as recorded in the Bible, also cited offenses against the community and their corresponding punishments. The Justinian Code of Emperor Justinian of the Byzantine or Eastern Roman Empire (529–565) organized many of the early codes.

As empires developed, the owners of large tracts of land, and later the rulers, wanted a more orderly legal system than blood feuds and thus established courts. Such courts often sentenced the offender to slavery in the victim's family for several years as restitution for the offense. Other punishments included laboring on public works projects, banishment, or even death.

## MEDIEVAL TIMES

As in ancient times, medieval Europe had very harsh punishments. Torture and death were commonly administered. From the depths of the "Dark Ages" came cruel instruments that tortured as they killed. For example, the rack stretched its victims until their bodies were torn apart. The Iron Maiden—a box thickly set with sharp spikes inside and on the inner side of its door—pierced its victims from front and back as it closed. People came to watch public executions to see the convicts burn, be hanged, or be beheaded.

### Confinement

Those arrested were usually confined (imprisoned) until they confessed to the crime and their physical punishment occurred. The medieval church sometimes used long-term incarceration to replace executions. Some wealthy landowners built private prisons to enhance their own power, imprisoning those who dared dispute their pursuit of power or oppose their whims. With the enactment of King Henry II's set of ordinances, called the Assize of Clarendon (England, 1166), many crimes were classified as offenses against the "king's peace" and were punished by the state and not by the church, the lord, or the victim's extended family. At this time the first prisons designed solely for incarceration were constructed.

### Prisons

The only comfort prisoners had in the cold, damp, filthy, rat- and roach-infested prisons of medieval Europe was what they could—or rather were required to—buy. The prison-keeper charged for blankets, mattresses, food, and even the manacles (chains). The prisoner had to pay for the privilege of being both booked (charged) and released. Wealthy prisoners could pay for plush quarters but most suffered in terrible conditions, often dying from malnutrition, disease, or victimization by other prisoners.

## THE RISE OF NATIONS

In Europe in the 1500s, while most jails still housed people waiting for trial or punishment, workhouses and debtors' prisons developed as sources of cheap labor or places to house insane or minor offenders. Those found guilty of serious crimes could be transported instead of executed. England transported many prisoners to colonial Georgia in the United States and later to colonial Australia; France sent many to South America. Although transportation was a less severe punishment than the death penalty, many prisoners did not survive the harsh conditions either on board the transport ships or life in the early colonies to which they were sent.

## COLONIAL AND EARLY POST-REVOLUTIONARY PERIODS

Just as in Europe, physical punishment was common in colonial America. Americans used stocks, pillories, branding, flogging, and maiming—such as cutting off an ear or slitting nostrils—to punish offenders. The death penalty was used frequently. In 1636 the Massachusetts Bay Colony listed thirteen crimes that warranted execution, including murder, practicing witchcraft, and worshipping idols. In early New York State, 20% of offenses, including pickpocketing, horse stealing, and robbery, were capital crimes (warranting the death penalty).

Jails were used to hold prisoners awaiting trial or sentencing or as debtors' prisons, but were not the punishment itself. The Puritans of Massachusetts believed that humans were naturally depraved, which made it easier for some of the colonies and the first states to enforce harsh punishments. In addition, since Puritans believed that humans had no control over their fate

(predestination), many early Americans felt there was no need for rehabilitation.

### Pennsylvania

The Quakers, led by William Penn, made colonial Pennsylvania an exception to the harsh practices often found in the other colonies. The early criminal code of colonial Pennsylvania abolished executions for all crimes except homicide, replaced physical punishments with imprisonment and hard labor, and did not charge the prisoners for their food and housing.

### Ideas of the Enlightenment

The philosophy of the Enlightenment (the Age of Reason) emphasized the importance of the individual. After the French Revolution of 1789, which was based on the ideas of the Enlightenment, western European countries abolished torture as a form of punishment and emphasized that the punishment should fit the individual's crime(s). Rather than inflicting pain as the main element of correction, the idea of changing the individual became the goal. The French Revolution, however, also introduced the guillotine, a sophisticated beheading machine.

In England, John Howard (1726–90) wrote *The State of the Prisons in England and Wales* (1777), in which he described the horrible treatment of prisoners. Howard thought that prisoners should not be harassed by keepers who extorted from them, nor should they have to suffer malnutrition and disease. He advocated segregating prisoners by age, sex, and type of crime; paying the staff; hiring medical officials and chaplains; and supplying prisoners with adequate food and clothing.

Howard called the facilities "penitentiaries" (from the word "penitent," meaning to be ashamed or sorry for committing a sin or offense) because he based his ideas on the Quakers' philosophy of people repenting, reflecting on their sins, and changing their ways. Public concern led the British Parliament to pass the Penitentiary Act of 1779; it called for the first secure and sanitary penitentiary. The law eliminated the charging of fees. Prisoners would live in solitary confinement at night and work together silently during the day. Nonetheless, although Parliament passed the law, it did not actually go into effect until the opening of Pentonville Penitentiary in North London in 1842.

## THE REFORM MOVEMENT

The idea of individual freedom and the concept that people could change society for the better by using reason permeated American society in the 1800s. Reformers worked to abolish slavery, secure women's rights, and prohibit liquor, as well as to change the corrections system.

## Pennsylvania System

In 1787 in Pennsylvania, a group campaigning for more humane treatment of prisoners established the Philadelphia Society for Alleviating the Miseries of Public Prisons. Led by Dr. Benjamin Rush, this organization, which included many Quakers, campaigned for the imprisonment of criminals rather than physical and capital punishment. The Quakers thought solitary confinement could reform criminals. In such cells the offenders could think over their wrongful ways, repent, and reform. In 1790 Pennsylvania established the Walnut Street Jail in Philadelphia for "hardened and atrocious offenders."

The association continued pressuring the legislature for more prisons. Eventually, in 1829, the state built the Western Penitentiary outside Pittsburgh and the Eastern Penitentiary near Philadelphia. The cells (12 by 8 by 10 feet in dimension) with individual exercise yards isolated inmates so they could work, read their Bibles, and contemplate in order to be rehabilitated. The only voice the inmates heard was that of the chaplain on Sunday.

The reformers thought solitary confinement not only allowed the offenders to repent but also served as a punishing experience since humans are social by nature. In addition, the system would be economical since, under these conditions, prisoners would not take long to see the error of their ways and fewer guards would be needed. However, many prisoners found the total isolation very difficult to endure, and the jails quickly became overcrowded warehouses for prisoners.

### Auburn System

The Auburn System (New York, 1819) used the Quaker idea of solitary confinement at night but used a system of congregating inmates in a common workroom during the day. The prisoners could neither talk nor look at one another. Any violation of the rules was met with immediate and strict discipline. Each supervisor had the right to flog an inmate who violated the rules.

Reformers perceived the system as economical because a single guard could watch a group of prisoners at work. The work of the inmates would help pay for their upkeep; they would learn about the benefits of work and have time to meditate and repent. Both the Pennsylvania and Auburn systems dictated that offenders should be isolated and have a disciplined routine. European countries tended to adopt the Pennsylvania system while most American states chose the Auburn system. While these methods made it easier to run a prison, they did little to rehabilitate prisoners.

After the American Civil War (1861–65) huge industrial prisons were built to house thousands of prisoners in the Northeast, Midwest, and California. The western states used their old territorial jails while the South relied on leasing out prisoners for farm labor.

## The Cincinnati Declaration

Because many prison administrators were corrupt, convicts were mistreated and used as cheap labor. However, a growing number of prison reformers were beginning to believe that the prison system should be more committed to reform. In 1870 the newly established National Prison Association (which later became the American Correctional Association) met in Cincinnati, Ohio, and issued a Declaration of Principles. The philosophy of the Auburn system (fixed sentences, silence, isolation, harsh punishment, lockstep work) was considered degrading and destructive to the human spirit. The values in the Declaration of Principles included the following:

- The penal system should be based on reformation, not suffering, and prisoners should be educated to be free, industrious citizens able to function in society, not orderly inmates controlled by the guards.

- Good conduct should be rewarded.

- Indeterminate sentencing (not a mandated exact sentence) should include the ability for prisoners to earn their freedom early through hard work and good behavior.

- Citizens should understand that society is responsible for the conditions that lead to crime.

- Prisoners should recognize that they can change their lives.

## ELMIRA REFORMATORY

The superintendent of the Elmira Reformatory in New York, Zebulon Brockway (1827–1920), used some of these ideas when New York opened the reformatory in 1876 for male offenders sixteen to thirty years old. Brockway believed that rehabilitation could be achieved through education.

Inmates who did well in both academic and moral subjects earned early release by accumulating points. Misbehavior and poor performance in the educational courses prolonged the individual's sentence. Brockway used this technique because the New York legislature had passed a law allowing indeterminate sentencing and the release of inmates on parole when they showed they had been reformed. Brockway recognized that it was difficult to distinguish between those inmates who had truly reformed and those who were pretending to be rehabilitated in order to be paroled.

## PRISON REFORM IN THE EARLY TWENTIETH CENTURY

By 1900 Brockway's correctional philosophy had spread throughout the nation. Nonetheless, by World War I (1914–18), the idea of using educational and rehabilitative approaches was being replaced by the use of strict discipline. The way the facilities were built, the lack of trained personnel, and the attitudes of the guards made Brockway's ideas difficult to implement. In addition, the introduction of a probation system kept the offenders easiest to rehabilitate out of the reformatories.

Despite this return to discipline, the reform movement survived. The progressives of the early twentieth century believed that if prisons applied the ideas of behavioral science to the inmates, prisoners could be rehabilitated. The progressives worked to change the social environment from which criminals came and to design ways to rehabilitate individual inmates. By the 1920s reformers were strongly advocating indeterminate sentencing, parole, and treatment programs as a way to rehabilitate offenders, but this approach to corrections was not put into practice until decades later.

While many of the reforms had merit, most could not be properly implemented due to inadequate funding or the unwillingness of prison officials to act. As each reform apparently failed to solve the problem of crime, many people became disillusioned.

## PRISONS AS WORKPLACES

Despite the efforts of reformers, most societies prefer that prisons pay their own way. To do this, prison administrators have at times constructed factories within prison walls or hired inmates out as laborers in "chain gangs." In rural areas inmates worked on prison-owned farms. In the South prisoners—predominantly African-American—were often leased out to local farmers. Prison superintendents justified the hard labor as teaching the offenders the value of work and self-discipline. Many free citizens, after all, earned their livings doing such work in factories and fields. Some penologists (those who study prison management) believe that the harshness of the prisons made these inmates more vindictive against society.

With the rise of labor unions in the North, the 1930s saw an end to the large-scale prison industry. Unions complained about competing with the inmates' free labor, especially amid the rising unemployment of the Great Depression. By 1940 the states had limited what inmates could produce. By 1970 the number of prison farms had decreased substantially because they were expensive to operate and the prisons found it cheaper to purchase food. In addition, agricultural work no longer prepared inmates for employment outside prison. Since the 1970s, however, support for prison factories as a way to train inmates for outside jobs has grown. Penologists believe that working in prison factories helps keep prisoners from being bored and idle and teaches them skills. While they believe prisoners benefit from work, they also assert that prisoners should not suffer the exploitation that characterized the factories of the 1920s.

## REHABILITATION MODEL

The rehabilitation model of corrections began in the 1930s and reached its high point in the 1950s. Qualified staff members were expected to diagnose the cause of an offender's criminal behavior, prescribe a treatment to change the individual, and determine when that individual had become rehabilitated. Group therapy, counseling, and behavior modification were all part of the approach. These techniques did not work with all inmates, especially with those convicted of violent crimes; most states did not budget enough money for their correctional institutions to achieve these goals; and there were too many prisoners for the prison staff to treat effectively.

## COMMUNITY CORRECTIONS

In response to an increase in crime during the 1960s, advocates of community corrections thought that rehabilitation needed to be done within the community, not in the prisons. They favored probation, educational courses, and job training. In 1965 the Commission on Law Enforcement and Administration of Justice, a panel of experts on crime and the justice system, recommended improvements to the correctional system and initiated the first standards for operating prison facilities. The task force recommended alternative community-based approaches, educational and vocational programs, and different treatments for special offender categories. As a result, the American Correctional Association's Commission of Accreditation established standards by which it assesses correctional facilities for voluntary accreditation.

## JUSTICE MODEL

As crime increased in the late 1980s, and the community corrections model seemed unsuccessful, the pendulum once again swung the other way. Pressure began mounting against rehabilitation, indeterminate sentencing, probation, parole, and treatment programs. Some penologists advocated putting criminals behind bars for a determinate amount of time, noting that offenders should be kept off the streets so that they cannot commit more crimes. As a result, the federal government and a growing number of states introduced mandatory sentencing and life terms for habitual criminals (often called "three strikes" laws after a baseball analogy, meaning that after three convictions "you're out"). They also limited the use of probation, parole, and time off for good behavior.

As Michael Tonry and Joan Petersilia pointed out in their study *Prisons Research at the Beginning of the 21st Century* (Washington, DC: National Institute of Justice, 1999), "The rapid increase in the 1990s in the numbers of people confined in prisons and jails coincided with falling crime rates." However, experts differed as to why this decrease in crime occurred. Some reasoned that imprisoning more criminals naturally led to less crime in society, while others believed that new policing strategies and tactics—such as community policing and zero-tolerance—reduced crime.

The rising number of offenders on parole and in prisons and jails has taxed the system. Facilities have become overcrowded and states have had problems securing sufficiently large budgets to build new prisons and jails or to supply the needed treatment and educational programs.

Meanwhile, state and federal courts have put caps on how many prisoners each facility can hold and have told states that certain basic services are required. With determinate sentencing often eliminating parole, prisons have turned to a system called gain-time to prevent overcrowding and maintain control. Gain-time, or good time, allows prison officials to deduct a specified number of days from an offender's sentence for every month served without the inmate breaking any rules.

## REHABILITTION OR PUNISHMENT—PUBLIC GOALS AND RECIDIVISM

According to a 1996 survey conducted by the College of Criminal Justice (CCJ) of Sam Houston State University in Texas, about half of the public sees the goal of prisons as rehabilitation (48.4%). A minority (14.6%) sees the goal as punishment, while the remaining third (33.1%) holds the opinion that prisons should prevent and deter crime.

Recidivism rates are an indirect indicator of the correctional system's performance in achieving the public goal of rehabilitation. The recidivism rate measures the relapse of a person into criminal behavior after incarceration. Unfortunately, no approach to prison reform has had much effect on the recidivism rate among released prisoners. Table 1.1 presents the recidivism rates for state prisoners released for the years 1983 and 1994 as published by Patrick A. Langan and David J. Levin in *Recidivism of Prisoners Released in 1994* (Washington, DC: Bureau of Justice Statistics, June 2002). Because of the long-term nature of a recidivism study—time must pass between a prisoner's release and rearrest—statistics on recidivism often lag several years behind other criminal justice statistics.

This sample, based on 108,580 state prisoners released in 1983 and 272,111 prisoners released in 1994, shows that nearly two-thirds of prisoners (62.5%) released in 1983 were arrested again within three years. Among those released in 1994, more than two-thirds (67.5%) were rearrested. The rearrest rate thus increased during the period studied. The highest recidivism rate was for property offenses for those released in 1994—73.8%, up from 68.1% for those released in 1983. The lowest rate was for violent offenses, 61.7% in 1994, up from 59.6% in 1983. Drug rearrests experienced the largest percentage growth, climbing from 50.4% in 1983 to 66.7% in 1994 for a change of 16.3%. In contrast, rearrests for violence grew 2.1% during that same timeframe.

*Recidivism Report: Inmates Released from Florida Prisons July 1995 to June 2001* (Tallahassee, FL: Florida Department of Corrections, Bureau of Research and Data Analysis, July 2003) provides more recent statistics on prisoners released in that state. This report shows that recidivism rates rise with the length of time a prisoner has been released. In the first six months following release, only 12.5% of male prisoners and 8.4% of female prisoners had committed a new offense, but by sixty months (five years) following release, those who had committed a new offense had risen to 48.7% for males and 42.8% for females. (See Table 1.2.)

A November 2003 study by Patrick A. Langan, Erica L. Schmitt, and Matthew R. Durose of the Bureau of Justice Statistics analyzed the recidivism

**TABLE 1.1**

**Recidivism rates of state prisoners released in 1983 and 1994**

| Most serious offense for which released | Percent of prisoners released in — | | Percent rearrested within 3 years, among prisoners released in — | | Percent reconvicted within 3 years, among prisoners released in — | |
|---|---|---|---|---|---|---|
| | 1983 | 1994 | 1983 | 1994 | 1983 | 1994 |
| All released prisoners | 100% | 100% | 62.5% | 67.5% | 46.8% | 46.9% |
| Violent | 34.6 | 22.5 | 59.6 | 61.7 | 41.9 | 39.9 |
| Property | 48.3 | 33.5 | 68.1 | 73.8 | 53.0 | 53.4 |
| Drug | 9.5 | 32.6 | 50.4 | 66.7 | 35.3 | 47.0 |
| Public-order | 6.4 | 9.7 | 54.6 | 62.2 | 41.5 | 42.0 |
| Other | 1.1 | 1.7 | 76.8 | 64.7 | 62.9 | 42.1 |
| Number of released prisoners | 108,580 | 272,111 | | | | |

SOURCE: Patrick A. Langan and David J. Levin, "Recidivism Rates by Offense Type and Year of Release," in *Recidivism of Prisoners Released in 1994*, Bureau of Justice Statistics, June 2002, http://www.ojp.usdoj.gov/bjs/pub/pdf/rpr94.pdf (accessed March 30, 2005)

rate specifically for sex offenders released from state prisons. *Recidivism of Sex Offenders Released from Prison in 1994* tracked 9,691 male sex offenders who had been released from prisons in fifteen states in 1994. Sex offenders include those arrested for rape, statutory rape, sexual assault, and child molestation. The study found that in the first three years following their release from prison, 5.3% of the released sex offenders were rearrested for a sex crime. However, during this same three-year period, a total of 43% of all released sex offenders were rearrested for any type of crime or for violating the terms of their parole. Within three years of their release 38.6% of the sex offenders in the study had been returned to prison following conviction on a new crime or because of a parole violation. Statutory rapists were more likely to be rearrested (49.9%) than child molesters (39.4%). (See Table 1.3 and Table 1.4.)

Recidivism rates for federal prisoners were lower. In a study published in September 2000, *Offenders Returning to Federal Prison, 1986–97*, William J. Sabol and his colleagues at the Bureau of Justice Statistics reported that the recidivism rate during that

**TABLE 1.2**

**Recidivism rates for inmates released from Florida prisons, July 1995–June 2001**

| Follow-up period (months since release) | Reoffense | | Reimprisonment | |
|---|---|---|---|---|
| | Male | Female | Male | Female |
| 6 | 12.5% | 8.4% | 1.3% | 0.6% |
| 12 | 21.5% | 15.2% | 6.4% | 3.0% |
| 18 | 28.2% | 21.1% | 12.5% | 6.3% |
| 24 | 33.2% | 25.7% | 18.0% | 9.1% |
| 36 | 40.5% | 33.3% | 26.7% | 15.5% |
| 48 | 45.4% | 39.1% | 33.2% | 20.2% |
| 60 | 48.7% | 42.8% | 38.1% | 24.6% |

SOURCE: Recidivism Rates, in *Recidivism Report: Inmates Released from Florida Prisons July 1995 to June 2001*, Florida Department of Corrections, July 2003, http://www.dc.state.fl.us/pub/recidivism/2003/exec.html (accessed March 30, 2005)

**TABLE 1.3**

**Recidivism rate of sex offenders released from prison in 1994, by type of recidivism measure, type of sex offender, and time after release**

[Cumulative percent of sex offenders released from prison in 1994]

| Time after 1994 release | All | Rapists | Sexual assaulters |
|---|---|---|---|
| **Rearrested for any type of crime within —** | | | |
| 6 months | 16.0% | 16.3% | 15.8% |
| 1 year | 24.2 | 25.8 | 23.4 |
| 2 years | 35.5 | 38.6 | 34.0 |
| 3 years | 43.0 | 46.0 | 41.5 |
| **Reconvicted for any type of crime within —ᵃ** | | | |
| 6 months | 3.6% | 4.3% | 3.3% |
| 1 year | 8.6 | 10.0 | 8.0 |
| 2 years | 17.2 | 19.9 | 15.9 |
| 3 years | 24.0 | 27.3 | 22.4 |
| **Returned to prison with a new sentence for any type of crime within —ᵇ** | | | |
| 6 months | 1.8% | 1.9% | 1.8% |
| 1 year | 4.0 | 4.1 | 3.9 |
| 2 years | 8.0 | 9.0 | 7.5 |
| 3 years | 11.2 | 12.6 | 10.5 |
| **Total released** | **9,691** | **3,115** | **6,576** |

Note: The 9,691 sex offenders were released in 15 states.
ᵃBecause of missing data, prisoners released in Ohio were excluded from the calculation of percent reconvicted.
ᵇ"New sentence" includes new sentences to state or federal prisons but not to local jails. Because of missing data, prisoners released in Ohio and Virginia were excluded from the calculation of percentage returned to prison with a new sentence.

SOURCE: Patrick A. Langan, Erica L. Schmitt and Matthew R. Durose, "Table 9. Recidivism Rate of Sex Offenders Released from Prison in 1994, by Type of Recidivism Measure, Type of Sex Offender, and Time after Release," in *Recidivism of Sex Offenders Released from Prison in 1994*, Bureau of Justice Statistics, November 2003, http://www.ojp.usdoj.gov/bjs/pub/pdf/rsorp94.pdf (accessed March 30, 2005)

**TABLE 1.4**

**Recidivism rate of child molesters and statutory rapists released from prison in 1994, by type of recidivism measure and time after release**

[Cumulative percent of sex offenders released from prison in 1994]

| Time after 1994 release | Child molesters | Statutory rapists |
|---|---|---|
| **Rearrested for any type of crime within —** | | |
| 6 months | 16.0% | 18.5% |
| 1 year | 22.9 | 29.8 |
| 2 years | 32.9 | 42.4 |
| 3 years | 39.4 | 49.9 |
| **Reconvicted for any type of crime within —ᵃ** | | |
| 6 months | 3.0% | 4.5% |
| 1 year | 7.1 | 13.6 |
| 2 years | 14.5 | 24.4 |
| 3 years | 20.4 | 32.7 |
| **Returned to prison with a new sentence for any type of crime within —ᵇ** | | |
| 6 months | 1.5% | 0.9% |
| 1 year | 3.1 | 4 |
| 2 years | 6.5 | 9.3 |
| 3 years | 9.1 | 13.2 |
| **Total released** | **4,295** | **443** |

Note: The 4,295 child molesters were released in 15 states; the 443 statutory rapists in 11 states. Because of overlapping definitions, all statutory rapists also appear under the column "child molesters."
ᵃBecause of missing data, prisoners released in Ohio were excluded from the calculation of percent reconvicted.
ᵇ"New sentence" includes new sentences to state or federal prisons but not to local jails. Because of missing data, prisoners released in Ohio and Virginia were excluded from the calculation of percentage returned to prison with a new sentence.

SOURCE: Patrick A. Langan, Erica L. Schmitt and Matthew R. Durose, "Table 10. Recidivism Rate of Child Molesters and Statutory Rapists Released from Prison in 1994, by Type of Recidivism Measure and Time after Release," in *Recidivism of Sex Offenders Released from Prison in 1994*, Bureau of Justice Statistics, November 2003, http://www.ojp.usdoj.gov/bjs/pub/pdf/rsorp94.pdf (accessed March 30, 2005)

TABLE 1.5

**Offenders returned to federal prison within 3 years of release, by sentencing policy and offense, 1986–97**

| | All offenders | | Applicable sentencing policy | | | |
|---|---|---|---|---|---|---|
| | | | Old law | | New law | |
| Offense of conviction | Number of first releases | Percent returned | Number of first releases | Percent returned | Number of first releases | Percent returned |
| All offenses* | 215,263 | 15.7% | 111,577 | 13.7% | 103,686 | 17.9% |
| Violent | 13,036 | 32.4 | 9,094 | 32.1 | 3,942 | 33.0 |
| Robbery | 8,880 | 36.3 | 6,646 | 35.8 | 2,234 | 37.9 |
| Other violent | 4,156 | 23.9 | 2,448 | 21.9 | 1,708 | 26.6 |
| Property | 48,428 | 16.6 | 27,451 | 13.6 | 20,977 | 20.6 |
| Fraud | 23,970 | 13.2 | 13,064 | 9.2 | 10,906 | 17.9 |
| Other property | 24,448 | 20.0 | 14,387 | 17.6 | 10,071 | 23.5 |
| Drugs | 72,728 | 13.4 | 40,063 | 11.7 | 32,665 | 15.4 |
| Public-order | 79,202 | 14.7 | 33,744 | 11.4 | 45,458 | 17.2 |
| Weapons | 9,203 | 24.2 | 4,372 | 16.3 | 4,831 | 31.3 |
| Immigration | 49,709 | 14.7 | 17,714 | 12.3 | 31,995 | 16.0 |
| Other public-order | 20,290 | 10.7 | 11,658 | 8.1 | 8,632 | 14.1 |

*Includes offenses with indeterminable offense category.

SOURCE: William J. Sabol, William P. Adams, Barbara Parthasarathy, and Yan Yuan, "Table 2. Offenders Returned to Federal Prison within 3 Years of Release from a U.S. District Court Commitment, by Applicable Sentencing Policy and Offense of Conviction, 1986–97," in *Offenders Returning to Federal Prison, 1986–97*, Bureau of Justice Statistics, 2000, http://www.ojp.usdoj.gov/bjs/pub/pdf/orfp97.pdf (accessed March 30, 2005)

period was 15.7% within three years of release. A total of 215,263 released prisoners were tracked. The highest recidivism rate was for prisoners sentenced originally for robbery, 36.3%. (See Table 1.5.)

## JUVENILES

By the late 1700s children ages seven years or younger were presumed to be incapable of criminal intent, a concept that has carried over to the present time. In the nineteenth century a movement arose based on sixteenth-century European educational reform movements that changed the concept of a child from a "miniature adult" to an individual with less fully developed cognitive capacity. This resulted in children being separated from adult offenders in many U.S. prisons and jails.

By passing the Juvenile Court Act of 1899, the state of Illinois established the first juvenile court, located in Cook County. Using the British doctrine of "parens patriae" (state as parent), this act formalized the right of the state to intervene in the lives of juveniles in a way that was different from the manner in which the state dealt with adults. The focus was placed on the welfare of the delinquent child, who was seen as in need of the justice system's benevolent intervention.

By 1925 most states had passed similar legislation. Unlike the adult criminal justice system, juvenile courts dealt with young delinquents by considering both legal and nonlegal factors, such as home environment and schooling. However, by the 1960s the juvenile court's success in rehabilitating young offenders was being called into question, largely due to the growing population of juveniles institutionalized indefinitely while being "reformed."

In 1974 Congress passed the Juvenile Justice and Delinquency Prevention Act. It required not only the segregation of juveniles from adults but also the separation of juvenile delinquents (those charged with a crime) from juvenile status offenders (truants and so-called "incorrigibles"). This led to the development and expansion of community-based programs in an effort to discourage institutionalization. A decade later the public's perception was that serious juvenile crime was on the rise again and that the system devised to protect juveniles had become too lenient. This perception led to a trend in the 1990s to exclude certain serious offenses from juvenile court jurisdiction. Juveniles charged with certain crimes could legally be tried in adult court, in some states at the sole discretion of the prosecuting agency.

According to *Juvenile Justice: A Century of Change* (*1999 National Report Series*, Office of Juvenile Justice and Delinquency Prevention), by 1997 most states had adopted new, stricter laws for dealing with juvenile offenders in one or more of the following areas:

- Transfer provisions—making it easier to transfer juvenile offenders to the adult criminal justice system.

- Sentencing authority—giving criminal and juvenile courts expanded sentencing options.

- Confidentiality—modifying or removing traditional juvenile court confidentiality by making records and proceedings more open.

- Victims' rights—increasing the role of victims of juvenile crime in the juvenile justice system.

- Correctional programming—allowing for the development of new detention programs for certain adult offenders and for juveniles transferred to the adult justice system.

In addition, many states have added language to their juvenile codes aimed at holding juveniles accountable for criminal behavior and imposing punishment consistent with the seriousness of the crime.

# CHAPTER 2
# EXPENDITURES

According to Lynn Bauer of the Bureau of Justice Statistics (BJS) in *Justice Expenditure and Employment in the United States, 2001* (May 2004), the total amount spent on corrections at the federal, state, and local levels rose from about $8.9 billion in 1982 to $57 billion in 2001, an increase of roughly 540%. During the same time period, total expenditures for police protection also increased—from $19 billion to $72.4 billion. Total judicial and legal costs rose by 385%—from $7.8 billion in 1982 to $37.8 billion in 2001. (See Table 2.1).

*Justice Expenditure and Employment in the United States, 2001* also reported that local governments paid for nearly half of all U.S. justice expenditures in 2001, including 70% of spending on police. State governments bore the largest share of corrections costs (67.8%). Table 2.2 presents justice spending by level of government and justice activity during fiscal year 2001.

Calculated on a per capita basis, in 1982 total spending on corrections cost each U.S. resident $39. By 2001 that figure had risen more than 400% to $200 per person. Adjusted for inflation, the increase was 222%. (See Table 2.1.) By comparison, the per capita cost of police protection, after inflation, rose by 109%, and judicial and legal costs rose 155%.

## INCARCERATION RATES RISING

The reasons for the escalating costs of corrections are simple enough:

- More people are being sent to prison

- Mandatory sentencing rules require that some criminals be held for longer periods

- Some courts are requiring stiffer sentences

The official crime rate, reported by the FBI in its *Uniform Crime Reports*, has declined since the 1980s and early 1990s, when it averaged an annual rate of more than 5,500 crimes per 100,000 population. After reaching 5,898 crimes per 100,000 in 1991, the national rate declined to 4,063 crimes per 100,000 population by 2003. During the same period, the incarceration rate as reported by the Bureau of Justice Statistics has increased from 313 per 100,000 in 1991 to 482 in 2003. These two trends appear paradoxical. Part of the explanation is that the official crime rate does not track drug offenses—or related money laundering offenses and illegal weapons violations—which have been growing at high rates. For this reason, the official crime rate and the incarceration rate do not always move in parallel. They do not reflect the same underlying facts.

According to *Prisoners in 2003* (Washington, DC: Bureau of Justice Statistics, November 2004), the number of sentenced prisoners under jurisdiction of state and federal correctional authorities increased from 1,585,586 in 1995 to 2,085,620 in 2003, an increase of 31.5%. The average annual increase during this period was 3.5%. (See Table 2.3.) In the western United States the percentage change between 1995 and 2003 was 35.4%, from 207,661 to 281,135, with Oregon (8.7%) seeing the biggest average annual percent change in its prison population. (See Table 2.4.) The Midwest saw a 28% increase, from 192,177 to 246,053, with North Dakota (9.8%) and Minnesota (6.2) experiencing the largest average annual percent changes. The prison population in the South grew 26.9%, from 446,491 in 1995 to 566,679 in 2003. West Virginia (8.3%) and Mississippi (7.7%) gained the most on an average annual basis. The Northeast had the least growth (5.46%), from 155,030 in 1995 to 163,494 in 2003. Maine (4.9%) and Vermont (3.7%) experienced the highest average annual percent change. Only two states witnessed a decline in prison population during that timeframe: Massachusetts, which decreased from 10,427 in 1995 to 8,814 in 2003, and New York, which had reduced its number of prisoners from 68,486 in 1995 to 65,198 in 2003.

TABLE 2.1

**Total and per capita justice expenditure across government and by function, selected years, 1982–2001**

| Year | Population | Justice expenditure across government and function | | Police protection expenditure | | Judicial and legal expenditure | | Corrections expenditure | |
|---|---|---|---|---|---|---|---|---|---|
| | | Total | Per capita | Total | Per capita | Total | Per capita | Total | Per capita |
| 2001 | 285,094,000 | $167,113,000,000 | $586 | $72,406,000,000 | $254 | $37,751,000,000 | $132 | $56,956,000,000 | $200 |
| 1997 | 267,784,000 | 129,793,000,000 | 485 | 57,754,000,000 | 216 | 28,529,000,000 | 107 | 43,511,000,000 | 162 |
| 1992 | 245,807,000 | 93,777,000,000 | 382 | 41,327,000,000 | 168 | 20,989,000,000 | 85 | 31,461,000,000 | 128 |
| 1987 | 243,400,000 | 58,879,000,000 | 242 | 28,778,000,000 | 118 | 12,539,000,000 | 52 | 17,562,000,000 | 72 |
| 1982 | 226,548,000 | 35,685,000,000 | 158 | 19,022,000,000 | 84 | 7,771,000,000 | 34 | 8,892,000,000 | 39 |

Note: Using the Consumer Price Index (CPI) to adjust the 2001 per capita figure of $586 for inflation would yield approximately $320 in 1982 dollars.

SOURCE: Lynn Bauer and Steven D. Owens, "Appendix Table. Total and Per Capita Justice Expenditure across Government and by Function, Selected Years, 1982–2001," in *Justice Expenditure and Employment in the United States, 2001*, Bureau of Justice Statistics, May 2004, http://www.ojp.usdoj.gov/bjs/pub/pdf/jeeus01.pdf (accessed March 30, 2005)

---

**TABLE 2.2**

**Expenditure for justice activities, by level of government and justice activity, fiscal year 2001**

[In millions]

| Activity | Amount spent fiscal year 2001 | | | |
|---|---|---|---|---|
| | All governments | Federal government | State governments | Local governments |
| Total justice system | — | $30,443 | $63,372 | $83,377 |
| Direct expenditure | $167,133 | 25,285 | 58,820 | 83,007 |
| Intergovernmental | — | 5,158 | 4,552 | 370 |
| Police protection | — | $15,014 | $10,497 | $50,718 |
| Direct expenditure | $72,406 | 12,470 | 9,220 | 50,716 |
| Intergovernmental | — | 2,544 | 1,277 | 1,519 |
| Judicial and legal | — | $10,230 | $14,444 | $15,938 |
| Direct expenditure | $37,751 | 8,497 | 13,523 | 15,732 |
| Intergovernmental | — | 1,733 | 921 | 207 |
| Corrections | — | $5,199 | $38,432 | $16,721 |
| Direct expenditure | $56,956 | 4,318 | 36,078 | 16,559 |
| Intergovernmental | — | 881 | 2,354 | 162 |

Notes: Detail may not add to total because of rounding. Local government data are estimates subject to sampling variability. The total lines for each justice activity, and for the total justice system, exclude duplicative intergovernmental amounts. Artificial inflation would result if an intergovernmental expenditure of a government were tabulated and then counted again when the recipient government(s) spent the amount. The intergovernmental expenditure lines are not totaled for the same reason.
—Not applicable.

SOURCE: Lynn Bauer and Steven D. Owens, "Table 3. Expenditure, by Level of Government and Justice Activity, Fiscal Year 2001," in *Justice Expenditure and Employment in the United States, 2001*, Bureau of Justice Statistics, 2004, http://www.ojp.usdoj.gov/bjs/pub/pdf/jeeus01.pdf (accessed March 30, 2005)

---

## FEDERAL CORRECTIONS

*The Budget of the United States for Fiscal Year 2006* proposes $4.75 billion in budget authority for corrections (Washington, DC: Office of Management and Budget, February 2005). Included in this proposal are $85 million to open three new federal prisons and to expand two other facilities, $37 million to pay for the added costs of almost 4,300 inmates in existing facilities, and $20 million for 1,600 new private contract beds. Historically, actual outlays tend to be slightly below authorizations as Congress debates the amounts to be spent.

## STATE CORRECTIONS

Based on data from the Bureau of Justice Statistics in *Justice Expenditure and Employment in the United States, 2001*, corrections represented about 3% of state and local direct expenditures in 2001. The criminal and justice system as a whole accounted for some 7% of state budgets, while 30% went to education, 14% to public welfare, and 7% to health and hospitals. These percentages have been remarkably steady since 1977. (See Figure 2.1.)

According to the U.S. Census Bureau, direct corrections expenditures by states in 2003 were $39.2 billion. (See Table 2.5.) The last year for which a complete breakdown of state prison expenses is available is 2001. According to James J. Stephan of the Bureau of Justice Statistics (*State Prison Expenditures 2001*, June 2004), a total of $38.2 billion was spent by state correctional systems in 2001. Of that amount, $29.5 billion was used for operating adult correctional facilities. The average annual operating cost per state inmate in 2001 was $22,650. (See Table 2.6.) State prisons in the Northeast spent the most on average per prisoner ($33,037), while those in the South spent the least ($16,479). State prisons cost each U.S. resident an average of $100 a year to operate. Prisons in the West cost the most per resident ($108), while those in the South cost the least ($91). Overall, Southern states spent the most money on prisons ($10 billion) and had the largest prison population (563,818).

Various factors, many out of the control of prison officials, influence the costs of running a state prison. Among such variables are climate (heating costs in the Northeast can be more expensive than in the South), local wage rates, and local cost of living. However, other costs are within the control of prison officials. State prisons with a high inmate-to-staff ratio, that is, with fewer guards, reported lower costs,

**TABLE 2.3**

**Number of inmates in prisons and jails, 1995 and 2000–03**

| | Total inmates in custody[a] | Prisoners in custody on December 31 | | Inmates in jail on June 30 | Incarceration rate[b] |
|---|---|---|---|---|---|
| | | **Federal** | **State** | | |
| 1995 | 1,585,586 | 89,538 | 989,004 | 507,044 | 601 |
| 2000 | 1,937,482 | 133,921 | 1,176,269 | 621,149 | 684 |
| 2001 | 1,961,247 | 143,337 | 1,180,155 | 631,240 | 685 |
| 2002 | 2,033,022 | 151,618 | 1,209,331 | 665,475 | 701 |
| 2003 | 2,085,620 | 161,673 | 1,226,175 | 691,301 | 714 |
| Percent change, 2002–2003 | 2.6% | 6.6% | 1.4% | 3.9% | |
| Average annual increase, 1995–2003 | 3.5% | 7.7% | 2.7% | 4.0% | |

Note: Counts include all inmates held in public and private adult correctional facilities.
[a]Total counts include federal inmates in non-secure privately operated facilities (6,471 in 2003, 6,598 in 2002, 6,515 in 2001 and 6,143 in 2000).
[b]Number of prison and jail inmates per 100,000 U.S. residents at year end.

SOURCE: Paige M. Harrison and Allen J. Beck, "Table 1. Number of Persons Held in State or Federal Prisons or in Local Jails, 1995, and 2000–2003," in *Prisoners in 2003*, Bureau of Justice Statistics, November 2004, http://www.ojp.usdoj.gov/bjs/pub/pdf/p03.pdf (accessed March 30, 2005)

while those with large staffs, some as high as one staff member for every 1.7 inmates, had heavy costs. States with a few large prison facilities tended to have lower overall operating costs than those with multiple, smaller facilities.

The $29.5 billion spent on state prison operations in 2001 was an increase of almost 23% from 1996, when $24 billion was spent, and a 150% increase from 1986, when a total of $11.7 billion was spent. The per capita rate for prison expenditures (cost per year to each U.S. resident) also rose during this period at an average annual rate of 6.4%. (See Table 2.7.) Compared to other state expenses, prison spending was relatively low. In 2001 the per capita rate for education was $1,315 and for public welfare, $914.

In 2001 salaries, wages, and benefits for state prison employees made up about two-thirds of state prison operating expenditures. Table 2.8 breaks down prison operating expenditures by state during that fiscal year. Operating costs include supplies, maintenance, and contractual services. About 4% is spent on new construction, renovations, major repairs, equipment, land, or buildings. Expenditures for new prison construction have been declining, from $1.5 billion in 1996 to $1.1 billion in 2001.

Other operating costs for state prisons include medical care, food service, and utilities. By far the largest of these costs was some $3.3 billion spent on prisoner medical care in 2001, followed by $1.2 billion for prisoner food, and $996 million for utilities. (See Table 2.9.) Nationwide, the average annual amount spent for medical care per prisoner was $2,625 (the average spent by U.S. citizens on their own health care is $4,370 per year.) The amount spent on prisoner medical care varied widely by state. Such factors as a high number of inmates with drug and alcohol abuse problems can raise costs, while operating larger prison

facilities, and thereby raising the average inmate-to-doctor ratio, can result in cost savings. In 2001 Maine spent the most on prisoner medical care ($5,601), while Louisiana spent the least ($860). By region, the West averaged the most spent on medical care ($3,672), and the South averaged the least ($2,025). Annual food service costs tended to be lowest in those states, such as Mississippi ($297 per prisoner) and North Carolina ($191 per prisoner), where prisons operated their own farms and grew their own fruits and vegetables. In addition, North Carolina prisoners operate their own cannery and meat processing plant.

## LOCAL JAIL EXPENDITURES BY COUNTIES AND MUNICIPALITIES

According to *Justice Expenditure and Employment in the United States, 2001* (Bureau of Justice Statistics, 2004), governments on the local level carry the bulk of justice system costs because police protection is primarily the responsibility of local communities. Some 59% of all justice system employees (1,357,153) are employed at the local level. (See Table 2.10.) In 2001, $50.7 billion, some 70% of all funds spent on police protection, came from county or municipal governments. (See Table 2.2.)

The Bureau of Justice Statistics reported in *Prison and Jail Inmates at Midyear 2003* (May 2004) that between 1995 and 2003, the number of inmates in local jails rose from 507,044 to 691,301. (See Table 2.11.) The average annual increase in jail inmates from December 31, 1995, to June 30, 2003, was 4%. However, at the end of June 2003, local jails were operating at 6% below their rated capacity. *Prison and Jail Inmates at Midyear 2003* also reported that local authorities supervised an additional 71,371 offenders in such alternative programs as work release, weekend reporting, electronic monitoring, and community service.

TABLE 2.4

## Sentenced prisoners under the jurisdiction of state or federal correctional authorities, yearend 1995, 2002, and 2003

| Region and jurisdiction | Sentenced prisoners | | | Percent change 2002–03 | Average change 1995–03[a] | Incarceration rate 2003[b] |
|---|---|---|---|---|---|---|
| | 2003 | 2002 | 1995 | | | |
| U.S. total | 1,409,280 | 1,380,516 | 1,085,022 | 2.1% | 3.3% | 482 |
| Federal | 151,919 | 143,040 | 83,663 | 6.2 | 7.7 | 52 |
| State | 1,257,361 | 1,237,476 | 1,001,359 | 1.6 | 2.9 | 430 |
| **Northeast** | 163,494 | 165,783 | 155,030 | −1.4% | 0.7% | 300 |
| Connecticut | 13,587 | 14,082 | 10,419 | −3.5 | 3.4 | 389 |
| Maine | 1,951 | 1,817 | 1,326 | 7.4 | 4.9 | 149 |
| Massachusetts[c] | 8,814 | 8,947 | 10,427 | −1.5 | −2.1 | 233 |
| New Hampshire | 2,434 | 2,451 | 2,015 | −0.7 | 2.4 | 188 |
| New Jersey[d] | 27,246 | 27,891 | 27,066 | −2.3 | 0.1 | 314 |
| New York | 65,198 | 67,065 | 68,486 | −2.8 | −0.6 | 339 |
| Pennsylvania | 40,880 | 40,164 | 32,410 | 1.8 | 2.9 | 330 |
| Rhode Island | 1,983 | 2,045 | 1,833 | −3.0 | 1.0 | 184 |
| Vermont | 1,401 | 1,321 | 1,048 | 6.1 | 3.7 | 226 |
| **Midwest** | 246,053 | 244,566 | 192,177 | 0.6% | 3.1% | 375 |
| Illinois[d] | 43,418 | 42,693 | 37,658 | 1.7 | 1.8 | 342 |
| Indiana | 23,007 | 21,542 | 16,046 | 6.8 | 4.6 | 370 |
| Iowa[d] | 8,546 | 8,398 | 5,906 | 1.8 | 4.7 | 290 |
| Kansas[d] | 9,132 | 8,935 | 7,054 | 2.2 | 3.3 | 334 |
| Michigan | 49,358 | 50,591 | 41,112 | −2.4 | 2.3 | 489 |
| Minnesota | 7,865 | 7,129 | 4,846 | 10.3 | 6.2 | 155 |
| Missouri | 30,275 | 30,080 | 19,134 | 0.6 | 5.9 | 529 |
| Nebraska | 3,976 | 3,972 | 3,006 | 0.1 | 3.6 | 228 |
| North Dakota | 1,147 | 1,025 | 544 | 11.9 | 9.8 | 181 |
| Ohio[d] | 44,778 | 45,646 | 44,663 | −1.9 | 0.0 | 391 |
| South Dakota | 3,016 | 2,911 | 1,871 | 3.6 | 6.1 | 393 |
| Wisconsin | 21,535 | 21,644 | 10,337 | −0.5 | [e] | 392 |
| **South** | 566,679 | 553,493 | 446,491 | 2.6% | 3.0% | 542 |
| Alabama | 28,612 | 27,532 | 20,130 | 3.9 | 4.5 | 635 |
| Arkansas | 13,013 | 12,999 | 8,520 | 0.1 | 5.4 | 476 |
| Delaware | 4,122 | 3,659 | 3,014 | 12.7 | 4.0 | 501 |
| Florida | 79,594 | 75,204 | 63,866 | 5.8 | 2.8 | 463 |
| Georgia | 47,200 | 47,424 | 34,168 | −0.5 | 4.1 | 539 |
| Kentucky | 16,190 | 15,572 | 12,060 | 4.0 | 3.7 | 392 |
| Louisiana | 36,047 | 36,032 | 25,195 | 0.0 | 4.6 | 801 |
| Maryland | 23,230 | 23,274 | 20,450 | −0.2 | 1.6 | 420 |
| Mississippi | 22,168 | 21,397 | 12,251 | 3.6 | 7.7 | 768 |
| North Carolina | 29,394 | 28,613 | 27,914 | 2.7 | 0.6 | 348 |
| Oklahoma[d] | 22,448 | 22,702 | 18,151 | −1.1 | 2.7 | 636 |
| South Carolina | 22,942 | 22,837 | 19,015 | 0.5 | 2.4 | 551 |
| Tennessee[d] | 25,403 | 24,989 | 15,206 | 1.7 | 6.6 | 433 |
| Texas[d] | 156,534 | 151,782 | 127,766 | 3.1 | 2.6 | 702 |
| Virginia | 35,067 | 34,973 | 27,260 | 0.3 | 3.2 | 472 |
| West Virginia | 4,715 | 4,504 | 2,483 | 4.7 | 8.3 | 260 |
| **West** | 281,135 | 273,634 | 207,661 | 2.7% | 3.9% | 419 |
| Alaska | 2,629 | 2,577 | 2,042 | 2.0 | 3.2 | 401 |
| Arizona | 29,722 | 28,008 | 20,291 | 6.1 | 4.9 | 525 |
| California | 162,678 | 159,984 | 131,745 | 1.7 | 2.7 | 455 |
| Colorado | 19,671 | 18,833 | 11,063 | 4.4 | 7.5 | 430 |
| Hawaii | 4,167 | 3,840 | 2,590 | 8.5 | 6.1 | 325 |
| Idaho | 5,887 | 5,746 | 3,328 | 2.5 | 7.4 | 427 |
| Montana | 3,620 | 3,323 | 1,999 | 8.9 | 7.7 | 393 |
| Nevada | 10,543 | 10,478 | 7,713 | 0.6 | 4.0 | 462 |
| New Mexico | 5,934 | 5,631 | 3,925 | 5.4 | 5.3 | 314 |
| Oregon | 12,695 | 12,080 | 6,515 | 5.1 | 8.7 | 354 |
| Utah | 5,681 | 5,475 | 3,447 | 3.8 | 6.4 | 240 |
| Washington | 16,036 | 15,922 | 11,608 | 0.7 | 4.1 | 260 |
| Wyoming | 1,872 | 1,737 | 1,395 | 7.8 | 3.7 | 372 |

[a]The average annual percentage increase from 1995 to 2003.
[b]Prisoners with sentences of more than 1 year per 100,000 residents.
[c]The incarceration rate includes an estimated 6,200 inmates sentenced to more than 1 year but held in local jails or houses of corrections.
[d]Includes some inmates sentenced to 1 year or less.
[e]Not calculated.

SOURCE: Paige M. Harrison and Allen J. Beck, "Table 4. Sentenced Prisoners under the Jurisdiction of State or Federal Correctional Authorities, Yearend 1995, 2002, and 2003," in *Prisoners in 2003*, Bureau of Justice Statistics, November 2004, http://www.ojp.usdoj.gov/bjs/pub/pdf/p03.pdf (accessed March 30, 2005)

**FIGURE 2.1**

**TABLE 2.5**

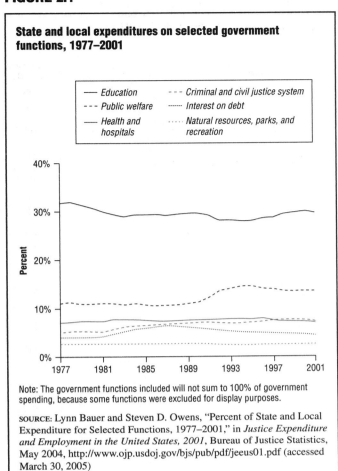

**State and local expenditures on selected government functions, 1977–2001**

— Education
--- Criminal and civil justice system
--- Public welfare
······ Interest on debt
— Health and hospitals
····· Natural resources, parks, and recreation

Note: The government functions included will not sum to 100% of government spending, because some functions were excluded for display purposes.

SOURCE: Lynn Bauer and Steven D. Owens, "Percent of State and Local Expenditure for Selected Functions, 1977–2001," in *Justice Expenditure and Employment in the United States, 2001*, Bureau of Justice Statistics, May 2004, http://www.ojp.usdoj.gov/bjs/pub/pdf/jeeus01.pdf (accessed March 30, 2005)

**State government finances, 2003**

[Dollar amounts in thousands. Per capita amounts in dollars.]

| Item | United States Amount | Per capita |
|---|---|---|
| Population (thousands, 2003) | 290,231 | X |
| **Total revenue** | **1,296,701,281** | **4,467.82** |
| General revenue | 1,113,391,406 | 3,836.22 |
| Intergovernmental revenue | 362,519,737 | 1,249.07 |
| Taxes | 548,990,867 | 1,891.57 |
| General sales | 184,596,707 | 636.03 |
| Selective sales | 89,214,514 | 307.39 |
| License taxes | 35,863,173 | 123.57 |
| Individual income tax | 181,932,513 | 626.85 |
| Corporate income tax | 28,384,474 | 97.80 |
| Other taxes | 28,999,486 | 99.92 |
| Current charges | 106,398,401 | 366.60 |
| Miscellaneous general revenue | 95,482,401 | 328.99 |
| Utility revenue | 12,517,945 | 43.13 |
| Liquor store revenue | 4,517,992 | 15.57 |
| Insurance trust revenue | 166,273,938 | 572.90 |
| **Total expenditure** | **1,358,964,865** | **4,682.36** |
| Intergovernmental expenditure | 382,781,397 | 1,318.89 |
| Direct expenditure | 976,183,468 | 3,363.47 |
| Current operation | 656,089,768 | 2,260.58 |
| Capital outlay | 92,186,403 | 317.63 |
| Insurance benefits and repayments | 168,978,731 | 582.22 |
| Assistance and subsidies | 25,888,450 | 89.20 |
| Interest on debt | 33,040,116 | 113.84 |
| Exhibit: Salaries and wages | 183,385,651 | 631.86 |
| **Total expenditure** | **1,358,964,865** | **4,682.36** |
| General expenditure | 1,163,884,688 | 4,010.20 |
| Intergovernmental expenditure | 382,781,397 | 1,318.89 |
| Direct expenditure | 781,103,291 | 2,691.32 |
| General expenditures, by function | | |
| Education | 411,501,528 | 1,417.84 |
| Public welfare | 313,230,417 | 1,079.25 |
| Hospitals | 38,394,884 | 132.29 |
| Health | 50,270,775 | 173.21 |
| Highways | 86,104,257 | 296.67 |
| Police protection | 11,158,200 | 38.45 |
| Correction | 39,226,109 | 135.15 |
| Natural resources | 18,623,901 | 64.17 |
| Parks and recreation | 5,857,213 | 20.18 |
| Government administration | 43,853,867 | 151.10 |
| Interest on general debt | 31,294,903 | 107.83 |
| Other and unallocable | 114,368,634 | 394.06 |
| Utility expenditure | 22,404,931 | 77.20 |
| Liquor store expenditure | 3,696,515 | 12.74 |
| Insurance trust expenditure | 168,978,731 | 582.22 |
| Debt at end of fiscal year | 697,929,028 | 2,404.74 |
| Cash and security holdings | 2,594,115,620 | 8,938.11 |

X=Not applicable

SOURCE: "State Government Finances: 2003," in *Federal State and Local Governments: 2003 State Government Finance Data,* U.S. Census Bureau, http://www.census.gov/govs/state/0300usst.html (accessed March 30, 2005)

## COSTS AND CONSEQUENCES

The costs of corrections for the United States have been rising in absolute terms, not simply as a reflection of a growing population. In the 1980–99 time period, the number of people held behind bars would have increased more than three-fold even if the U.S. population had remained unchanged. In 1980 some 139 people were in state and federal prisons for every 100,000 U.S. residents. By 2003 that ratio had increased to 482 people, according to *Prisoners in 2003* (Bureau of Justice Statistics, November 2004). *Justice Expenditure and Employment in the United States, 2001* (Bureau of Justice Statistics, 2004) reports that in 1982, correctional expenditures amounted to $39 for every man, woman, and child in the United States; by 2001 that cost had climbed to $200. During this period, the phenomenon of crime has increased in absolute terms, and more of the nation's resources have had to be expended on its consequences than in previous times.

Responses to rising costs have been variable and include some of the following:

Authorities have responded to budgetary pressures by crowding more people into available space and have thus caused increased crowding in correctional facilities. Crowding has been most serious in federal facilities, somewhat less so on average in state prison systems, and least in local jails, especially the smallest ones.

The number of adult correctional facilities increased from 1,464 in 1995, to 1,668 in 2000, according to

TABLE 2.6

**Expenditures and operating costs per state inmate and per U.S. resident, fiscal year 2001**

| Region and state | Expenditures (1,000's of dollars) | | | Annual operating costs | | Prisoners under state authority on 6/30/01 |
|---|---|---|---|---|---|---|
| | Total | Operating | Capital | Per inmate | Per U.S. resident | |
| **Total** | **$29,491,268** | **$28,374,273** | **$1,116,995** | **$22,650** | **$100** | **1,252,743** |
| **Northeast** | **$6,056,762** | **$5,712,994** | **$343,769** | **$33,037** | **$106** | **172,925** |
| Connecticut[a] | 523,960 | 506,905 | 17,055 | 26,856 | 148 | 18,875 |
| Maine | 76,479 | 75,133 | 1,346 | 44,379 | 58 | 1,693 |
| Massachusetts | 413,071 | 404,862 | 8,209 | 37,718 | 63 | 10,734 |
| New Hampshire | 62,754 | 60,279 | 2,475 | 25,949 | 48 | 2,323 |
| New Jersey | 799,560 | 768,661 | 30,899 | 27,347 | 91 | 28,108 |
| New York | 2,807,259 | 2,547,452 | 259,807 | 36,835 | 134 | 69,158 |
| Pennsylvania | 1,203,219 | 1,183,668 | 19,551 | 31,900 | 96 | 37,105 |
| Rhode Island[a] | 124,333 | 121,167 | 3,165 | 38,503 | 114 | 3,147 |
| Vermont[a] | 46,128 | 44,867 | 1,261 | 25,178 | 73 | 1,782 |
| **Midwest** | **$6,327,346** | **$5,952,214** | **$375,132** | **$24,779** | **$92** | **240,213** |
| Illinois | 1,011,311 | 996,738 | 14,573 | 21,844 | 80 | 45,629 |
| Indiana | 477,628 | 449,406 | 28,222 | 21,841 | 73 | 20,576 |
| Iowa | 188,391 | 186,298 | 2,093 | 22,997 | 64 | 8,101 |
| Kansas | 199,843 | 182,655 | 17,189 | 21,381 | 68 | 8,543 |
| Michigan | 1,582,611 | 1,573,273 | 9,338 | 32,525 | 157 | 48,371 |
| Minnesota | 253,385 | 239,953 | 13,432 | 36,836 | 48 | 6,514 |
| Missouri | 436,081 | 362,429 | 73,652 | 12,867 | 64 | 28,167 |
| Nebraska | 126,857 | 99,865 | 26,992 | 25,321 | 58 | 3,944 |
| North Dakota | 26,796 | 24,219 | 2,577 | 22,425 | 38 | 1,080 |
| Ohio | 1,277,622 | 1,201,269 | 76,354 | 26,295 | 106 | 45,684 |
| South Dakota | 37,529 | 37,030 | 499 | 13,853 | 49 | 2,673 |
| Wisconsin | 709,292 | 599,080 | 110,212 | 28,622 | 111 | 20,931 |
| **South** | **$10,002,325** | **$9,750,580** | **$251,745** | **$16,479** | **$91** | **563,818** |
| Alabama | 228,871 | 221,774 | 7,097 | 8,128 | 50 | 27,286 |
| Arkansas | 199,003 | 192,611 | 6,392 | 15,619 | 72 | 12,332 |
| Delaware[a] | 166,327 | 162,397 | 3,930 | 22,802 | 204 | 7,122 |
| Dist. of Columbia[b] | 143,700 | 143,700 | e | 26,670 | 251 | 5,388 |
| Florida | 1,484,799 | 1,453,799 | 31,000 | 20,190 | 89 | 72,007 |
| Georgia | 923,505 | 900,918 | 22,586 | 19,860 | 107 | 45,363 |
| Kentucky | 288,438 | 274,404 | 14,034 | 17,818 | 67 | 15,400 |
| Louisiana | 479,260 | 459,686 | 19,573 | 12,951 | 103 | 35,494 |
| Maryland | 645,620 | 632,749 | 12,872 | 26,398 | 118 | 23,970 |
| Mississippi | 266,196 | 264,503 | 1,693 | 12,795 | 93 | 20,672 |
| North Carolina | 863,892 | 840,347 | 23,545 | 26,984 | 103 | 31,142 |
| Oklahoma | 384,060 | 377,378 | 6,682 | 16,309 | 109 | 23,139 |
| South Carolina | 405,238 | 373,249 | 31,989 | 16,762 | 92 | 22,267 |
| Tennessee[c] | 421,807 | 421,807 | e | 18,206 | 73 | 23,168 |
| Texas | 2,315,899 | 2,270,959 | 44,940 | 13,808 | 106 | 164,465 |
| Virginia | 723,767 | 699,104 | 24,663 | 22,942 | 97 | 30,473 |
| West Virginia | 61,944 | 61,194 | 750 | 14,817 | 34 | 4,130 |

*Census of State and Federal Correctional Facilities, 2000* (Bureau of Justice Statistics, 2003).

Privately run prisons and jails have been created on the theory that the private sector can do the job at lower cost. Because privately run prisons would be free of the bureaucracy and politics of state-run prisons, and not subject to mandatory use of unionized labor, it was believed they could be more cost effective than public prisons. So far, studies have shown mixed results, with some communities reporting great savings while others report no significant differences. A 1996 study by the U.S. Government Accounting Office, reported in *Emerging Issues on Privatized Prisons* (Washington, DC:

Bureau of Justice Assistance, 2001), shows no clear evidence that privatization saves money. Despite the uncertainty, the privately run prison population has grown at a faster rate than the correctional population as a whole. At year-end in 2003, according to the Bureau of Justice Statistics (*Prisoners in 2003*), 95,522 prisoners were in privately operated facilities. (See Table 2.12.) Nationwide, some 6.5% of all prisoners are in privately run prisons, most in the South and West. The six states having at least 25% of their prison population housed in private prisons are New Mexico (44.2%), Alaska (30.6%), Montana (29.3%), Oklahoma (26.4%), and Wyoming (26.3%).

**TABLE 2.6**

## Expenditures and operating costs per state inmate and per U.S. resident, fiscal year 2001 [CONTINUED]

| Region and state | Expenditures (1,000's of dollars) | | | Annual operating costs | | Prisoners under state authority on 6/30/01 |
| | Total | Operating | Capital | Per inmate | Per U.S. resident | |
|---|---|---|---|---|---|---|
| West | $7,104,834 | $6,958,485 | $146,349 | $25,231 | $108 | 275,787 |
| Alaska[a] | 154,650 | 154,156 | 494 | 36,730 | 243 | 4,197 |
| Arizona | 618,571 | 609,910 | 8,661 | 22,476 | 115 | 27,136 |
| California | 4,166,573 | 4,107,844 | 58,729 | 25,053 | 119 | 163,965 |
| Colorado | 466,551 | 435,037 | 31,514 | 25,408 | 98 | 17,122 |
| Hawaii[a,d] | 117,101 | 117,101 | [e] | 21,637 | 96 | 5,412 |
| Idaho | 95,494 | 92,821 | 2,673 | 16,319 | 70 | 5,688 |
| Montana | 71,994 | 71,169 | 825 | 21,898 | 79 | 3,250 |
| Nevada | 182,092 | 180,834 | 1,258 | 17,572 | 86 | 10,291 |
| New Mexico | 149,077 | 148,249 | 828 | 28,035 | 81 | 5,288 |
| Oregon | 404,255 | 399,436 | 4,819 | 36,060 | 115 | 11,077 |
| Utah | 133,963 | 133,683 | 281 | 24,574 | 59 | 5,440 |
| Washington | 488,314 | 459,814 | 28,500 | 30,168 | 77 | 15,242 |
| Wyoming | 56,199 | 48,431 | 7,768 | 28,845 | 98 | 1,679 |

Note: Forty-six states and the District of Columbia began their fiscal years in July and ended them in June. Exceptions included Albama and Michigan, October to September; New York, April to March; and Texas, September to August. Detail may not add to total because of rounding.
[a]States have integrated jail-prison systems.
[b]The District of Columbia reported no capital outlays during fiscal year 2001, a transition period during which its sentenced felons were being transferred to the Federal Bureau of Prisons.
[c]During fiscal year 2001 Tennessee spent capital amounts from sources outside its Department of Corrections.
[d]Hawaii's Department of Public Safety, Corrections Division had nonrecurring expenditures which state budget officials excluded from the capital category.
[e]Not reported.

SOURCE: James J. Stephan, "Table 2. Total, Operating, and Capital Expenditures, and Operating Costs per State Inmate and per U.S. Resident, Fiscal Year 2001," in *State Prison Expenditures 2001*, Bureau of Justice Statistics, June 2004, http://www.ojp.usdoj.gov/bjs/pub/pdf/spe01.pdf (accessed March 31, 2005)

**TABLE 2.7**

## Annual per capita costs for selected state expenditures, 1986–2001

[In 2001 constant dollars]

| Fiscal year | State expenditures as costs per resident | | | | | |
| | Total corrections | Prisons | Health | Education | Public welfare | Natural resources |
|---|---|---|---|---|---|---|
| 1986 | $65 | $49 | $78 | $842 | $425 | $44 |
| 1991 | 98 | 76 | 109 | 998 | 632 | 52 |
| 1996 | 119 | 91 | 141 | 1,143 | 849 | 56 |
| 2001 | 134 | 104 | 154 | 1,315 | 914 | 61 |
| Average annual percent change,1986–2001* | 6.2% | 6.4% | 5.8% | 4.2% | 6.4% | 3.3% |

*Based on total expenditures.

SOURCE: James J. Stephan, "Table 1. Annual per Capita Costs, in 2001 Constant Dollars, for Selected State Expenditures, 1986–2001," in *State Prison Expenditures 2001*, Bureau of Justice Statistics, June 2004, http:// www.ojp.usdoj.gov/bjs/pub/pdf/spe01.pdf (accessed March 30, 2005)

TABLE 2.8

## Components of state prison operating expenditures, fiscal year 2001

| Region and jurisdiction | Operating expenditures (1,000's of dollars) | | |
| --- | --- | --- | --- |
| | Total | Salaries, wages and benefits | Other operating costs |
| **Total** | **$28,374,273** | **$18,583,923** | **$9,790,350** |
| **Northeast** | $5,712,994 | $4,014,190 | $1,698,803 |
| Connecticut* | 506,905 | 316,497 | 190,408 |
| Maine | 75,133 | 51,147 | 23,986 |
| Massachusetts | 404,862 | 297,405 | 107,457 |
| New Hampshire | 60,279 | 42,476 | 17,803 |
| New Jersey | 768,661 | 443,235 | 325,426 |
| New York | 2,547,452 | 1,969,750 | 577,702 |
| Pennsylvania | 1,183,668 | 765,038 | 418,629 |
| Rhode Island* | 121,167 | 101,999 | 19,168 |
| Vermont* | 44,867 | 26,643 | 18,224 |
| **Midwest** | $5,952,214 | $3,960,772 | $1,991,442 |
| Illinois | 996,738 | 713,339 | 283,399 |
| Indiana | 449,406 | 304,310 | 145,096 |
| Iowa | 186,298 | 149,039 | 37,260 |
| Kansas | 182,655 | 107,721 | 74,934 |
| Michigan | 1,573,273 | 1,116,883 | 456,390 |
| Minnesota | 239,953 | 159,981 | 79,971 |
| Missouri | 362,429 | 220,790 | 141,639 |
| Nebraska | 99,865 | 64,327 | 35,538 |
| North Dakota | 24,219 | 13,734 | 10,485 |
| Ohio | 1,201,269 | 760,668 | 440,601 |
| South Dakota | 37,030 | 19,956 | 17,074 |
| Wisconsin | 599,080 | 330,025 | 269,055 |
| **South** | $9,750,580 | $6,017,146 | $3,733,434 |
| Alabama | 221,774 | 153,077 | 68,697 |
| Arkansas | 192,611 | 108,960 | 83,651 |
| Delaware* | 162,397 | 110,751 | 51,646 |
| District of Columbia | 143,700 | 63,545 | 80,155 |
| Florida | 1,453,799 | 955,791 | 498,008 |
| Georgia | 900,918 | 678,964 | 221,954 |
| Kentucky | 274,404 | 124,787 | 149,617 |
| Louisiana | 459,686 | 196,078 | 263,609 |
| Maryland | 632,749 | 351,870 | 280,879 |
| Mississippi | 264,503 | 125,045 | 139,458 |
| North Carolina | 840,347 | 603,932 | 236,415 |
| Oklahoma | 377,378 | 189,432 | 187,946 |
| South Carolina | 373,249 | 266,518 | 106,732 |
| Tennessee | 421,807 | 168,295 | 253,511 |
| Texas | 2,270,959 | 1,343,459 | 927,500 |
| Virginia | 699,104 | 539,590 | 159,514 |
| West Virginia | 61,194 | 37,052 | 24,142 |
| **West** | $6,958,485 | $4,591,814 | $2,366,671 |
| Alaska* | 154,156 | 81,508 | 72,648 |
| Arizona | 609,910 | 408,558 | 201,352 |
| California | 4,107,844 | 2,873,065 | 1,234,778 |
| Colorado | 435,037 | 275,095 | 159,942 |
| Hawaii* | 117,101 | 64,813 | 52,288 |
| Idaho | 92,821 | 52,401 | 40,420 |
| Montana | 71,169 | 35,677 | 35,492 |
| Nevada | 180,834 | 123,037 | 57,798 |
| New Mexico | 148,249 | 75,527 | 72,723 |
| Oregon | 399,436 | 197,265 | 202,171 |
| Utah | 133,683 | 82,152 | 51,531 |
| Washington | 459,814 | 299,391 | 160,423 |
| Wyoming | 48,431 | 23,326 | 25,105 |

Note: Detail may not add to total because of rounding.
*States have integrated jail-prison systems.

SOURCE: James J. Stephan, "Table 3. Components of State Prison Operating Expenditures, Fiscal Year 2001," in *State Prison Expenditures 2001*, Bureau of Justice Statistics, June 2004, http://www.ojp.usdoj.gov/bjs/pub/pdf/spe01.pdf (accessed March 31, 2005)

TABLE 2.9

## State prison expenditures for medical care, food service, and utilities, fiscal year 2001

| Region and jurisdiction | 1,000's of dollars | | | Cost per inmate in 2001 | | |
|---|---|---|---|---|---|---|
| | Medical care | Food service | Utilities | Medical care | Food service | Utilities |
| Total | $3,288,200 | $1,195,854 | $996,027 | $2,625 | $955 | $795 |
| Northeast | $590,935 | $210,400 | $203,294 | $3,417 | $1,217 | $1,176 |
| Connecticut[a] | 68,330 | 23,451 | 19,838 | 3,620 | 1,242 | 1,051 |
| Maine | 9,483 | 3,107 | 2,781 | 5,601 | 1,835 | 1,643 |
| Massachusetts | 43,460 | 9,497 | 21,266 | 4,049 | 885 | 1,981 |
| New Hampshire | 3,964 | 2,035 | 3,393 | 1,706 | 876 | 1,461 |
| New Jersey | 91,652 | 22,760 | 31,140 | 3,261 | 810 | 1,108 |
| New York | 219,735 | 66,618 | 85,824 | 3,177 | 963 | 1,241 |
| Pennsylvania | 137,291 | 77,083 | 37,452 | 3,700 | 2,077 | 1,009 |
| Rhode Island[a,b] | 11,820 | 4,107 | 636 | 3,756 | 1,305 | 202 |
| Vermont[a] | 5,199 | 1,741 | 963 | 2,918 | 977 | 540 |
| Midwest | $543,001 | $290,949 | $198,432 | $2,260 | $1,211 | $826 |
| Illinois | 73,235 | 52,481 | 38,355 | 1,605 | 1,150 | 841 |
| Indiana | 37,601 | 19,965 | 19,018 | 1,827 | 970 | 924 |
| Iowa | 16,713 | 14,225 | 7,253 | 2,063 | 1,756 | 895 |
| Kansas | 22,835 | 11,975 | 7,592 | 2,673 | 1,402 | 889 |
| Michigan | 137,414 | 48,148 | 37,970 | 2,841 | 995 | 785 |
| Minnesota | 25,458 | 10,843 | 7,930 | 3,908 | 1,665 | 1,217 |
| Missouri | 50,207 | 21,144 | 19,050 | 1,782 | 751 | 676 |
| Nebraska | 12,406 | 5,627 | 2,568 | 3,145 | 1,427 | 651 |
| North Dakota | 2,892 | 1,803 | 939 | 2,678 | 1,670 | 870 |
| Ohio | 111,693 | 75,445 | 40,729 | 2,445 | 1,651 | 892 |
| South Dakota | 5,465 | 4,173 | 1,225 | 2,044 | 1,561 | 458 |
| Wisconsin | 47,082 | 25,119 | 15,802 | 2,249 | 1,200 | 755 |
| South | $1,141,489 | $411,988 | $377,792 | $2,025 | $731 | $670 |
| Alabama | 28,700 | 7,152 | 12,616 | 1,052 | 262 | 462 |
| Arkansas | 19,924 | 5,233 | 4,843 | 1,616 | 424 | 393 |
| Delaware[a] | 14,762 | 9,624 | 6,651 | 2,073 | 1,351 | 934 |
| District of Columbia | 10,425 | 2,955 | 2,688 | 1,935 | 549 | 499 |
| Florida | 242,132 | 78,483 | 44,792 | 3,363 | 1,090 | 622 |
| Georgia | 117,384 | 52,174 | 36,280 | 2,588 | 1,150 | 800 |
| Kentucky | 14,782 | 8,688 | 8,338 | 960 | 564 | 541 |
| Louisiana | 30,535 | 12,381 | 11,584 | 860 | 349 | 326 |
| Maryland | 52,193 | 15,316 | 28,454 | 2,177 | 639 | 1,187 |
| Mississippi | 25,946 | 6,142 | 7,149 | 1,255 | 297 | 346 |
| North Carolina | 45,558 | 5,935 | 31,165 | 1,463 | 191 | 1,001 |
| Oklahoma | 46,457 | 23,395 | 9,691 | 2,008 | 1,011 | 419 |
| South Carolina | 28,716 | 9,679 | 15,533 | 1,290 | 435 | 698 |
| Tennessee | 35,943 | 25,552 | 12,969 | 1,551 | 1,103 | 560 |
| Texas | 329,162 | 104,871 | 103,449 | 2,001 | 638 | 629 |
| Virginia | 87,320 | 39,856 | 39,293 | 2,866 | 1,308 | 1,289 |
| West Virginia | 11,550 | 4,550 | 2,296 | 2,797 | 1,102 | 556 |
| West | $1,012,775 | $282,516 | $216,508 | $3,672 | $1,024 | $785 |
| Alaska[a] | 16,987 | 5,242 | 6,930 | 4,047 | 1,249 | 1,651 |
| Arizona | 75,024 | 32,461 | 19,840 | 2,765 | 1,196 | 731 |
| California | 720,436 | 140,922 | 125,890 | 4,394 | 859 | 768 |
| Colorado | 43,509 | 24,399 | 13,242 | 2,541 | 1,425 | 773 |
| Hawaii[a] | 9,788 | 9,615 | 5,207 | 1,809 | 1,777 | 962 |
| Idaho | 9,757 | 3,660 | 2,579 | 1,715 | 643 | 453 |
| Montana | 2,997 | 1,380 | 1,094 | 922 | 425 | 337 |
| Nevada | 29,546 | 14,414 | 8,023 | 2,871 | 1,401 | 780 |
| New Mexico | 24,669 | 4,514 | 3,339 | 4,665 | 854 | 632 |
| Oregon | 14,222 | 7,359 | 8,865 | 1,284 | 664 | 800 |
| Utah | 7,308 | 5,214 | 3,280 | 1,343 | 958 | 603 |
| Washington | 51,998 | 31,617 | 16,672 | 3,412 | 2,074 | 1,094 |
| Wyoming | 6,533 | 1,719 | 1,547 | 3,891 | 1,024 | 921 |

[a]States have integrated jail-prison systems.
[b]The Rhode Island State Department of Health and Hospitals operated a centralized power plant that provided utilities to prisons and other government agencies. Utilities were unmetered and costs were allocated on the basis of square footage.

SOURCE: James J. Stephan, "Table 5. State Prison Expenditures for Medical Care, Food Service, and Utilities, Fiscal Year 2001," in *State Prison Expenditures 2001*, Bureau of Justice Statistics, June 2004, http://www.ojp.usdoj.gov/bjs/pub/pdf/spe01.pdf (accessed March 31, 2005)

**TABLE 2.10**

Employment and monthly payroll of the justice system, by activity and level of government, March 2001

| Activity | All governments | Federal | State | Local | Percent distribution Total | Percent distribution Federal | Percent distribution State | Percent distribution Local |
|---|---|---|---|---|---|---|---|---|
| **Total justice system** | | | | | | | | |
| Total employees | 2,295,423 | 197,263 | 741,007 | 1,357,153 | 100% | 8.6% | 32.3% | 59.1% |
| 2001 March payroll* | $8,150 | $1,035 | $2,513 | $4,602 | | 12.7 | 30.8 | 56.5 |
| **Police protection** | | | | | | | | |
| Total employees | 1,060,219 | 106,337 | 104,657 | 849,225 | 100% | 10.0% | 9.9% | 80.1% |
| 2001 March payroll | $4,003 | $581 | $407 | $3,016 | | 14.5 | 10.2 | 75.3 |
| **Judicial and legal** | | | | | | | | |
| Total employees | 488,143 | 57,953 | 162,982 | 267,208 | 100% | 11.9% | 33.4% | 54.7% |
| 2001 March payroll | $1,798 | $318 | $639 | $841 | | 17.7 | 35.5 | 46.8 |
| **Corrections** | | | | | | | | |
| Total employees | 747,061 | 32,973 | 473,368 | 240,720 | 100% | 4.4% | 63.4% | 32.2% |
| 2001 March payroll | $2,349 | $137 | $1,468 | $744 | | 5.8 | 62.5 | 31.7 |

*Payroll is in millions. Detail may not add to total because of rounding.

SOURCE: Lynn Bauer and Steven D. Owens, "Table 4. Employment and Monthly Payroll of the Justice System, by Activity and Level of Government, March 2001," in *Justice Expenditure and Employment in the United States, 2001*, Bureau of Justice Statistics, 2004, http://www.ojp.usdoj.gov/bjs/pub/pdf/jeeus01.pdf (accessed March 30, 2005)

**TABLE 2.11**

Average daily population and the number of men, women, and juveniles in local jails, midyear, selected years 1995–2003

| | 1995 | 2000 | 2002 | 2003 |
|---|---|---|---|---|
| **Average daily population[a]** | 509,828 | 618,319 | 652,082 | 680,760 |
| **Number of inmates, June 30** | 507,044 | 621,149 | 665,475 | 691,301 |
| Adults | 499,300 | 613,534 | 658,228 | 684,431 |
| Male | 448,000 | 543,120 | 581,411 | 602,781 |
| Female | 51,300 | 70,414 | 76,817 | 81,650 |
| Juveniles[b] | 7,800 | 7,615 | 7,248 | 6,869 |
| Held as adults[c] | 5,900 | 6,126 | 6,112 | 5,484 |
| Held as juveniles | 1,800 | 1,489 | 1,136 | 1,385 |

Note: Data are for June 30 in 1995, 2000, and 2003; for June 29 in 2001; and June 28, for 2002. Detailed data for 1995 were estimated and rounded to the nearest 100.
[a]The average daily population is the sum of the number of inmates in a jail each day for a year, divided by the total number of days in the year.
[b]Juveniles are persons held under the age of 18.
[c]Includes juveniles who were tried or awaiting trial as adults.

SOURCE: Paige M. Harrison and Jennifer C. Karberg, "Table 9. Average Daily Population and the Number of Men, Women, and Juveniles in Local Jails, Midyear 1995, 2000, and 2002–2003," in *Prison and Jail Inmates at Midyear 2003*, Bureau of Justice Statistics, May 2004, http://www.ojp.usdoj.gov/bjs/pub/pdf/pjim03.pdf (accessed April 2, 2005)

TABLE 2.12

**State and federal prisoners held in private facilities and local jails, by jurisdiction, yearend 2002 and 2003**

| Region and jurisdiction | Private facilities | | | Local jails | | |
|---|---|---|---|---|---|---|
| | 2003 | 2002 | Percent of all inmates, 2003[a] | 2003 | 2002 | Percent of all inmates, 2003[a] |
| U.S. total | 95,522 | 93,912 | 6.5% | 73,343 | 72,550 | 5.0% |
| Federal[b] | 21,865 | 20,274 | 12.6 | 3,278 | 3,377 | 1.9 |
| State | 73,657 | 73,638 | 5.7 | 70,065 | 69,173 | 5.4 |
| **Northeast** | 3,201 | 3,146 | 1.8% | 1,911 | 2,234 | 1.1% |
| Connecticut | 0 | 0 | 0.0 | d | d | d |
| Maine | 30 | 8 | 1.5 | 0 | 0 | 0.0 |
| Massachusetts | 0 | 0 | 0.0 | 361 | 375 | 3.5 |
| New Hampshire | 0 | 0 | 0.0 | 7 | 11 | 0.3 |
| New Jersey[c] | 2,636 | 2,601 | 9.7 | 1,542 | 1,528 | 5.7 |
| New York | 0 | 0 | 0.0 | 1 | 320 | 0.0 |
| Pennsylvania | 535 | 537 | 1.3 | 0 | 0 | 0.0 |
| Rhode Island[c] | 0 | 0 | 0.0 | d | d | d |
| Vermont[c] | 0 | 0 | 0.0 | d | d | d |
| **Midwest** | 4,957 | 6,748 | 2.0% | 2,386 | 1,801 | 1.0% |
| Illinois | 0 | 0 | 0.0 | 0 | 0 | 0.0 |
| Indiana | 652 | 843 | 2.8 | 1,724 | 1,262 | 7.5 |
| Iowa | 0 | 0 | 0.0 | 0 | 0 | 0.0 |
| Kansas | 0 | 0 | 0.0 | 0 | 0 | 0.0 |
| Michigan | 480 | 460 | 1.0 | 42 | 30 | 0.1 |
| Minnesota | 0 | 0 | 0.0 | 283 | 221 | 3.6 |
| Missouri | 0 | 0 | 0.0 | 0 | 0 | 0.0 |
| Nebraska | 0 | 0 | 0.0 | 0 | 0 | 0.0 |
| North Dakota | 0 | 23 | 0.0 | 44 | 9 | 3.6 |
| Ohio | 1,901 | 1,927 | 4.2 | 0 | 0 | 0.0 |
| South Dakota | 25 | 32 | 0.8 | 29 | 12 | 1.0 |
| Wisconsin | 1,899 | 3,463 | 8.4 | 264 | 267 | 1.2 |
| **South** | 48,222 | 46,091 | 8.2% | 60,810 | 60,036 | 10.3% |
| Alabama | 1,698 | 0 | 5.8 | 1,340 | 2,449 | 4.6 |
| Arkansas | 0 | 0 | 0.0 | 1,016 | 1,172 | 7.8 |
| Delaware | 0 | 0 | 0.0 | d | d | d |
| Florida | 4,330 | 4,173 | 5.4 | 48 | 47 | 0.1 |
| Georgia | 4,589 | 4,573 | 9.7 | 4,949 | 4,975 | 10.5 |
| Kentucky | 1,640 | 1,635 | 9.9 | 3,969 | 3,657 | 23.9 |
| Louisiana | 2,918 | 2,929 | 8.1 | 16,549 | 16,022 | 45.9 |
| Maryland | 122 | 127 | 0.5 | 234 | 168 | 1.0 |
| Mississippi | 3,463 | 3,435 | 14.9 | 4,724 | 4,550 | 20.4 |
| North Carolina | 215 | 186 | 0.6 | 0 | 0 | 0.0 |
| Oklahoma | 6,022 | 6,470 | 26.4 | 1,869 | 1,497 | 8.2 |
| South Carolina | 44 | 21 | 0.2 | 424 | 415 | 1.8 |
| Tennessee | 5,049 | 4,200 | 19.9 | 6,283 | 6,717 | 24.7 |
| Texas | 16,570 | 16,773 | 9.9 | 13,331 | 12,375 | 8.0 |
| Virginia | 1,562 | 1,569 | 4.5 | 5,106 | 5,024 | 14.6 |
| West Virginia | 0 | 0 | 0.0 | 968 | 968 | 20.3 |
| **West** | 17,277 | 17,653 | 6.0% | 4,958 | 5,102 | 1.7% |
| Alaska | 1,386 | 1,360 | 30.6 | d | d | d |
| Arizona | 2,323 | 1,965 | 7.5 | 174 | 232 | 0.6 |
| California | 3,507 | 4,649 | 2.1 | 2,415 | 2,591 | 1.5 |
| Colorado | 3,013 | 2,452 | 15.3 | 221 | 160 | 1.1 |
| Hawaii | 1,478 | 1,347 | 25.4 | d | d | d |
| Idaho | 1,267 | 1,266 | 21.5 | 239 | 295 | 4.1 |
| Montana | 1,059 | 963 | 29.3 | 567 | 419 | 15.7 |
| Nevada | 0 | 434 | 0.0 | 190 | 177 | 1.8 |
| New Mexico | 2,751 | 2,690 | 44.2 | 0 | 0 | 0.0 |
| Oregon | 0 | 0 | 0.0 | 0 | 0 | 0.0 |
| Utah | 0 | 0 | 0.0 | 1,065 | 1,170 | 18.5 |
| Washington[c] | 0 | 0 | 0.0 | 0 | 0 | 0.0 |
| Wyoming | 493 | 527 | 26.3 | 87 | 58 | 4.6 |

[a]Based on the total number of inmates under state or federal jurisdiction.
[b]Includes federal inmates in non-secure privately operated facilities (6,471 in 2003, and 6,598 in 2002).
[c]Inmates held in other state facilities include interstate compact cases.
[d]Not applicable. Prison and jails form an integrated system.

SOURCE: Paige M. Harrison and Allen J. Beck, "Table 7. State and Federal Prisoners Held in Private Facilities and Local Jails, by Jurisdiction, Yearend 2002 and 2003," in *Prisoners in 2003*, Bureau of Justice Statistics, November 2004, http://www.ojp.usdoj.gov/bjs/pub/pdf/p03.pdf (accessed March 30, 2005)

# CHAPTER 3
# JAILS

Corrections institutions are organized in tiers by level of government and, at each level (federal, state, and local), specific types of institutions provide corrections functions based on the relative severity of the offenses committed. The most restrictive form of corrections is incarceration in a prison. Both the federal and the state governments operate their own prison systems; within the federal government, the military maintains its own prisons. Prison inmates serve time for serious offenses and are incarcerated for a year or longer.

In contrast, most people sentenced to jail serve less than a year for misdemeanors and offenses against the public order. Jails are operated at the local level—by cities and counties. The federal government operates some jails as well, and within the federal government, the Bureau of Immigration and Customs Enforcement has its own detention facilities. In some states, jails and prisons are operated under a single state authority, but the distinction—prisons for long terms and for serious offenses, jails for lesser terms and for less serious offenses—is still maintained.

Probation is the most common form of corrections without incarceration and is one form of what is known as "community corrections." In addition to holding offenders for short terms of confinement, jails also serve other purposes, including:

- Receiving individuals pending arraignment and holding them awaiting trial, conviction, or sentencing

- Readmitting probation, parole, and bail-bond violators and absconders

- Temporarily detaining juveniles pending transfer to juvenile authorities

- Holding mentally ill persons pending their movement to appropriate health facilities

- Holding individuals for the military, for protective custody, for contempt, and for the courts as witnesses

- Releasing convicted inmates to the community upon completion of sentence

- Transferring inmates to federal, state, or other authorities

- Housing inmates for federal, state, or other authorities because of crowding of their facilities

- Operating community-based programs as alternatives to incarceration

- Holding inmates sentenced to short terms (generally under one year)

## NUMBER OF JAIL INMATES

People in jail represent the smallest percentage of individuals in custody. According to Paige M. Harrison and Jennifer C. Karberg in *Prison and Jail Inmates at Midyear 2003* (Bureau of Justice Statistics, May 2004), on June 30, 2003, the nation's jails held or supervised 762,672 inmates, more than 90% of those (691,301 inmates) were behind bars and the rest (71,371 inmates) were supervised outside the jail in community service, work release, weekend reporting, electronic monitoring, and other alternative programs. The jail population was up 3.9% from the year before as reported in *Prison and Jail Inmates at Midyear 2003*. (See Table 3.1.) The increase was just below the average annual growth of 4% experienced between 1995 and 2003.

According to Harrison and Karberg, the jail inmate population rose from 193 per 100,000 U.S. residents in 1995 to 238 per 100,000 in 2003. (See Table 3.2.) The average daily jail population for 2003 was 680,760, an increase of 4.4% from 652,082 in 2002 and up 33.5% from 509,828 in 1995. (See Table 2.11 in Chapter 2.)

Significant changes have occurred in the profile of this population in the eight-year period shown in Table 2.11. Men represented the overwhelming majority of the

TABLE 3.1

**Number of persons held in state or federal prisons or in local jails, 1995–2003**

| Year | Total inmates in custody | Prisoners in custody | | Inmates held in local jails | Total incarceration rate[a] |
|---|---|---|---|---|---|
| | | Federal | State | | |
| 1995 | 1,585,586 | 89,538 | 989,004 | 507,044 | 601 |
| 1999[b] | 1,893,115 | 125,682 | 1,161,490 | 605,943 | 672 |
| 2000[c] | 1,935,919 | 133,921 | 1,176,269 | 621,149 | 683 |
| 2001[c] | 1,961,247 | 143,337 | 1,180,155 | 631,240 | 685 |
| 2002[c] | | | | | |
| June 30 | 2,020,969 | 148,783 | 1,199,949 | 665,475 | 703 |
| December 31 | d | 151,618 | 1,209,640 | d | |
| 2003[c] | | | | | |
| June 30 | 2,078,570 | 159,275 | 1,221,501 | 691,301 | 715 |
| Percent change, 6/30/02–6/30/03 | 2.9% | 7.1% | 1.8% | 3.9% | |
| Annual average increase, 12/31/95–6/30/03 | 3.7% | 8.0% | 2.9% | 4.0% | |

Note: Jail counts are for mid-year (June 30) and exclude persons who were supervised outside of a jail facility. State and federal prisoner counts for 1995–2003 are for December 31.
[a]Persons in custody per 100,000 residents in each reference year.
[b]The incarceration rate for 1999 was adjusted based on the resident population estimated for December 31, 1999, using the *2000 Census of Population and Housing.*
[c]Total counts include federal inmates in non-secure privately operated facilities (6,143 in 2000, 6,192 in 2001, and 6,762 (June) and 6,598 (December) in 2002, and 6,493 in 2003) and exclude those District of Columbia inmates reported in the Annual Survey of Jails.
[d]Not available.

SOURCE: Paige M. Harrison and Jennifer C. Karberg, "Table 1. Number of Persons Held in State or Federal Prisons or in Local Jails, 1995–2003," in *Prison and Jail Inmates at Midyear 2003*, Bureau of Justice Statistics, May 2004, http://www.ojp.usdoj.gov/bjs/pub/pdf/pjim03.pdf (accessed April 2, 2005)

TABLE 3.2

**Number held in jail and incarceration rate, 1995 and 1999–2003**

| Year | Number held in jail | Jail incarceration rate* |
|---|---|---|
| 2003 | 691,301 | 238 |
| 2002 | 665,475 | 231 |
| 2001 | 631,240 | 222 |
| 2000 | 621,149 | 220 |
| 1999 | 605,943 | 215 |
| 1995 | 507,044 | 193 |

*Number of jail inmates per 100,000 U.S. residents on July 1 of each year.

SOURCE: Paige M. Harrison and Jennifer C. Karberg, "Jail Incarceration Rates Rose in Last 12-Month Period," in *Prison and Jail Inmates at Midyear 2003*, Bureau of Justice Statistics, May 2004, http://www.ojp.usdoj.gov/bjs/pub/pdf/pjim03.pdf (accessed April 2, 2005)

the period 1990–2001, total estimated arrests first rose from 14.2 million in 1990 to 15.3 million in 1997, the peak year in this timeframe. Thereafter, arrests declined every year to reach 13.7 million in 2003. For the period as a whole, arrests decreased at the rate of 0.3% a year—versus a growth in jail population of 4% a year in the same period. The overall arrest rate, therefore, does not explain the increase in jail population. Individuals are jailed for periods of less than a year, and therefore a peak in arrests in 1997 does not influence the jail population in 2003.

Table 3.3 shows arrests by categories for 2003. The largest single category is "drug abuse violations." The even larger classification, "all other offenses" is an aggregation of offenses against specific state and local statutes that are not used elsewhere in the tabulation. Arrests for drug abuse violations were up by 22.4% in the ten-year period from 1994 to 2003. Other categories showed a decline during this period. Murders were down 36.2%, robbery 25%, and forcible rape 22.3%. More rigorous prosecution of drug violations may, in part, explain why the rate of growth in jail populations is higher than the growth rate of total arrests.

### Sentencing Status and Procedural Delays

According to Doris J. James in *Profile of Jail Inmates, 2002* (Bureau of Justice Statistics, July 2004), 28.2% of jail inmates in 2002 were detained awaiting arraignment or trial, and about 15% were held on a prior sentence but also awaiting arraignment or trial on a new charge. These percentages are in line with data shown in the Bureau's publication *Felony Sentences in State*

jail population throughout the period, but the proportion of women has increased. In 1995 women represented 10.2% of the local jail population; in 2003 they were 11.9%. In addition, the female population grew at an average annual rate of 6.4%, compared to the male jail population's 3.9% average annual growth rate in 2003. While the overall number of inmates in local jails has been rising, the number of juveniles in jail has dropped from 7,800 in 1995 to 6,869 in 2003.

### REASONS FOR THE GROWING INMATE POPULATION

#### Arrest Statistics

The FBI collects data on arrests and publishes the numbers in its *Crime in the United States* series. During

TABLE 3.3

**Estimated number of arrests, 2003**

| | |
|---|---:|
| Total[a] | 13,639,479 |
| Murder and nonnegligent manslaughter | 13,190 |
| Forcible rape | 26,350 |
| Robbery | 107,553 |
| Aggravated assault | 449,933 |
| Burglary | 290,956 |
| Larceny-theft | 1,145,074 |
| Motor vehicle theft | 152,934 |
| Arson | 16,163 |
|     Violent crime[b] | 597,026 |
|     Property crime[b] | 1,605,127 |
| Other assaults | 1,246,698 |
| Forgery and counterfeiting | 111,823 |
| Fraud | 299,138 |
| Embezzlement | 16,826 |
| Stolen property; buying, receiving, possessing | 126,775 |
| Vandalism | 273,431 |
| Weapons; carrying, possessing, etc. | 167,972 |
| Prostitution and commercialized vice | 75,190 |
| Sex offenses (except forcible rape and prostitution) | 91,546 |
| Drug abuse violations | 1,678,192 |
| Gambling | 10,954 |
| Offenses against the family and children | 136,034 |
| Driving under the influence | 1,448,148 |
| Liquor laws | 612,079 |
| Drunkenness | 548,616 |
| Disorderly conduct | 639,371 |
| Vagrancy | 28,948 |
| All other offenses | 3,665,543 |
| Suspicion | 7,163 |
| Curfew and loitering law violations | 136,461 |
| Runaways | 123,581 |

[a]Does not include suspicion.
[b]Violent crimes are offenses of murder, forcible rape, robbery, and aggravated assault. Property crimes are offenses of burglary, larceny-theft, motor vehicle theft, and arson.

SOURCE: "Table 29. Estimated Number of Arrests: United States, 2003," in *Crime in the United States, 2003*, U.S. Department of Justice, Federal Bureau of Investigation,2004, http://www.fbi.gov/ucr/cius_03/pdf/03sec4.pdf (accessed April 2, 2005)

*Courts, 2002* (Matthew R. Durose and Patrick A. Langan, Bureau of Justice Statistics, December 2004). In the period between 1992 and 2002, the median number of days required to dispose of all cases increased from 138 days to 184 days. In 2002 the median time between arrest and sentencing for violent offenses was 218 days; for property offenses, 172 days; and for drug offenses, 175 days. Of all persons convicted of a felony in state courts, 78% were sentenced within one year following arrest.

## LARGEST JAIL JURISDICTIONS

In *Prison and Jail Inmates at Midyear 2003*, Harrison and Karberg reported that in 2003 the country's fifty largest jail jurisdictions held about one-third (31.2%) of all jail inmates, accounting for a total jail population of 215,729. Twenty states had jails that made the top fifty based on average daily population. Some states had more than one among the largest fifty jails: California (twelve), Florida (eight), Texas (seven), Georgia (three), Ohio (two), Pennsylvania (two), and Tennessee (two). Los Angeles County and New York City together accounted for 33,700 inmates, or 5% of the national total. The top five jail jurisdictions by number of prisoners were Los Angeles County; New York City; Cook County, Illinois; Maricopa County, Arizona; and Harris County, Texas.

According to *Prison and Jail Inmates at Midyear 2003*, seventeen of the fifty largest jurisdictions had a drop in jail population. Those with the largest decreases were Contra Costa County, California (down 15.7%); Travis County, Texas (down 15.5%); and Milwaukee County, Wisconsin (down 12.9%). Conversely, eleven jail jurisdictions of the fifty largest experienced double-digit growth. The largest increase was seen in Fresno County, California (up 43.1%). Other jail jurisdictions with large increases included Fulton County, Georgia (up 22.7%); Hillsborough County, Florida (up 19.1%); and De Kalb County, Georgia (up 14.9%).

## RATED CAPACITY

State or local rating officials define "rated capacity" as the maximum number of beds or inmates that may be housed in a jail. In 2003 U.S. jails added 22,572 beds to total jail capacity, bringing it to 736,471, according to Harrison and Karberg in *Prison and Jail Inmates at Midyear 2003*. (See Table 3.4.) This was the smallest annual increase since 1995. Capacity utilization had dropped to 90% in 2001 but increased to 94% in 2003. During that period the number of beds increased but not at the same rate as inmates.

TABLE 3.4

**Rated capacity of local jails and percent of capacity occupied, 1990 and 1995–2003**

| Year | Rated capacity[a] | Amount of capacity added[b] | Percent of capacity occupied[c] |
|---|---:|---:|---:|
| 2003 | 736,471 | 22,572 | 94% |
| 2002 | 713,899 | 14,590 | 93 |
| 2001 | 699,309 | 21,522 | 90 |
| 2000 | 677,787 | 25,466 | 92 |
| 1999 | 652,321 | 39,541 | 93 |
| 1998 | 612,780 | 26,216 | 97 |
| 1997 | 586,564 | 23,593 | 97 |
| 1996 | 562,971 | 17,208 | 92 |
| 1995 | 545,763 | 41,439 | 93 |
| 1990 | 389,171 | | 104 |
| Average annual increase, 1995–2003 | 3.8% | 23,839 | |

[a]Rated capacity is the number of beds or inmates assigned by a rating official to facilities within each jurisdiction.
[b]The number of beds added during the 12 months ending June 30 of each year.
[c]The number of inmates divided by the rated capacity times 100.

SOURCE: Paige M. Harrison and Jennifer C. Karberg, "Table 11. Rated Capacity of Local Jails and Percent of Capacity Occupied, 1990 and 1995–2003," in *Prison and Jail Inmates at Midyear 2003*, Bureau of Justice Statistics, May 2004, http://www.ojp.usdoj.gov/bjs/pub/pdf/pjim03.pdf (accessed April 2, 2005)

## TABLE 3.5

**Jail occupancy as a percent of capacity, 2002–03**

| Size of jurisdiction* | Percent of capacity occupied | |
|---|---|---|
| | 2003 | 2002 |
| Total | 94% | 93% |
| Fewer than 50 inmates | 67 | 68 |
| 50–99 | 90 | 89 |
| 100–249 | 92 | 93 |
| 250–499 | 94 | 95 |
| 500–999 | 99 | 98 |
| 1,000 or more | 96 | 95 |

*Based on the average daily population in the year ending June 30.

SOURCE: Paige M. Harrison and Jennifer C. Karberg, "At Midyear 2003, 94% of Jail Capacity Occupied," in *Prison and Jail Inmates at Midyear 2003*, Bureau of Justice Statistics, May 2004, http://www.ojp.usdoj.gov/bjs/pub/pdf/pjim03.pdf (accessed April 2, 2005)

## TABLE 3.6

**Gender, race, Hispanic origin, and conviction status of local jail inmates, midyear, selected years 1995–2003**

| Characteristic | Percent of jail inmates | | | |
|---|---|---|---|---|
| | 1995 | 2000 | 2002 | 2003 |
| **Total** | **100%** | **100%** | **100%** | **100%** |
| **Gender** | | | | |
| Male | 89.8% | 88.6% | 88.4% | 88.1% |
| Female | 10.2 | 11.4 | 11.6 | 11.9 |
| **Race/Hispanic origin** | | | | |
| White[a] | 40.1% | 41.9% | 43.8% | 43.6% |
| Black[a] | 43.5 | 41.3 | 39.8 | 39.2 |
| Hispanic | 14.7 | 15.1 | 14.7 | 15.4 |
| Other[b] | 1.7 | 1.6 | 1.6 | 1.8 |
| **Conviction status (adults only)** | | | | |
| Convicted | 44.0% | 44.0% | 40.0% | 39.4% |
| Male | 39.7 | 39.0 | 35.4 | 34.7 |
| Female | 4.3 | 5.0 | 4.6 | 4.7 |
| Unconvicted | 56.0 | 56.0 | 59.9 | 60.6 |
| Male | 50.0 | 50.0 | 53.0 | 53.5 |
| Female | 6.0 | 6.0 | 6.9 | 7.1 |

Note: Detail may not add to total because of rounding.
[a]Non-Hispanic only.
[b]Includes Asians, American Indians, Alaska Natives, Native Hawaiians, and other Pacific Islanders.

SOURCE: Paige M. Harrison and Jennifer C. Karberg, "Table 10. Gender, Race, Hispanic Origin, and Conviction Status of Local Jail Inmates, Midyear 1995, 2000, and 2002–2003," in *Prison and Jail Inmates at Midyear 2003*, Bureau of Justice Statistics, May 2004, http://www.ojp.usdoj.gov/bjs/pub/pdf/pjim03.pdf (accessed April 2, 2005)

## TABLE 3.7

**Gender and race of jail inmates, 2003**

| | Estimated count | Jail incarceration rate[a] |
|---|---|---|
| Total | 691,301 | 238 |
| **Gender** | | |
| Male | 609,132 | 426 |
| Female | 82,169 | 56 |
| **Race/Hispanic origin** | | |
| White[b] | 301,200 | 151 |
| Black[b] | 271,000 | 748 |
| Hispanic | 106,600 | 269 |
| Other[c] | 12,500 | 80 |

Note: Inmate counts were estimated and rounded to the nearest 100. Resident population figures were estimated for July 1, 2003, based on the *2000 Census of Population and Housing*.
[a]Number of jail inmates per 100,000 residents in each group.
[b]Non-Hispanic only.
[c]Includes Asians, American Indians, Alaska Natives, Native Hawaiians, and other Pacific Islanders.

SOURCE: Paige M. Harrison and Jennifer C. Karberg, "Characteristics of Jail Inmate Population Changing Gradually," in *Prison and Jail Inmates at Midyear 2003*, Bureau of Justice Statistics, May 2004, http://www.ojp.usdoj.gov/bjs/pub/pdf/pjim03.pdf (accessed April 2, 2005)

At midyear 2003 jail systems with 500 to 999 beds reported the highest occupancy rate, 99%. (See Table 3.5.) The occupancy rate was 96% in jail systems with an average daily population of one thousand or more inmates, higher than in 2002, when the rate was 95%. All jurisdictions with fifty or more beds had occupancy rates of at least 90%. Jurisdictions with fewer than fifty inmates had a 67% capacity experience, down slightly from a rate of 68% the year before.

## JAIL INMATE CHARACTERISTICS

### Gender and Race

At midyear 2003, according to Harrison and Karberg in *Prison and Jail Inmates at Midyear 2003*, the jail incarceration rate for women was 119 per 100,000 female residents in the United States. At the same time, the rate for men was 1,331 per 100,000 adult male residents. In 1995 females represented 10.2% of jail inmates, and in 2003, 11.9%. (See Table 3.6.)

Most local jail inmates in 2003 were minorities, according to *Prison and Jail Inmates at Midyear 2003*. Table 3.6 shows that the percentage of whites and African-Americans experienced slight declines, while Hispanics saw a proportional increase. At midyear 2003, non-Hispanic whites made up 43.6% of the jail population, down from 43.8% at midyear 2002. Non-Hispanic African-Americans were 39.2% of jail inmates, down from 39.8% in 2002 and 43.5% in 1995. Hispanics were 15.4%, up from 14.7% in 2002, and other races (Asians/Pacific Islanders, Native Americans, and Alaska Natives) were 1.8%, up from 1.6% the previous year.

Relative to their proportion in the U.S. population, African-Americans were five times more likely than whites to be held in local jails, according to *Prison and Jail Inmates at Midyear 2003*. In addition, African-

Americans were nearly three times more likely than Hispanics to be held in jail and over nine times more likely than persons of other races. On a per capita basis, men were about eight times more likely than women to have been in a jail in 2003. (See Table 3.7.)

**TABLE 3.8**

**Prior alcohol use of jail inmates, 2002 and 1996**

| | Percent of jail inmates who drank alcohol | | | |
|---|---|---|---|---|
| | Regularly[a] | | At the time of the offense[b] | |
| Characteristics | 2002 | 1996 | 2002 | 1996 |
| **Total** | **66.0%** | **66.3%** | **33.4%** | **40.8%** |
| **Gender** | | | | |
| Male | 67.4% | 67.7% | 34.9% | 41.9% |
| Female | 55.4 | 54.5 | 22.2 | 31.1 |
| **Race/Hispanic origin[c]** | | | | |
| White[d] | 75.3% | 76.5 | 38.5% | 48.2% |
| Black[d] | 62.2 | 61.0 | 29.3 | 33.6 |
| Hispanic | 56.1 | 56.9 | 30.1 | 38.2 |
| **Most serious offense** | | | | |
| Violent | 65.7% | 67.7% | 37.6% | 40.7% |
| Property | 65.9 | 64.3 | 28.5 | 33.1 |
| Drug | 62.9 | 59.8 | 22.4 | 28.9 |
| Public-order, excluding driving while intoxicated | 65.0 | 68.6 | 26.1 | 32.7 |

[a]Includes inmates who reported ever drinking at least once a week for a month, as well as drinking daily or at least once a week during the year before the current offense.
[b]Includes all inmates with a current conviction or prior conviction.
[c]Jail inmates who identified more than one race not shown.
[d]Non-Hispanic inmates.

SOURCE: Doris J. James, "Table 11. Prior Alcohol Use of Jail Inmates, 2002 and 1996," in *Profile of Jail Inmates, 2002*, Bureau of Justice Statistics, July 2004, http://www.ojp.usdoj.gov/bjs/pub/pdf/pji02.pdf (accessed April 2, 2005)

## Drug and Alcohol Abuse

According to *Profile of Jail Inmates, 2002*, the majority of jail inmates reported that they were regular users of alcohol and drugs before they were arrested. Table 3.8 shows that in 2002, 66% of all inmates said that before their arrest, they had drunk alcohol regularly, defined as at least once a week for at least a month. This number is down slightly from 66.3% reported in 1996. One-third (33.4%) of all inmates had been drinking alcohol at the time of their arrest. The number of male inmates who had used alcohol at the time of their arrest was higher (34.9%) than for female inmates (22.2%). Of those arrested for violent offenses, 37.6% had been using alcohol at the time of their arrest.

Drug use among jail inmates was also common. In 2002, 54.6% of jail inmates had used drugs in the month prior to their arrest. In 1996 the number had been virtually the same, 54%. (See Table 3.9.) The most popular drugs used were marijuana or hashish, cocaine or crack, and methamphetamines. Almost 29% of all jail inmates had been using drugs at the time of their arrest, a decline from 34.9% in 1996. Combining the data on alcohol and drug use, almost half of all jail inmates (49.7%) were using alcohol or drugs at the time of their arrest. (See Table 3.10.) Male inmates were more likely to have been using alcohol at the time of their arrest (34.9%) than using drugs (28%). Female inmates were more likely to have been using drugs (34.4%) than using alcohol (22.2%).

Drug use often continues behind bars as well. According to *Drug Use, Testing, and Treatment in Jails* (Bureau of Justice Statistics, May 2000), facilities regularly testing inmates for drugs reported that about 10% of those tested were found to be positive.

## Juveniles in Jail

According to the Bureau of Justice Statistics in *Key Facts at a Glance* (May 28, 2004), the number of juveniles in jail rose from 2,301 in 1990 to 6,869 juveniles in 2003. (See Table 3.11.) The number hit its peak in 1999

**TABLE 3.9**

**Prior drug use of jail inmates, by type of drug, 2002 and 1996**

| | Percent of jail inmates who used drugs | | | | | | | |
|---|---|---|---|---|---|---|---|---|
| | All inmates | | | | Convicted inmates[a] | | | |
| | Ever | | Regularly[b] | | In the month before the offense | | At the time of the offense | |
| Type of drug | 2002 | 1996 | 2002 | 1996 | 2002 | 1996 | 2002 | 1996 |
| **Any drug** | 82.2% | 82.4% | 68.7% | 64.2% | 54.6% | 54.0% | 28.8% | 34.9% |
| Marijuana or hashish | 75.7% | 78.2% | 58.5% | 54.9 | 37.5% | 36.0% | 13.6% | 18.0% |
| Cocaine or crack | 48.1 | 50.4 | 30.9 | 31.0 | 20.7 | 22.8 | 10.6 | 14.3 |
| Heroin/opiates | 20.7 | 23.9 | 12.0 | 11.8 | 7.8 | 7.9 | 4.1 | 5.1 |
| Depressants[c] | 21.6 | 29.9 | 10.7 | 10.4 | 6.1 | 5.3 | 2.4 | 2.2 |
| Stimulants[d] | 27.8 | 33.6 | 17.1 | 16.5 | 11.4 | 9.6 | 5.2 | 5.6 |
| Hallucinogens[e] | 32.4 | 32.2 | 13.4 | 10.5 | 5.9 | 4.2 | 1.6 | 1.4 |
| Inhalants | 12.7 | 16.8 | 4.2 | 4.8 | 1.0 | 0.9 | 0.2 | 0.3 |

[a]Includes all inmates with a current conviction or with a prior conviction, but no new conviction for the current charge.
[b]Used drugs at least once a week for at least a month.
[c]Depressants include barbiturates, tranquilizers, and quaaludes.
[d]Stimulants include amphetamines and methamphetamines.
[e]Hallucinogens include LSD, ecstasy, and PCP.

SOURCE: Doris J. James, "Table 12. Prior Drug Use of Jail Inmates, by Type of Drug, 2002 and 1996," in *Profile of Jail Inmates, 2002*, Bureau of Justice Statistics, July 2004, http://www.ojp.usdoj.gov/bjs/pub/pdf/pji02.pdf (accessed April 2, 2005)

TABLE 3.10

**Convicted jail inmates using drugs or alcohol at the time of the offense, by characteristics of inmates, 2002 and 1996**

| Characteristic | Alcohol or drugs | | Alcohol | | Drugs | |
|---|---|---|---|---|---|---|
| | 2002 | 1996 | 2002 | 1996 | 2002 | 1996 |
| Total | 49.7% | 58.8% | 33.4% | 40.8% | 28.8% | 33.4% |
| **Gender** | | | | | | |
| Male | 50.2% | 58.9% | 34.9% | 41.4% | 28.0% | 32.4% |
| Female | 46.3 | 58.4 | 22.2 | 32.9 | 34.4 | 42.5 |
| **Race/Hispanic origin** | | | | | | |
| White* | 58.8 | 67.1% | 38.5 | 46.7 | 33.2 | 30.3 |
| Black* | 43.2 | 51.1 | 29.3 | 34.2 | 27.3 | 39.2 |
| Hispanic | 44.2 | 57.4 | 30.1 | 36.4 | 23.8 | 30.6 |
| **Most serious offense** | | | | | | |
| Violent | 47.2% | 52.9% | 37.6% | 40.9% | 21.8% | 24.1% |
| Property | 46.8 | 53.0 | 28.5 | 33.7 | 32.5 | 37.0 |
| Drug | 51.7 | 63.1 | 22.4 | 27.6 | 43.2 | 60.3 |
| Public-order, excluding driving while intoxicated | 37.2 | 45.4 | 26.1 | 33.7 | 19.8 | 22.7 |

Note: Includes all inmates with a current conviction or a prior conviction.
*Non-Hispanic inmates

SOURCE: Doris J. James, "Table 13. Convicted Jail Inmates Using Drugs or Alcohol at the Time of the Offense, by Characteristics of Inmates, 2002 and 1996," in *Profile of Jail Inmates, 2002*, Bureau of Justice Statistics, July 2004, http://www.ojp.usdoj.gov/bjs/pub/pdf/pji02.pdf (accessed April 2, 2005)

when 9,458 juveniles were in jail. Since that year, the numbers have been falling.

Of the 6,869 juveniles held in adult jails, according to *Prison and Jail Inmates at Midyear 2003*, 80% (5,484) had been convicted or were being held for trial as adults. Most states require that persons under eighteen be subject to juvenile court jurisdiction, but exceptions are made based on the severity of the offense or the offender's criminal history.

**TABLE 3.11**

**Jail populations by age and gender, 1990–2003**

[one-day count]

| Year | Adult males | Adult females | Juveniles |
|---|---|---|---|
| 1990 | 365,821 | 37,198 | 2,301 |
| 1991 | 384,628 | 39,501 | 2,350 |
| 1992 | 401,106 | 40,674 | 2,804 |
| 1993 | 411,500 | 44,100 | 4,300 |
| 1994 | 431,300 | 48,500 | 6,700 |
| 1995 | 448,000 | 51,300 | 7,800 |
| 1996 | 454,700 | 55,700 | 8,100 |
| 1997 | 498,678 | 59,296 | 9,105 |
| 1998 | 520,581 | 63,791 | 8,090 |
| 1999 | 528,998 | 67,487 | 9,458 |
| 2000 | 543,120 | 70,414 | 7,615 |
| 2001 | 551,007 | 72,621 | 7,613 |
| 2002 | 581,411 | 76,817 | 7,248 |
| 2003 | 602,781 | 81,650 | 6,869 |

SOURCE: "Jail Populations by Age and Gender, 1990–2003," *Demographic Trends in Jail Populations*, Bureau of Justice Statistics, May 28, 2004, http://www.ojp.usdoj.gov/bjs/glance/tables/jailagtab.htm (accessed April 2, 2005)

**Adult Conviction Status**

Convicted inmates include those awaiting sentencing, serving a sentence, or returned to jail for a violation of probation or parole. As shown at the bottom of Table 3.6, less than half (39.4%) of all adults under supervision by jail authorities had been convicted of their current charges in 2003. This figure is down from 44% in 2000. Harrison and Karberg reported in *Prison and Jail Inmates at Midyear 2003* that convicted female inmates comprised 4.7% of the inmate population in 2003, up from 4.6% in 2002. Adult inmates who were unconvicted at year-end 2003 made up 60.6% of the jail population; 53.5% of the jail population were unconvicted males, and unconvicted females comprised 7.1%.

**Confinement Status**

In 1995, for the first time, the Bureau of Justice Statistics' *Annual Survey of Jails* obtained the count of the number of offenders under community supervision. Respondents were asked if their jail jurisdictions operated any community-based programs and how many persons participated in them.

From June 30, 1995, to June 30, 2003, the number of persons supervised outside a jail facility rose from 34,869 to 71,371. (See Table 3.12.) The largest number of persons supervised outside a jail facility (17,102 or 24%) were sentenced to community service. Next were persons sentenced to electronic monitoring (12,678 or about 18%), people who wear electronic bracelets from which their location can be determined. The next largest category (12,111 or 17%) comprised individuals who were sentenced to spend their weekends in jail.

**TABLE 3.12**

**Persons under jail supervision, by confinement status and type of program, midyear 1995 and 2000–03**

| Confinement status and type of program | Number of persons under jail supervision | | | | |
|---|---|---|---|---|---|
| | 1995 | 2000 | 2001 | 2002 | 2003 |
| Total | 541,913 | 687,033 | 702,044 | 737,912 | 762,672 |
| Held in jail | 507,044 | 621,149 | 631,240 | 665,475 | 691,301 |
| Supervised outside | | | | | |
| a jail facility[a] | 34,869 | 65,884 | 70,804 | 72,437 | 71,371 |
| Weekender programs | 1,909 | 14,523 | 14,381 | 17,955 | 12,111 |
| Electronic monitoring | 6,788 | 10,782 | 10,017 | 9,706 | 12,678 |
| Home detention[b] | 1,376 | 332 | 539 | 1,037 | 594 |
| Day reporting | 1,283 | 3,969 | 3,522 | 5,010 | 7,965 |
| Community service | 10,253 | 13,592 | 17,561 | 13,918 | 17,102 |
| Other pretrial supervision | 3,229 | 6,279 | 6,632 | 8,702 | 11,452 |
| Other work programs[c] | 9,144 | 8,011 | 5,204 | 5,190 | 4,498 |
| Treatment programs[d] | [e] | 5,714 | 5,219 | 1,256 | 1,891 |
| Other/unspecified | 887 | 2,682 | 7,729 | 9,663 | 3,080 |

[a]Excludes persons supervised by a probation or parole agency.
[b]Includes only those without electronic monitoring.
[c]Includes persons in work release programs, work gangs, and other work alternative programs.
[d]Includes persons under drug, alcohol, mental health, and other medical treatment.
[e]Not available.

SOURCE: Paige M. Harrison and Jennifer C. Karberg, "Table 8. Persons under Jail Supervision, by Confinement Status and Type of Program, Midyear 1995 and 2000–2003," in *Prison and Jail Inmates at Midyear 2003*, Bureau of Justice Statistics, May 2004, http://www.ojp.usdoj.gov/bjs/pub/pdf/pjim03.pdf (accessed April 2, 2005)

Other offenders participated in drug, alcohol, or mental treatment programs, work release, day reporting, or home detention.

## PAYING FOR SERVICES

### Inmate Fees

The last comprehensive survey of statutory state authority permitting jails to charge fees for some kinds of services was conducted by the National Institute of Corrections (NIC), U.S. Department of Justice, in 1997 and published as *Fees Paid by Jail Inmates: Findings from the Nation's Largest Jails*. Data from that study indicate that most states authorized some kind of fee for services to inmates. An explanation of such fees follows:

- Medical services—collecting copayments or other fees for medical care

- Per diem fees—requiring jail inmates to reimburse the county for all or a portion of their daily incarceration costs, including housing, food, and basic programs

- Other nonprogram functions—charging for services such as bonding, telephone use, haircuts, release escort, and drug testing

- Participation in programs—imposing a fee or collecting a portion of any compensation earned by inmates in programs, such as work release, weekend incarceration, and electronic monitoring; or charging for participation in rehabilitation programs such as education or substance abuse treatment

### Jurisdiction Fees

The NIC's 1997 survey was an update of earlier work tracking what has become a major trend in the management of jails, a trend that was still strong in 2003 as evidenced by a review of journalistic reports of new proposals on the Internet. However, the trend has not been surveyed authoritatively in recent years. Jails are also attempting to finance a portion of their operations by charging other jurisdictions for housing inmates, as noted earlier. In the *Census of Jails, 1999* (Bureau of Justice Statistics, August 2001), the Department of Justice reported that at that time about 71% of all jail systems had established charges for keeping inmates for other jurisdictions. Fees charged averaged $48 a day for federal prisoners, $36 for state prisoners, and $38 for jail inmates held for other local jails.

## THE 1999 CENSUS OF JAILS

The BJS conducted its census of jails in 1999 and published the results in 2001. The Bureau usually reports on jails only as part of an annual survey of prisons and jails combined. The 1999 census provides a slightly dated but comprehensive look at jail staffing, facilities, and privately run jails. More recent data on some topics is also found in *Profile of Jail Inmates, 2002* and *Prison and Jail Inmates at Midyear 2003*.

### Facilities and Staffing

The number of jails across the country has remained relatively steady since 1983, rising from 3,338 in that year to 3,365 in 2002. There are 3,043 counties in the United States. The number of jails is roughly one per county plus additional jails in large urban areas. However, while the total facilities increased by just twenty-seven jails between 1983 and 2002, their capacity to house offenders has increased significantly. In 1983 rated capacity of the nation's jails was 261,556 or about seventy-eight beds per jail on average. In 2003 capacity had increased to 736,471. Jails, therefore, have grown in size if not significantly in number. The utilization of available jail capacity increased from 85% occupancy in 1983 to 101% crowding in 1988. Capacity growth then began, reflected in decreasing jail utilization: 97% of capacity was being used in 1993, 93% in 1999. Ninety-four percent of capacity was being used in 2003, but it had been as low as 90% in 2001.

The nation's publicly operated local jails employed 207,600 people in 1999, up from 64,560 in 1983, a 222% increase, more than matching the 171% increase in jail inmates, which stood in 1999 at 605,943 inmates, up from 223,551. In 1999 there was a staff member present for every 2.9 prisoners and a correctional officer for every 4.3 prisoners. Staff and guards had more inmates to administer in 1983 when there were 3.5 inmates per member of staff and 5.0 per correctional officer.

Two-thirds of jail staff members in 1999 were male; 66% of staffers were white, 24% were African-American, 8% were Hispanic, and 2% were of other races. Eighty-nine percent of inmates in 1999 were male; 41% of inmates were white, 42% African-American, 15% Hispanic (Hispanics may be of any race), and 2% of other races. In the data presented here, African-Americans and whites are non-Hispanics.

## Privately Operated Jails

In 1993 there were seventeen privately operating jails. Six years later, the number had increased to forty-seven jails, with 16,656 offenders. Of these, 13,814 were inmates in the private jails and 2,842 were supervised but not confined. On average, private jails were bigger than those operated by public agencies. Excluding offenders supervised but not confined, the average population of the forty-seven private jails in 1999 was 294 inmates. Most inmates were male, as in the public jails, 89%. The racial composition was somewhat different from public facilities: whites were 31.7%, African-Americans 38%, Hispanics 16%, and other races 14.2% of the population. Among private jail staff, women accounted for nearly half (46.3% of total staff, 40.8% of correctional officers). Private jail staffs supervised 3.3 inmates per person, a somewhat higher workload than in publicly run jails (2.9 inmates per staff). Private correctional officers supervised 5.3 inmates each, one more than publicly employed guards (4.3).

## Federal Jails

While the emergence of private jails is often mentioned in the press, less known is the fact that the federal government operates jails of its own—in addition to the much better known federal penitentiaries—and federal jails have also grown in number. The government increased such facilities from seven in 1993 to eleven in 1999. In 1999 they held nearly as many inmates as private jails—11,209, up from 5,899 in 1993, a near doubling of the federal jail population. Federal jail inmates were overwhelmingly male (93%). The majority, 63%, were white; 32% were African-American, and 5% were of all other races. Federal jail staff was 74.5% male. The total employee-to-inmate ratio in 1999 was 3.6, and each correctional officer supervised 6.7 inmates. Federal jails were crowded; they operated 39% above rated capacity—but the 1999 results were better than in 1993 when federal jails were 55% above capacity.

## JAIL INDUSTRIES

The National Institute of Justice defines a jail industry as one that uses inmate labor to create a product or provide a service that has value to a public or private client and for which the inmates receive compensation, whether it be pay, privileges, or other benefits. This definition describes a variety of activities. If a convict cuts the grass in front of the jail and thereby earns permission to watch television for an extra hour, the elements of labor, service provision, value, and compensation are all present. At the other end of the spectrum are those jail inmates who work for private-sector industry and earn real dollars.

Jail officials hoped these programs would develop inmate work habits and skills, generate revenues or reduce costs for the county, reduce inmate idleness, and meet needs in the community. The 1984 Justice Assistance Act (PL 98-473) removed some of the longstanding restrictions on interstate commerce of prisoner-made goods, thereby opening new opportunities for prison labor to work for the private sector. Both state prisons and county jails have entered into private-sector work programs.

In most programs, inmates receive no or low wages. In some instances, a portion of the money they earn is used to pay child support, victim restitution, or other obligations. Some receive extra food, longer recreation time, or more frequent visits from family. Their work often serves the public sector, and they are usually credited with "good time." Thus, the offenders pay for their crimes with public service labor, and their early release makes scarce bed space available for other offenders.

In 1992 the Bureau of Justice Assistance began funding the BJA Jail Work and Industry Center, which serves as a national clearinghouse for information and assistance about jail industries. According to *Developing a Jail Industry: A Workbook* (Bureau of Justice Assistance, Washington, DC, August 2002), many counties have experienced positive results from developing their own jail industries. These results include:

- Becoming self-sufficient (and sometimes profitable)
- Providing inmates with meaningful work experience and income
- Reducing inmate idleness
- Reducing inmate tension and misconduct
- Improving skills for postrelease employment
- Providing positive publicity
- Relieving crowding
- Providing an inmate management tool that promotes better inmate behavior

- Increasing inmate incentives

- Contributing to the community

## Jail Industries at Work

The Bureau of Justice Assistance recommends jail industries to even smaller facilities, explaining that many opportunities do not require much space to operate. Among those industries suitable for jails with little spare space are data entry, mailing, and clothing repair. (See Table 3.13.)

In an effort to help inmates learn new skills and establish solid work habits, the Santa Clara County Department of Correction in California (http://www.scvmed.org/site/0,4760,sid%253D11277,00.html) offers a jail industry program. As of spring 2005, inmates manufactured a range of products, including computer and office desks, bookshelves, benches, and toys. The items were sold to government and nonprofit organizations throughout the United States.

In 2005 inmates in Clark County, Washington, provided several services, including a computer recycling program (http://www.clark.wa.gov/sheriff/custody/jailindust.html). The service was geared toward training inmates in electronics, reducing the number of discarded computers that become hazardous waste in landfills, and providing rebuilt computers to nonprofit organizations, which distribute the rebuilt machines to low-income families. Programs in other regions included habitat restoration and enhancement as well as litter cleanup.

One factor that has limited the development of jail industries is that individuals sentenced to jail serve relatively short periods of time compared with those in prison (who serve for one year or longer). Continuity of employment in jail industries is therefore difficult to maintain. Work undertaken must call for skills widely distributed in the population; projects must be of short duration; and organization of the workplace and of the workflow must accommodate relatively rapid turnover. These considerations limit the usefulness of jail industries, as compared with prison industries, as training places for offenders intending to acquire new skills to be used as part of their rehabilitation after release.

**TABLE 3.13**

**Ten jail industries that can operate in a closet**

- Data entry
- Mailing
- Disassembly of small items
- Assembly of small items
- Sewing
- Engraving
- Shoe repair
- Refinishing small furniture items
- Clothing repair
- Answering telephone

SOURCE: Rod Miller, George Sexton, and Vic Jacobsen, "Exhibit 4–4. Ten Jail Industries That Can Operate in a Closet," in *Developing a Jail Industry: A Workbook*, Bureau of Justice Assistance, August 2002, http://www.ncjrs.org/pdffiles1/bja/182506.pdf (accessed April 2, 2005)

# CHAPTER 4

# PRISONS

In *Prisoners in 2003* (Washington, DC: Bureau of Justice Statistics, November 2004), Paige M. Harrison and Allen J. Beck reported that the prison population increased 2.1% between 2002 and 2003, although at a lower rate than the average annual growth rate of 3.4% since 1995. According to Harrison and Beck, the number of individuals under state jurisdiction grew by 20,370 (1.6%) between 2002 and 2003, and the number of those under federal jurisdiction by 9,531 (5.8%). The rate of increase has declined both for those in custody and those under prison jurisdiction since 1995. (See Table 4.1.)

The incarceration rate of prisoners in 2003 was 482 per 100,000 residents, an increase from 411 in 1995. Among those states exceeding the national incarceration rate were Louisiana (801), Mississippi (768), Texas (702), and Oklahoma (636). Maine (149), Minnesota (155), and North Dakota (181) were among the lowest rates. (See Table 4.2.)

## RATE OF INCARCERATION

The inmate population in the United States is measured by the rate of incarceration—that is, the number of people sent by the courts to prisons and jails per 100,000 people in the general population. As reported by The Sentencing Project, an advocacy group promoting alternatives to incarceration, in *U.S. Prison Populations— Trends and Implications* (Washington, DC, December 2004), the United States had the highest incarceration rate in the world in 2003 with 714 individuals confined in prisons or jails per 100,000 population, higher than Russia (548), South Africa (402), Israel (209), Mexico (169), England (141), China (119), Germany (96), or Japan (58).

The incarceration rate for federal and state prisoners in the United States, excluding those in jail, has risen from a low of seventy-nine in 1925 to 482 in 2003. (See Table 4.3 for data from earlier years.) Beginning in 1925,

the rate of incarceration of U.S. prisoners rose steadily for fifteen years to a peak of 137 in 1939. The rate declined somewhat and more or less leveled out to between 100 and 120 for the next thirty-five years. Then, in the early 1970s, the rate began to rise steadily. From 1974 to 2002, the rate increased more than four-fold. The rate for males jumped from about 200 inmates per 100,000 people in the mid-1970s to over 900 per 100,000 at the turn of the century. Female incarceration rates began to rise in the mid-1980s, growing to become 6.9% of the prison population in 2003.

Prison incarceration rates and prison populations vary widely by state and region of the country. In 2003 some smaller states experienced the largest growth in their prison populations. North Dakota led with growth of 11.4%, followed by Minnesota (10.3%), Montana (8.9%), Wyoming (7.8%), and Hawaii (7.5%). Despite leading in percentage of growth in prison population, North Dakota had a total prison population of 1,239 inmates, the smallest in the country. (See Table 4.4.)

## PRISONS AND THEIR CAPACITIES

The Bureau of Justice Statistics conducts a census of prisons at five-year intervals. As reported in *Census of State and Federal Correctional Facilities, 2000* (Bureau of Justice Statistics, August 2003), 1,320 state prisons housed 1,101,202 inmates and eighty-four federal facilities housed 110,974—for a total count of 1,404 prisons and slightly more than 1.2 million prisoners. State prisons were up from 1,277 in 1995, and federal facilities had increased from a total of seventy-seven in 1995. At the state level, the biggest growth was in facilities labeled minimum security (16.4%), followed by medium-security facilities (14.6%); at the federal level, the increase was in the minimum-security category (up 42.1%). To the 1,404 state and federal prisons must be added 264 privately operated

TABLE 4.1

**Change in the state and federal prison populations, 1995–2003**

| | Annual increase in the number of prisoners | | |
| | Custody | Jurisdiction | Percent change* |
|---|---|---|---|
| 1995 | 88,395 | 71,172 | 6.7% |
| 1996 | 49,222 | 57,494 | 5.1 |
| 1997 | 48,800 | 58,785 | 5.0 |
| 1998 | 47,905 | 58,420 | 4.7 |
| 1999 | 36,957 | 43,796 | 3.4 |
| 2000 | 25,182 | 18,191 | 1.3 |
| 2001 | 14,647 | 15,521 | 1.1 |
| 2002 | 37,457 | 36,112 | 2.6 |
| 2003 | 26,899 | 29,901 | 2.1 |
| Average annual increase, 1995–2003 | 41,718 | 43,266 | 3.4% |

Note: Counts based on comparable methods were used to calculate the annual increase and percent change.
*Change in the number of prisoners under state and federal jurisdiction.

SOURCE: Paige M. Harrison and Allen J. Beck, "Table 2. Change in the State and Federal Prison Populations, 1995–2003," in *Prisoners in 2003*, Bureau of Justice Statistics, November 2004, http://www.ojp.usdoj.gov/bjs/pub/pdf/p03.pdf (accessed March 31, 2005)

prisons with 93,077 inmates in 2000. When private prisons are added, the count of facilities in 2000 was 1,668.

## Crowding in Prisons

From 1995 to 2003, the number of state and federal prisons increased, and capacity in the state-run or state-supervised prison system increased. Old prisons were replaced with new ones; more prisoners were housed in privately operated prisons; and additions to capacity at existing sites added new beds. In 1995 states operated their prisons at 14% above capacity. According to *Prisoners in 2003*, twenty-three states were operating at or above capacity. Federal capacity, already strained in 1995, decreased further. In the federal sector, prisons operated at 125% of capacity in 1995 and 139% of capacity in 2003.

What does crowding mean? The American Correctional Association guidelines, *Standards for Adult Correctional Institutions*, call for a standard cell area of sixty square feet and for inmates spending no more than ten hours per day in their cells (Lanham, MD: American Correctional Association, 2003). In many prisons, inmates are double-bunked in cells designed for one or sleep on mattresses in unheated prison gyms or on the floors of dayrooms, halls, or basements. Some are housed in tents; others share the same bunks at different times of the day. Crowding makes it more difficult to segregate violent from nonviolent prisoners and contributes to the spread of such communicable diseases as tuberculosis. Overcrowded conditions can also cause tension, which can lead to fights and injuries.

## State and Federal Prisoners Held Elsewhere

**IN PRIVATELY RUN PRISONS.** At the end of 2003 a total of 95,522 prisoners under the jurisdiction of federal and state correctional authorities were housed in private facilities. This was an increase from 90,542 in 2000 and accounted for 5.7% of all state inmates and 12.6% of federal prisoners.

While the number of state prisoners in private facilities dropped slightly (1.8%) from 2000 to 2003, the number of federal prisoners increased from 15,524 in 2000 to 21,865 in 2003, a jump of some 40%. The states with the highest percentage of prisoners under private management were New Mexico (44.2%), Alaska (30.6%), and Montana (29.3%). Twenty states had no prisoners in privately operated facilities.

**IN LOCAL JAILS.** 73,343 prisoners were housed in local jails in 2003, 1.9% of all federal prisoners and 5.4% of state prisoners. Louisiana, with 45.9% of its prisoners in jails rather than in prisons, led this category, followed by Tennessee (24.7%) and Kentucky (23.9%).

## RISING PRISON POPULATIONS

Felonies, the most serious type of crime, are often punished with a prison sentence. Data on felony convictions at the state level tend to be reported later than data on prisoners, but trends can be discerned after a lag in time. Between 1994 and 2002, felony convictions in state courts increased from 872,220 to 1,051,000, an increase of 20%. (See Table 4.5.) During the same period, prisoners held in state and federal facilities increased from 1,016,691 to 1,380,516 (as shown in Table 4.3). Of those convicted of a felony, 45% received a prison sentence in 1994; in 1998 this percentage dropped to 44%; and in 2002 it had dropped to 41%. As shown in Figure 4.1, conviction rates for all major crimes decreased between 1994 and 2002. Prison populations are therefore rising despite the fact that fewer felons are being sentenced to prison time. The explanation for these contradictory trends lies with other factors such as the types of offenses being committed and the lengths of prison sentences.

## Drug Offenses and Violent Crimes Are Up

The rise in drug offenders confined to federal prison has contributed dramatically to the overcrowding of those prisons. According to data issued by the U.S. Bureau of Prisons (http://www.albany.edu/sourcebook/pdf/t654.pdf), of 20,686 total sentenced federal prisoners in 1970, some 3,384, or 16.3%, were drug offenders. By 1980, such offenders had climbed to 24.9% of the federal prison population. The percentage of sentenced drug offenders reached its peak in 1994 at 61.3% of the federal prison population. By 2002 the number of drug offenders had tapered off to comprise 54.7% of all federal

TABLE 4.2

## State and federal prisoners, by region and jurisdiction, yearend 1995, 2002, and 2003

| Region and jurisdiction | Sentenced prisoners | | | Percent change 2002–03 | Average change 1995–03[a] | Incarceration rate 2003[b] |
|---|---|---|---|---|---|---|
| | 2003 | 2002 | 1995 | | | |
| U.S. total | 1,409,280 | 1,380,516 | 1,085,022 | 2.1% | 3.3% | 482 |
| Federal | 151,919 | 143,040 | 83,663 | 6.2 | 7.7 | 52 |
| State | 1,257,361 | 1,237,476 | 1,001,359 | 1.6 | 2.9 | 430 |
| Northeast | 163,494 | 165,783 | 155,030 | −1.4% | 0.7% | 300 |
| Connecticut | 13,587 | 14,082 | 10,419 | −3.5 | 3.4 | 389 |
| Maine | 1,951 | 1,817 | 1,326 | 7.4 | 4.9 | 149 |
| Massachusetts[c] | 8,814 | 8,947 | 10,427 | −1.5 | −2.1 | 233 |
| New Hampshire | 2,434 | 2,451 | 2,015 | −0.7 | 2.4 | 188 |
| New Jersey[d] | 27,246 | 27,891 | 27,066 | −2.3 | 0.1 | 314 |
| New York | 65,198 | 67,065 | 68,486 | −2.8 | −0.6 | 339 |
| Pennsylvania | 40,880 | 40,164 | 32,410 | 1.8 | 2.9 | 330 |
| Rhode Island | 1,983 | 2,045 | 1,833 | −3.0 | 1.0 | 184 |
| Vermont | 1,401 | 1,321 | 1,048 | 6.1 | 3.7 | 226 |
| Midwest | 246,053 | 244,566 | 192,177 | 0.6% | 3.1% | 375 |
| Illinois[d] | 43,418 | 42,693 | 37,658 | 1.7 | 1.8 | 342 |
| Indiana | 23,007 | 21,542 | 16,046 | 6.8 | 4.6 | 370 |
| Iowa[d] | 8,546 | 8,398 | 5,906 | 1.8 | 4.7 | 290 |
| Kansas[d] | 9,132 | 8,935 | 7,054 | 2.2 | 3.3 | 334 |
| Michigan | 49,358 | 50,591 | 41,112 | −2.4 | 2.3 | 489 |
| Minnesota | 7,865 | 7,129 | 4,846 | 10.3 | 6.2 | 155 |
| Missouri | 30,275 | 30,080 | 19,134 | 0.6 | 5.9 | 529 |
| Nebraska | 3,976 | 3,972 | 3,006 | 0.1 | 3.6 | 228 |
| North Dakota | 1,147 | 1,025 | 544 | 11.9 | 9.8 | 181 |
| Ohio[d] | 44,778 | 45,646 | 44,663 | −1.9 | 0.0 | 391 |
| South Dakota | 3,016 | 2,911 | 1,871 | 3.6 | 6.1 | 393 |
| Wisconsin | 21,535 | 21,644 | 10,337 | −0.5 | — | 392 |
| South | 566,679 | 553,493 | 446,491 | 2.6% | 3.0% | 542 |
| Alabama | 28,612 | 27,532 | 20,130 | 3.9 | 4.5 | 635 |
| Arkansas | 13,013 | 12,999 | 8,520 | 0.1 | 5.4 | 476 |
| Delaware | 4,122 | 3,659 | 3,014 | 12.7 | 4.0 | 501 |
| Florida | 79,594 | 75,204 | 63,866 | 5.8 | 2.8 | 463 |
| Georgia | 47,200 | 47,424 | 34,168 | −0.5 | 4.1 | 539 |
| Kentucky | 16,190 | 15,572 | 12,060 | 4.0 | 3.7 | 392 |
| Louisiana | 36,047 | 36,032 | 25,195 | 0.0 | 4.6 | 801 |
| Maryland | 23,230 | 23,274 | 20,450 | −0.2 | 1.6 | 420 |
| Mississippi | 22,168 | 21,397 | 12,251 | 3.6 | 7.7 | 768 |
| North Carolina | 29,394 | 28,613 | 27,914 | 2.7 | 0.6 | 348 |
| Oklahoma[d] | 22,448 | 22,702 | 18,151 | −1.1 | 2.7 | 636 |
| South Carolina | 22,942 | 22,837 | 19,015 | 0.5 | 2.4 | 551 |
| Tennessee[d] | 25,403 | 24,989 | 15,206 | 1.7 | 6.6 | 433 |
| Texas[d] | 156,534 | 151,782 | 127,766 | 3.1 | 2.6 | 702 |
| Virginia | 35,067 | 34,973 | 27,260 | 0.3 | 3.2 | 472 |
| West Virginia | 4,715 | 4,504 | 2,483 | 4.7 | 8.3 | 260 |
| West | 281,135 | 273,634 | 207,661 | 2.7% | 3.9% | 419 |
| Alaska | 2,629 | 2,577 | 2,042 | 2.0 | 3.2 | 401 |
| Arizona | 29,722 | 28,008 | 20,291 | 6.1 | 4.9 | 525 |
| California | 162,678 | 159,984 | 131,745 | 1.7 | 2.7 | 455 |
| Colorado | 19,671 | 18,833 | 11,063 | 4.4 | 7.5 | 430 |
| Hawaii | 4,167 | 3,840 | 2,590 | 8.5 | 6.1 | 325 |
| Idaho | 5,887 | 5,746 | 3,328 | 2.5 | 7.4 | 427 |
| Montana | 3,620 | 3,323 | 1,999 | 8.9 | 7.7 | 393 |
| Nevada | 10,543 | 10,478 | 7,713 | 0.6 | 4.0 | 462 |
| New Mexico | 5,934 | 5,631 | 3,925 | 5.4 | 5.3 | 314 |
| Oregon | 12,695 | 12,080 | 6,515 | 5.1 | 8.7 | 354 |
| Utah | 5,681 | 5,475 | 3,447 | 3.8 | 6.4 | 240 |
| Washington | 16,036 | 15,922 | 11,608 | 0.7 | 4.1 | 260 |
| Wyoming | 1,872 | 1,737 | 1,395 | 7.8 | 3.7 | 372 |

—Not calculated.

[a]The average annual percentage increase from 1995 to 2003.

[b]Prisoners with sentences of more than 1 year per 100,000 residents.

[c]The incarceration rate includes an estimated 6,200 inmates sentenced to more than 1 year but held in local jails or houses of corrections.

[d]Includes some inmates sentenced to 1 year or less.

SOURCE: Paige M. Harrison and Allen J. Beck, "Table 4. Sentenced Prisoners under the Jurisdiction of State or Federal Correctional Authorities, by Region and Jurisdiction, Yearend 1995, 2002, and 2003," in *Prisoners in 2003*, Bureau of Justice Statistics, November 2004, http://www.ojp.usdoj.gov/bjs/pub/pdf/p03.pdf (accessed March 31, 2005)

TABLE 4.3

## Number and rate of sentenced state and federal prisoners, yearend 1925–2003

[By sex. Rate per 100,000 resident population in each group.]

| | Total | Rate | Male Number | Male Rate | Female Number | Female Rate |
|---|---|---|---|---|---|---|
| 1925 | 91,669 | 79 | 88,231 | 149 | 3,438 | 6 |
| 1926 | 97,991 | 83 | 94,287 | 157 | 3,704 | 6 |
| 1927 | 109,983 | 91 | 104,983 | 173 | 4,363 | 7 |
| 1928 | 116,390 | 96 | 111,836 | 182 | 4,554 | 8 |
| 1929 | 120,496 | 98 | 115,876 | 187 | 4,620 | 8 |
| 1930 | 129,453 | 104 | 124,785 | 200 | 4,668 | 8 |
| 1931 | 137,082 | 110 | 132,638 | 211 | 4,444 | 7 |
| 1932 | 137,997 | 110 | 133,573 | 211 | 4,424 | 7 |
| 1933 | 136,810 | 109 | 132,520 | 209 | 4,290 | 7 |
| 1934 | 138,316 | 109 | 133,769 | 209 | 4,547 | 7 |
| 1935 | 144,180 | 113 | 139,278 | 217 | 4,902 | 8 |
| 1936 | 145,038 | 113 | 139,990 | 217 | 5,048 | 8 |
| 1937 | 152,741 | 118 | 147,375 | 227 | 5,366 | 8 |
| 1938 | 160,285 | 123 | 154,826 | 236 | 5,459 | 8 |
| 1939 | 179,818 | 137 | 173,143 | 263 | 6,675 | 10 |
| 1940 | 173,706 | 131 | 167,345 | 252 | 6,361 | 10 |
| 1941 | 165,439 | 124 | 159,228 | 239 | 6,211 | 9 |
| 1942 | 150,384 | 112 | 144,167 | 217 | 6,217 | 9 |
| 1943 | 137,220 | 103 | 131,054 | 202 | 6,166 | 9 |
| 1944 | 132,456 | 100 | 126,350 | 200 | 6,106 | 9 |
| 1945 | 133,649 | 98 | 127,609 | 193 | 6,040 | 9 |
| 1946 | 140,079 | 99 | 134,075 | 191 | 6,004 | 8 |
| 1947 | 151,304 | 105 | 144,961 | 202 | 6,343 | 9 |
| 1948 | 155,977 | 106 | 149,739 | 205 | 6,238 | 8 |
| 1949 | 163,749 | 109 | 157,663 | 211 | 6,086 | 8 |
| 1950 | 166,123 | 109 | 160,309 | 211 | 5,814 | 8 |
| 1951 | 165,680 | 107 | 159,610 | 208 | 6,070 | 8 |
| 1952 | 168,233 | 107 | 161,994 | 208 | 6,239 | 8 |
| 1953 | 173,579 | 108 | 166,909 | 211 | 6,670 | 8 |
| 1954 | 182,901 | 112 | 175,907 | 218 | 6,994 | 8 |
| 1955 | 185,780 | 112 | 178,655 | 217 | 7,125 | 8 |
| 1956 | 189,565 | 112 | 182,190 | 218 | 7,375 | 9 |
| 1957 | 195,414 | 113 | 188,113 | 221 | 7,301 | 8 |
| 1958 | 205,643 | 117 | 198,208 | 229 | 7,435 | 8 |
| 1959 | 208,105 | 117 | 200,469 | 228 | 7,636 | 8 |
| 1960 | 212,953 | 117 | 205,265 | 230 | 7,688 | 8 |
| 1961 | 220,149 | 119 | 212,268 | 234 | 7,881 | 8 |
| 1962 | 218,830 | 117 | 210,823 | 229 | 8,007 | 8 |
| 1963 | 217,283 | 114 | 209,538 | 225 | 7,745 | 8 |
| 1964 | 214,336 | 111 | 206,632 | 219 | 7,704 | 8 |
| 1965 | 210,895 | 108 | 203,327 | 213 | 7,568 | 8 |
| 1966 | 199,654 | 102 | 192,703 | 201 | 6,951 | 7 |
| 1967 | 194,896 | 98 | 188,661 | 195 | 6,235 | 6 |
| 1968 | 187,914 | 94 | 182,102 | 187 | 5,812 | 6 |
| 1969 | 196,007 | 97 | 189,413 | 192 | 6,594 | 6 |
| 1970 | 196,429 | 96 | 190,794 | 191 | 5,635 | 5 |
| 1971 | 198,061 | 95 | 191,732 | 189 | 6,329 | 6 |
| 1972 | 196,092 | 93 | 189,823 | 185 | 6,269 | 6 |
| 1973 | 204,211 | 96 | 197,523 | 191 | 6,004 | 6 |
| 1974 | 218,466 | 102 | 211,077 | 202 | 7,389 | 7 |
| 1975 | 240,593 | 111 | 231,918 | 220 | 8,675 | 8 |
| 1976 | 262,833 | 120 | 252,794 | 238 | 10,039 | 9 |
| 1977[a] | 278,141 | 126 | 267,097 | 249 | 11,044 | 10 |
| 1977[b] | 285,456 | 129 | 274,244 | 255 | 11,212 | 10 |
| 1978 | 294,396 | 132 | 282,813 | 261 | 11,583 | 10 |
| 1979 | 301,470 | 133 | 289,465 | 264 | 12,005 | 10 |
| 1980 | 315,974 | 139 | 303,643 | 275 | 12,331 | 11 |
| 1981 | 353,673 | 154 | 339,375 | 304 | 14,298 | 12 |
| 1982 | 395,516 | 171 | 379,075 | 337 | 16,441 | 14 |
| 1983 | 419,346 | 179 | 401,870 | 354 | 17,476 | 15 |
| 1984 | 443,398 | 188 | 424,193 | 370 | 19,205 | 16 |
| 1985 | 480,568 | 202 | 459,223 | 397 | 21,345 | 17 |
| 1986 | 522,084 | 217 | 497,540 | 426 | 24,544 | 20 |
| 1987 | 560,812 | 231 | 533,990 | 453 | 26,822 | 22 |
| 1988 | 603,732 | 247 | 573,587 | 482 | 30,145 | 24 |
| 1989 | 680,907 | 276 | 643,643 | 535 | 37,264 | 29 |
| 1990 | 739,980 | 297 | 699,416 | 575 | 40,564 | 32 |
| 1991 | 789,610 | 313 | 745,808 | 606 | 43,802 | 34 |
| 1992 | 846,277 | 332 | 799,776 | 642 | 46,501 | 36 |
| 1993 | 932,074 | 359 | 878,037 | 698 | 54,037 | 41 |
| 1994 | 1,016,691 | 389 | 956,566 | 753 | 60,125 | 45 |
| 1995 | 1,085,022 | 411 | 1,021,059 | 789 | 63,963 | 47 |
| 1996 | 1,137,722 | 427 | 1,068,123 | 819 | 69,599 | 51 |
| 1997 | 1,194,581 | 444 | 1,120,787 | 853 | 73,794 | 54 |
| 1998 | 1,245,402 | 461 | 1,167,802 | 885 | 77,600 | 57 |
| 1999 | 1,304,074 | 463[c] | 1,221,611 | 913 | 82,463 | 59 |
| 2000 | 1,331,278 | 469[c] | 1,246,234 | 915 | 85,044 | 59 |
| 2001 | 1,345,217 | 470 | 1,260,033 | 896 | 85,184 | 58 |
| 2002 | 1,380,516 | 476 | 1,291,450 | 906 | 89,066 | 60 |
| 2003[d] | 1,409,280 | 482 | 1,316,495 | 915 | 92,785 | 62 |

Note: Prison population data are compiled by a year end census of prisoners in state and federal institutions. Data for 1925 through 1939 include sentenced prisoners in state and federal prisons and reformatories whether committed for felonies or misdemeanors. Data for 1940 through 1970 include all adult felons serving sentences in state and federal institutions. Since 1971, the census has included all adults or youthful offenders sentenced to a state or federal correctional institution with maximum sentences of over 1 year.

[a]Custody counts.
[b]Jurisdiction counts.
[c]Rates have been revised and are now based on population estimates from the 2000 decennial census.
[d]Preliminary; subject to revision.

SOURCE: Adapted from Kathleen Maguire and Ann L. Pastore, editors, "Table 6.22. Number and Rate (per 100,000 Resident Population in Each Group) of Sentenced Prisoners under Jurisdiction of State and Federal Correctional Authorities on December 31 United States, by Sex, 1925–2003," in *Sourcebook of Criminal Justice Statistics*, Bureau of Justice Statistics, August 2004, http://www.albany.edu/sourcebook/pdf/t622.pdf (accessed March 31, 2005).

7.5% a year, imprisoned drug offenders increased at an average rate of 14% a year. Federal prisoners, however, are a small fraction of total prisoners.

As reported by the Bureau of Justice Statistics (*Prison Statistics*, http://www.ojp.usdoj.gov/bjs/prisons.htm), the state prison population grew between 1995 and 2001 because of two factors. While 15% of that growth was because of a growing number of drug offenders entering state prisons, the growing number of violent offenders accounted for 63% of the total growth.

## More Time Is Served

Prison populations are influenced both by the length of a sentence a court imposes and by the percentage of the sentence the felon actually serves. As reported by Matthew R. Durose and Patrick A. Langan in *Felony Sentences in State Courts, 2002* (Bureau of Justice Statistics, December 2004), between 1994 and 2002 the average sentence imposed for all offenses fell from seventy-one months in 1994 to fifty-three months in

prisoners. (See Table 4.6.) Using data in this table, one can calculate that in the 1988 to 1998 period, during which state and federal prison populations increased

**TABLE 4.4**

Highest and lowest jurisdictions for selected characteristics of the prison population, yearend 2003

| Prison population | Number of inmates | Incarceration rate, 12/31/03 | | Inmates per 100,000 residents* | | Growth, 12/31/02 to 12/31/03 | | Percent change |
|---|---|---|---|---|---|---|---|---|
| **5 highest** | | | | | | | | |
| Federal | 173,059 | Louisiana | | 801 | | North Dakota | | 11.4% |
| Texas | 166,911 | Mississippi | | 768 | | Minnesota | | 10.3 |
| California | 164,487 | Texas | | 702 | | Montana | | 8.9 |
| Florida | 79,594 | Oklahoma | | 636 | | Wyoming | | 7.8 |
| New York | 65,198 | Alabama | | 635 | | Hawaii | | 7.5 |
| **5 lowest** | | | | | | | | |
| North Dakota | 1,239 | Maine | | 149 | | Connecticut | | −4.2% |
| Wyoming | 1,872 | Minnesota | | 155 | | New York | | −2.8 |
| Vermont | 1,944 | North Dakota | | 181 | | Michigan | | −2.4 |
| Maine | 2,013 | Rhode Island | | 184 | | New Jersey | | −2.3 |
| New Hampshire | 2,434 | New Hampshire | | 188 | | Ohio | | −1.9 |

*Prisoners with a sentence of more than 1 year per 100,000 in the resident population.

SOURCE: Paige M. Harrison and Allen J. Beck, "Smaller States Had High Rates of Prison Population Growth during 2003," in *Prisoners in 2003*, Bureau of Justice Statistics, November 2004, http://www.ojp.usdoj.gov/bjs/pub/pdf/p03.pdf (accessed March 31, 2005)

**TABLE 4.5**

Number of felony convictions in state courts, 1994–2002

| | Estimated number of felony convictions |
|---|---|
| 1994 | 872,220 |
| 1996 | 997,970 |
| 1998 | 927,720 |
| 2000 | 924,740 |
| 2002 | 1,051,000 |

SOURCE: Matthew R. Durose and Patrick A. Langan, "Estimated Number of Felony Convictions," in *Felony Sentences in State Courts, 2002*, Bureau of Justice Statistics, December 2004, http://www.ojp.usdoj.gov/bjs/pub/pdf/fssc02.pdf (accessed March 31, 2005)

2002. However, at the same time, the percentage of time actually served increased from 38% of the sentence in 1994 to 51% in 2002. The net effect of these averages was to increase the time actually served for several important categories of crime. The percentage of sentenced time actually served for murder, for example, rose from 47% in 1994 to 63% in 2002, while the actual time served for murder rose from 127 months in 1994 to 142 months in 2002. (See Table 4.7.)

Comparing the percent of imposed prison sentence actually served for 1994 and 2002 as shown in Table 4.7, all six offense categories have risen dramatically. Comparing the estimated actual time to be served in prison for 1994 and 2002, four out of the six offense categories have risen while the remaining two have stayed the same. The net effect of sentencing and time served between 1994 and 2002, therefore, was to increase the prison population because violent and property crimes represented the largest proportions of all felonies—while drug offenses were growing more rapidly.

## Truth-in-Sentencing Laws

Beginning in the mid-1980s, the federal government and many states passed truth-in-sentencing laws as part of a widespread movement to "get tough on crime." The idea behind these laws was to ensure that all or a substantial portion of each sentence imposed would actually be served. States operating under federal truth-in-sentencing guidelines require that 85% of sentences are served. Forty-two states, the District of Columbia, and the federal government operate under such statutes. Their effect has been longer retention of prisoners and thus a growth in prison populations.

## Parole Violators

The rising incidence of rearrest of those who have been paroled is yet another cause of a rising prison population. In 1990, 29.1% of all admissions to state prison systems were parole violators. According to *Prison and Jail Inmates Midyear 2003*, that proportion had increased to 33.6% of all admissions by 2002— 207,251 prisoners out of 615,377. (See Table 4.8.) Although statistics on why parolees are recommitted to prison are not routinely collected by the Bureau of Justice Statistics, a survey conducted in 1997 and reported in *Trends in State Parole, 1990–2000* (Bureau of Justice Statistics, October 2001) indicated that 69.9% of imprisoned parolees had committed a new offense. Some 16% of parolees were rearrested for drug violations.

## PRIVATIZATION OF PRISONS

Rising prison populations and the need to expand the prison system in the states has led to calls for privatization in this sphere as in others (telecommunications,

FIGURE 4.1

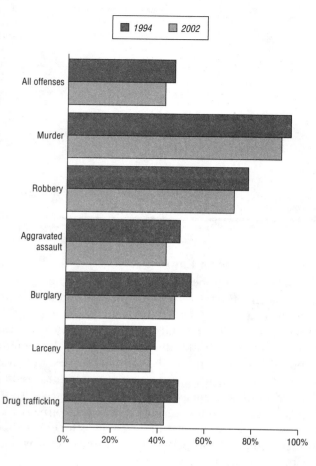

Percent of convicted felons who received a prison sentence, 1994–2002

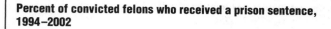

| | 1994 | 1998 | 2002 |
|---|---|---|---|
| **All offenses** | 45% | 44% | 41% |
| Murder | 95 | 94 | 91 |
| Robbery | 77 | 76 | 71 |
| Aggravated assault | 48 | 46 | 42 |
| Burglary | 53 | 54 | 46 |
| Larceny | 38 | 40 | 36 |
| Drug trafficking | 48 | 45 | 42 |

SOURCE: Adapted from Matthew R. Durose and Patrick A. Langan, "Percent of Convicted Felons Who Received a Prison Sentence, 1994–2002," in *Felony Sentences in State Courts, 2002,* Bureau of Justice Statistics, December 2004, http://www.ojp.usdoj.gov/bjs/pub/pdf/fssc02.pdf (accessed March 31, 2005)

TABLE 4.6

Drug offenders in the federal prison population, 1970–2002

| | | Sentenced population | | |
|---|---|---|---|---|
| | | | Drug offenses | |
| | Total sentenced and unsentenced population | Total | Number | Percent of total |
| 1970 | 21,266 | 20,686 | 3,384 | 16.3% |
| 1971 | 20,891 | 20,529 | 3,495 | 17.0 |
| 1972 | 22,090 | 20,729 | 3,523 | 16.9 |
| 1973 | 23,336 | 22,038 | 5,652 | 25.6 |
| 1974 | 23,690 | 21,769 | 6,203 | 28.4 |
| 1975 | 23,566 | 20,692 | 5,540 | 26.7 |
| 1976 | 27,033 | 24,135 | 6,425 | 26.6 |
| 1977 | 29,877 | 25,673 | 6,743 | 26.2 |
| 1978 | 27,674 | 23,501 | 5,981 | 25.4 |
| 1979 | 24,810 | 21,539 | 5,468 | 25.3 |
| 1980 | 24,252 | 19,023 | 4,749 | 24.9 |
| 1981 | 26,195 | 19,765 | 5,076 | 25.6 |
| 1982 | 28,133 | 20,938 | 5,518 | 26.3 |
| 1983 | 30,214 | 26,027 | 7,201 | 27.6 |
| 1984 | 32,317 | 27,622 | 8,152 | 29.5 |
| 1985 | 36,042 | 27,623 | 9,491 | 34.3 |
| 1986 | 37,542 | 30,104 | 11,344 | 37.7 |
| 1987 | 41,609 | 33,246 | 13,897 | 41.8 |
| 1988 | 41,342 | 33,758 | 15,087 | 44.7 |
| 1989 | 47,568 | 37,758 | 18,852 | 49.9 |
| 1990 | 54,613 | 46,575 | 24,297 | 52.2 |
| 1991 | 61,026 | 52,176 | 29,667 | 56.9 |
| 1992 | 67,768 | 59,516 | 35,398 | 59.5 |
| 1993 | 76,531 | 68,183 | 41,393 | 60.7 |
| 1994 | 82,269 | 73,958 | 45,367 | 61.3 |
| 1995 | 85,865 | 76,947 | 46,669 | 60.7 |
| 1996 | 89,672 | 80,872 | 49,096 | 60.7 |
| 1997 | 95,513 | 87,294 | 52,059 | 59.6 |
| 1998 | 104,507 | 95,323 | 55,984 | 58.7 |
| 1999 | 115,024 | 104,500 | 60,399 | 57.8 |
| 2000 | 123,141 | 112,329 | 63,898 | 56.9 |
| 2001 | 131,419 | 120,829 | 67,037 | 55.5 |
| 2002 | 139,183 | 128,090 | 70,009 | 54.7 |

Note: These data represent inmates housed in Federal Bureau of Prisons facilities; inmates housed in contract facilities are not included. Data for 1970–76 are for June 30; beginning in 1977, data are for September 30.

SOURCE: Kathleen Maguire and Ann L. Pastore, editors, "Table 6.54. Federal Prison Population, and Number and Percent Sentenced for Drug Offenses," in *Sourcebook of Criminal Justice Statistics*, Bureau of Justice Statistics, August 2004, http://www.albany.edu/sourcebook/pdf/t654.pdf (accessed March 31, 2005)

electric power). The basic assumption behind this movement is that the private sector is inherently more efficient and flexible than public bureaucracies because it is less constrained by regulations and is more cost effective. Private facilities also save the public the initial costs of prison construction, since those costs are assumed by private contractors. This saves the government from taking on long-term debt in order to build housing for more prisoners. In this view, a privatized or even a partially privatized corrections system would cost taxpayers less

money. Corrections functions, however, are ultimately vested in governmental hands, and private prisons must operate under established rules and regulations. The complexity of corrections activities is such that comparisons between private and public facilities are very difficult to make, and the cost savings achieved by private corrections are in dispute because the evidence is inconclusive.

Speaking before the National Conference of State Legislatures in July 2000 in Chicago, J. Michael Quinlan of the Corrections Corporation of America, the leading private prison company, cited statistics from the *1999 Corrections Yearbook* (Middletown, CT: Criminal Justice Institute, Inc., 1999) stating that, in 1998, public prisons cost $56.51 per day to operate per prisoner whereas private prison costs were $43.00 per

TABLE 4.7

**Sentences imposed and time served, 1994, 1998, and 2002**

| | 1994 | 1998 | 2002 |
|---|---|---|---|
| **Average imposed prison sentence length (in months)** | | | |
| **All offenses** | 71 mo | 57 mo | 53 mo |
| Murder | 269 | 263 | 225 |
| Robbery | 116 | 106 | 91 |
| Aggravated assault | 79 | 66 | 54 |
| Burglary | 69 | 52 | 50 |
| Larceny | 45 | 37 | 34 |
| Drug trafficking | 66 | 54 | 55 |
| **Percent of imposed prison sentence actually served** | | | |
| **All offenses** | 38% | 47% | 51% |
| Murder | 47 | 52 | 63 |
| Robbery | 44 | 51 | 58 |
| Aggravated assault | 46 | 57 | 66 |
| Burglary | 35 | 45 | 49 |
| Larceny | 37 | 45 | 52 |
| Drug trafficking | 32 | 41 | 45 |
| **Estimated actual time to be served in prison (in months)** | | | |
| **All offenses** | 27 mo | 27 mo | 27 mo |
| Murder | 127 | 136 | 142 |
| Robbery | 51 | 54 | 53 |
| Aggravated assault | 36 | 38 | 36 |
| Burglary | 24 | 24 | 24 |
| Larceny | 17 | 17 | 18 |
| Drug trafficking | 21 | 22 | 24 |

SOURCE: Adapted from Matthew R. Durose and Patrick A. Langan, "Sentences Imposed and Time Served, 1994, 1998, and 2002," in *Felony Sentences in State Courts, 2002*, Bureau of Justice Statistics, December 2004, http://www.ojp.usdoj.gov/bjs/pub/pdf/fssc02.pdf (accessed March 31, 2005)

diem. Survey results, however, are not universally accepted in the field of corrections because too many variables make generalizations impossible. While now somewhat dated, *Private and Public Prisons—Studies Comparing Operational Costs and/or Quality of Service* (Washington, DC: GAO/GGD-96-158, 1996) remains the most comprehensive report on state-sponsored investigations comparing private and public prisons. The following paragraph from the summary provides insight into the difficulties of comparing private and public facilities:

> Three of the studies we reviewed (California, Tennessee, and Washington) made comparisons of costs between reasonably matched private and public facilities that were operating within each state that was studied. Of the four private/public comparisons reported in these three studies, two showed no significant differences in operational costs, one showed a 7% difference in favor of the private facility, and the other reported the private facility to be more costly than one public facility but less costly than another public facility. One additional study (Texas) reported a 14% to 15% savings from privatization; however, the analysis for the Texas study was problematic because the comparison was based on hypothetical public facilities, not existing ones. We could not conclude from these studies that privatization of correctional facilities will not save money. However, these studies do not offer substantial evidence that savings have occurred.

TABLE 4.8

**Number of sentenced inmates admitted to state prisons, by type of admission, 1990–2002**

| Year | State prison admissions | | |
|---|---|---|---|
| | All* | New court commitments | Parole violators |
| 1990 | 460,739 | 323,069 | 133,870 |
| 1995 | 521,970 | 337,492 | 175,726 |
| 1998 | 565,291 | 347,270 | 206,152 |
| 1999 | 575,415 | 345,648 | 198,636 |
| 2000 | 584,643 | 350,431 | 203,569 |
| 2001 | 593,838 | 365,714 | 215,450 |
| 2002 | 615,377 | 392,717 | 207,251 |

*Based on inmates with a sentence of more than 1 year. Excludes escapes, AWOL's (absent without leave), and transfers to and from other jurisdictions.

SOURCE: Paige M. Harrison and Jennifer C. Karberg, "Number of Sentenced Inmates Admitted to State Prisons, by Type of Admission, 1990–2002," in *Prison and Jail Inmates at Midyear 2003*, Bureau of Justice Statistics, May 2004, http://www.ojp.usdoj.gov/bjs/pub/pdf/pjim03.pdf (accessed March 31, 2005)

A study conducted by the Bureau of Justice Assistance (*Emerging Issues on Privatized Prisons*, February 2001) found that cost savings were less than anticipated but that the prospect of privatization often was of benefit to those wanting to reform public prisons:

> It was discovered that, rather than the projected 20% savings, the average saving from privatization was only about 1%, and most of that was achieved through lower labor costs. Nevertheless, there were indications that the mere prospect of privatization had a positive effect on prison administration, making it more responsive to reform.

Despite resistance to the concept by those who champion government prisons, private prisons have become a growing alternative in many states and in the federal prison system as well. The Bureau of Justice Statistics has been tracking private prisons and prison populations on a consistent basis since 2000. These data show that as a percentage of all inmates under state and federal jurisdiction, the percentage of prisoners in private prisons has stayed at a steady 6.5%. (See Table 4.9.) According to *Prisoners in 2003*, private prisons held 5.7% of all state prisoners and 12.6% of all federal prisoners.

Table 4.9 also shows that while the overall percentage of private prisoners has remained the same, their numbers have been increasing along with the general prison population. The privately managed prison population grew from 90,542 in 2000 to 95,522 in 2003. Private prisons are estimated to have increased from sixty-seven in 1990 to 264 in 2000, according to the *Census of State and Federal Correctional Facilities, 2000* (Bureau of Justice Statistics, August 2003).

**TABLE 4.9**

**Number of inmates in privately operated facilities, 2000–03**

|  | Total | State | Federal | Percent of inmates |
|------|--------|--------|---------|--------------------|
| 2003 | 95,522 | 73,657 | 21,865 | 6.5% |
| 2002 | 93,912 | 73,638 | 20,274 | 6.5 |
| 2001 | 91,953 | 72,702 | 19,251 | 6.5 |
| 2000 | 90,542 | 75,018 | 15,524 | 6.5 |

SOURCE: Paige M. Harrison and Allen J. Beck, "Number of Inmates in Privately Operated Facilities, 2000 to 2003," in *Prisoners in 2003*, Bureau of Justice Statistics, November 2004, http://www.ojp.usdoj.gov/bjs/pub/pdf/p03.pdf (accessed March 31, 2005)

While privatization appears to be driven by a need to find solutions to the high costs of housing prisoners, not least the high capital expenditures required to build new prisons in an era of severe budgetary shortfalls at the state level, it is also evident from the public debate that the privatization issue transcends budgets and cost effectiveness and mirrors the opposing views of those who would rely upon the private sector and those who prefer that officials responsive to the voting public manage the public's business. Both sides acknowledge that the ultimate responsibility for corrections rests with the government. Therefore, government cannot completely privatize corrections; it must always retain at minimum a supervisory responsibility, whereas the private sector cannot act as a purely private entity but must do so as the agent of government under statutes and regulations. Some of the arguments for and against private prisons are presented in Table 4.10.

## PRISON WORK PROGRAMS AND INDUSTRIES

Work in fields, laundries, and kitchens has always been a part of many inmates' lives; some even participate in work-release programs. According to the 1995 BJS census of correctional facilities, the last such census published, more than 94% of all prisons operated inmate work programs. About 63% of state inmates and 90% of federal inmates participated in some type of work program.

State and local governments prevent prisoners from working at some jobs because they would be in competition with private enterprise or workers. In 1936 Congress barred convicts from working on federal contracts worth more than $10,000. In 1940 Congress made it illegal to transport convict-made goods in interstate commerce.

These rules were changed in 1979 when Congress established the Prison Industry Enhancement Certification Program (PIECP). The PIECP allows state correctional industries that meet certain requirements to sell inmate-produced goods to the federal government and in interstate commerce. According to the Bureau of Justice Assistance (http://www.ncjrs.org/html/bja/piecp/bja-prison-industr.html#background), the PIECP was created to:

> encourage states and units of local government to establish employment opportunities for inmates that approximate private-sector work opportunities. The program is designed to place inmates in a realistic work environment, pay them the prevailing local wage for similar work, and enable them to acquire marketable skills to increase their potential for successful rehabilitation and meaningful employment upon release.

**TABLE 4.10**

**Public strategies for private prisons**

| Reasons to privatize | Reasons not to privatize |
|---|---|
| 1. Private operators can provide construction financing options that allow the government client to pay only for capacity as needed in lieu of encumbering long-term debt. | 1. There are certain responsibilities that only the government should meet, such as public safety and environmental protection. To provide incarceration, the government has legal, political, and moral obligations. Major constitutional competition among both public and private issues revolves around the deprivation of liberty, discipline, and preserving the constitutional rights of inmates. Related issues include use of force, loss of time credit, and segregation. |
| 2. Private companies offer modern state-of-the-art correctional facility designs that are efficient to operate and built based upon value engineering specifications. | 2. Few private companies are available from which to choose. |
| 3. Private operators typically design and construct a new correctional facility in half the time of a comparable government construction project. | 3. Private operators may be inexperienced with key corrections issues. |
| 4. Private vendors provide government clients with the convenience and accountability of one entity for all compliance issues. | 4. Operator may become a monopoly through political ingratiation, favoritism, etc. |
| 5. Private corrections management companies are able to mobilize rapidly and to specialize in unique facility missions. | 5. Government may lose the capability to perform the function over time. |
| 6. Private corrections management companies provide economic development opportunities by hiring locally and, to the extent possible, purchasing locally. | 6. The profit motive will inhibit the proper performance of duties. Private prisons have financial incentives to cut corners. |
| 7. Government can reduce or share its liability exposure by contracting with private corrections companies. | 7. Procurement process is slow, inefficient, and open to risks. |
| 8. The government can retain flexibility by limiting the contract duration and by specifying facility mission. | 8. Creating a good, clear contract is a daunting task. |
| 9. Adding other service providers injects competition among both public and private organizations. | 9. Lack of enforcement remedies in contracts leaves only termination or lawsuits as recourse. |

SOURCE: James Austin and Garry Coventry, "Table 6. Public Strategies for Private Prisons," in *Emerging Issues on Privatized Prisons*, Bureau of Justice Assistance, February 2001, http://www.ncjrs.org/pdffiles1/bja/181249.pdf (accessed March 31, 2005). Data by Cunningham (1999).

In 1999 PIECP wage guidelines were enacted. According to the *Federal Register* (April 7, 1999):

PIECP inmate workers must receive wages at a rate which is not less than that paid for work of a similar nature in the locality in which the work is to be performed. This requirement benefits society by allowing for the development of prison industries while protecting the private sector labor force and business from unfair competition that could otherwise stem from the flow of low-cost, prisoner-made goods into the marketplace.

Correctional facilities interested in participating in PIECP must meet the following requirements, as listed by the Bureau of Justice Assistance (http://www.ncjrs.org/html/bja/piecp/bja-prison-industr.html#background):

1. Eligibility. Authority to involve the private sector in the production and sale of inmate-made goods on the open market.

2. Wages. Authority to pay wages at a rate not less than that paid for work of a similar nature in the locality in which the work is performed.

3. Non-inmate worker displacement. Written assurances that PIECP will not result in the displacement of employed workers; be applied in skills, crafts, or trades in which there is a surplus of available gainful labor in the locality; or significantly impair existing contracts.

4. Benefits. Authority to provide inmate workers with benefits comparable to those made available by the federal or state government to similarly situated private-sector employees, including workers' compensation and, in some circumstances, Social Security.

5. Deductions. Corrections departments may opt to take deductions from inmate worker wages. Permissible deductions are limited to taxes, room and board, family support, and victims' compensation. If victims' compensation deductions are taken, written assurances that the deductions will be not less than 5% and not more than 20% of gross wages and that all deductions will not total more than 80% of gross wages.

6. Voluntary participation. Written assurances that inmate participation is voluntary.

7. Consultation with organized labor. Written proof of consultation with organized labor prior to program startup.

8. Consultation with local private industry. Written proof of consultation with local private industry prior to program startup.

9. National Environmental Policy Act (NEPA). Written proof of compliance with NEPA requirements prior to program startup.

## Wages

Some private industries pay minimum wage, but many prisons take most of prisoners' wages to pay for room and board, restitution, family support, and taxes. The Bureau of Justice Assistance reported that from December 1979 through June 30, 2003, PIECP participants had paid wages of $264 million. After deductions for victims programs ($24 million), room and board ($70 million), family support ($15.6 million), and taxes ($35.6 million), inmates had earned $146.3 million.

Many prison administrators generally favor work programs. Some believe that work keeps prisoners productive and occupied, thus leading to a safer prison environment. Another cited benefit is that work programs prepare prisoners for re-entry into the noninstitutionalized world by helping them develop job skills and solid work habits that will be needed for post-incarceration employment. Some prisons report that inmates who work in industry are less likely to cause problems in prison or be rearrested after release than convicts who do not participate in work programs.

Generally, it is believed that the new skills developed through prison work programs, as well as educational opportunities, give prisoners an added edge in helping them readjust to normal life.

In addition, many inmates report that they like the opportunity to work. They assert that it provides relief

**TABLE 4.11**

**UNICOR sales by business segment, 2002–04**

[In thousands]

| Business segment | Fiscal year | | |
|---|---|---|---|
| | 2004 | 2003 | 2002 |
| **Electronics** | | | |
| Sales | $255,171 | $152,357 | $132,662 |
| Earnings | $80,143 | $38,576 | $27,353 |
| **Fleet management** | | | |
| Sales | $129,068 | $123,272 | $99,054 |
| Earnings | $517 | $3,355 | ($301) |
| **Graphics** | | | |
| Sales | $23,681 | $23,658 | $26,006 |
| Earnings | $2,692 | $2,943 | $783 |
| **Industrial products** | | | |
| Sales | $45,846 | $36,759 | $27,782 |
| Earnings | ($194) | ($3,510) | ($9,545) |
| **Office furniture** | | | |
| Sales | $140,935 | $151,996 | $217,852 |
| Earnings | ($1,878) | ($2,205) | $22,342 |
| **Recycling activities** | | | |
| Sales | $10,004 | $8,083 | $3,359 |
| Earnings | $2,818 | $4 | ($229) |
| **Services** | | | |
| Sales | $13,550 | $12,239 | $12,210 |
| Earnings | $789 | $729 | $2,509 |
| **Clothing and textiles** | | | |
| Sales | $184,465 | $158,399 | $159,730 |
| Earnings | $35,540 | $25,344 | $28,473 |
| **Corporate total** | | | |
| Sales | $802,720 | $666,763 | $678,655 |
| Earnings | $120,427 | $65,236 | $71,385 |

SOURCE: "UNICOR Sales, 2002–2004, by Business Segment," in *U.S. Department of Justice Federal Prison Industries, Inc. FY2004 Annual Report*, 2004, http://www.unicor.gov/information/publications/pdfs/corporate/catar2004f.pdf (accessed March 31, 2005)

from boredom and gives them some extra money. Inmates find that the money they earn helps them to meet financial obligations for their families even while they are in prison.

## UNICOR

UNICOR is the trade name for Federal Prison Industries, Inc., the government corporation that employs inmates in federal prisons. UNICOR should not be confused with state prison industry programs administered by the states. Under UNICOR, established in 1934, federal inmates get job training by producing goods and services for federal agencies. In 2005 items produced by inmates included industrial products (lockers, fencing, filtration products, storage cabinets, shelving), clothing and textile products (draperies, towels, mattresses, canvas goods, military clothing), graphics and services (data entry, text editing, road signs), electronics (lighting systems, circuit boards, cable assemblies, connectors, power distribution systems), office furniture, and recycling activities.

UNICOR products and services must be purchased by federal agencies and are not for sale in interstate commerce or to nonfederal entities. UNICOR is not permitted to compete with private industry. If UNICOR cannot make the needed product or provide the required service, federal agencies may buy the product from the private sector through a waiver issued by UNICOR.

According to the agency's 2004 Annual Report, UNICOR employed 19,337 inmates in 102 factories at seventy-one prison locations. Approximately 13% of all inmates in Bureau of Prisons facilities work for UNICOR. The agency's goal is to employ 25% of all work-eligible prisoners who have no existing job skills. UNICOR had 2004 sales of $802.7 million, up from $678.6 million in 2002. (See Table 4.11.)

UNICOR is a self-supporting government corporation that may borrow funds from the U.S. Treasury and use the proceeds to purchase equipment, pay wages to inmates and staff, and invest in expansion of facilities. No funds are appropriated for UNICOR operations.

## CHAPTER 5
# CHARACTERISTICS OF INMATES

*Prisoners overwhelmingly represent societal "failures," young men (and a small percentage of women and older men) who have had unsuccessful experiences in their families, schools, military services, and labor force. They suffer disproportionately from child abuse, alcohol and drug abuse, poor self-concept, and deficient social skills. They tend to be hostile to others, and especially to authority.*

— James B. Jacobs, "Inside Prisons," *Crime File Study Guide* (Washington, DC: National Institute of Justice, not dated)

## RACE, ETHNICITY, AGE, AND GENDER

In 2003 some 1.3 million men and 92,785 women were serving sentences in state and federal prisons, according to Paige M. Harrison and Allen J. Beck in *Prisoners in 2003* (Washington, DC: Bureau of Justice Statistics, November 2004). (See Table 5.1.) Expressed in percentages of total prisoners 35% were non-Hispanic whites, 44% non-Hispanic African-Americans, 19% were Hispanics, and 1.9% were of other races (Asians, American Indians, Alaskan Natives, Native Hawaiians, and other Pacific Islanders). About 93% were men.

Among white prisoners, 8.6% were women, among African-Americans 5.9%, and among Hispanics 6.4%. The age group with the highest number of male prisoners in 2003 was twenty-five to twenty-nine years old (231,400). Women were most numerous in the thirty-five- to thirty-nine-year-old age group across all races. Among men, whites were more numerous in the group aged thirty-five to thirty-nine years (75,400), while African-Americans (111,400) and Hispanics (54,700) were more predominant in the twenty-five- to twenty-nine-year-old age group.

The largest overall number of prisoners were African-Americans. Among men, African-Americans outnumbered whites in every age group except those aged forty-five to fifty-four and fifty-five and older.

Among women, whites were more numerous than African-Americans in every age category except those aged eighteen and nineteen.

According to *Prisoners in 2003*, incarceration rates (measured as the number of prisoners per 100,000 residents of a gender/age group) indicate that, overall, 465 white males aged eighteen and older were in prison per 100,000 resident males of the same age group. For African-Americans this number was 3,405, for Hispanics 1,231. The rates for women were thirty-eight for whites, 185 for African-Americans, and eighty-four for Hispanics. Whites and African-Americans in this context are non-Hispanic. (See Table 5.2.) These data, translated into percentages, indicate that 9.3% of African-American males aged twenty-five to twenty-nine were in prison in 2003 compared to 1.1% of white males in that age range and 2.6% of Hispanic males.

A somewhat expanded data set, prisoners under the *jurisdiction* of state and federal correctional authorities (a grouping that includes people on probation and parole), shows correctional population trends for men and women since 1995. (See Table 5.3.) These data, reported in *Prisoners in 2003*, indicate that 1,368,866 men and 101,179 women made up the correctional population in 2003. Men increased 2% from 2002 to 2003 with an annual average rate of 3.3% from 1995 to 2003. The female correctional population increased by 3.6% from 2002 to 2003 and grew 5% on average each year from 1995 to 2003. Numbers for prisoners sentenced to more than one year show that the male correctional population in this category grew 1.9% from 2002 to 2003 while the female population increased by 4.2%. The incarceration rate for men was 789 per 100,000 residents in 1995 and 915 in 2003. The corresponding rate for women was forty-seven in 1995 and sixty-two in 2003.

TABLE 5.1

**Number of state and federal prisoners, by gender, race, Hispanic origin, and age, 2003**

| | Number of sentenced prisoners | | | | | | | |
|---|---|---|---|---|---|---|---|---|
| | Males | | | | Females | | | |
| | Total[a] | White[b] | Black[b] | Hispanic | Total[a] | White[b] | Black[b] | Hispanic |
| Total | 1,316,495 | 454,300 | 586,300 | 251,900 | 92,785 | 39,100 | 35,000 | 16,200 |
| 18–19 | 25,200 | 7,100 | 12,600 | 4,900 | 1,100 | 400 | 500 | 200 |
| 20–24 | 208,300 | 59,400 | 99,900 | 46,200 | 11,100 | 4,400 | 4,200 | 2,300 |
| 25–29 | 231,400 | 63,100 | 111,400 | 54,700 | 13,900 | 5,600 | 5,300 | 2,600 |
| 30–34 | 221,000 | 70,300 | 100,000 | 47,900 | 17,200 | 7,200 | 6,500 | 3,100 |
| 35–39 | 209,400 | 75,400 | 91,900 | 37,800 | 18,800 | 7,800 | 7,300 | 3,200 |
| 40–44 | 182,300 | 71,700 | 78,100 | 27,900 | 15,600 | 6,800 | 5,800 | 2,500 |
| 45–54 | 178,400 | 74,800 | 73,900 | 24,800 | 12,400 | 5,400 | 4,700 | 1,800 |
| 55 or older | 57,700 | 31,900 | 17,200 | 7,200 | 2,600 | 1,400 | 700 | 300 |

Note: Based on custody counts by race and Hispanic origin from National Prisoner Statistics (NPS-1A) and updated from jurisdiction counts by gender at yearend. Estimates by age were derived from the National Corrections Reporting Program, 2002. Estimates were rounded to the nearest 100.
[a]Includes American Indians, Alaska Natives, Asians, Native Hawaiians, and other Pacific Islanders.
[b]Excludes Hispanics.

SOURCE: Paige M. Harrison and Allen J. Beck, "Table 11. Number of Sentenced Prisoners under State or Federal Jurisdiction, by Gender, Race, Hispanic Origin, and Age, 2003," in *Prisoners in 2003*, Bureau of Justice Statistics, November 2004, http://www.ojp.usdoj.gov/bjs/pub/pdf/p03.pdf (accessed April 2, 2005)

TABLE 5.2

**Number of sentenced state or federal prisoners per 100,000 residents, by gender, race, Hispanic origin, and age, 2003**

| | Number of sentenced prisoners per 100,000 residents of each group | | | | | | | |
|---|---|---|---|---|---|---|---|---|
| | Males | | | | Females | | | |
| Age | Total[a] | White[b] | Black[b] | Hispanic | Total[a] | White[b] | Black[b] | Hispanic |
| Total | 915 | 465 | 3,405 | 1,231 | 62 | 38 | 185 | 84 |
| 18–19 | 597 | 266 | 2,068 | 692 | 28 | 15 | 80 | 39 |
| 20–24 | 1,996 | 932 | 7,017 | 2,267 | 112 | 71 | 286 | 138 |
| 25–29 | 2,380 | 1,090 | 9,262 | 2,592 | 147 | 99 | 406 | 152 |
| 30–34 | 2,074 | 1,042 | 7,847 | 2,440 | 164 | 109 | 456 | 181 |
| 35–39 | 1,895 | 1,017 | 6,952 | 2,226 | 170 | 106 | 491 | 209 |
| 40–44 | 1,584 | 873 | 5,854 | 1,995 | 133 | 82 | 386 | 192 |
| 45–54 | 899 | 501 | 3,500 | 1,329 | 60 | 36 | 190 | 97 |
| 55 or older | 208 | 141 | 747 | 397 | 8 | 5 | 22 | 16 |

Note: Based on estimates of the U.S. resident population on July 1, 2003, using intercensal estimates for July 1, 2002 (by gender, race, and Hispanic origin) and adjusted to the July 1, 2003, estimates by gender.
[a]Includes American Indians, Alaska Natives, Asians, Native Hawaiians, and other Pacific Islanders.
[b]Excludes Hispanics.

SOURCE: Paige M. Harrison and Allen J. Beck, "Table 12. Number of Sentenced Prisoners under State or Federal Jurisdiction per 100,000 Residents, by Gender, Race, Hispanic Origin, and Age, 2003," in *Prisoners in 2003*, Bureau of Justice Statistics, November 2004, http://www.ojp.usdoj.gov/bjs/pub/pdf/p03.pdf (accessed April 1, 2005)

## TYPES OF CRIMES

### State Prisons

Between 1980 and 2001, the number of people in the state correctional system increased by 309%, including an increase of 76.8% between 1990 and 2001, according to *Key Facts at a Glance* (Bureau of Justice Statistics, July 27, 2003). Most inmates were in state prisons rather than in federal facilities or local jails. Figure 5.1 shows a twenty-year history of state incarcerations divided by type of crime committed. The largest category was violent crime, which accounted for more than half of the increase in state prison population since 1995. Prisoners incarcerated for drug offenses grew from 19,000 in 1980 to 246,100 in 2001 as measured by state prison population. Between 1990 and 2001, the group confined for crimes against the public order increased from 45,500 prisoners to 129,900 prisoners. These crimes include illegal weapons possession, drunken driving, flight to escape prosecution, obstruction of justice, liquor law violations, and others.

According to the Bureau of Justice Statistics in *Key Facts at a Glance* (http://www.ojp.usdoj.gov/bjs/glance/tables/corrtyptab.htm), nearly half (49.4%) of all prison inmates were serving time for violent crimes in 2001.

## TABLE 5.3

**State and federal prisoners, by gender, yearend 1995, 2002, and 2003**

| | Men | Women |
|---|---|---|
| **All inmates** | | |
| 2003 | 1,368,866 | 101,179 |
| 2002 | 1,342,513 | 97,631 |
| 1995 | 1,057,406 | 68,468 |
| Percent change, 2002–2003 | 2.0% | 3.6% |
| Average annual 1995–2003 | 3.3% | 5.0% |
| **Sentenced to more than 1 year** | | |
| 2003 | 1,316,495 | 92,785 |
| 2002 | 1,291,450 | 89,066 |
| Percent change, 2002–2003 | 1.9% | 4.2% |
| **Incarceration rate\*** | | |
| 2003 | 915 | 62 |
| 1995 | 789 | 47 |

\*The number of prisoners with sentences of more than 1 year per 100,000 residents on December 31.

SOURCE: Paige M. Harrison and Allen J. Beck, "Table 5. Prisoners under the Jurisdiction of State or Federal Correctional Authorities, by Gender, Yearend 1995, 2002, and 2003," in *Prisoners in 2003*, Bureau of Justice Statistics, November 2004, http://www.ojp.usdoj.gov/bjs/pub/pdf/p03.pdf (accessed April 2, 2005)

## FIGURE 5.1

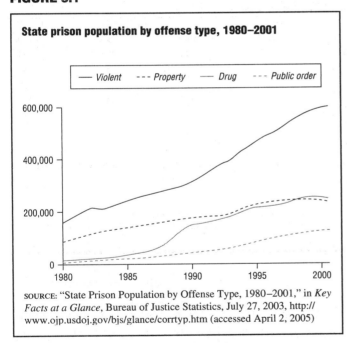

**State prison population by offense type, 1980–2001**

— Violent    - - - Property    —— Drug    - - - Public order

SOURCE: "State Prison Population by Offense Type, 1980–2001," in *Key Facts at a Glance*, Bureau of Justice Statistics, July 27, 2003, http://www.ojp.usdoj.gov/bjs/glance/corrtyp.htm (accessed April 2, 2005)

A fifth of all prisoners (20.4%) were serving for drug offenses, and another fifth (19.3%) for property crimes. The remaining 10.9% of prisoners have been convicted of offenses against the public order.

The distribution of offenses has changed somewhat over the period shown in Figure 5.1, dramatically in some instances. Thus in 1980 inmates incarcerated for drug offenses accounted for less than 7% of total prisoners; by

## TABLE 5.4

**Federal prisoners by type of offense, 2005**

| Types of offenses | |
|---|---|
| Drug offenses: | 88,960 (53.8%) |
| Weapons, explosives, arson: | 21,475 (13.0%) |
| Immigration: | 18,325 (11.1%) |
| Robbery: | 10,078 (6.1%) |
| Burglary, larceny, property offenses: | 6,784 (4.1%) |
| Extortion, fraud, bribery: | 6,856 (4.1%) |
| Homicide, aggravated assault, and kidnapping offenses: | 5,326 (3.2%) |
| Miscellaneous: | 3,478 (2.1%) |
| Sex offenses: | 1,732 (1.0%) |
| Banking and insurance, counterfeit, embezzlement: | 1,013 (0.6%) |
| Courts or corrections: | 709 (0.4%) |
| Continuing criminal enterprise: | 603 (0.4%) |
| National security: | 103 (0.1%) |

SOURCE: "Federal Prisoners by Type of Offense," in *Federal Bureau of Prisons Quick Facts*, Federal Bureau of Prisons, February 26, 2005, http://www.bop.gov//about/facts.jsp#4 (accessed April 2, 2005)

1990 they reached a peak of 22%, declining slightly thereafter. Violent crimes represented 59% of all incarcerations in 1980, dropped to a low in this period of 46% in 1990, but have been increasing in share of total offenses since. The largest drop in share has been in property crime. The category dropped from 30% in 1980 to 26% in 1990 and finally to less than 20% of total inmates in 2001.

### Federal Prisons

In 2003 there were nearly eight people in state prison for every one in federal facilities. While in state prisons a fifth of all inmates were held for drug offenses, the Federal Bureau of Prisons reported at its Web site (http://www.bop.gov/about/facts.jsp#4) that at the federal level more than half (53.8%) were imprisoned for drug violations as of March 2005. (See Table 5.4.) The next three categories of inmates in terms of percentage were: weapons violations, explosives charges, and arson (13% of offenders), immigration violations (11.1%), and robbery (6.1%).

According to the Federal Bureau of Prisons' Quick Facts (http://www.bop.gov/news/quick.jsp), most federal inmates were male (93.2%) in March 2005. The inmate population at that time comprised 56.7% whites, 40% African-Americans, 1.7.% Native Americans, and 1.6% Asians. In addition, the Federal Bureau of Prisons reported that among those incarcerated in federal prisons, 71.5% were American citizens, 17.2% were citizens of Mexico, 1.9% were Colombian citizens, 1.9% were citizens of the Dominican Republic, and 1% were Cuban citizens. The remaining 6.5% were either of unknown or other citizenship.

## EDUCATION OF PRISON AND JAIL INMATES

Early in 2003, the Bureau of Justice Statistics issued a special report, *Education and Correctional Populations*, on the educational attainment of prison and jail inmates. Data on prisoners are for the benchmark years of 1991 and 1997. The study utilized surveys of inmates in correctional facilities for those two years, surveys of local jail inmates conducted in 1989 and 1996, *Current Population Survey* data for 1997, and data from the 1992 *Adult Literacy Survey* sponsored by the National Center of Educational Statistics. Although the data are somewhat dated, this study is the most recent to take a comprehensive consideration of the education of inmates. *Profile of Jail Inmates, 2002* (Bureau of Justice Statistics, July 2004), provides some updated statistics on the educational levels of jail inmates in 2002.

## Educational Attainment

In 1997, 11.4% of state prisoners had "postsecondary/some college" education or were "college graduates or more." Federal prisoners in the same categories represented 23.9% of the federal prison population. In contrast, 48.4% of the general population had postsecondary education or a college degree or higher. Prisoners with less than a high school education comprised 39.7% of the state prison population and 26.5% of the federal prison population in 1997—compared to only 18.4% of the general population that had attained less than a high school education.

In 1997, 33.2% of the general population had achieved a high school diploma as their highest level of education. By contrast, only 20.5% of the state prison population and 27% of the federal prison population were high school graduates. More than a fifth of the prison population had a General Education Development (GED) certificate—28.5% in state prisons, 22.7% in federal prisons. No comparable data for the general population were available. Concerning those in the state prisons without a high school education, *Education and Correctional Population* presented the following summary:

> The groups of state prison inmates who had not completed high school or the GED included:
>
> 40% of males and 42% of females
>
> 27% of whites, 44% of African-Americans, and 53% of Hispanics
>
> 52% of inmates 24 or younger and 35% of inmates 45 or older
>
> 61% of noncitizens and 38% of U.S. citizens
>
> 59% with a speech disability, 66% with a learning disability, and 37% without a reported disability
>
> 47% of drug offenders
>
> 12% of those with military service and 44% with no military service.

According to Doris J. James of the Bureau of Justice Statistics in *Profile of Jail Inmates, 2002*, jail inmates in 2002 with less than a high school education include 31.6% with "some high school" and 12.3% with eighth grade or less, for a total of 43.9% of all inmates. Forty-three percent of jail inmates had attained either a high school diploma or GED as their highest level of education. Thirteen percent of jail inmates had either "some college" or had graduated from college. (See Table 5.5.)

## Women and Men

Among state prison inmates in 1997, 41.8% of women had an educational attainment of less than high school compared with 39.6% for men ("eighth grade or less" and "some high school"). Nearly 22% of women had only a high school diploma, 20.4% of men. However, if GED-certified prisoners are combined with high school graduates, men in these categories represented 49.3% of the prison population, women 43.9%. Proportionately more women had an educational attainment exceeding the high school level: 14.3% had postsecondary education, some college, or were college graduates; 11.1% of males fell into these categories. A slightly smaller percentage of women participated in educational programs offered in state prisons than men, 50.1% versus the male participation rate of 52%.

## Education by Race and Ethnicity

A breakdown of the state prison population by race and ethnicity shows that 27.2% of whites, 44.1% of African-Americans, and 53% of Hispanics had less than a high school education in 1997—all significantly higher than the same group in the general population (18.4%). For 58% of the white prison population, a high school diploma or GED was their highest educational attainment while 14.9% had at least some college education. Among African American prisoners 45.8% had a high school diploma or GED as their highest educational attainment and 10% had at least some college. Among Hispanics, 39.6% had a high school diploma or GED but no further education and 7.4% had at least some college education.

## Education Programs

Most prisons offer some kind of educational programs to inmates including basic adult education, secondary education, college courses, special education, vocational training, and study release programs. According to *State of the Bureau 2003: Accomplishments and Goals* (Washington, DC: Federal Bureau of Prisons, 2004), in September 2003 there were 21,000 federal prisoners enrolled in GED programs. During 2003, 5,313 inmates graduated from the program and received GEDs. In addition, the Bureau of Prisons also operated or supported 325 occupational training programs, 514 apprenticeship programs, and 158 advanced occupational training programs. Some 10,000 federal prisoners were enrolled in these educational programs during 2003. The Bureau estimated that during 2003 some 35% of all federal prisoners were enrolled in one or another of the available educational programs.

TABLE 5.5

**Selected characteristics of jail inmates, by conviction status, 2002 and 1996**

| | Percent of jail inmates, 2002 | | | | 1996 |
|---|---|---|---|---|---|
| | Total | Convicted | Unconvicted | Both[a] | |
| **Gender** | | | | | |
| Male | 88.4% | 87.7% | 89.2% | 89.6% | 89.8% |
| Female | 11.6 | 12.3 | 10.8 | 10.4 | 10.2 |
| **Race/Hispanic origin[b]** | | | | | |
| White[c] | 36.0% | 39.4% | 31.0% | 33.3% | 37.4% |
| Black[c] | 40.1 | 37.3 | 43.0 | 44.1 | 40.9 |
| Hispanic | 18.5 | 18.5 | 19.6 | 16.6 | 18.5 |
| American Indian/Alaska Native | 1.3 | 1.2 | 1.4 | 1.6 | 2.4 |
| Asian/Pacific Islander | 1.1 | 0.9 | 1.7 | 0.9 | 0.9 |
| More than one race[d] | 3.0 | 2.6 | 3.3 | 3.6 | — |
| **Age** | | | | | |
| 17 or younger | 1.8% | 1.2% | 2.9% | 1.6% | 2.3% |
| 18–24 | 28.1 | 28.3 | 28.9 | 26.4 | 28.5 |
| 25–34 | 31.9 | 31.0 | 31.8 | 35.4 | 37.4 |
| 35–44 | 26.0 | 27.1 | 24.2 | 25.2 | 23.9 |
| 45–54 | 10.0 | 10.2 | 9.4 | 10.4 | 6.3 |
| 55 or older | 2.2 | 2.2 | 2.8 | 1.0 | 1.5 |
| **Marital status** | | | | | |
| Married | 16.2% | 15.8% | 16.5% | 17.3% | 15.7% |
| Widowed | 1.2 | 1.1 | 1.5 | 1.1 | 1.4 |
| Divorced | 15.7 | 16.3 | 14.7 | 15.5 | 15.6 |
| Separated | 6.7 | 7.5 | 5.6 | 6.3 | 8.7 |
| Never married | 60.1 | 59.3 | 61.7 | 59.8 | 58.6 |
| **Education** | | | | | |
| 8th grade or less | 12.3% | 11.8% | 14.3% | 10.6% | 13.1% |
| Some high school | 31.6 | 30.6 | 32.7 | 33.4 | 33.4 |
| General equivalency diploma | 17.1 | 18.2 | 14.1 | 18.6 | 14.1 |
| High school diploma | 25.9 | 26.1 | 26.2 | 24.6 | 25.9 |
| Some college | 10.1 | 10.5 | 9.7 | 9.6 | 10.3 |
| College graduate or more | 2.9 | 2.8 | 2.9 | 3.1 | 3.2 |
| **U.S. citizenship** | | | | | |
| Citizen | 92.2% | 92.6% | 89.5% | 95.8% | 91.8% |
| Noncitizen | 7.8 | 7.4 | 10.5 | 4.2 | 8.2 |
| **Number of jail inmates[e]** | **631,241** | **394,039** | **182,754** | **100,495** | **507,026** |

[a]Includes inmates with a prior conviction, but no new conviction for the current charge.
[b]Excludes 0.3% of inmates in 1996 and 2002 who did not specify a race.
[c]Non-Hispanic inmates.
[d]Includes 1.6% of jail inmates who specified black and other races; 1.3%, American Indian/Alaskan Native and other races; and 0.1%, Asian and other races.
[e]The survey totals were weighted to midyear estimates from the *Annual Survey of Jails* in 1995 and 2001.

SOURCE: Doris J. James, "Table 1. Selected Characteristics of Jail Inmates, by Conviction Status, 2002 and 1996," in *Profile of Jail Inmates, 2002*, Bureau of Justice Statistics, July 2004, http://www.ojp.usdoj.gov/bjs/pub/ pdf/pji02.pdf (accessed April 2, 2005)

## PAST ABUSE AND FAMILY BACKGROUND

The Bureau of Justice Statistics published a special report titled *Prior Abuse Reported by Inmates and Probationers* in 1999. The report was prepared from survey data collected from state and federal prisoners in 1997, inmates of local jails in 1996, and the 1995 *Survey of Adults on Probation*. The special report found that 18.7% of state prisoners, 9.5% of federal prisoners, 16.4% of jail inmates, and 15.7% of probationers had experienced abuse before being admitted to prison. The survey relied on the respondents' own definitions of physical and sexual abuse.

A more recent study of abuse among jail inmates is reported in *Profile of Jail Inmates, 2002*. According to Table 5.6, 18.2% of all jail inmates reported having been either physically or sexually abused. While 13.4% of male inmates reported prior abuse, well over half (55.3%) of female inmates had been abused. Of those men who reported abuse, 11.2% said they had been physically abused, while 4% said it was sexual abuse. For women, the percentages were much higher: 44.9% had been physically abused and 35.9% had been sexually abused. Overall more inmates reported in 2002 that the abuse had occurred before the age of eighteen; however, among female inmates in 2002, more reported abuse after age eighteen. More than 92% knew their abuser, and a parent or guardian had been the abuser in 47.9% of the cases overall.

The same study found that over 46% of jail inmates reported having a close relative who had also been in jail. Over 18% of jail inmates said their father had been incarcerated, 31.4% a brother, and 8.9% a sister. (See Table 5.7.) Nearly 20% of inmates reported that a parent or guardian had abused alcohol when they were growing

**TABLE 5.6**

**Prior physical or sexual abuse of jail inmates, 2002 and 1996**

| | Percent of all jail inmates | | | | | |
|---|---|---|---|---|---|---|
| | All | | Male | | Female | |
| | 2002 | 1996 | 2002 | 1996 | 2002 | 1996 |
| **Ever physically or sexually abused** | 18.2% | 16.4% | 13.4% | 12.9% | 55.3% | 47.5% |
| Before age 18 | 10.9 | 11.6 | 9.7 | 10.6 | 20.3 | 20.8 |
| After age 18 | 4.9 | 2.0 | 2.3 | 1.0 | 25.2 | 10.9 |
| Both | 2.3 | 2.7 | 1.4 | 1.3 | 9.7 | 15.8 |
| Physically abused | 15.1% | 13.3% | 11.2% | 10.7% | 44.9% | 37.2% |
| Sexually abused | 7.7 | 8.7 | 4.0 | 5.6 | 35.9 | 37.1 |
| **Relationship to abuser** | Percent of abused inmates | | | | | |
| **Knew abuser** | 92.4% | 86.6% | 92.5% | 87.9% | 92.1% | 90.3% |
| Parent/guardian | 47.9 | 53.2 | 59.7 | 60.1 | 25.7 | 36.3 |
| Intimate* | 30.0 | 16.6 | 10.5 | 3.5 | 66.7 | 47.7 |
| Other relatives | 17.3 | 24.4 | 16.4 | 21.6 | 18.9 | 31.3 |
| Friend/acquaintance | 20.7 | 23.1 | 13.9 | 21.7 | 33.5 | 26.4 |
| **Did not know abuser** | **7.6%** | **13.4%** | **7.5%** | **12.1%** | **7.9%** | **17.9%** |

Note: Details adds to more than total because more than 1 person may have abused inmates; or some inmates were both physically and sexually abused.
*Includes (ex) spouse, (ex) boyfriend, and (ex) girlfriend.

SOURCE: Doris J. James, "Table 17. Prior Physical or Sexual Abuse of Jail Inmates, 2002 and 1996," in *Profile of Jail Inmates, 2002*, Bureau of Justice Statistics, July 2004, http://www.ojp.usdoj.gov/bjs/pub/pdf/pji02.pdf (accessed April 2, 2005)

**TABLE 5.7**

**Family background of jail inmates, 2002 and 1996**

| | 2002 | 1996 |
|---|---|---|
| **Person(s) lived with most of the time while growing up:** | | |
| Both parents | 43.6% | 39.7% |
| Mother only | 39.2 | 43.3 |
| Father only | 4.4 | 4.9 |
| Grandparents | 10.3 | 7.0 |
| Other | 2.5 | 5.2 |
| **Ever lived in a foster home, agency, or institution while growing up** | 11.5% | 13.6% |
| **Family member ever incarcerated** | | |
| Total* | 46.3% | 46.1% |
| Father | 18.6 | 17.1 |
| Mother | 7.1 | 4.4 |
| Brother | 31.4 | 30.3 |
| Sister | 8.9 | 6.2 |
| Spouse | 1.8 | 3.3 |
| Child | 3.5 | 1.3 |
| **Parent or guardian ever abused alcohol or drugs while inmate was growing up** | | |
| Alcohol | 19.9% | 23.1% |
| Drugs | 2.1 | 1.3 |
| Both alcohol and drugs | 8.6 | 6.9 |

*Details may not add to total because more than one response was possible.

SOURCE: Doris J. James, "Table 15. Family Background of Jail Inmates, 2002 and 1996," in *Profile of Jail Inmates, 2002*, Bureau of Justice Statistics, July 2004, http://www.ojp.usdoj.gov/bjs/pub/pdf/pji02.pdf (accessed April 2, 2005)

**TABLE 5.8**

**Jail inmates with a restraining order, 2002**

| | Percent of jail inmates | | |
|---|---|---|---|
| **Restraining order** | All | Violent | Non-violent |
| Ever under order | 18.6% | 24.3% | 16.7% |
| At admission | 5.1 | 7.3 | 4.4 |
| Ever violated | 4.4% | 5.1% | 4.1% |
| Violation charge at admission | 1.5 | 2.0 | 1.3 |
| | Percent of inmates ever under a restraining order | | |
| **Person who sought order*** | | | |
| Parent | 3.8% | 5.1% | 3.1% |
| Intimate* | 75.1 | 73.1 | 76.4 |
| Other relative | 2.3 | 2.7 | 2.2 |
| Other nonrelative | 20.5 | 22.1 | 19.3 |

Note: Details add to more than total because more than one person may have sought restraining order.
*Includes (ex-) spouse, (ex-) boyfriend, and (ex-) girlfriend.

SOURCE: Doris J. James, "Table 18. Experience of Jail Inmates with a Restraining Order, 2002," in *Profile of Jail Inmates, 2002*, Bureau of Justice Statistics, July 2004, http://www.ojp.usdoj.gov/bjs/pub/pdf/pji02.pdf (accessed April 2, 2005)

up. In addition, 2.1% reported that a parent or guardian had abused drugs, and 8.6% reported the use of both drugs and alcohol by a parent or guardian. Less than half of all inmates (43.6%) had been raised in a two-parent family.

*Profile of Jail Inmates, 2002* also reported that 18.6% of jail inmates had been under a restraining order at some time. (See Table 5.8.) A restraining order is issued by a court and forbids a named individual from visiting or even approaching the person who has asked for the order. Restraining orders are usually requested by those who fear they may be violently attacked by a former spouse or boyfriend. Over 75% of the restraining orders against jail inmates had been requested by their intimate partners.

**TABLE 5.9**

**Estimated number of state and federal prisoners with minor children, by gender, 1991 and 1999**

| | State prisoners | | | Federal prisoners | | |
|---|---|---|---|---|---|---|
| | **Total** | **Male** | **Female** | **Total** | **Male** | **Female** |
| **Number of parents** | | | | | | |
| 1991 | 413,100 | 386,500 | 26,600 | 39,400 | 36,500 | 2,900 |
| 1999 | 642,300 | 593,800 | 48,500 | 79,200 | 74,100 | 5,100 |
| **Number of minor children** | | | | | | |
| 1991 | 852,300 | 794,500 | 57,800 | 84,200 | 78,300 | 5,900 |
| 1999 | 1,324,900 | 1,209,400 | 115,500 | 173,900 | 163,300 | 10,600 |

Note: Numbers are estimates based on responses to the 1991 and 1997 Surveys of Inmates in State and Federal Correctional Facilities, and custody counts from the National Prisoner Statistics program.

SOURCE: Christopher J. Mumola, "Table 2. Estimated Number of State and Federal Prisoners with Minor Children, by Gender, 1991 and 1999," in *Incarcerated Parents and Their Children*, Bureau of Justice Statistics, August 2000, http://www.ojp.usdoj.gov/bjs/pub/pdf/iptc.pdf (accessed April 2, 2005)

## PRISONERS AND THEIR CHILDREN

In 1999, the latest year for which statistics are available, some 1.5 million children had a parent in prison (Christopher J. Mumola, *Incarcerated Parents and Their Children*, Bureau of Justice Statistics, August 2000). At the state level, 642,300 prisoners had 1.325 million minor children being taken care of by others. In federal prisons, 79,200 prisoners had left 173,900 children in others' care. (See Table 5.9.) Among state prisoners, males were parents to 92% of the minor children, female prisoners accounted for 8% of children left behind. In federal prisons, female prisoners were parents to 6% of minor children left behind, while male prisoners accounted for 94%.

Looking at state prisons only, the number of prisoners' children had increased by 55% since 1991. Prisoners with children had on average 2.1 children both in 1991 and 1999. Male parents in state prison increased 54%; the number of their children increased by 52%. The female-parent prison population rose 82%; the children they had left doubled in number in this eight-year period.

Data for federal prisons show a somewhat different picture. Children with parents in federal prisons more than doubled—a 106.5% increase; federal prisoners with children increased 101%. Children with a male parent in prison increased 108.6% (from 78,300 to 163,300), those with a female parent in prison by 79.7% (from 5,900 children in 1991 to 10,600 in 1999).

According to Mumola in *Incarcerated Parents and Their Children*:

Half of the parents in state prison were never married.

Fewer than half of the parents in state prison lived with their minor children before incarceration.

One-third of mothers in prison had been living alone with their children in the months before arrest.

Fathers cite the child's mother as the current caregiver; mothers cite the child's grandparents or other relatives.

About 40% of fathers and 60% of mothers in state prison had at least weekly contact with their children.

A majority of parents in prison were violent offenders or drug traffickers.

## PRISON GANGS

There are a number of active gangs operating among the inmates in prisons. "The environment in most U.S. prisons is ripe for recruiting and controlling gang members because inmates tend to form associations for self-protection along racial, ethnic, and cultural lines," according to the *National Gang Threat Assessment* (National Alliance of Gang Investigators Associations, February 2000, http://www.nagia.org/table_of_contents. htm). In addition to providing mutual protection, prison gangs are also involved in selling drugs and other contraband. They routinely use violence and intimidation to dominate other inmates.

The BJS defines gangs as groups that commit illegal acts and have five or six of the following characteristics:

- Formal membership with a required initiation or rules for members

- A recognized leader or certain members whom others follow

- Common clothing or group colors, symbols, tattoos, or special language

- A group name

- Members from the same neighborhood, street, or school

- Turf or territory where the group is known and where group activities take place

The Florida Department of Corrections (http:// www.dc.state.fl.us/pub/gangs/prison.html) identified six major gangs operating in prisons in early 2005. They are: Neta (Puerto Rican inmates), the Aryan brotherhood (white inmates), the Black Guerrilla Family (African-American male inmates), the Mexican Mafia, La Nuestra Familia, and the Texas Syndicate (all Mexican-American inmates). While these gangs operate in prisons nationwide, such street gangs as the Crips, Bloods, Latin Kings, Barrio Aztecas, Black Gangster Disciples, and Nazi Low Riders are known to be operating in prisons as well.

# CHAPTER 6
# INMATE HEALTH

*Through the mid-1990s, a number of studies, limited in scope, found a higher prevalence of certain infectious diseases, chronic diseases, and mental illness among prison and jail inmates. Further, each year the nation's prisons and jails release more than 11.5 million inmates. The potential that ex-offenders may be contributing to the spread of infectious disease in the community became of increasing concern. In addition, as these ex-offenders' diseases get worse, society may have to pay substantially more to treat them than if these conditions had been treated at an earlier stage— or prevented altogether—while these individuals were still incarcerated.*

— Edward A. Harrison, CCHP, President, National Commission on Correctional Health Care

## DEATH RATES OF PRISONERS

Data on the health status of inmates in prisons and jails are not routinely collected by the Bureau of Justice Statistics (BJS). There are some exceptions. Surveys of prisoners conducted at intervals include questions about health. Since 1990 BJS has also collected data on the prevalence of Human Immunodeficiency Virus and Acquired Immune Deficiency Syndrome (HIV/AIDS) and has reported its findings on an annual basis. Estimates of prisoners' health conditions were developed by the National Commission on Correctional Health Care (NCCHC) and published in a report to Congress (*The Health Status of Soon-to-Be-Released Inmates*, Chicago, IL, 2002). These estimates, however, were not based on actual examinations of prison or jail inmates but were, instead, projections developed using studies of the general population with the results allocated to the prison population based on the economic, gender, and racial/ethnic composition of prisoners and inmates of jails.

An indirect measure of the health status of inmates is provided by mortality data that BJS makes available as part of its HIV/AIDS reporting. Table 6.1 shows deaths and death rates by cause of death in state prisons for the years 1995 and 2002. In 2002 the death rate from natural causes, excluding AIDS, was 190 per 100,000 inmates. When deaths from AIDS are added, the rate was 207. In federal prisons (see Table 6.2), the 2002 death rate from natural causes, excluding AIDS, was 179 per 100,000 inmates. When deaths from AIDS are added, the rate was 190.

In the 1995–2002 period, the overall death rate (all causes combined) generally dropped in prisons as in the general population. The state prison overall death rate declined from 311 per 100,000 inmates in 1995 to 246 in 2002. Within the state prison population, the most dramatic change was the sharply dropping death rate from AIDS. Deaths per 100,000 declined from one hundred in 1995 to seventeen in 2002, with the rates dropping every year.

## MEDICAL CONDITIONS, SURVEYED AND MEASURED

The *Census of State and Federal Adult Correctional Facilities* (2000) included survey questions on inmate health and is the most recent survey of the health status of state and federal prisoners, but the Bureau of Justice Statistics has not yet published the results. Data from the 1997 survey provide a self-assessment of prisoners' state of health. To that the BJS has added data from official prison records for 2000. These data are shown for federal prisoners in Table 6.3 together with benchmark measures on the health status of the general public for selected conditions.

Federal prison records in 2000 showed that 4.4% of inmates suffered from asthma; 0.9% of inmates in the 1997 survey reported asthma as a medical problem; data for 1998 for the general public showed that 8.9% of the public suffered from asthma. Fewer prisoners report ailments than prison records show that they have, and, with the exception of HIV/AIDS, prisoners experience lower incidents of ailments than the general public. The data shown here are, of

## TABLE 6.1

**Inmate deaths in state prisons, by cause, 1995 and 2002**

| Cause of death | Deaths of state inmates | | | |
| | Number* | | Rate per 100,000 inmates | |
| | 2002 | 1995 | 2002 | 1995 |
|---|---|---|---|---|
| **Total** | **3,105** | **3,133** | **246** | **311** |
| Natural causes other than AIDS | 2,405 | 1,569 | 190 | 156 |
| AIDS | 215 | 1,010 | 17 | 100 |
| Suicide | 166 | 160 | 13 | 16 |
| Accident | 41 | 48 | 3 | 5 |
| Execution | 70 | 56 | 6 | 6 |
| By another person | 53 | 86 | 4 | 9 |
| Other/unspecified | 155 | 204 | 12 | 20 |

*Detail may not add to total due to rounding.

SOURCE: Laura M. Maruschak, "Table 4. Inmate Deaths in State Prisons, by Cause, 1995 and 2002," in *HIV in Prisons and Jails, 2002*, Bureau of Justice Statistics, December 2004, http://www.ojp.usdoj.gov/bjs/pub/pdf/hivpj02.pdf (accessed April 1, 2005)

## TABLE 6.2

**Inmate deaths in federal prisons, by cause, 2001–02**

| Cause of death | Deaths of federal inmates | | | |
| | Number | | Rate per 100,000 inmates* | |
| | 2002 | 2001 | 2002 | 2001 |
|---|---|---|---|---|
| **Total** | **335** | **303** | **207** | **198** |
| Natural causes other than AIDS | 289 | 247 | 179 | 162 |
| AIDS | 17 | 22 | 11 | 14 |
| Suicide | 17 | 18 | 11 | 12 |
| Accident | 5 | 6 | 3 | 4 |
| Execution | 0 | 2 | 0 | 1 |
| By another person | 3 | 8 | 2 | 5 |
| Other/unspecified | 4 | 0 | 2 | 0 |

*Detail may not add to total due to rounding.

SOURCE: Laura M. Maruschak, "Table 5. Inmate Deaths in Federal Prisons, by Cause, 2001 and 2002," in *HIV in Prisons and Jails, 2002*, Bureau of Justice Statistics, December 2004, http://www.ojp.usdoj.gov/bjs/pub/pdf/hivpj02.pdf (accessed April 1, 2005)

## TABLE 6.3

**Medical problems among federal inmates and in the general public, 1997, 1998, 2000**

| Medical problem | Percent of federal inmates | | Percent of general public, 1998[b] |
| | Official records, midyear 2000[a] | 1997 survey data | |
|---|---|---|---|
| Asthma | 4.4% | 0.9% | 8.9% |
| Diabetes | 3.6 | 1.5 | 6.2 |
| Heart | 2.6 | 1.3 | 11.4 |
| High blood pressure | 7.8 | 1.7 | 19.0 |
| HIV/AIDS | 1.0 | 0.5 | 0.178[d] |
| Mental health | 4.8 | 4.8 | — |

[a]Based on the clinical status on July 29, 2000, except for asthma, which was counted on September 20, 2000. Inmate totals were based on average daily population in each month.
[b]Unless otherwise noted, values are from J.R. Pleis and R. Coles, *Summary Health Statistics for U.S. Adults: National Health Interview Survey, 1998*, National Center for Health Statistics. Vital Health Statistics 10(209). 2002.
[c]Value is for 2000 from National Diabetes Information Clearinghouse, National Institutes of Health, obtained from http://www.niddk.nih.gov/health/diabetes/pubs/dmstats/dmstats.htm#7.
[d]Value is for 2001 from "Table 1: Persons reported to be living with HIV infection and with AIDS," in HIV/AIDS Surveillance Report, 2001; 13 (No. 2), Centers for Disease Control and Prevention, Atlanta, GA, accessible at http://www.cdc.gov/hiv/stats/hasr1302/table1.htm. Rate calculated using 2001 population projections, middle series, from the U.S. Census Bureau.
—Not reported.

SOURCE: Adapted from Laura M. Maruschak and Allen J. Beck, "Comparing Estimates Based on Self-Reported Data to Official Records," in *Medical Problems of Inmates, 1997*, Bureau of Justice Statistics, January 2001, http://www.ojp.usdoj.gov/bjs/pub/pdf/mpi97.pdf (accessed April 1, 2005)

The prisoners, assessing themselves, significantly underestimated their actual medical problems compared with measurements taken in prison infirmaries and hospitals. The exception was mental health problems. The most common form of diabetes, late-onset Type II, takes a long time to result in symptoms and requires blood-sugar testing for early detection. Only prisoners who experienced acute heart episodes were likely to know they had problems. Similarly, high blood pressure does not have symptoms.

These data are for the federal prison population, which is a small part (11%) of the total prison population. With the exception of data on HIV/AIDS, the absence of data for the larger state prison population (data such as those shown in Table 6.3) illustrates indirectly some of the problems with health care in prisons. However, there have been several selective studies done of health care in prisons nationwide or in particular state prisons. In 2004 the BJS released statistics about the screening for and treating of hepatitis C in state prisons. Hepatitis C is a virus that can cause lifelong infection, cirrhosis (scarring) of the liver, cancer, liver failure, and death. It is spread most often through infected blood transferred by shared needles when using illegal drugs. Allen J. Beck and Laura M. Maruschak of the BJS reported in *Hepatitis Testing and Treatment in State Prisons* (April 2004) that 1,209 of the 1,584 state public and private prisons had

course, for different years and are therefore only indicative of patterns. Asthma illustrates well the differences between the prison population—predominantly young adults—and the general public. The prevalence of asthma is much higher in the general public, which includes children and seniors; children are absent from prison, and seniors are underrepresented. Diabetes, heart disease, and high blood pressure (hypertension) are conditions that manifest later in life, hence the lower levels of such diseases in the prison population. The one sexually transmitted disease charted (HIV/AIDS) is substantially higher in prison than in the general public: 1% of federal inmates had been diagnosed with the condition compared with 0.18% of the general public as determined by the Centers for Disease Control and Prevention (CDC).

TABLE 6.4

**Testing for hepatitis C in state prisons, July 1, 1999–June 30, 2000**

| | Facilities | | Inmates | |
|---|---|---|---|---|
| Testing | Number | Percent | Number | Percent |
| Total | 1,584 | 100% | 1,194,279 | 100% |
| Tests conducted | 1,209 | 79.0% | 1,113,035 | 94.3% |
| Broad coverage | 132 | 8.6% | 71,208 | 6.0% |
| All at some time | 73 | 4.8 | 29,951 | 2.5 |
| At admission | 61 | 4.0 | 38,540 | 3.3 |
| Random sample | 27 | 1.8 | 29,117 | 2.5 |
| Targeted group only | 1,064 | 69.5% | 1,033,862 | 87.6% |
| High risk | 492 | 32.1 | 566,369 | 48.0 |
| Upon inmate request | 604 | 39.5 | 666,004 | 56.4 |
| Clinical indication | 1,000 | 65.3 | 1,023,368 | 86.7 |
| Other | 13 | 0.8% | 7,965 | 0.7% |
| Do not conduct tests | 322 | 21.0% | 66,822 | 5.7% |
| Not reported | 53 | | 14,422 | |

Note: Detail may sum to more than total because facilities may report more than one policy.

SOURCE: Allen J. Beck and Laura M. Maruschak, "Table 1. Testing for Hepatitis C in State Prisons, July 1, 1999, through June 30, 2000," in *Hepatitis Testing and Treatment in State Prisons*, Bureau of Justice Statistics, April 2004, http://www.ojp.usdoj.gov/bjs/pub/pdf/httsp.pdf (accessed April 1, 2005)

TABLE 6.5

**Confirmed positive hepatitis C tests among state and federal inmates, July I, 1999–June 30, 2000**

| | Hepatitis C tests | |
|---|---|---|
| Testing policy | Number | Percent positive |
| Any | 57,018 | 31% |
| Broad coverage | 9,165 | 27 |
| Targeted group only | 46,479 | 33 |
| Other | 1,374 | 4 |

SOURCE: Allen J. Beck and Laura M. Maruschak, "Nearly a Third of Hepatitis C Tests Confirmed Positive," in *Hepatitis Testing and Treatment in State Prisons*, Bureau of Justice Statistics, April 2004, http://www.ojp.usdoj.gov/bjs/pub/pdf/httsp.pdf (accessed April 1, 2005)

tested inmates for hepatitis C between July 1, 1999, and June 30, 2000. (See Table 6.4.) Of the 1,584 total state facilities, 69.5% of them tested only those prisoners who were targeted as being at high risk from the disease; 4.8% tested all prisoners in some way. Table 6.5 shows that regardless of approach, those state prisons where testing was done for hepatitis C found that an average of 31% of prisoners had the disease.

A more wide-ranging study of prison health was conducted by the Department of Pediatrics, University of Texas Health Science Center at San Antonio. *The Disease Profile of Texas Prison Inmates* (April 2002) examined 170,215 inmates who were in the Texas prison system any time between August 1997 and July 1998. Based on the initial medical examination each prisoner received upon entering the system, and any subsequent

visits for medical treatment, the study showed that 29.6% of the prisoners had an infectious disease, 14% displayed a disease of the circulatory system, and 10.8% had a mental illness. The most common infectious disease was tuberculosis. (See Table 6.6.)

In 2002 the National Commission on Correctional Health Care, a nonprofit organization, identified some of the problems involved in measuring prisoners' health and delivering services. The following four items are quoted from the NCCHC's Report to Congress, taken from page xiv. The issues highlight barriers to effective prevention, screening, and treatment:

- **Lack of leadership**, such as failure to recognize the need for improved health care services, reluctance to consider that improving public health is a correctional responsibility, and unwillingness of public health agencies to advocate for improving correctional health care or to collaborate to promote improvement.

- **Logistical barriers**, such as short periods of incarceration, security-conscious administration procedures for distributing medications, and difficulty coordinating discharge planning.

- **Limited resources** that require difficult budgeting decisions to meet the high cost of many health care services and some medications, and that make it difficult to provide adequate space for medical services.

- **Correctional policies**, such as failure to specify minimum levels of required care in contracts with private health care vendors, delays caused by the need to escort inmates to medical treatment, poor communication between public health agencies and prisons and jails, and lack of adequate clinical guidelines.

## HIV/AIDS

An HIV-positive person is infected with the Human Immunodeficiency Virus. HIV interferes with and eventually destroys the body's immune system. Once the late stage of the disease is reached, the person has Acquired Immune Deficiency Syndrome. AIDS is incurable and leads to death. HIV/AIDS is transmitted in sexual contact, through breast-feeding of babies by an infected mother, and by blood. A common pathway is the use of unclean needles when injecting drugs. HIV can be treated but not cured. A very small percentage of those infected turn out to be so-called "nonprogressors," indicating that their bodies are able to overcome the virus; they do not "progress" and acquire AIDS.

According to Maruschak in *HIV in Prisons and Jails, 2002* (Bureau of Justice Statistics, December 2004), the number of HIV-positive inmates hit its highest level in 1999 (25,801). Since then, the numbers have been declining. In 2002, 23,864 prisoners were HIV-positive.

TABLE 6.6

**Prevalence of major disease categories in the Texas prison system, 1997–98***

| Disease | Overall (n=170,215) | | Males (n=155,947) | | Females (n=14,268) | |
|---|---|---|---|---|---|---|
| | Frequency | Prevalence | Frequency | Prevalence | Frequency | Prevalence |
| Infective and parasitic disease | 50,366 | 29.6 | 45,144 | 28.9 | 5,288 | 37.0 |
| Neoplasms | 1,239 | 0.7 | 1,116 | 0.7 | 123 | 0.9 |
| Endocrine, metabolic, nutritional and allergic diseases | 5,569 | 3.3 | 4,996 | 3.2 | 573 | 4.0 |
| Diseases of the blood and blood-forming organs | 838 | 0.5 | 731 | 0.5 | 107 | 0.8 |
| Mental disorders | 18,368 | 10.8 | 15,539 | 10.0 | 2,828 | 19.8 |
| Diseases of the nervous system and sense organs | 7,132 | 4.2 | 6,409 | 4.1 | 723 | 5.1 |
| Diseases of the circulatory system | 23,828 | 14.0 | 22,066 | 14.2 | 1,762 | 12.4 |
| Diseases of the respiratory system | 10,808 | 6.3 | 9,665 | 6.2 | 1,143 | 8.0 |
| Diseases of the digestive system | 10,034 | 5.9 | 9,045 | 5.8 | 989 | 6.9 |
| Diseases of the genitourinary system | 1,267 | 0.7 | 952 | 0.6 | 315 | 2.2 |
| Diseases of the skin and subcutaenous tissue | 4,114 | 2.4 | 3,745 | 2.4 | 369 | 2.6 |
| Diseases of the musculoskeletal system and connective tissue | 6,093 | 15.3 | 23,917 | 15.3 | 2,174 | 15.2 |
| Congenital anomalies | 689 | 0.4 | 652 | 0.4 | 37 | 0.3 |

*Prevalence estimates represent the percentage of inmates with a given disease during the study period

SOURCE: "Table 2. Prevalence of Major Disease Categories in the TDCJ Prison System," in *The Disease Profile of Texas Prison Inmates*, Department of Pediatrics, University of Texas Health Science Center at San Antonio, April 2002, http://www.ncjrs.org/pdffiles1/nij/grants/194052.pdf (accessed April 1, 2005)

(See Table 6.7.) Nearly half of the HIV-positive prisoners were found in three states: New York (5,000), Florida (2,848), and Texas (2,528). Female prisoners had a higher HIV-positive rate (3%) than did male prisoners (1.9%).

Table 6.7 further shows that the prevalence of HIV infection was 1.9% among state and federal prisoners in 2002—2% among state prison inmates and 1.1% among federal prisoners. Among state prisoners, the percentage of those with HIV has dropped from a high of 2.3% in 1999. Among federal prisoners, the rate has varied from 0.9% to 1.1%. (See Table 6.8.) Confirmed AIDS cases were nearly 3.5 times higher in the prison population in 2002 than in the general public, 0.48% of prisoners and 0.14% of the general public. The differences between these two populations are narrowing. While the HIV rate among the general public has been slowly rising, from a low of 0.8% in 1995, the rate for prisoners has been dropping since 1999. (See Table 6.9.)

**Higher Prevalence in Women**

In 2002 women prisoners were more likely to be HIV-positive than male prisoners—2.9% of female inmates in state prisons, or 2,164 women, were found to be HIV-positive compared to 1.9% of male prisoners, or 20,273 men. (Table 6.10.) Between 1998 and 2002, the rate of infection for both male and female prisoners declined. For men, it fell from 2.2%, while for women, it fell from 3.8%. The New York prison system had the largest number of female HIV-positive inmates (410). Florida had 340, followed by Texas, with 267. Among federal prisoners in 2002, 1.2% of females (116 inmates) were HIV-positive. (See Table 6.11.)

**Race and Ethnicity**

While there are no recent figures for the race and ethnicity of those inmates who are HIV-positive in prison, the BJS has published data on the race and ethnicity of HIV-positive prisoners in the nation's jails. Table 6.12, from *HIV in Prisons and Jails, 2002*, shows that in 2002, 2.9% of Hispanic jail inmates, 0.8% of white inmates, and 1.2% of African-American inmates were HIV-positive. African-American females (3%) had the highest rate of infection, while white males (0.6%) had the lowest. The forty-five-and-older age group had the highest rate of HIV infection (2.7%), with the twenty-four-or-younger age group having the least (0.2%).

**MENTAL ILLNESS IN PRISON**

Beginning in the 1970s, there was a movement to de-institutionalize the mentally ill and reintegrate them into society. This widespread trend resulted in the closing of many large-scale mental hospitals and treatment centers. With fewer options open to them, the mentally ill more often came into contact with law enforcement authorities. Morris L. Thigpen, Director of the National Institute of Corrections, wrote in *Effective Prison Mental Health Services: Guidelines to Expand and Improve Treatment* (Washington, DC: National Institute of Corrections, May 2004): "Since the early 1990s, an increasing number of adults with mental illness have become involved with the criminal justice system. State and federal prisons, in particular, have undergone a dramatic transformation, housing a growing number of inmates with serious mental disorders. Complicating this situation is the high proportion of mentally ill inmates who have co-occurring substance use disorders."

According to the National Institute of Mental Health (NIMH), about 22.1% of the American public suffer from a diagnosable mental disorder. The U.S. prison population, at least as measured by looking at its largest component, the state prison population, experiences a prevalence of mental illness very much in line with that of the general population. Beck and Maruschak reported in *Mental Health Treatment in State Prisons, 2000* (Bureau of Justice Statistics, July 2001) that the prevalence of mental illness, broadly defined, was between 22% and 24% in the prison population.

*Effective Prison Mental Health Services* reported in 2004 that, of state public and private prisons, 95% provided some sort of mental health services to their inmates, with 84% providing professional therapy or counseling. Most (78%) screened newly arrived inmates for mental problems.

## Prisoner Characteristics

The most recent comprehensive survey of the prison population's mental health was issued in 1999 (*Mental Health and Treatment of Inmates and Probationers*, BJS, July 1999). It was based on the 1997 *Survey of Inmates in State and Federal Correctional Facilities*, the 1996 *Survey of Inmates in Local Jails*, and the 1995 *Survey of Adults on Probation*. Although the data are now aging, they bring into focus the differences between prison inmates with mental problems and those who do not have them.

**TABLE 6.7**

**State and federal inmates known to be HIV-positive, 2000–02**

| Jurisdiction | Total known to be HIV positive[a] | | | HIV/AIDS cases as a percent of total custody population[b] | | |
|---|---|---|---|---|---|---|
| | 2002 | 2001 | 2000 | 2002 | 2001 | 2000 |
| **U.S. total** | | | | | | |
| Reported[c] | 23,864 | 24,147 | 25,333 | 1.9% | 1.9% | 2.0% |
| Comparable reporting[d] | 23,848 | 24,011 | 25,198 | | | |
| Federal | 1,547 | 1,520 | 1,302 | 1.1% | 1.2% | 1.0% |
| State | 22,317 | 22,627 | 24,031 | 2.0 | 2.0 | 2.2 |
| **Northeast** | 7,620 | 8,136 | 8,721 | 4.6% | 4.9% | 5.2% |
| Connecticut | 666 | 604 | 593 | 3.6 | 3.5 | 3.6 |
| Maine | † | 15 | 11 | † | 0.9 | 0.7 |
| Massachusetts | 290 | 307 | 313 | 2.9 | 3.0 | 3.0 |
| New Hampshire | 16 | 17 | 23 | 0.6 | 0.7 | 1.0 |
| New Jersey | 756 | 804 | 771 | 3.2 | 3.4 | 3.2 |
| New York | 5,000 | 5,500 | 6,000 | 7.5 | 8.1 | 8.5 |
| Pennsylvania | 800 | 735 | 900 | 2.0 | 2.0 | 2.4 |
| Rhode Island | 86 | 148 | 90 | 2.5 | 4.4 | 2.6 |
| Vermont | 6 | 6 | 20 | 0.4 | 0.4 | 1.5 |
| **Midwest** | 2,133 | 2,135 | 2,252 | 1.0% | 1.0% | 1.1% |
| Illinois | 570 | 593 | 619 | 1.3 | 1.3 | 1.4 |
| Indiana | † | † | † | † | † | † |
| Iowa | 33 | 27 | 27 | 0.4 | 0.3 | 0.3 |
| Kansas | 48 | 41 | 49 | 0.5 | 0.5 | 0.6 |
| Michigan | 591 | 584 | 585 | 1.2 | 1.2 | 1.2 |
| Minnesota | 37 | 33 | 42 | 0.5 | 0.5 | 0.7 |
| Missouri | 262 | 262 | 267 | 0.9 | 0.9 | 1.0 |
| Nebraska | 24 | 24 | 18 | 0.6 | 0.6 | 0.5 |
| North Dakota | 4 | 4 | 2 | 0.4 | 0.4 | 0.2 |
| Ohio | 417 | 398 | 478 | 1.0 | 0.9 | 1.1 |
| South Dakota | 6 | 5 | 4 | 0.2 | 0.2 | 0.2 |
| Wisconsin | 141 | 164 | 161 | 0.8 | 0.9 | 1.0 |
| **South** | 10,656 | 10,392 | 10,767 | 2.2% | 2.2% | 2.3% |
| Alabama | 276 | 302 | 419 | 1.1 | 1.2 | 1.8 |
| Arkansas | 100 | 108 | 101 | 0.8 | 0.9 | 0.9 |
| Delaware | 128 | 143 | 127 | 1.9 | 2.1 | 1.9 |
| District of Columbia[e] | † | † | 126 | † | † | 3.3 |
| Florida | 2,848 | 2,602 | 2,640 | 3.8 | 3.6 | 3.7 |
| Georgia | 1,123 | 1,150 | 938 | 2.4 | 2.5 | 2.1 |
| Kentucky | † | 105 | 124 | † | 1.1 | 1.3 |
| Louisiana | 503 | 514 | 500 | 2.5 | 2.6 | 2.6 |
| Maryland | 967 | 830 | 998 | 4.0 | 3.5 | 4.3 |
| Mississippi | 224 | 234 | 230 | 1.9 | 2.0 | 2.1 |
| North Carolina | 602 | 573 | 588 | 1.8 | 1.8 | 1.9 |
| Oklahoma | 146 | 130 | 145 | 0.9 | 0.9 | 1.0 |
| South Carolina | 544 | 559 | 560 | 2.4 | 2.6 | 2.7 |
| Tennessee | 218 | 231 | 215 | 1.5 | 1.7 | 1.6 |
| Texas | 2,528 | 2,388 | 2,492 | 1.9 | 1.8 | 1.8 |
| Virginia | 425 | 507 | 550 | 1.4 | 1.7 | 1.9 |
| West Virginia | 24 | 16 | 14 | 0.7 | 0.5 | 0.5 |

TABLE 6.7

**State and federal inmates known to be HIV-positive, 2000–02** [CONTINUED]

| Jurisdiction | Total known to be HIV positive[a] | | | HIV/AIDS cases as a percent of total custody population[b] | | |
|---|---|---|---|---|---|---|
| | 2002 | 2001 | 2000 | 2002 | 2001 | 2000 |
| **West** | 1,908 | 1,964 | 2,291 | 0.7% | 0.8% | 0.9% |
| Alaska | 16 | 16 | [f] | 0.5 | 0.5 | [f] |
| Arizona | 130 | 122 | 110 | 0.4 | 0.4 | 0.4 |
| California | 1,181 | 1,305 | 1,638 | 0.7 | 0.8 | 1.0 |
| Colorado | 182 | 173 | 146 | 1.1 | 1.2 | 1.0 |
| Hawaii | 22 | 13 | 19 | 0.6 | 0.3 | 0.5 |
| Idaho | 18 | 14 | 14 | 0.4 | 0.4 | 0.3 |
| Montana | 8 | 11 | 11 | 0.4 | 0.6 | 0.7 |
| Nevada | 113 | 127 | 151 | 1.2 | 1.4 | 1.6 |
| New Mexico | 30 | 27 | 28 | 0.5 | 0.5 | 0.5 |
| Oregon | 42 | 30 | 41 | 0.4 | 0.3 | 0.4 |
| Utah | 58 | 34 | 37 | 1.4 | 0.8 | 0.9 |
| Washington | 101 | 88 | 90 | 0.6 | 0.6 | 0.6 |
| Wyoming | 7 | 4 | 6 | 0.6 | 0.4 | 0.5 |

[a]Counts published in previous reports have been revised.
[b]Percentages are based on custody counts, except for New Mexico. New Mexico's percentages are based on its year end jurisdiction count.
[c]Excludes inmates in jurisdictions that did not report data.
[d]Excludes data from Maine, Kentucky, and Alaska for all 3 years due to incomplete reporting.
[e]At year end 2001 responsibility for housing District of Columbia sentenced felons was transferred to the Federal Bureau of Prisons.
[f]Not reported.

SOURCE: Laura M. Maruschak, "Table 1. Inmates in Custody of State or Federal Prison Authorities and Known to Be Positive for the Human Immunodeficiency Virus, 2000–2002," in *HIV in Prisons and Jails, 2002*, Bureau of Justice Statistics, December 2004, http://www.ojp.usdoj.gov/bjs/pub/pdf/hivpj02.pdf (accessed March 31, 2005)

TABLE 6.8

**Percent of custody population known to be HIV positive, 1998–2002**

| Year | State | Federal |
|---|---|---|
| 1998 | 2.3% | 1.0% |
| 1999 | 2.3 | 0.9 |
| 2000 | 2.2 | 1.0 |
| 2001 | 2.0 | 1.2 |
| 2002 | 2.0 | 1.1 |

SOURCE: Laura M. Maruschak, "Percent of Custody Population Known to Be HIV Positive," in *HIV in Prisons and Jails, 2002*, Bureau of Justice Statistics, December 2004, http://www.ojp.usdoj.gov/bjs/pub/pdf/hivpj02.pdf (accessed April 1, 2005)

TABLE 6.9

**Percent of the general population and prison population with confirmed AIDS, 1995–2002**

| Year | U.S. general population | State and federal prisoners |
|---|---|---|
| 1995 | 0.08% | 0.51% |
| 1996 | 0.09 | 0.54 |
| 1997 | 0.10 | 0.55 |
| 1998 | 0.11 | 0.53 |
| 1999 | 0.12 | 0.60 |
| 2000 | 0.13 | 0.53 |
| 2001 | 0.14 | 0.52 |
| 2002 | 0.14 | 0.48 |

Note: The percent of the general population with confirmed AIDS in each year may be overestimated due to delays in death reports.

SOURCE: Laura M. Maruschak, "Percent of Population with Confirmed AIDS," in *HIV in Prisons and Jails, 2002*, Bureau of Justice Statistics, December 2004, http://www.ojp.usdoj.gov/bjs/pub/pdf/hivpj02.pdf (accessed April 1, 2005)

A higher percentage of women were identified as mentally ill than men in 1998: 23.6% in state prisons and 12.5% in federal prisons. This contrasts with men, of whom 15.8% (state) and 7% (federal) were mentally ill. Some 22.6% of whites in state prisons and 11.8% in federal facilities were mentally ill. Among African-American prisoners, the prevalence was lower, 13.5% (state) and 5.6% (federal). Hispanics had the lowest rates: 11% in state and 4.1% in federal facilities. (See Table 6.13.)

## Guidelines for Treating the Mentally Ill in Prison

The National Commission on Correctional Health Care (http://www.ncchc.org/) has issued guidelines that prisons should follow to provide adequate mental health treatment to inmates:

- Inmates must be screened for mental health problems by a qualified health professional within two hours of admission.

- Inmates must be informed within twenty-four hours of arrival of the types of mental health services available and how to access them.

- Inmates must have a health appraisal within seven days of arrival that includes taking a history of any prior mental health problems, hospitalizations, psychotropic medications, suicide attempts, and alcohol and other drug abuse.

**TABLE 6.10**

**HIV-positive prison inmates by gender, 1998–2002**

| | State prison inmates | |
|---|---|---|
| Year | Estimated number of HIV-positive inmates* | Percent HIV/AIDS in custody population |
| **Male inmates** | | |
| 1998 | 22,045 | 2.2% |
| 1999 | 22,175 | 2.2 |
| 2000 | 21,894 | 2.1 |
| 2001 | 20,415 | 1.9 |
| 2002 | 20,273 | 1.9 |
| **Female inmates** | | |
| 1998 | 2,552 | 3.8% |
| 1999 | 2,402 | 3.5 |
| 2000 | 2,472 | 3.4 |
| 2001 | 2,212 | 3.1 |
| 2002 | 2,164 | 2.9 |

*To provide year-to-year comparisons, estimates were made for states not reporting a gender breakdown. For each state, estimates were made by applying the same percent breakdown by gender from the most recent year when data were provided.

SOURCE: Laura M. Maruschak, "HIV-Positive Prison Inmates by Gender, 1998–2002," in *HIV in Prisons and Jails, 2002*, Bureau of Justice Statistics, December 2004, http://www.ojp.usdoj.gov/bjs/pub/pdf/hivpj02.pdf (accessed April 1, 2005)

- Inmates must receive a mental health evaluation within fourteen days of arrival that includes a complete mental health history and current mental status and screening for mental retardation and other developmental disabilities.

- Treatment plans must be created for inmates who are identified as having serious mental health needs and who are developmentally disabled.

- Inmates should be seen by a qualified professional within forty-eight hours of a request for nonemergency mental health services (seventy-two hours on a weekend).

- Prison procedures must address psychiatric emergencies and suicide attempts.

- Mental health treatment should occur in private (except for high security risks) and with respect for the offender's dignity and feelings.

## Suicide in Prison

Broadly defined, mental illness is a leading cause of suicide in prison. According to *Juvenile Suicide in Confinement: A National Survey* (Washington, DC: National Center on Institutions and Alternatives, February 2004), there were 110 juvenile suicides in confinement between 1995 and 1999. These deaths occurred in training schools, detention centers, and residential treatment centers, among other correctional facilities. The study found that "a history of mental illness was found in 65.8% of the victims, with the vast majority (65.3%) suffering from depression at the time of their deaths."

Suicide among adult inmates in prison is also an unfortunately common occurrence. *Prison Suicide: An Overview and Guide to Prevention* (Washington, DC: National Institute of Corrections, June 1995) contains a report on a ten-year survey of prison suicides conducted by the National Center on Institutions and Alternatives (NCIA) from 1984 through 1993. This survey found that prisoners committed suicide at a much higher rate than does the general population. During the ten-year period, prison suicides occurred at a rate of twenty-one per 100,000 inmates per year, while suicides in jails occurred at the rate of 107 per 100,000 inmates. The rate of suicide in the general population during this period was 12.2 per 100,000. The study did find that prison suicide rates

**TABLE 6.11**

**State and federal inmates known to be HIV-positive, by gender, yearend 2002**

| | Male HIV cases | | Female HIV cases | |
|---|---|---|---|---|
| Jurisdiction[a] | Number | Percent of population | Number | Percent of population |
| **U.S. total** | | | | |
| Estimated[b] | 21,704 | | 2,280 | |
| Reported | 20,728 | 1.9% | 2,169 | 2.8% |
| Federal | 1,431 | 1.1% | 116 | 1.2% |
| State | 19,297 | 1.9 | 2,053 | 3.0 |
| **Northeast** | 6,920 | 4.4% | 700 | 8.1% |
| Connecticut | 563 | 3.3 | 103 | 7.2 |
| Maine | c | c | c | c |
| Massachusetts | 249 | 2.7 | 41 | 5.9 |
| New Hampshire | 15 | 0.6 | 1 | 0.6 |
| New Jersey | 691 | 3.1 | 65 | 5.1 |
| New York | 4,590 | 7.2 | 410 | 13.6 |
| Pennsylvania | 738 | 2.0 | 62 | 3.5 |
| Rhode Island | 68 | 2.1 | 18 | 9.3 |
| Vermont | 6 | 0.5 | 0 | 0 |
| **Midwest** | 1,841 | 1.0% | 151 | 1.2% |
| Illinois | 520 | 1.3 | 50 | 2.0 |
| Indiana | c | c | c | c |
| Iowa | 29 | 0.4 | 4 | 0.6 |
| Kansas | 41 | 0.5 | 7 | 1.2 |
| Michigan | 544 | 1.1 | 47 | 2.1 |
| Minnesota | 37 | 0.6 | 0 | 0 |
| Missouri | 250 | 0.9 | 12 | 0.5 |
| Nebraska | 23 | 0.6 | 1 | 0.3 |
| North Dakota | 4 | 0.4 | 0 | 0 |
| Ohio | 388 | 1.0 | 29 | 1.0 |
| South Dakota | 5 | 0.2 | 1 | 0.4 |
| Wisconsin | c | c | c | c |
| **South** | 8,786 | 2.2% | 1,044 | 3.5% |
| Alabama | 252 | 1.1 | 24 | 1.5 |
| Arkansas | 89 | 0.8 | 11 | 1.4 |
| Delaware | 116 | 1.9 | 12 | 2.3 |
| Florida | 2,508 | 3.6 | 340 | 7.4 |
| Georgia | 1,023 | 2.3 | 100 | 3.2 |
| Kentucky | c | c | c | c |
| Louisiana | 472 | 2.5 | 31 | 3.0 |
| Maryland | 815 | 3.6 | 152 | 12.1 |
| Mississippi | c | c | c | c |
| North Carolina | c | c | c | c |
| Oklahoma | 138 | 1.0 | 8 | 0.5 |
| South Carolina | 502 | 2.4 | 42 | 2.6 |
| Tennessee | 194 | 1.5 | 24 | 2.1 |
| Texas | 2,261 | 1.8 | 267 | 2.7 |
| Virginia | 394 | 1.4 | 31 | 1.5 |
| West Virginia | 22 | 0.7 | 2 | 0.8 |

TABLE 6.11

**State and federal inmates known to be HIV-positive, by gender, yearend 2002** [CONTINUED]

| | Male HIV cases | | Female HIV cases | |
|---|---|---|---|---|
| Jurisdiction[a] | Number | Percent of population | Number | Percent of population |
| **West** | 1,750 | 0.7% | 158 | 0.9% |
| Alaska | 14 | 0.5 | 2 | 0.8 |
| Arizona | 117 | 0.4 | 13 | 0.5 |
| California | 1,107 | 0.7 | 74 | 0.8 |
| Colorado | 156 | 1.1 | 26 | 1.7 |
| Hawaii | 21 | 0.6 | 1 | 0.2 |
| Idaho | 17 | 0.5 | 1 | 0.2 |
| Montana | 7 | 0.4 | 1 | 0.5 |
| Nevada | 98 | 1.1 | 15 | 4.2 |
| New Mexico | 27 | 0.5 | 3 | 0.6 |
| Oregon | 42 | 0.4 | 0 | 0 |
| Utah | 48 | 1.2 | 10 | 3.4 |
| Washington | 91 | 0.6 | 10 | 0.8 |
| Wyoming | 5 | 0.5 | 2 | 2.2 |

[a]At yearend 2001 responsibility for housing District of Columbia sentenced felons was transferred to the Federal Bureau of Prisons.
[b]Includes estimate of the number of inmates with HIV/AIDS by gender for Maine, Wisconsin, Kentucky, Mississippi, and North Carolina. Estimates were based on the most recent data available by gender.
[c]Not reported.

SOURCE: Laura M. Maruschak, "Table 2. Inmates in Custody of State and Federal Prison Authorities Known to Be Positive for the Human Immunodeficiency Virus, by Gender, Yearend 2002," in *HIV in Prisons and Jails, 2002*, Bureau of Justice Statistics, December 2004, http://www.ojp.usdoj.gov/bjs/pub/pdf/hivpj02.pdf (accessed April 1, 2005)

declined from 1985 through 1993. In 1995 state prisons reported 160 inmate suicides; the number in 2002 was 166. In federal prisons, the number for 2001 was eighteen suicides; in 2002 it was seventeen.

Methods of preventing suicide in prison have been advanced by several organizations. The American Correctional Association (ACA) has developed suicide prevention standards that are now used in many prisons across the country:

- A written policy and procedures to ensure that all special management inmates are directly observed at least every thirty minutes.

- More frequent observation for inmates who are violent or have a mental illness than for inmates who are not violent and do not have mental illness.

- Continual observation for actively suicidal inmates.

- A written suicide prevention and intervention program approved by a qualified medical or mental health professional.

- Training for all correctional staff in the suicide prevention and intervention program.

- Intake screening, identification, and supervision of inmates who may be prone to suicide.

TABLE 6.12

**Jail inmates ever tested for HIV and results, by selected characteristics, 2002**

| | Tested inmates who reported results | |
|---|---|---|
| Characteristic | Number | Percent HIV positive |
| **All inmates** | 374,711 | 1.3% |
| **Gender** | | |
| Male | 324,370 | 1.2% |
| Female | 50,340 | 2.3 |
| **Race/Hispanic origin** | | |
| White | 136,069 | 0.8% |
| Male | 113,671 | 0.6 |
| Female | 22,398 | 1.6 |
| Black | 163,219 | 1.2 |
| Male | 144,330 | 1.0 |
| Female | 18,889 | 3.0 |
| Hispanic | 55,938 | 2.9 |
| Male | 49,819 | 2.9 |
| Female | 6,120 | 2.9 |
| **Age** | | |
| 24 or younger | 101,362 | 0.2% |
| 25–34 | 126,607 | 1.1 |
| 35–44 | 103,566 | 2.1 |
| 45 or older | 43,176 | 2.7 |
| **Marital status** | | |
| Married | 56,397 | 1.0% |
| Widowed/divorced | 67,281 | 1.9 |
| Separated | 26,747 | 1.7 |
| Never married | 223,706 | 1.2 |
| **Education** | | |
| Less than high school | 143,272 | 1.6% |
| GED | 90,300 | 1.3 |
| High school or more | 140,341 | 1.1 |

Note: Data are from the 2002 Survey of Inmates in Local Jails.

SOURCE: Laura M. Maruschak, "Table 9. Jail Inmates Ever Tested for the Human Immunodeficiency Virus and Results, by Selected Characteristics, 2002," in *HIV in Prisons and Jails, 2002*, Bureau of Justice Statistics, December 2004, http://www.ojp.usdoj.gov/bjs/pub/pdf/hivpj02.pdf (accessed April 1, 2005)

## INJURIES IN PRISON

Data on injuries suffered by prisoners, whether in accidents or in fights, also date back to the 1997 survey of state and federal prisons. BJS has not published any new data since *Medical Problems of Inmates, 1997*, a report by Laura M. Maruschak and Allen J. Beck that was published in January 2001. The 1997 BJS data includes statistics on injuries and is based on prisoner reporting. In the report, Maruschak and Beck present statistics on prison inmates who reported injuries by time served in months. Both accidental injuries and injuries sustained in fights are reported.

*Medical Problems of Inmates, 1997* indicates that 13.2% of state prisoners and 17% of federal prisoners, both with less than twelve months of time served, had suffered injuries. Of these, 2.9% of state and 0.8% of federal prisoners reported being injured in fights, while 10.2% of state and 15.6% of federal prisoners were injured in accidents in this group. Prisoners who had served twelve to twenty-three months had higher

**TABLE 6.13**

**Inmates and probationers identified as mentally ill, by gender, race, Hispanic origin, and age, 1998**

| Offender characteristic | Percent identified as mentally ill | | | |
|---|---|---|---|---|
| | State inmates | Federal inmates | Jail inmates | Probationers |
| **Gender** | | | | |
| Male | 15.8% | 7.0% | 15.6% | 14.7% |
| Female | 23.6 | 12.5 | 22.7 | 21.7 |
| **Race/Hispanic origin** | | | | |
| White* | 22.6% | 11.8% | 21.7% | 19.6% |
| Black* | 13.5 | 5.6 | 13.7 | 10.4 |
| Hispanic | 11.0 | 4.1 | 11.1 | 9.0 |
| **Age** | | | | |
| 24 or younger | 14.4% | 6.6% | 13.3% | 13.8% |
| 25–34 | 14.8 | 5.9 | 15.7 | 13.8 |
| 35–44 | 18.4 | 7.5 | 19.3 | 19.8 |
| 45–54 | 19.7 | 10.3 | 22.7 | 21.1 |
| 55 or older | 15.6 | 8.9 | 20.4 | 16.0 |

*Excludes Hispanics.

SOURCE: Paula M. Ditton, "Table 4. Inmates and Probationers Identified as Mentally Ill, by Gender, Race/Hispanic Origin, and Age, 1998," in *Mental Health and Treatment of Inmates and Probationers*, Bureau of Justice Statistics, July 1999, http://www.ojp.usdoj.gov/bjs/pub/pdf/mhtip.pdf (accessed April 1, 2005)

incidence of injury: 19.8% of state prisoners and 22% of federal inmates reported an injury since admission. The longer prisoners serve, the higher the percentage of those injured. The survey format used by the BJS researchers produces what amounts to a cumulative measure of injury over time. (See Table 6.14.)

## RAPE IN PRISONS

In September 2003 President George W. Bush signed into law the Prison Rape Elimination Act. This act mandates that the Bureau of Justice Statistics begin a comprehensive program to monitor the prevalence of rape in prisons and develop a set of guidelines to reduce such crimes. While the problem is acknowledged to be a major one, few studies have been conducted on the subject of rape in prison, and those have been typically small in scale and limited in scope. Victims of same-sex rape are often reluctant to discuss the event with authorities. Inmates attacked by guards often fear retribution if they speak of the matter. The Prison Rape Elimination Act was instituted to get accurate numbers from which effective measures can be determined. Under the act's provisions, those prisons with both the highest and lowest rates of sexual assault will be studied to determine what measures have been the least and most effective in preventing such crimes.

According to *Data Collections for the Prison Rape Elimination Act of 2003* (Bureau of Justice Statistics, June 2004), the primary objectives of the bureau's data collection are to determine:

- The number of reported incidents of inmate-on-inmate sexual violence and staff-on-inmate sexual misconduct, by gender

- How prison systems and facilities record these incidents (e.g., in disciplinary, grievance, investigative, or medical files)

- What information is recorded (e.g., allegations, confirmed incidents, only incidents involving serious bodily harm, or threats)

- Where the incidents occur (e.g., in the victim's cell/room, in a common area, or outside of the facility)

- What additional data are available (for purposes of administrative collections in future years)

## REDUCING THE COST AND IMPROVING THE AVAILABILITY OF TREATMENT

Telecommunications links make it possible for physicians and other health care specialists to evaluate and treat patients who are hundreds or thousands of miles away. This technology, called telemedicine, offers the prospect of providing prisoners with cost-effective health care. For example, telemedicine makes it possible for

**TABLE 6.14**

**Injuries reported by state and federal inmates since admission, by time served, 1997**

| Time since admission | Percent of inmates who reported an injury since admission | | | | | |
|---|---|---|---|---|---|---|
| | Total | | Injured in an accident | | Injured in a fight | |
| | State | Federal | State | Federal | State | Federal |
| Less than 12 months | 13.2% | 17.0% | 10.2% | 15.6% | 2.9% | 0.8% |
| 12–23 months | 19.8 | 22.0 | 14.8 | 20.1 | 5.3 | 1.8 |
| 24–47 months | 26.7 | 26.3 | 19.0 | 24.3 | 9.2 | 2.1 |
| 48–71 months | 36.8 | 30.2 | 26.3 | 25.3 | 13.8 | 5.4 |
| 72 months or more | 45.9 | 31.6 | 31.7 | 26.3 | 19.7 | 5.3 |

SOURCE: Laura M. Maruschak and Allen J. Beck, "Table 4. Injuries Reported by State and Federal Inmates since Admission, by Time Served, 1997," in *Medical Problems of Inmates, 1997*, Bureau of Justice Statistics, January 2001, http://www.ojp.usdoj.gov/bjs/pub/pdf/mpi97.pdf (accessed April 1, 2005)

physicians to examine prisoners without the inconvenience of traveling to prison facilities, often located in remote or isolated areas. Likewise, the cost and security concerns of transporting prisoners to physicians are also eliminated.

In "Can Telemedicine Reduce Spending and Improve Health Care?" (*National Institute of Justice Journal*, April 1999), authors Douglas McDonald, Andrea Hassol, and Kenneth Carlson reported on a demonstration program to evaluate a telemedicine system in prison. The pilot project was conducted jointly at four federal prisons:

- U.S. Penitentiary, Lewisburg, PA. Maximum security. Houses an average of 1,300 male prisoners

- U.S. Penitentiary, Allenwood, PA. Maximum security. Houses an average of 1,000 male prisoners

- Federal Correction Institution, Allenwood, PA. Low and medium security. Houses an average of 1,100 male prisoners

- Federal Medical Center, Lexington, KY. Medium and minimum security. Houses an average of 1,450 mostly male prisoners with chronic illnesses

The pilot program was conducted from September 1996 to December 1997. It did not replace routine medical care provided by prison staff. As reported, the goal of the telemedicine test program was to reduce three types of care:

- Consultations with specialty physicians who would normally visit the prison

- Prisoner trips to hospitals or off-site physicians

- Transfers of prisoners to federal medical centers for intensive or long-term treatment

At each prison a dedicated telemedicine room was equipped with interactive video-conferencing equipment, specialized medical cameras, an electronic stethoscope, and a computer workstation with appropriate software. For most examinations a medical staff member from the prison (usually a physician's assistant) presented the inmate patient to an off-site specialist linked via video-conferencing and equipped with remote controls that enabled the specialist to manipulate cameras located in the patient examination room.

During the fifteen months of the demonstration project, physicians made approximately one hundred telemedicine consultations each month, for a total of 1,321 consultations. About 58% of the telemedicine "visits" were for psychiatric consultations, followed by dermatology (13.3%), orthopedics (10.7%), dietary (6.4%), and podiatry (4.7%). The remaining 6.5% of telemedicine consultations were with specialists from other disciplines, including infectious diseases, cardiology, and neurology.

Four specialties were selected for purposes of comparing conventional medical care in prisons with telemedicine consultations—psychiatry, orthopedics, dermatology, and cardiology. Specialists in these four fields were among the most frequently consulted prior to the pilot project, and that frequently increased with the implementation of telemedicine.

During the pilot program, the cost of in-prison consultations decreased from approximately $108 per conventional consultation to $71 per telemedicine consultation, a savings of $37 per consultation. However, because there was not a one-for-one substitution of regular consultations and telemedicine consultations, the total number of consultations increased with the addition of telemedicine.

Some thirty-five trips for inmates to visit specialists outside of prison were eliminated through telemedicine for a total savings of about $27,500. Some trips were unavoidable when inmates required invasive tests, surgery, or intensive trauma care. The Bureau of Prisons estimated that it saved an additional $59,134 because, in certain cases, telemedicine eliminated the need for air transfers of inmates to federal medical centers. Most of the averted air transfers were for psychiatric patients who required intensive monitoring that was made possible through telemedicine consultations.

There were other nonfinancial benefits to the implementation of telemedicine consultations. Waiting time to see specialists decreased and new services became available, including more specialized HIV/AIDS care. Also, inmate patients reported feeling that the quality of care improved with telemedicine.

As a result of the success of this pilot program, the National Institute of Justice (NIJ) began studies using telemedicine in jails. It also funds a program to inform corrections staff of the benefits of telemedicine and to help prison administrators decide if telemedicine will succeed at their facilities. Some of the points to consider are space constraints and access to nearby medical centers. In addition, the program suggests ways to develop and launch prison telemedicine systems. Designing such systems is discussed in *Implementing Telemedicine in Correctional Facilities* by Peter L. Nacci and others (Washington, DC: U.S. Department of Justice and U.S. Department of Defense, May 2002).

One of the new systems implemented in 2003 involves the University of Texas Medical Branch (UTMB) and the Federal Medical Center in Lexington, Kentucky. Under the telemedicine agreement, medical specialists in Galveston treat inmates in Lexington nearly 1,000 miles away. Among the specialties offered are orthopedics and urology.

# CHAPTER 7
# JUVENILE CONFINEMENT

*Since 1992, forty-five states have passed or amended legislation making it easier to prosecute juveniles as adults. The result is that the number of youths under eighteen confined in adult prisons has more than doubled in the past decade. This phenomenon is challenging the belief, enshrined in our justice system a century ago, that children and young adolescents should be adjudicated and confined in a separate system focused on their rehabilitation.*

— Nancy E. Gist, Director, Bureau of Justice Assistance, 2003

## WHO IS A JUVENILE?

In most states offenders age eighteen or younger are considered juveniles and fall under the jurisdiction of juvenile courts rather than adult criminal courts. However, all states will prosecute juveniles as adults under some circumstances. According to the National Center for Juvenile Justice (http://ncjj.servehttp.com/NCJJWebsite/main.htm) in 2005:

- "Forty-six states have judicial waiver provisions, in which juvenile court judges clear the way for criminal court prosecutions by waiving jurisdiction over individual juveniles. Under a waiver law, a case against an offender of juvenile age must at least originate in juvenile court; it cannot be channeled elsewhere without a juvenile court judge's formal approval. While all states prescribe standards that must be consulted in waiver decision-making, most leave the decision largely to the judge's discretion (forty-five states). However, some set up presumptions in favor of waiver in certain classes of cases (fifteen states), and some even specify circumstances under which waiver is mandatory (fifteen states)."

- "Fifteen states have direct file laws, which leave it up to prosecutors to decide, at least in specified classes of cases, whether to initiate cases in juvenile or criminal courts."

- "Twenty-nine states have statutory exclusion provisions that grant criminal courts original jurisdiction over certain classes of cases involving juveniles. Legislatures in these states have essentially predetermined the question of the appropriate forum for prosecution—taking the decision out of both prosecutors' and judges' hands."

As of March 2005, the *OJJDP Statistical Briefing Book*, maintained on the Internet by the Office of Juvenile Justice and Delinquency Prevention (OJJDP), indicated that most states retain juvenile court jurisdiction over offenders seventeen years of age and younger. Those older are considered to be adults. In ten states, those sixteen and younger are juveniles. In Connecticut, New York, and North Carolina, juveniles are fifteen and younger. (See Table 7.1.)

According to the National Center for Juvenile Justice, since 1992 many states have tightened their laws concerning the criminal prosecution of juveniles. Between 1998 and 2002, eighteen states expanded the number of offenses that could transfer a juvenile's case into criminal court. In most cases, the change was an addition to the transfer-eligible list of offenses. Because of the shootings at Columbine High School in Littleton, Colorado, in 1999, for example, three states (Illinois, Nevada, and New York) changed their transfer laws to include violent crimes committed on school property. Illinois, Maryland, and North Carolina changed their laws so that juveniles who have previously been tried as adults are ineligible to ever be tried in juvenile court.

## CHANGING APPROACHES TO JUVENILE DELINQUENCY

Juvenile courts date to the late nineteenth century when Cook County, Illinois, established the first juvenile court under the Juvenile Court Act of 1899 passed by the state. The underlying concept was that if parents failed to

## TABLE 7.1

**Oldest age for original juvenile court jurisdiction in delinquency matters, 1999**

| Age | State |
|-----|-------|
| 15 | Connecticut, New York, North Carolina |
| 16 | Georgia, Illinois, Louisiana, Massachusetts, Michigan, Missouri, New Hampshire, South Carolina, Texas, Wisconsin |
| 17 | Alabama, Alaska, Arizona, Arkansas, California, Colorado, Delaware, District of Columbia, Florida, Hawaii, Idaho, Indiana, Iowa, Kansas, Kentucky, Maine, Maryland, Minnesota, Mississippi, Montana, Nebraska, Nevada, New Jersey, New Mexico, North Dakota, Ohio, Oklahoma, Oregon, Pennsylvania, Rhode Island, South Dakota, Tennessee, Utah, Vermont, Virginia, Washington, West Virginia, Wyoming |

SOURCE: Howard N. Snyder and Melissa Sickmund, "Oldest Age for Juvenile Court Jurisdiction in Delinquency Matters," in *Juvenile Offenders and Victims: 1999 National Report*, U.S. Department of Justice, Office of Justice Programs, Office of Juvenile Justice and Delinquency Prevention, September 1999, http://ojjdp.ncjrs.org/ojstatbb/structure_process/qa04101.asp?qaDate= 20020425 (accessed April 3, 2005)

provide children with proper care and supervision, the state had the right to intervene benevolently. Other states followed Illinois's initiative. Juvenile courts were in operation in most states by 1925. Juvenile courts favored a rehabilitative rather than a punitive approach and evolved less formal approaches than those in place in adult courts. They had exclusive jurisdiction over juveniles. Adult courts could try a juvenile only if the juvenile court waived its jurisdiction.

This approach began to change in the 1950s and 1960s because rehabilitation techniques were judged to be ineffective. A growing number of juveniles were being institutionalized until they reached adulthood because "treatment" did not seem to modify their behavior. Under the impetus of a number of U.S. Supreme Court decisions, juvenile courts became more formal to protect juveniles' rights in waiver situations or if they were to be confined. Congress passed the Juvenile Delinquency Prevention and Control Act in 1968. The act suggested that so-called "status offenders" (noncriminal offenders such as runaways) no longer be handled inside the court system. The Juvenile Justice and Delinquency Prevention Act of 1974 mandated that juvenile offenders be separated from adult offenders. The act was amended in 1980; part of the amendment required that juveniles be removed from adult jails. In the 1970s the national policy became community-based management of juvenile delinquents.

Public perception changed again during the 1980s. Juvenile crime was growing, and the systems in place were perceived as being too lenient in dealing with delinquents. According to the Office of Juvenile Justice and Delinquency Prevention (*Juvenile Offenders and Victims: 1999 National Report*) public opinion was based on a "substantial misperception regarding increases in juvenile crime." Nonetheless, according to *Juvenile Offenders and Victims*, state legislatures responded in various ways:

Some laws removed certain classes of offenders from the juvenile justice system and handled them as adult criminals in criminal court. Others required the juvenile justice system to be more like the criminal justice system and to treat certain classes of juvenile offenders as criminals but in juvenile court.

As a result, offenders charged with certain offenses are *excluded* from juvenile court jurisdiction or face *mandatory* or *automatic waiver* to criminal court. In some states, concurrent jurisdiction provisions give prosecutors the discretion to file certain juvenile cases directly in criminal court. . . . In some states, some adjudicated juvenile offenders face *mandatory sentences*.

— *Juvenile Offenders and Victims: 1999 National Report*, Chapter 4, p. 86.

From 1992 to 1997, forty-seven states and the District of Columbia changed their laws. Between 1998 and 2002, thirty-one states made further revisions, according to the National Center for Juvenile Justice. Nearly all states took significant steps to toughen up their laws by making it easier to transfer juveniles to criminal court. These legislative changes ushered in an era of incarcerating juvenile offenders at historically high rates.

## TRENDS IN JUVENILE ARRESTS

During the period when the majority of states enacted tougher transfer, sentencing, and confidentiality statutes relating to juveniles, juveniles age ten to under eighteen declined as a proportion of total population from 13,482 per 100,000 in 1980 to 11,540 in 2000. Juvenile arrest and incarceration trends are thus not simply a reflection of a growing population of people in their teens—pure demographics, in other words—but some mix in behavior and the legislative/law enforcement response to that behavior.

Juvenile arrest rates for the crimes included in the FBI's Property Crime Index and Violent Crime Index are charted in Figure 7.1 and Figure 7.2 for the same period—during which the juvenile incarceration rate began to rise. Measured as arrests per 100,000 juveniles in the ten-to-seventeen age bracket, the data show both property and violent crime arrests decreasing at first from 1980 to around 1984. Property crime arrests then began increasing gradually while violent arrest rates began to climb more sharply by 1988. Arrest rates began to drop again in 1994 for both property and violent crimes, more steeply for violent crimes. The 2002 rates for both property and violent crimes were the lowest they had ever been during the twenty-two-year period covered.

Table 7.2 shows that 2.2 million juveniles were arrested in 2003. Thirty-two percent of these juveniles were under fifteen years of age. The majority of juveniles (463,300) were arrested for property crimes, while 92,300 were arrested for violent crimes. Of the violent

**FIGURE 7.1**

### Juvenile arrest rate for property crimes, 1980–2002

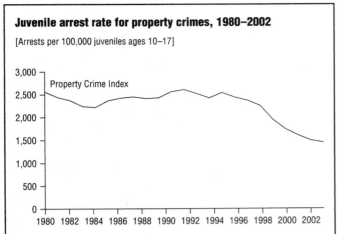

[Arrests per 100,000 juveniles ages 10–17]

Note: The juvenile arrest rate for Property Crime Index offenses in 2002 was nearly 40% below its levels in the early 1980s.

SOURCE: Howard N. Snyder, "After Years of Relative Stability, the Juvenile Property Crime Index Arrest Rate Began a Decline in the Mid-1990s That Continued through 2002," in *Juvenile Arrests in 2002*, U.S. Department of Justice, Office of Justice Programs, Office of Juvenile Justice and Delinquency Prevention, September 2004, http://www.ncjrs.org/pdffiles1/ojjdp/204608.pdf (accessed April 3, 2005)

**FIGURE 7.2**

### Juvenile arrest rate for violent crimes, 1980–2002

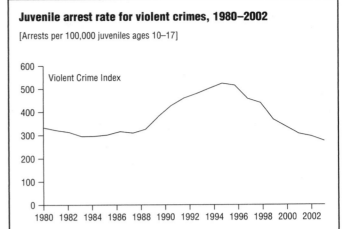

[Arrests per 100,000 juveniles ages 10–17]

Note: In comparison with the juvenile Violent Crime Index arrest rate, the rate for young adults (persons ages 18–24) that peaked in 1992 had fallen only 28% by 2002, remaining above the rates of the early 1980s.

SOURCE: Howard N. Snyder, "The Juvenile Violent Crime Index Arrest Rate in 2002 Was Lower than in Any Year since at Least 1980 and 47% below the Peak Year of 1994," in *Juvenile Arrests in 2002*, U.S. Department of Justice, Office of Justice Programs, Office of Juvenile Justice and Delinquency Prevention, September 2004, http://www.ncjrs.org/pdffiles1/ojjdp/204608.pdf (accessed April 3, 2005)

**TABLE 7.2**

### Estimated number of juvenile arrests, 2003

| Most serious offense | Number of juvenile arrests | Percent of total juvenile arrests | | Percent change | | |
|---|---|---|---|---|---|---|
| | | Female | Under age 15 | 1994–03 | 1999–03 | 2002–03 |
| Total | 2,220,300 | 29% | 32% | −18% | −11% | 0% |
| **Violent Crime Index** | 92,300 | 18 | 33 | −32 | −9 | 0 |
| Murder and nonnegligent manslaughter | 1,130 | 9 | 11 | −68 | −18 | 10 |
| Forcible rape | 4,240 | 2 | 37 | −25 | −11 | 9 |
| Robbery | 25,440 | 9 | 25 | −43 | −8 | 3 |
| Aggravated assault | 61,490 | 24 | 36 | −26 | −9 | 0 |
| **Property Crime Index** | 463,300 | 32 | 37 | −38 | −15 | 3 |
| Burglary | 85,100 | 12 | 35 | −40 | −15 | 1 |
| Larceny—theft | 325,600 | 39 | 38 | −35 | −15 | 3 |
| Motor vehicle theft | 44,500 | 17 | 25 | −52 | −15 | 4 |
| Arson | 8,200 | 12 | 61 | −36 | −12 | 3 |
| **Nonindex** | | | | | | |
| Other assaults | 241,900 | 32 | 43 | 10 | 5 | 5 |
| Forgery and counterfeiting | 4,700 | 35 | 13 | −47 | −36 | 8 |
| Fraud | 8,100 | 33 | 18 | −29 | −37 | 9 |
| Embezzlement | 1,200 | 40 | 6 | 15 | −30 | 17 |
| Stolen property (buying, receiving, possessing) | 24,300 | 15 | 27 | −46 | −19 | 5 |
| Vandalism | 107,700 | 14 | 44 | −33 | −11 | 2 |
| Weapons (carrying, possessing, etc.) | 39,200 | 11 | 36 | −41 | −6 | 11 |
| Prostitution and commercialized vice | 1,400 | 69 | 14 | 31 | 23 | 11 |
| Sex offenses (except forcible rape and prostitution) | 18,300 | 9 | 51 | 2 | 3 | 3 |
| Drug abuse violations | 197,100 | 16 | 17 | 19 | −3 | 4 |
| Gambling | 1,700 | 2 | 15 | −59 | 46 | 1 |
| Offenses against the family and children | 7,000 | 39 | 35 | 19 | −24 | 19 |
| Driving under the influence | 21,000 | 20 | 2 | 33 | −9 | 4 |
| Liquor law violations | 136,900 | 35 | 10 | 4 | −22 | 6 |
| Drunkenness | 17,600 | 23 | 13 | −11 | −19 | 6 |
| Disorderly conduct | 193,000 | 31 | 41 | 13 | 0 | 6 |
| Vagrancy | 2,300 | 25 | 25 | −50 | −20 | 9 |
| All other offenses (except traffic) | 379,800 | 27 | 28 | −2 | −12 | 1 |
| Suspicion | 1,500 | 24 | 26 | −77 | −74 | 53 |
| Curfew and loitering | 136,500 | 30 | 29 | −1 | −18 | 8 |
| Runaways | 123,600 | 59 | 36 | −42 | −18 | 2 |

SOURCE: "Estimated Number of Juvenile Arrests, 2003," in *OJJDP Statistical Briefing Book*, U.S. Department of Justice, Office of Justice Programs, Office of Juvenile Justice and Delinquency Prevention, February 28, 2005, http://ojjdp.ncjrs.org/ojstatbb/crime/qa05101.asp?qaDate=20050228 (accessed April 3, 2005)

FIGURE 7.3

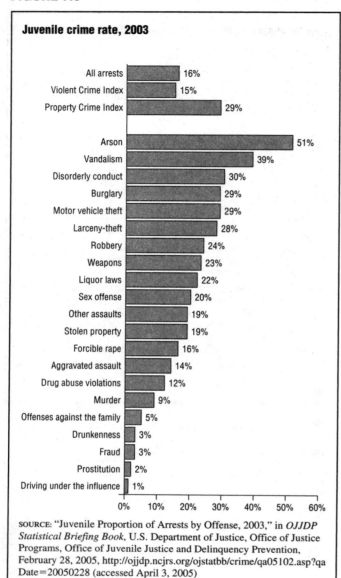

**Juvenile crime rate, 2003**

| Offense | Percent |
|---|---|
| All arrests | 16% |
| Violent Crime Index | 15% |
| Property Crime Index | 29% |
| Arson | 51% |
| Vandalism | 39% |
| Disorderly conduct | 30% |
| Burglary | 29% |
| Motor vehicle theft | 29% |
| Larceny-theft | 28% |
| Robbery | 24% |
| Weapons | 23% |
| Liquor laws | 22% |
| Sex offense | 20% |
| Other assaults | 19% |
| Stolen property | 19% |
| Forcible rape | 16% |
| Aggravated assault | 14% |
| Drug abuse violations | 12% |
| Murder | 9% |
| Offenses against the family | 5% |
| Drunkenness | 3% |
| Fraud | 3% |
| Prostitution | 2% |
| Driving under the influence | 1% |

SOURCE: "Juvenile Proportion of Arrests by Offense, 2003," in *OJJDP Statistical Briefing Book*, U.S. Department of Justice, Office of Justice Programs, Office of Juvenile Justice and Delinquency Prevention, February 28, 2005, http://ojjdp.ncjrs.org/ojstatbb/crime/qa05102.asp?qa Date=20050228 (accessed April 3, 2005)

## Arrest Rates by Gender

Data on juvenile arrest rates for three types of violent crime and for drug abuse (see Figure 7.4) show that the majority of juveniles arrested were males, but arrest rates for females grew proportionately more than for males. According to Howard N. Snyder in *Juvenile Arrests in 2002* (Office of Juvenile Justice and Delinquency Prevention, September 2004), between 1980 and 2002, the female juvenile arrest rate for aggravated assault grew by 99%, while the male rate grew by 14%. The female rate for simple assault grew by 258% during the same period, while the male rate grew by 99%; and the female rate for weapons law violations grew by 125% versus the male growth rate of 7%. In 2002, 29% of juveniles arrested were female. Data for females are shown graphed both with males, indicating much lower female involvement, as well as separately to show the trend lines more clearly than is possible in combination with the much more numerous male arrests in each category.

## Juvenile Offenders by Race

According to *Juvenile Arrests in 2002*, the majority of all juveniles arrested in 2002 were white, representing 55% of violent crime arrests and 70% of property crime arrests. Forty-three percent of violent crime arrests and 27% of arrests for property crimes involved African-Americans. Asians/Pacific Islanders comprised 1% of those arrested for violent crimes and 2% of those arrested for property crimes; Native Americans represented 1% of arrests in each category. Table 7.3 shows the African-American proportion of juveniles arrested for a variety of both violent and property offenses. Of all juveniles arrested for murder, for example, half were African-American. African-Americans comprised 36% of those juveniles arrested for forcible rape, 59% of those arrested for robbery, and 38% of those arrested for motor vehicle theft.

Figure 7.5 compares the juvenile arrest rates for African-Americans and whites from 1980 to 2002. The respective rates for violent crimes have narrowed over this period, according to Snyder in *Juvenile Arrests in 2002*. In 1980 the African-American juvenile Violent Crime Index arrest rate was 6.3 times the white rate; in 2002, the rate disparity had declined to 3.8. Arrest rates for murder showed a particularly sharp decline. The murder arrest rate for white juveniles dropped by two-thirds between 1993 and 2002; the rate for African-American juveniles dropped by 80%. The 2002 murder rates were lower than any year in the 1980s or 1990s for both white and African-American juveniles. Property crime also showed dramatic drops during this period. The 2002 Property Crime Index arrest rates for both white juveniles and African-American juveniles were only half of what they had been in 1980.

crimes, aggravated assault was the most common (61,490 arrests), followed by robbery (25,440 arrests). Substance abuse was the cause of many arrests: 197,100 were arrested on drug abuse violations, 136,900 for liquor law violations, 21,000 for driving under the influence, and 17,600 for drunkenness.

In 2003 juvenile arrests made up 16% of all arrests in the nation, according to the *OJJDP Statistical Briefing Book* (Washington, DC: Office of Juvenile Justice and Delinquency Prevention, February 28, 2005). (See Figure 7.3.) Juveniles were arrested for 15% of all Violent Crime Index offenses and for 29% of all Property Crime Index offenses. Juveniles made up a particularly large percentage of the arrests for arson (51%), vandalism (39%), disorderly conduct (30%), motor vehicle theft, and burglary (both 29%).

**FIGURE 7.4**

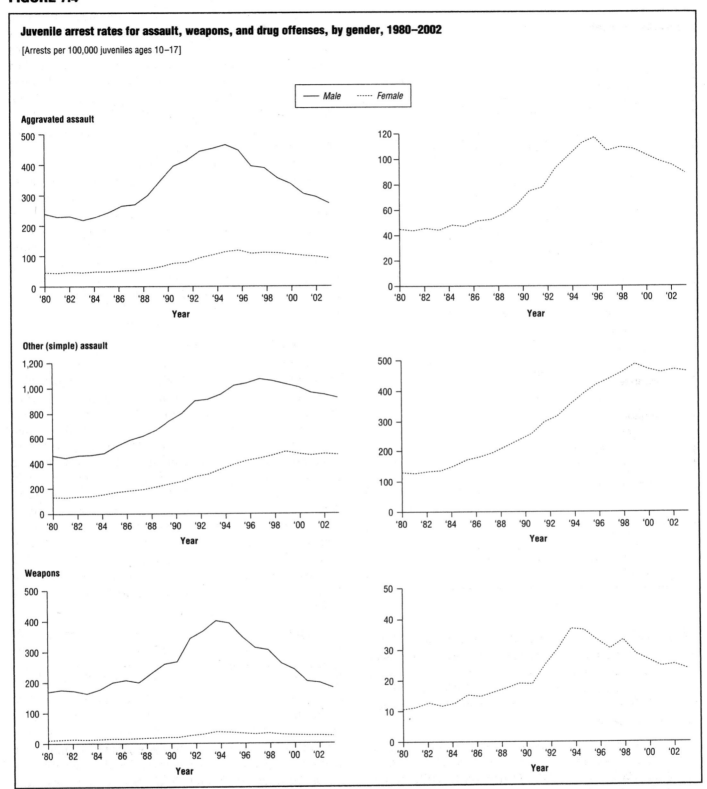

**Juvenile arrest rates for assault, weapons, and drug offenses, by gender, 1980–2002**

[Arrests per 100,000 juveniles ages 10–17]

## Disposition of Juveniles Arrested

A change in the disposition of juveniles arrested appeared in the 1970s. In 1972, 50.8% of those arrested were referred to juvenile courts; 45% were handled within police departments and released; only 1.3% were transferred by referral to criminal or adult courts, according to the *Sourcebook of Criminal Justice Statistics, 2002* (Bureau of Justice Statistics, August 2004). By 2002, cases handled internally (followed by release) had dropped to 18.1%. The majority of cases were referred to juvenile court (72.8%). The cases

**FIGURE 7.4**

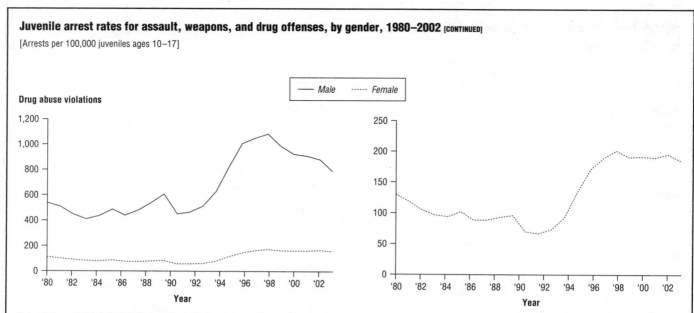

**Juvenile arrest rates for assault, weapons, and drug offenses, by gender, 1980–2002** [CONTINUED]

[Arrests per 100,000 juveniles ages 10–17]

Notes: Between 1980 and 2002, the increase in the female juvenile arrest rate was greater than the increase in the male rate for aggravated assault (99% vs. 14%), simple assault (258% vs. 99%), and weapons law violations (125% vs. 7%).
In contrast, the increase in the female juvenile arrest rate between 1980 and 2002 was comparable with the increase in the male rate for drug abuse violations (42% vs. 47%).

SOURCE: Howard N. Snyder, "Male Juvenile Arrest Rates for Aggravated Assault and Simple Assault Fell from the Mid-1990s through 2002, while Female Rates Remained Near Their Highest Levels," in *Juvenile Arrests in 2002*, U.S. Department of Justice, Office of Justice Programs, Office of Juvenile Justice and Delinquency Prevention, September 2004, http://www.ncjrs.org/pdffiles1/ojjdp/204608.pdf (accessed April 3, 2005)

**TABLE 7.3**

**Arrests of African-American youths as a percentage of all juvenile arrests, 2002**

| Most serious offense | Black proportion of juvenile arrests in 2002 |
|---|---|
| Murder | 50% |
| Forcible rape | 36 |
| Robbery | 59 |
| Aggravated assault | 37 |
| Burglary | 25 |
| Larceny-theft | 26 |
| Motor vehicle theft | 38 |
| Weapons | 31 |
| Drug abuse violations | 25 |
| Curfew and loitering | 29 |
| Runaways | 18 |

SOURCE: Howard N. Snyder, "Black Proportion of Juvenile Arrests in 2002," in *Juvenile Arrests in 2002*, U.S. Department of Justice, Office of Justice Programs, Office of Juvenile Justice and Delinquency Prevention, September 2004, http://www.ncjrs.org/pdffiles1/ojjdp/204608.pdf (accessed April 3, 2005)

referred to adult jurisdictions had escalated to 7% of all cases. (See Table 7.4.)

## JUVENILES IN JAIL AND PRISON

In 2003, 9,875 juveniles were in jail or prison, according to *Prison and Jail Inmates at Midyear 2003* (Bureau of Justice Statistics, May 2004). Of these juveniles, 6,869 were in jail (5,484 held as adults) and 3,006 were in state

prisons. (See Table 7.5 and Table 2.11 in Chapter 2.) Juvenile males (2,880) far outnumbered females (126) in state prisons. The number of incarcerated juveniles has dropped since 1995. In that year, 7,800 juveniles were in jail, of whom 5,900 were being held as adults. In 1995, 5,309 juveniles were held in state prisons.

The most recent survey of the characteristics of juveniles in adult confinement was conducted by the U.S. Justice Department's Office of Justice Programs in 1998, published in *Juveniles in Adult Prisons and Jails* in 2000. For purposes of this survey, juveniles were defined as those seventeen and younger; the survey also collected matching data for the adult population. The federal prison system did not participate in the survey so the results are for state prisons and a number of local jail systems. Among juvenile offenders held in adult facilities, 3.3% were female, significantly lower than youths held in juvenile residential facilities (13%).

Table 7.6 shows the offenses for which youths and adults surveyed were incarcerated in state prison, the racial and ethnic composition of these two groups, and the manner in which they were housed. The major difference between the juvenile and the adult populations in 1998 was that only one in ten youths but one in five adults were serving time for drug offenses. Proportionally, therefore, more youths were held for offenses against persons and for property crimes than adults. A larger percentage of the juvenile population was

**FIGURE 7.5**

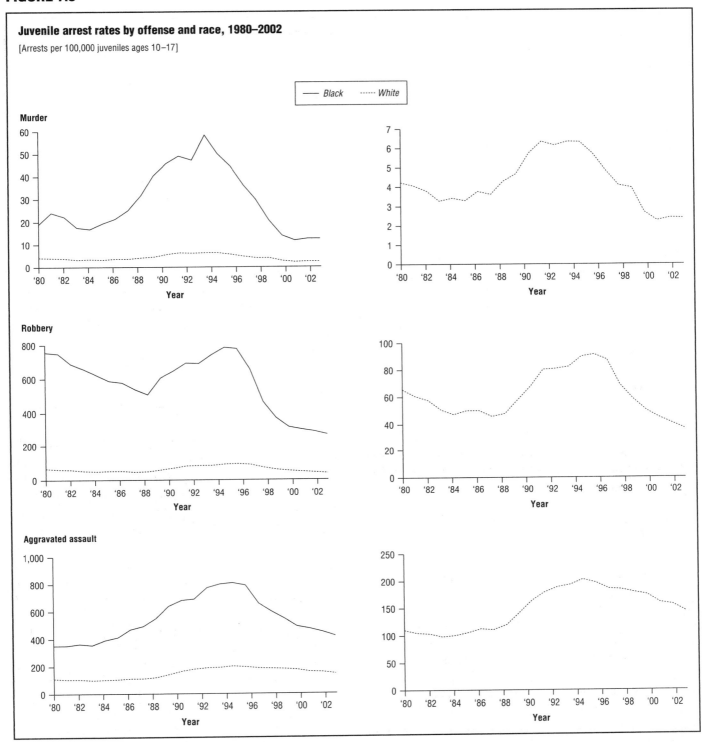

Juvenile arrest rates by offense and race, 1980–2002

[Arrests per 100,000 juveniles ages 10–17]

African-American (55% versus 48% of adults), a smaller percentage was white (26% versus 35%), and a significantly higher percentage (4% versus 1% among adults) was Native American. A higher proportion of juveniles occupied single cells (30% versus 22% for adults) and slept in dormitories (51% versus 43% for the adult population).

## JUVENILES IN RESIDENTIAL PLACEMENT

The almost 10,000 juveniles in jail and prison in 2003 were but a fraction of all juveniles in confinement. They represented those youths transferred to the jurisdiction of adult courts, usually by waiver or under statutorily mandated rules. In 2002 *Juvenile Residential Facility Census, 2000: Selected Findings* was published by the

FIGURE 7.5

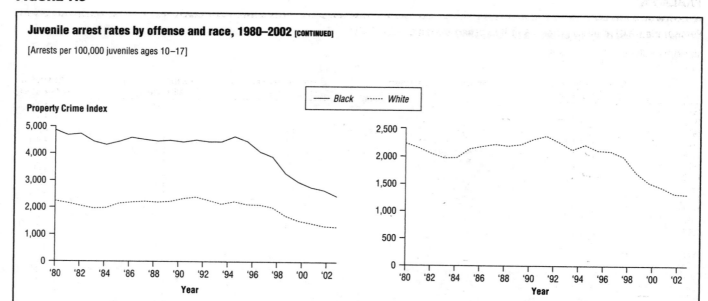

**Juvenile arrest rates by offense and race, 1980–2002** [CONTINUED]

[Arrests per 100,000 juveniles ages 10–17]

Notes: Murder arrest rates in 2002 were lower than in any year in the 1980s and 1990s for both white and black juveniles. The murder arrest rate for white juveniles in 2002 was just one-third of what it had been in 1993, while the 2002 rate for black juveniles was just one-fifth of its 1993 value.
The decline in robbery arrest rates between 1980 and 2002 was greater for black juveniles than white juveniles (64% vs. 43%).
The Property Crime Index arrest rates for both white juveniles and black juveniles in 2002 were about half of what they were in 1980.

SOURCE: Howard N. Snyder, "The Decline in Juvenile Arrest Rates from the Mid-1990s through 2002 Was Proportionally Greater for Black Youth than White Youth," in *Juvenile Arrests in 2002*, U.S. Department of Justice, Office of Justice Programs, Office of Juvenile Justice and Delinquency Prevention, September 2004, http://www.ncjrs.org/pdffiles1/ojjdp/204608.pdf (accessed April 3, 2005)

Office of Juvenile Justice and Delinquency Prevention. Authored by Melissa Sickmund, this study reported that 110,284 offenders under the age of twenty-one were being held in public and private juvenile detention, correctional, and shelter facilities. This category excludes prisons and jails. In October 2000 there were 1,203 public and 1,848 private, residential facilities in the nation.

The vast majority of juveniles in residential placement were delinquents (96%), the rest were confined for status offenses, according to Sickmund in *Juvenile Offenders in Residential Placement, 1997–1999* (Office of Juvenile Justice and Delinquency Prevention, March 2002). Status offenders are runaways, truants from school, youths who are beyond the control of their parents, curfew violators, and those who violate other noncriminal ordinances and rules. The largest number of youths in residential placement were held for burglary (11%), followed by two violent crime categories, aggravated assault (9%) and robbery (8%). Robbery involves the use or threat of force. Categories of offense with the greatest increase since 1997 were offenses against other persons (a 50% increase) and sexual assault (up 34%). Offenses against other persons, according to Sickmund, "include kidnapping, violent sex acts other than forcible rape (e.g., incest, sodomy), custody interference, unlawful restraint, false imprisonment, reckless endangerment, harassment, and attempts to commit any such acts." The greatest decreases were in status offenses

(down 32%), in criminal homicide (down 21%), and robbery (down 13%). (See Table 7.7.)

The largest populations of juveniles in residential placement were in California, Texas, Florida, Pennsylvania, and New York, in that order, according to *Juvenile Residential Facility Census, 2000*. (See Table 7.8.) Those five states housed 40.9% of all juveniles in residential detention in the United States in October 2000. Seventy percent of all juveniles were held in public and 30% in private facilities.

The 2000 survey of residential facilities showed that crowding is also an issue in juvenile confinement: 2,875 of 3,061 facilities reported on the availability of "standard beds," a category that excludes informal sleeping arrangements such as sofas, mattresses on the floor, and cots. Thirty-nine percent of all reporting facilities had fewer standard beds than inmates, 37% of public and 40% of private facilities. The most crowded conditions in public facilities were reported in Delaware and Rhode Island, where all public facilities had fewer beds than inmates. In Mississippi all private facilities reported a shortfall in beds for juveniles housed.

**Placement Status**

Juveniles in residential placement are classified by the OJJDP into three categories. The largest group in 1999, 73.8% of the confined youths, were *committed* by

**TABLE 7.4**

**Percent distribution of juveniles taken into police custody, 1972–2002**

[By method of disposition]*

| | Referred to juvenile court jurisdiction | Handled within department and released | Referred to criminal or adult court | Referred to other police agency | Referred to welfare agency |
|---|---|---|---|---|---|
| 1972 | 50.8% | 45.0% | 1.3% | 1.6% | 1.3% |
| 1973 | 49.5 | 45.2 | 1.5 | 2.3 | 1.4 |
| 1974 | 47.0 | 44.4 | 3.7 | 2.4 | 2.5 |
| 1975 | 52.7 | 41.6 | 2.3 | 1.9 | 1.4 |
| 1976 | 53.4 | 39.0 | 4.4 | 1.7 | 1.6 |
| 1977 | 53.2 | 38.1 | 3.9 | 1.8 | 3.0 |
| 1978 | 55.9 | 36.6 | 3.8 | 1.8 | 1.9 |
| 1979 | 57.3 | 34.6 | 4.8 | 1.7 | 1.6 |
| 1980 | 58.1 | 33.8 | 4.8 | 1.7 | 1.6 |
| 1981 | 58.0 | 33.8 | 5.1 | 1.6 | 1.5 |
| 1982 | 58.9 | 32.5 | 5.4 | 1.5 | 1.6 |
| 1983 | 57.5 | 32.8 | 4.8 | 1.7 | 3.1 |
| 1984 | 60.0 | 31.5 | 5.2 | 1.3 | 2.0 |
| 1985 | 61.8 | 30.7 | 4.4 | 1.2 | 1.9 |
| 1986 | 61.7 | 29.9 | 5.5 | 1.1 | 1.8 |
| 1987 | 62.0 | 30.3 | 5.2 | 1.0 | 1.4 |
| 1988 | 63.1 | 29.1 | 4.7 | 1.1 | 1.9 |
| 1989 | 63.9 | 28.7 | 4.5 | 1.2 | 1.7 |
| 1990 | 64.5 | 28.3 | 4.5 | 1.1 | 1.6 |
| 1991 | 64.2 | 28.1 | 5.0 | 1.0 | 1.7 |
| 1992 | 62.5 | 30.1 | 4.7 | 1.1 | 1.7 |
| 1993 | 67.3 | 25.6 | 4.8 | 0.9 | 1.5 |
| 1994 | 63.2 | 29.5 | 4.7 | 1.0 | 1.7 |
| 1995 | 65.7 | 28.4 | 3.3 | 0.9 | 1.7 |
| 1996 | 68.6 | 23.3 | 6.2 | 0.9 | 0.9 |
| 1997 | 66.9 | 24.6 | 6.6 | 0.8 | 1.1 |
| 1998 | 69.2 | 22.2 | 6.8 | 0.9 | 1.0 |
| 1999 | 69.2 | 22.5 | 6.4 | 1.0 | 0.8 |
| 2000 | 70.8 | 20.3 | 7.0 | 1.1 | 0.8 |
| 2001 | 72.4 | 19.0 | 6.5 | 1.4 | 0.7 |
| 2002 | 72.8 | 18.1 | 7.0 | 1.4 | 0.7 |

Note: These data include all offenses except traffic and neglect cases.
*Because of rounding, percents may not add to 100.

SOURCE: "Table 4.26. Percent Distribution of Juveniles Taken into Police Custody," in *2002 Sourcebook of Criminal Justice Statistics 2002*, Bureau of Justice Statistics, August 2004, http://www.albany.edu/sourcebook/pdf/t426.pdf (accessed April 3, 2005)

juvenile courts. Most of the rest, 25.2%, were *detained* and represented a transitory population. Some of these juveniles may well have ended up in jails and prisons later. They were in residential placement awaiting their hearings, waiting for the disposition of their cases, or waiting to be transferred to some other kind of facility. The remaining 1% of residents were in juvenile confinement voluntarily as a consequence of so-called *diversion* agreements. Under such agreements a juvenile may opt to enter a juvenile facility voluntarily in lieu of judicial proceedings in juvenile court. The offender profiles of those committed and those detained were quite similar in most regards. A smaller percentage of detainees were being held for offenses against persons than those committed (29.1% versus 36.8%). Detainees were also proportionately less involved in property offenses (25.9% versus the committed population's 30.5%). A significantly higher proportion of detainees were being held for technical violations, which involve such matters as parole violations and failure to follow court orders. Those in juvenile homes voluntarily, the diversionary group, were proportionately less delinquent than either the committed or the detained population

(71.1% versus 95.6% of those committed). This small group, however, had a disproportionately high number (28.9%) in the "status offense" category—youths who run away, fail to attend school, are incorrigible, etc.

## JUVENILE BOOT CAMPS

Boot camps for juvenile offenders began around 1985, when such a program was established in Orleans Parish, Louisiana. By 1995, states operated thirty juvenile boot camps, while larger counties across the country operated another eighteen camps in local jails. Boot camps for juveniles are typically intended for "mid-range" offenders—those who have failed with lesser sanctions like probation but are not yet hardened criminals. Juvenile programs typically exclude some types of offenders, such as sex offenders, armed robbers, and youths with a record of serious violence. Definitions of terms like "nonviolent" vary from program to program. Boot camps initially had three main goals: reducing recidivism among juvenile offenders, reducing prison populations, and reducing costs.

## TABLE 7.5

**Number of inmates under age 18 held in state prisons, by gender, selected years 1990–2003**

| Year | Inmates under age 18 | | |
|---|---|---|---|
| | Total | Male | Female |
| 2003 | 3,006 | 2,880 | 126 |
| 2002 | 3,038 | 2,927 | 111 |
| 2001 | 3,147 | 3,010 | 137 |
| 2000 | 3,896 | 3,721 | 175 |
| 1999 | 4,194 | 4,027 | 167 |
| 1995 | 5,309 | * | * |
| 1990 | 3,600 | * | * |

Note: Federal prisons held 39 inmates under age 18 in 1990, but none in 1995 and 1999 to 2003.
*Not available.

SOURCE: Paige M. Harrison and Jennifer C. Karberg, "Table 5. Number of Inmates under Age 18 Held in State Prisons, by Gender, June 30, 1990, 1995, and 1999–2003," in *Prison and Jail Inmates at Midyear 2003*, Bureau of Justice Statistics, May 2004, http://www.ojp.usdoj.gov/bjs/pub/pdf/pjim03.pdf (accessed April 3, 2005)

## TABLE 7.6

**Characteristics of youths and adults in state prisons, 1998**

| | Youths | | Adults | | |
|---|---|---|---|---|---|
| | Number | Percentage | Number | Percentage | Total |
| **Offense/crime** | | | | | |
| Persons | 2,772 | 57% | 473,821 | 44% | 476,544 |
| Property | 974 | 21% | 216,756 | 20% | 217,730 |
| Alcohol related | 135 | 3% | 20,457 | 2% | 20,592 |
| Drug related | 467 | 10% | 210,975 | 20% | 211,442 |
| Public order | 185 | 4% | 40,468 | 4% | 40,653 |
| Parole/probation | 79 | 2% | 90,260 | 8% | 90,339 |
| Unknown | 92 | 2% | 5,676 | 1% | 5,768 |
| Other | 85 | 2% | 13,327 | 1% | 13,412 |
| Total | 4,739 | 100% | 1,071,740 | 100% | 1,076,479 |
| **Race/ethnicity** | | | | | |
| Asian | 65 | 1% | 11,056 | 1% | 11,121 |
| Black | 2,706 | 55% | 497,343 | 48% | 500,050 |
| White | 1,309 | 26% | 355,960 | 35% | 357,269 |
| Hispanic | 689 | 14% | 156,782 | 15% | 157,471 |
| Native American | 176 | 4% | 9,421 | 1% | 9,597 |
| Total | 4,945 | 100% | 1,030,562 | 100% | 1,035,507 |
| **Housing type*** | | | | | |
| Single cell | 1,019 | 30% | 120,221 | 22% | 121,240 |
| Double cell | 670 | 19% | 193,754 | 35% | 194,424 |
| Dormitory | 1,757 | 51% | 237,801 | 43% | 239,559 |
| Total | 3,446 | 100% | 551,776 | 100% | 555,222 |

Note: Discrepancies in totals are due to rounding.
*Housing type statistics are reported for 21 states that house juveniles in adult correctional facilities.

SOURCE: James Austin, Kelly Dedel Johonson, and Maria Gregoriou, "Table 7. Characteristics of State Prison Inmates, 1998," in *Juveniles in Adult Prisons and Jails: A National Assessment*, U.S. Department of Justice, Office of Justice Programs, October 2000, http://www.ncjrs.org/pdffiles1/bja/182503.pdf (accessed April 3, 2005)

## TABLE 7.7

**Juvenile offenders in residential placement, by offense, 1999**

| Most serious offense | Juvenile offenders in residential placement | | Percent change 1997–99 |
|---|---|---|---|
| | Number | Percent | |
| **Total juvenile offenders** | **108,931** | **100** | **3** |
| **Delinquency** | 104,237 | 96 | 5 |
| Person | 38,005 | 35 | 7 |
| Criminal homicide | 1,514 | 1 | −21 |
| Sexual assault | 7,511 | 7 | 34 |
| Robbery | 8,212 | 8 | −13 |
| Aggravated assault | 9,984 | 9 | 5 |
| Simple assault | 7,448 | 7 | 12 |
| Other person[a] | 3,336 | 3 | 50 |
| Property | 31,817 | 29 | −1 |
| Burglary | 12,222 | 11 | −3 |
| Theft | 6,944 | 6 | −5 |
| Auto theft | 6,225 | 6 | −5 |
| Arson | 1,126 | 1 | 23 |
| Other property | 5,300 | 5 | 13 |
| Drug | 9,882 | 9 | 6 |
| Drug trafficking | 3,106 | 3 | 2 |
| Other drug | 6,776 | 6 | 9 |
| Public order | 10,487 | 10 | 8 |
| Weapons | 4,023 | 4 | −4 |
| Other public order | 6,464 | 6 | 17 |
| Technical violation[b] | 14,046 | 13 | 12 |
| Violent Crime Index[b] | 27,221 | 25 | 3 |
| Property Crime Index[b] | 26,517 | 24 | −3 |
| **Status offense** | 4,694 | 4 | −32 |

[a]Offenses against other persons include kidnapping, violent sex acts other than forcible rape (e.g., incest, sodomy), custody interference, unlawful restraint, false imprisonment, reckless endangerment, harassment, and attempts to commit any such acts.
[b]Technical violations include violations of probation, parole, and valid court orders. Violent Crime Index offenses include criminal homicide, sexual assault, robbery, and aggravated assault. Property Crime Index offenses include burglary, theft, auto theft, and arson.

SOURCE: Melissa Sickmund, "More than One–Third of Juvenile Offenders in Residential Placement Were Held for Person Offenses," in "Juvenile Offenders in Residential Placement, 1997–1999," in *Juvenile Offenders and Victims National Report Series Fact Sheet #07*, U.S. Department of Justice, Office of Justice Programs, Office of Juvenile Justice and Delinquency Prevention, March 2002, http://www.ncjrs.org/pdffiles1/ojjdp/fs200207.pdf (accessed April 3, 2005)

tance. Boot camps emphasize vigorous physical activity, drill and ceremony, and manual labor. The offenders are allowed little free time and strictly enforced rules govern all aspects of conduct and appearance. Because of state-mandated education rules, programs spend a minimum of three hours daily on academic education. Most programs also include some vocational education, work-skills training, or job preparation.

In a study of three boot camps in Cleveland, Ohio, Denver, Colorado, and Mobile, Alabama, the Office of Juvenile Justice and Delinquency Prevention found high rates of program completion among those randomly assigned to the camps. There were also improvements in the academic performance of boot camp participants, with over 80% of those attending the Mobile camp showing a rise of one grade level. Unfortunately, the recidivism rates between the experimental groups who attended boot camp and control groups who did not attend showed that the boot

Most juvenile boot camps share the 90–120-day duration typical of military boot camps. They employ military customs and have correctional officers acting as uniformed drill instructors who initially use intense verbal tactics designed to break down inmates' resis-

**TABLE 7.8**

## Juvenile residential facilities by state, 2000

| State | Juvenile facilities | | | Offenders younger than 21 | | |
|---|---|---|---|---|---|---|
| | All facilities | Public | Private | All facilities | Public | Private |
| U.S. total* | 3,061 | 1,203 | 1,848 | 110,284 | 77,662 | 32,464 |
| Alabama | 46 | 12 | 34 | 1,583 | 926 | 657 |
| Alaska | 19 | 5 | 14 | 339 | 261 | 78 |
| Arizona | 51 | 16 | 35 | 2,248 | 1,752 | 398 |
| Arkansas | 45 | 11 | 34 | 639 | 295 | 344 |
| California | 285 | 116 | 169 | 19,286 | 17,551 | 1,735 |
| Colorado | 73 | 12 | 61 | 2,054 | 1,112 | 940 |
| Connecticut | 26 | 5 | 21 | 1,360 | 900 | 460 |
| Delaware | 7 | 3 | 4 | 295 | 246 | 49 |
| Dist. of Columbia | 17 | 3 | 14 | 272 | 159 | 113 |
| Florida | 166 | 53 | 113 | 7,278 | 3,269 | 4,009 |
| Georgia | 50 | 29 | 21 | 3,270 | 2,593 | 677 |
| Hawaii | 7 | 3 | 4 | 122 | 107 | 15 |
| Idaho | 22 | 14 | 8 | 580 | 470 | 110 |
| Illinois | 46 | 26 | 20 | 3,402 | 3,074 | 328 |
| Indiana | 97 | 41 | 56 | 3,334 | 2,239 | 1,095 |
| Iowa | 76 | 18 | 60 | 1,166 | 395 | 771 |
| Kansas | 51 | 17 | 34 | 1,185 | 831 | 354 |
| Kentucky | 58 | 31 | 27 | 950 | 757 | 193 |
| Louisiana | 64 | 20 | 44 | 2,663 | 2,105 | 558 |
| Maine | 17 | 3 | 14 | 300 | 248 | 52 |
| Maryland | 43 | 11 | 32 | 1,492 | 690 | 802 |
| Massachusetts | 71 | 18 | 53 | 1,481 | 567 | 914 |
| Michigan | 108 | 42 | 66 | 3,896 | 1,782 | 2,114 |
| Minnesota | 121 | 22 | 99 | 1,922 | 986 | 936 |
| Mississippi | 20 | 19 | 1 | 787 | 785 | 2 |
| Missouri | 65 | 57 | 8 | 1,540 | 1,290 | 250 |
| Montana | 18 | 8 | 10 | 260 | 173 | 65 |
| Nebraska | 23 | 6 | 17 | 789 | 577 | 212 |
| Nevada | 15 | 10 | 5 | 1,176 | 750 | 426 |
| New Hampshire | 8 | 2 | 6 | 193 | 123 | 70 |
| New Jersey | 57 | 45 | 12 | 2,274 | 2,171 | 103 |
| New Mexico | 27 | 19 | 8 | 885 | 838 | 47 |
| New York | 210 | 59 | 151 | 5,081 | 2,883 | 2,198 |
| North Carolina | 67 | 27 | 40 | 1,555 | 1,237 | 318 |
| North Dakota | 13 | 4 | 9 | 203 | 105 | 98 |
| Ohio | 106 | 71 | 35 | 4,890 | 4,342 | 548 |
| Oklahoma | 52 | 14 | 38 | 1,034 | 535 | 479 |
| Oregon | 48 | 27 | 21 | 1,637 | 1,415 | 222 |
| Pennsylvania | 163 | 29 | 134 | 5,085 | 1,241 | 3,844 |
| Rhode Island | 11 | 1 | 10 | 360 | 211 | 149 |
| South Carolina | 42 | 16 | 26 | 1,592 | 1,072 | 520 |
| South Dakota | 22 | 9 | 13 | 646 | 365 | 265 |
| Tennessee | 63 | 28 | 35 | 1,824 | 1,041 | 783 |
| Texas | 138 | 77 | 61 | 8,354 | 6,475 | 1,879 |
| Utah | 51 | 17 | 34 | 1,135 | 453 | 682 |
| Vermont | 5 | 1 | 4 | 158 | 26 | 132 |
| Virginia | 74 | 62 | 12 | 2,868 | 2,616 | 252 |
| Washington | 42 | 31 | 11 | 2,064 | 1,938 | 126 |
| West Virginia | 27 | 6 | 21 | 381 | 241 | 140 |
| Wisconsin | 94 | 27 | 67 | 2,017 | 1,271 | 746 |
| Wyoming | 24 | 2 | 22 | 379 | 173 | 206 |

Note: State is the state where the facility is located. Offenders sent to out-of-state facilities are counted in the state where the facility is located, not the state where their offense occurred.

*U.S. total includes 158 offenders in 10 tribal facilities. These offenders were located in Arizona, Colorado, Montana, Oklahoma, and South Dakota.

SOURCE: Melissa Sickmund, "In October 2000, 4 in 10 Juvenile Facilities Were Publicly Operated and Held 70% of Juvenile Offenders in Custody," in *Juvenile Residential Facility Census, 2000: Selected Findings*, U.S. Department of Justice, Office of Justice Programs, Office of Juvenile Justice and Delinquency Prevention, December 2002, http://www.ncjrs.org/pdffiles1/ojjdp/196595.pdf (accessed April 3, 2005)

camp experience had little effect. As for saving costs, a 1999 study of boot camps in four states (*Final Report: Boot Camps' Impact on Confinement Bed Space Requirements*, National Institute of Justice, Washington, DC, August 30, 1999) showed some savings in the number of prison beds required in three of the four states: "Washington and South Dakota saved a substantial number of prison beds, while Oregon's boot camp achieved a modest bed space savings."

Several factors seem to have a direct bearing on the success or failure rates for boot camp participants, including the length of the sessions and the amount of post-release supervision. In a study of many boot camps across the country (*Correctional Boot Camps: Lessons from a Decade of Research*, U.S. Department of Justice, Office of Justice Programs, June 2003), it was reported that:

- Participants reported positive short-term changes in attitudes and behaviors; they also had better problem-solving and coping skills.

- With few exceptions, these positive changes did not lead to reduced recidivism. The boot camps that did produce lower recidivism rates offered more treatment services, had longer sessions, and included more intensive post-release supervision. However, not all programs with these features had successful results.

- Under a narrow set of conditions, boot camps can lead to small relative reductions in prison populations and correctional costs.

## JUVENILES AND THE DEATH PENALTY

On March 1, 2005, the U.S. Supreme Court struck down the death penalty for juveniles. The ruling found that state laws authorizing capital punishment for those under eighteen years old who commit murder violate the Eighth Amendment's provision against cruel and unusual punishment and are therefore unconstitutional. Juveniles who commit serious crimes can now be sentenced to a maximum of life in prison. The ruling changes the law in twenty-one states that had authorized the death penalty for juvenile offenders and took seventy-two prisoners off of death row. An online version of the ruling is located at http://wid.ap.org/documents/scotus/050301roper.pdf.

Historically, it was rare for a juvenile to be sentenced to death. According to the BJS, in sixteen states allowing the death penalty in 2003, the minimum age authorized for capital punishment was eighteen years. (See Table 7.9.) Those states included California, Colorado, Connecticut, Illinois, Indiana, Kansas, Maryland, Missouri, Nebraska, New Jersey, New Mexico, New York, Ohio, Oregon, Tennessee, and Washington. The federal system observed eighteen years as well. However, five states—Florida, Georgia, New Hampshire, North

Carolina, and Texas— had authorized the death penalty at seventeen years. The minimum age for capital punishment was sixteen years or less in thirteen other states. Alabama, Delaware, Kentucky, Mississippi, Nevada, Oklahoma, and Wyoming set sixteen years as the minimum, while Arkansas, Utah, and Virginia used fourteen years. States without specific age limits were Arizona, Idaho, Louisiana, Montana, Pennsylvania, South Carolina, and South Dakota.

**TABLE 7.9**

**Minimum age authorized for capital punishment, 2003**

| Age 16 or less | Age 17 | Age 18 | None specified |
|---|---|---|---|
| Alabama (16) | Florida | California | Arizona |
| Arkansas (14) | Georgia | Colorado | Idaho |
| Delaware (16) | New Hampshire | Connecticut | Louisiana |
| Kentucky (16) | North Carolina[a] | Federal system | Montana[b] |
| Mississippi (16)[c] | Texas | Illinois | Pennsylvania |
| Nevada (16) | | Indiana | South Carolina |
| Oklahoma (16) | | Kansas | South Dakota[d] |
| Utah (14)[e] | | Maryland | |
| Virginia (14)[e] | | Missouri[f] | |
| Wyoming (16) | | Nebraska | |
| | | New Jersey | |
| | | New Mexico | |
| | | New York | |
| | | Ohio | |
| | | Oregon | |
| | | Tennessee | |
| | | Washington | |

Note: Reporting by states reflects interpretations by state attorney generals' offices and may differ from previously reported ages.

[a]Age required is 17 unless the murderer was incarcerated for murder when a subsequent murder occurred; then the age may be 14.

[b]Montana law specifies that offenders tried under the capital sexual assault statute be 18 or older. Age may be a mitigating factor for other capital crimes.

[c]The minimum age defined by statute is 13, but the effective age is 16 based on interpretation of U.S. Supreme Court decisions by the Mississippi Supreme Court.

[d]Juveniles may be transferred to adult court. Age can be a mitigating factor.

[e]The minimum age for transfer to adult court by statute is 14, but the effective age is 16 based on interpretation of U.S. Supreme Court decisions by the state attorney general's office.

[f]The minimum age defined by statute is 16, but the effective age is 18 based on interpretation of the 8th Amendment of the U.S. Constitution by the Missouri Supreme Court.

SOURCE: Thomas P. Bonczar and Tracy L. Snell, "Table 3. Minimum Age Authorized for Capital Punishment, 2003," in *Capital Punishment, 2003*, Bureau of Justice Statistics, November 2004, http://www.ojp.usdoj.gov/bjs/pub/pdf/cp03.pdf (accessed April 3, 2005)

# CHAPTER 8
# PROBATION AND PAROLE

*Any society that depends on only two sentencing options—confinement or nothing at all—is unsafe and unjust. We need a full array of effective sentencing tools that actually suit our various sentencing purposes.*

— Michael Smith, Vera Institute of Justice

Most of the correctional population of the United States—those under the supervision of correctional authorities—are walking about freely. They are people on probation or people on parole. According to Lauren E. Glaze and Seri Palla in *Probation and Parole in the United States, 2003* (Washington, DC: Bureau of Justice Statistics, July 2004), 4,024,087 people were on probation, 774,588 were on parole, and 2.1 million were in jail or prison in 2003. For every person behind bars, more than two people convicted of crimes were on the street, 70%, all told. Probationers and parolees, however, were nonetheless under official supervision, and most had to satisfy requirements placed on them as a condition of freedom or of early release from correctional facilities. Table 8.1 shows the number of adults under correctional supervision by region and jurisdiction, as of December 31, 2003.

A probationer is someone who has been convicted of a crime and sentenced—but the person's sentence has been suspended on condition that he or she behaves in the manner ordered by the court. Probation sometimes follows a brief period of incarceration; more often it is granted by the court immediately.

A parolee is an individual who has served a part of his or her sentence in jail and prison but, because of good behavior or by legislative mandate, has been granted freedom before the sentence is fully served. The sentence remains in effect, however, and the parolee continues to be under the jurisdiction of a parole board. If the person fails to live up to the conditions of the release, the parolee may be confined again.

The number of persons on probation has grown from 1.1 million in 1980 to four million in 2003. (See Figure 8.1.) Since 1995, according to *Probation and Parole in the United States, 2003*, the number of persons on probation has grown by 32.4%, with an average annual increase of 2.9%. (See Table 8.2.) The increase from 2002 to 2003 was 1.2%, less than half the average growth rate. During the 1980–2003 period, those on parole increased from 220,000 to 774,000. Since 1995, the number of persons on parole increased by 14%, with an annual average increase of 1.7%. (See Table 8.3.)

## PROBATION
### Characteristics of Probationers

Those whom the courts release for probation are deemed to be the least dangerous among those arrested and most likely to stay clear of the justice system in the future, although only 59% of those on probation appear to succeed. (See Table 8.4.) Whereas all persons in prison serve sentences for felonies, only 49% of probationers were felons in 2003; 49% had been sentenced for misdemeanors, the rest for other infractions. In 1995 the majority (54%) had felony sentences while only 44% had misdemeanors.

According to *Probation and Parole in the United States, 2003*, among those entering probation in 2003, 73% did so without any incarceration; among those leaving this status, 59% had completed their probation successfully—a far higher percentage than those leaving parole (47%). Among those leaving probation in 2003, be it by reason of completing probation or failing to do so successfully, 16% returned to incarceration or were incarcerated for the first time. By contrast, 38% of those leaving parole were put behind bars again for failure to live up to the rules or committing a new offense. The single largest category of serious offense committed by probationers was a drug violation (25%) followed by driving while intoxicated (17%).

TABLE 8.1

## Adults under correctional supervision, by region and jurisdiction, 2003

| Region and jurisdiction | Total under correctional supervision, 12/31/03 | Number on probation or parole,[a] 12/31/03 | Number in prison or jail, 6/30/03 | Supervision rate per 100,000 adults[b] | Percent of correctional population incarcerated |
|---|---|---|---|---|---|
| U.S. total | 6,889,800 | 4,811,200 | 2,078,600 | 3,173 | 30.2% |
| Federal | 282,800 | 117,100 | 165,800 | 130 | 58.6% |
| State | 6,607,000 | 4,694,100 | 1,912,800 | 3,042 | 29.0 |
| **Northeast** | 1,067,000 | 792,700 | 274,200 | 2,588 | 25.7% |
| Connecticut | 74,100 | 54,800 | 19,300 | 2,815 | 26.0 |
| Maine | 13,400 | 9,900 | 3,500 | 1,341 | 26.4 |
| Massachusetts | 153,300 | 130,800 | 22,500 | 3,117 | 14.6 |
| New Hampshire | 9,400 | 5,300 | 4,100 | 974 | 43.6 |
| New Jersey | 183,600 | 137,500 | 46,100 | 2,817 | 25.1 |
| New York | 278,400 | 180,100 | 98,200 | 1,925 | 35.3 |
| Pennsylvania | 315,000 | 239,500 | 75,600 | 3,339 | 24.0 |
| Rhode Island | 27,700 | 24,200 | 3,500 | 3,357 | 12.8 |
| Vermont | 12,000 | 10,600 | 1,400 | 2,559 | 11.9 |
| **Midwest** | 1,418,300 | 1,055,300 | 363,000 | 2,918 | 25.6% |
| Illinois | 244,400 | 179,500 | 65,000 | 2,609 | 26.6 |
| Indiana | 155,300 | 118,600 | 36,700 | 3,373 | 23.6 |
| Iowa | 36,200 | 24,000 | 12,200 | 1,638 | 33.7 |
| Kansas | 34,400 | 18,700 | 15,700 | 1,715 | 45.7 |
| Michigan | 263,100 | 195,800 | 67,400 | 3,527 | 25.6 |
| Minnesota | 127,900 | 114,300 | 13,600 | 3,411 | 10.6 |
| Missouri | 110,600 | 70,800 | 39,800 | 2,595 | 36.0 |
| Nebraska | 25,800 | 19,100 | 6,800 | 2,009 | 26.2 |
| North Dakota | 5,700 | 3,700 | 1,900 | 1,189 | 34.0 |
| Ohio | 301,400 | 236,300 | 65,000 | 3,530 | 21.6 |
| South Dakota | 11,600 | 7,200 | 4,400 | 2,069 | 38.2 |
| Wisconsin | 101,800 | 67,300 | 34,500 | 2,491 | 33.9 |
| **South** | 2,730,900 | 1,879,100 | 851,800 | 3,485 | 31.2% |
| Alabama | 74,200 | 45,100 | 29,100 | 2,202 | 39.2 |
| Arkansas | 59,600 | 41,800 | 17,800 | 2,924 | 29.9 |
| Delaware | 26,200 | 19,400 | 6,800 | 4,235 | 25.9 |
| District of Columbia[c] | 15,400 | 12,300 | 3,100 | 3,440 | 20.3 |
| Florida | 423,900 | 289,100 | 134,900 | 3,197 | 31.8 |
| Georgia | 533,500 | 446,500 | 87,000 | d | d |
| Kentucky | 63,100 | 35,700 | 27,400 | 2,028 | 43.4 |
| Louisiana | 106,600 | 58,100 | 48,400 | 3,255 | 45.5 |
| Maryland | 128,400 | 91,600 | 36,800 | 3,117 | 28.6 |
| Mississippi | 47,500 | 20,900 | 26,600 | 2,264 | 56.0 |
| North Carolina | 165,500 | 115,800 | 49,600 | 2,589 | 30.0 |
| Oklahoma | 62,100 | 32,400 | 29,700 | 2,372 | 47.9 |
| South Carolina | 79,400 | 43,300 | 36,200 | 2,547 | 45.5 |
| Tennessee | 90,900 | 49,400 | 41,400 | 2,054 | 45.6 |
| Texas | 738,000 | 524,200 | 213,800 | 4,609 | 29.0 |
| Virginia | 102,500 | 46,500 | 56,000 | 1,827 | 54.6 |
| West Virginia | 14,000 | 6,900 | 7,100 | 991 | 50.5 |
| **West** | 1,390,800 | 967,000 | 423,800 | 2,840 | 30.5% |
| Alaska | 10,900 | 6,300 | 4,500 | 2,382 | 41.7 |
| Arizona | 112,700 | 71,200 | 41,600 | 2,717 | 36.9 |
| California | 725,600 | 485,000 | 240,500 | 2,791 | 33.2 |
| Colorado | 84,700 | 56,800 | 27,900 | 2,486 | 33.0 |
| Hawaii | 25,200 | 19,900 | 5,300 | 2,600 | 21.0 |
| Idaho | 43,600 | 34,500 | 9,100 | d | d |
| Montana | 12,500 | 7,700 | 4,800 | 1,817 | 38.1 |
| Nevada | 32,400 | 16,300 | 16,100 | 1,909 | 49.7 |
| New Mexico | 30,100 | 17,000 | 13,100 | 2,211 | 43.6 |
| Oregon | 83,100 | 64,500 | 18,600 | 3,082 | 22.4 |
| Utah | 22,400 | 11,900 | 10,500 | 1,397 | 46.9 |
| Washington | 199,500 | 170,600 | 28,900 | 4,350 | 14.5 |
| Wyoming | 8,100 | 5,200 | 2,900 | 2,186 | 35.5 |

Note: Counts were rounded to the nearest 100. Jail counts by state were estimated, using the average daily population from *Deaths in Custody, 2002* and the *Annual Survey of Jails, 2003.*
[a]Excludes by state and region 25,497 probationers in jail and 11,872 probationers in prison.
[b]Based on the estimated number of adult state residents on December 31, 2003, using the *2000 Census of Population and Housing* and adjusting for population change since April 2000.
[c]Excludes inmates held by the Federal Bureau of Prisons.
[d]Not calculated.

SOURCE: Lauren E. Glaze and Seri Palla, "Table 8. Total under Adult Correctional Supervision and Number Supervised per 100,000 Adult Residents, by Jurisdiction, 2003," in *Probation and Parole in the United States, 2003*, Bureau of Justice Statistics, July 2004, http://www.ojp.usdoj.gov/bjs/pub/pdf/ppus03.pdf (accessed April 3, 2005).

## FIGURE 8.1

### Adult correctional populations, 1980–2003

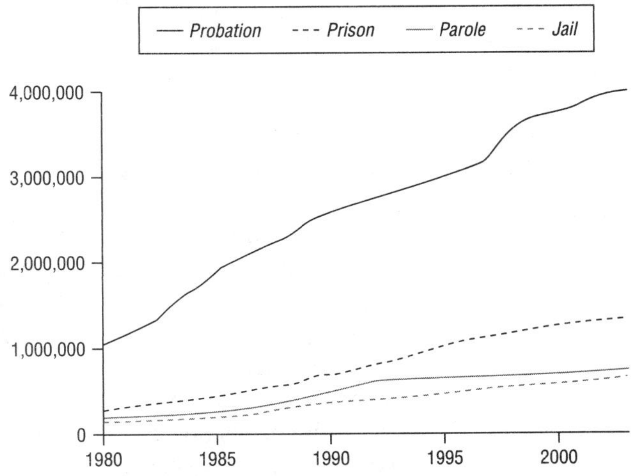

SOURCE: "Adult Correctional Populations, 1980–2003," in *Key Facts at a Glance, Correctional Populations*, Bureau of Justice Statistics, August 20, 2002, http://www.ojp.usdoj.gov/bjs/glance/corr2.htm (accessed April 2, 2005)

## TABLE 8.2

### Change in the number of adults on probation, 1995–2003

| Year | Annual increase | |
| | Number | Percent change |
| --- | --- | --- |
| 1995 | 96,839 | 3.2% |
| 1996 | 87,135 | 2.8 |
| 1997 | 101,841 | 3.2 |
| 1998[a] | 121,100 | 3.7 |
| 1999[a] | 109,481 | 3.0 |
| 2000 | 46,287 | 1.2 |
| 2001 | 105,522 | 2.8 |
| 2002 | 92,336 | 2.4 |
| 2003 | 49,920 | 1.2 |
| **Total increase, 1995–2003[b]** | **996,126** | **32.4%** |
| **Average annual increase, 1995–2003[c]** | **100,315** | **2.9%** |

[a]Survey coverage was expanded to include 186 additional agencies in 1998 and 1999. Annual increases reflect comparable reporting agencies in each year.
[b]Based on overall survey counts, 1995 and 2003.
[c]Based on comparable reporting agencies, excluding 193,607 probationers in 2003 who were in agencies added since 1995.

SOURCE: Lauren E. Glaze and Seri Palla, "Table 3. Change in the Number of Adults on Probation, 1995–2003," in *Probation and Parole in the United States, 2003*, Bureau of Justice Statistics, July 2004, http://www.ojp.usdoj.gov/bjs/pub/pdf/ppus03.pdf (accessed April 2, 2005)

In comparison with state and federal prisoners, a larger proportion of probationers were female (23% versus 6.9% of prisoners) and white (56% versus 35% of those in prison) in 2003. A smaller proportion of probationers were African-American (30% of probationers, 44.1% of prisoners) and of Hispanic origin (12% of probationers, 19% of prisoners).

## TABLE 8.3

### Change in the number of adults on parole, 1995–2003

| Year | Annual increase | |
| | Number | Percent change |
| --- | --- | --- |
| 1995 | −10,950 | −1.6% |
| 1996 | 312 | 0.0 |
| 1997 | 15,054 | 2.2 |
| 1998 | 1,598 | 0.2 |
| 1999 | 18,072 | 2.6 |
| 2000 | 9,441 | 1.3 |
| 2001 | 8,435 | 1.2 |
| 2002 | 18,601 | 2.5 |
| 2003 | 23,654 | 3.1 |
| **Total increase, 1995–2003** | **95,167** | **14.0%** |
| **Average annual increase, 1995–2003** | **11,896** | **1.7%** |

SOURCE: Lauren E. Glaze and Seri Palla, "Table 6. Change in the Number of Adults on Parole, 1995–2003," in *Probation and Parole in the United States, 2003*, Bureau of Justice Statistics, July 2004, http://www.ojp.usdoj.gov/bjs/pub/pdf/ppus03.pdf (accessed April 2, 2005)

### Geographical Distribution

On average across the nation, nearly two people of every 100 (1,876 per 100,000 adults) were under probation, but rates varied considerably state to state and region to region, according to *Probation and Parole in the United States, 2003*. In broad terms, populations of probationers paralleled the general population with some differences. (See Table 8.5.) The South and the Midwest had proportionally more probationers. In the South, 2,135 per 100,000 adults were on probation. In the Midwest, the rate was 1,926 per 100,000. The West (1,672 per 100,000) and the Northeast (1,491 per 100,000) had proportionately fewer probationers.

Table 8.5 shows these data for all states and the District of Columbia for 2003. Rankings are provided in Table 8.6. Texas leads in probationer population (431,989) but is second in total population. California is second in probationers (374,701), first in people. Florida (287,641), Ohio (219,658), and Michigan (176,392) round out the top five.

Kentucky (17.2%), Mississippi (14.9%), Nebraska (11.8%), and New Hampshire (11.6%) had the greatest increases in probationers between 2002 and 2003. Washington (3,767 per 100,000 adult population), Rhode Island (3,143), Delaware (3,058), Minnesota (2,953), Texas (2,698), and Massachusetts (2,585) had the highest rates of probationers to population. The state of Washington also had the largest percentage (3.8%) of its population under some form of community supervision. The states with the fewest probationers per 100,000 adult U.S. residents were New Hampshire (426), West Virginia (487), and Utah (646). (See Table 8.6.)

**TABLE 8.4**

## Characteristics of adults on probation, 1995, 2000, and 2003

| Characteristics of adults on probation | 1995 | 2000 | 2003 |
|---|---|---|---|
| Total | 100% | 100% | 100% |
| **Gender** | | | |
| Male | 79% | 78% | 77% |
| Female | 21 | 22 | 23 |
| **Race** | | | |
| White | 53% | 54% | 56% |
| Black | 31 | 31 | 30 |
| Hispanic | 14 | 13 | 12 |
| American Indian/Alaska Native | 1 | 1 | 1 |
| Asian/Pacific Islander[a] | d | 1 | 1 |
| **Status of probation** | | | |
| Direct imposition | 48% | 56% | 54% |
| Split sentence | 15 | 11 | 8 |
| Sentence suspended | 26 | 25 | 25 |
| Imposition suspended | 6 | 7 | 10 |
| Other | 4 | 1 | 3 |
| **Status of supervision** | | | |
| Active | 79% | 76% | 71% |
| Residential/other treatment program | c | c | 1 |
| Inactive | 8 | 9 | 9 |
| Absconder | 9 | 9 | 11 |
| Warrant status | c | c | 4 |
| Supervised out of state | 2 | 3 | 2 |
| Other | 2 | 3 | 2 |
| **Type of offense** | | | |
| Felony | 54% | 52% | 49% |
| Misdemeanor | 44 | 46 | 49 |
| Other infractions | 2 | 2 | 2 |
| **Most serious offense** | | | |
| Sexual assault | c | c | 3% |
| Domestic violence | c | c | 7 |
| Other assault | c | c | 9 |
| Burglary | c | c | 5 |
| Larceny/theft | c | c | 12 |
| Fraud | c | c | 4 |
| Drug law violations | c | 24 | 25 |
| Driving while intoxicated | 16 | 18 | 17 |
| Minor traffic offenses | c | 6 | 6 |
| Other | 84 | 52 | 12 |
| **Adults entering probation** | | | |
| Without incarceration | 72% | 79% | 73% |
| With incarceration | 13 | 16 | 22 |
| Other types | 15 | 5 | 6 |
| **Adults leaving probation** | | | |
| Successful completions | 62% | 60% | 59% |
| Returned to incarceration | 21 | 15 | 16 |
| With new sentence | 5 | 3 | 5 |
| With the same sentence | 13 | 8 | 7 |
| Unknown | 3 | 4 | 4 |
| Absconder[b] | c | 3 | 4 |
| Discharge to custody, detainer, or warrant | c | 1 | 1 |
| Other unsuccessful[b] | c | 11 | 13 |
| Death | 1 | 1 | 1 |
| Other | 16 | 9 | 7 |

Note: For every characteristic there were persons of unknown status or type. Detail may not sum to total because of rounding.
[a]Includes Native Hawaiians.
[b]In 1995 "absconder" and "other unsuccessful" statuses were reported among "other."
[c]Not available.
[d]Less than 0.5%.

SOURCE: Lauren E. Glaze and Seri Palla, "Table 4. Characteristics of Adults on Probation, 1995, 2000, and 2003," in *Probation and Parole in the United States, 2003*, Bureau of Justice Statistics, July 2004, http://www.ojp.usdoj.gov/bjs/pub/pdf/ppus03.pdf (accessed April 2, 2005)

## Federal Probation Violations

Probation can be a successful sentencing approach. In 2002 some 79.5% of federal probationers did not violate the terms of their probation, according to *Compendium of Federal Justice Statistics, 2002* (Bureau of Justice Statistics, September 2004). Of the 20.5% who did violate probation, most had either committed a new crime (6.6% of all probationers) or had used drugs (3.7%). (See Table 8.7.) Those who had been convicted of violent offenses were most likely to violate probation by committing a new crime (11.7%). Those who had been previously convicted of murder were the most likely to commit a new crime (23.5%). More male probationers (7.6%) committed a new crime than did female probationers (4.1%). (See Table 8.8.) The youngest probationers (sixteen to eighteen years old) were most likely to violate probation, either by committing a new crime (17.2%) or by using drugs (10.2%). Hispanics (12.9%) were more likely than non-Hispanics (5.4%) to violate probation by committing a new crime. Measuring by educational attainment, those with less than a high school education had the highest number of probation violations.

## Probation Officers

Community corrections has a cost to the community—although it is lower than the cost of housing and feeding prisoners and providing them with health care. A major part of that cost is the employment of skilled probation officers to supervise probationers.

In 1975 the U.S. government employed 1,377 probation officers to supervise 64,261 federal probationers, a ratio of one officer per forty-seven probationers. By 2003, 4,560 officers supervised 110,621 probationers, for a ratio of about twenty-four per officer. (See Table 8.9.) The federal government was expending resources to lower the ratio of probationers to officers. Between 2000 and 2005, the number of probationers increased 10%, while officers increased by 14.5%.

## SUPERVISED RELEASE

The Sentencing Reform Act of 1984 created an alternative to parole and probation for federal offenders—supervised release—which occurs after an offender's term of imprisonment is completed. Following his or her release, an offender is sentenced to a period of supervision in the community. The Sentencing Reform Act calls for supervised release to follow any term of imprisonment that exceeds one year or if required by a specific statute. The court also may order supervised release to follow imprisonment in any other case. Offenders on supervised release are supervised by probation officers. During 2002, according to data from the BJS, some 70% (73,229) of federal offenders on community supervision were serving a term of supervised release. (See Table 8.10.) Most offenders sentenced to supervised release (54%) were convicted of trafficking in drugs. Only 6.2% had been convicted of violent offenses.

Table 8.11 shows that in 2002 there were 27,678 offenders who terminated their supervised release. Most (62.2%) had not violated the terms of their release and successfully completed their sentence. A little over 13% had violated their supervised release by committing a new crime; 8.4% had used drugs. Men were more likely to violate the terms of their supervised release than were women. Nearly 60% of men successfully completed their sentence; women were successful 73.6% of the time. (See Table 8.12.) Of those sentenced to supervised release, the youngest (nineteen and twenty year olds) and the least educated (less than high school) had the highest percentages of those who violated the terms of their sentence.

## PAROLE

### Trends in Parole

Since the mid-1990s there has been a trend among the states to abolish discretionary paroles in favor of mandatory paroles. Discretionary parole is administered by parole boards. Their members examine the criminal history of prisoners and the candidates' prison records and reach decisions on whether to release a prisoner from incarceration now or not. Mandatory parole is legislatively imposed at the state level and, with some exceptions, takes away the discretion of parole boards. Mandatory parole provisions ensure that sentences for the same crime require

**TABLE 8.5**

**Adults on probation, by region and jurisdiction, 2003**

| Region and jurisdiction | Probation population, 1/1/03 | 2003 Entries | 2003 Exits | Probation population, 12/31/03 | Percent change, 2003 | Number on probation per 100,000 adult residents, 12/31/03 |
|---|---|---|---|---|---|---|
| **U.S. total** | **4,024,067** | **2,229,668** | **2,179,847** | **4,073,987** | **1.2%** | **1,876** |
| Federal | 31,330 | 13,989 | 14,449 | 30,599 | −2.3% | 14 |
| State | 3,992,737 | 2,215,679 | 2,165,398 | 4,043,388 | 1.3 | 1,862 |
| **Northeast** | 629,503 | 233,044 | 247,722 | 614,825 | −2.3% | 1,491 |
| Connecticut | 50,984 | 24,384 | 23,176 | 52,192 | 2.4 | 1,983 |
| Maine | 9,446 | 6,625 | 6,216 | 9,855 | 4.3 | 984 |
| Massachusetts[a,b,c] | 131,319 | 56,933 | 61,117 | 127,135 | h | 2,585 |
| New Hampshire[d] | 3,702 | 1,480 | 1,052 | 4,130 | 11.6 | 426 |
| New Jersey | 134,290 | 40,601 | 50,610 | 124,281 | −7.5 | 1,907 |
| New York[b] | 132,966 | 39,590 | 48,261 | 124,295 | −6.5 | 859 |
| Pennsylvania[c] | 130,786 | 52,072 | 45,652 | 137,206 | 4.9 | 1,454 |
| Rhode Island | 25,914 | 6,451 | 6,436 | 25,929 | 0.1 | 3,143 |
| Vermont | 10,096 | 4,908 | 5,202 | 9,802 | −2.9 | 2,085 |
| **Midwest** | 937,378 | 606,152 | 607,511 | 936,387 | −0.1% | 1,926 |
| Illinois | 141,544 | 63,000 | 60,090 | 144,454 | 2.1 | 1,542 |
| Indiana | 114,209 | 94,741 | 97,324 | 111,626 | −2.3 | 2,424 |
| Iowa | 19,970 | 14,600 | 13,685 | 20,885 | 4.6 | 945 |
| Kansas[c] | 15,217 | 23,315 | 23,981 | 14,551 | −4.4 | 725 |
| Michigan[c,d] | 174,577 | 130,857 | 129,029 | 176,392 | 1.0 | 2,364 |
| Minnesota | 122,692 | 59,517 | 71,484 | 110,725 | −9.8 | 2,953 |
| Missouri | 54,584 | 26,512 | 25,486 | 55,610 | 1.9 | 1,305 |
| Nebraska | 16,468 | 15,845 | 13,901 | 18,412 | 11.8 | 1,432 |
| North Dakota | 3,229 | 2,332 | 2,059 | 3,502 | 8.5 | 737 |
| Ohio[c,d] | 215,186 | 146,723 | 142,616 | 219,658 | 2.1 | 2,573 |
| South Dakota | 5,088 | 3,261 | 3,129 | 5,236 | 2.9 | 933 |
| Wisconsin | 54,614 | 25,449 | 24,727 | 55,336 | 1.3 | 1,354 |
| **South** | 1,623,038 | 960,243 | 910,074 | 1,673,206 | 3.1% | 2,135 |
| Alabama | 39,713 | 15,152 | 15,213 | 39,652 | −0.2 | 1,177 |
| Arkansas | 27,377 | 9,168 | 8,419 | 28,126 | 2.7 | 1,380 |
| Delaware | 20,201 | 13,962 | 15,242 | 18,921 | −6.3 | 3,058 |
| District of Columbia[c,d] | 9,389 | 6,597 | 8,755 | 7,231 | h | 1,612 |
| Florida[c,d] | 291,315 | 257,539 | 261,212 | 287,641 | −1.3 | 2,169 |
| Georgia[c,e] | 367,349 | 230,686 | 173,650 | 424,385 | h | h |
| Kentucky[c] | 24,480 | 16,165 | 11,949 | 28,696 | 17.2 | 921 |
| Louisiana | 36,257 | 13,875 | 13,455 | 36,677 | 1.2 | 1,120 |
| Maryland | 81,982 | 39,037 | 43,144 | 77,875 | −5.0 | 1,890 |
| Mississippi[c,f] | 16,633 | 8,773 | 6,290 | 19,116 | 14.9 | 911 |
| North Carolina | 112,900 | 60,782 | 60,521 | 113,161 | 0.2 | 1,770 |
| Oklahoma[d] | 29,881 | 15,299 | 16,854 | 28,326 | −5.2 | 1,082 |
| South Carolina | 41,574 | 14,760 | 16,287 | 40,047 | −3.7 | 1,285 |
| Tennessee[c] | 42,712 | 24,256 | 24,132 | 42,836 | 0.3 | 968 |
| Texas | 434,486 | 200,450 | 202,947 | 431,989 | −0.6 | 2,698 |
| Virginia | 40,359 | 30,669 | 29,365 | 41,663 | 3.2 | 743 |
| West Virginia[c] | 6,430 | 3,072 | 2,638 | 6,864 | 6.7 | 487 |

**TABLE 8.5**

**Adults on probation, by region and jurisdiction, 2003** [CONTINUED]

| Region and jurisdiction | Probation population, 1/1/03 | 2003 Entries | 2003 Exits | Probation population, 12/31/03 | Percent change, 2003 | Number on probation per 100,000 adult residents, 12/31/03 |
|---|---|---|---|---|---|---|
| **West** | 802,818 | 416,241 | 400,092 | 818,970 | 2.0% | 1,672 |
| Alaska | 5,229 | 973 | 796 | 5,406 | 3.4 | 1,185 |
| Arizona[d] | 66,485 | 39,115 | 39,795 | 65,805 | −1.0 | 1,586 |
| California[d] | 358,121 | 180,636 | 164,059 | 374,701 | 4.6 | 1,441 |
| Colorado[c,d] | 57,328 | 28,954 | 30,985 | 55,297 | −3.5 | 1,623 |
| Hawaii | 16,772 | 7,006 | 6,126 | 17,652 | 5.2 | 1,822 |
| Idaho[d,g] | 31,361 | 25,360 | 24,501 | 32,220 | 2.7 | [h] |
| Montana | 6,703 | 3,898 | 3,687 | 6,914 | 3.1 | 1,006 |
| Nevada | 12,290 | 5,869 | 6,000 | 12,159 | −1.1 | 716 |
| New Mexico | 16,287 | 7,662 | 7,813 | 16,136 | −0.9 | 1,186 |
| Oregon | 45,397 | 16,275 | 16,847 | 44,825 | −1.3 | 1,662 |
| Utah | 10,646 | 5,429 | 5,696 | 10,379 | −2.5 | 646 |
| Washington[c,d] | 171,603 | 93,132 | 91,921 | 172,814 | 0.7 | 3,767 |
| Wyoming | 4,596 | 1,932 | 1,866 | 4,662 | 1.4 | 1,255 |

Note: Because of incomplete data, the population for some jurisdictions on December 31, 2003, does not equal the population on January 1, 2003, plus entries, minus exits.
[a]Data are for June 30, 2002, and 2003. Some data for June 30, 2002, were estimated.
[b]Due to change in reporting criteria, data are not comparable to previous reports.
[c]Data for entries and exits were estimated for nonreporting agencies.
[d]All data were estimated.
[e]Counts include private agency cases and may overstate the number under supervision.
[f]Data are for year ending December 1, 2003.
[g]Counts include estimates for misdemeanors based on admissions.
[h]Not calculated.

SOURCE: Lauren E. Glaze and Seri Palla, "Table 2. Adults on Probation, 2003," in *Probation and Parole in the United States*, 2003, Bureau of Justice Statistics, July 2004, http://www.ojp .usdoj.gov/bjs/pub/pdf/ppus03.pdf (accessed April 2, 2005)

---

**TABLE 8.6**

**Probation population statistics, 2003**

| 10 states with the largest 2003 community corrections populations | Number supervised | 10 states with the largest percent increase | Percent increase, 2002–03 | 10 states with the highest rates of supervision, 2003 | Persons supervised per 100,000 adult U.S. residents* | 10 states with the lowest rates of supervision, 2003 | Persons supervised per 100,000 adult .residents* |
|---|---|---|---|---|---|---|---|
| Texas | 431,989 | Kentucky | 17.2% | Washington | 3,767 | New Hampshire | 426 |
| California | 374,701 | Mississippi | 14.9 | Rhode Island | 3,143 | West Virginia | 487 |
| Florida | 287,641 | Nebraska | 11.8 | Delaware | 3,058 | Utah | 646 |
| Ohio | 219,658 | New Hampshire | 11.6 | Minnesota | 2,953 | Nevada | 716 |
| Michigan | 176,392 | North Dakota | 8.5 | Texas | 2,698 | Kansas | 725 |
| Washington | 172,814 | West Virginia | 6.7 | Massachusetts | 2,585 | North Dakota | 737 |
| Illinois | 144,454 | Hawaii | 5.2 | Ohio | 2,573 | Virginia | 743 |
| Pennsylvania | 137,206 | Pennsylvania | 4.9 | Indiana | 2,424 | New York | 859 |
| Massachusetts | 127,135 | California | 4.6 | Michigan | 2,364 | Mississippi | 911 |
| New York | 124,295 | Iowa | 4.6 | Florida | 2,169 | Kentucky | 921 |

Note: This table excludes the District of Columbia, a wholly urban jurisdiction, Georgia probation counts, which included probation case-based counts for private agencies, and Idaho in which misdemeanor probation counts were not reported in 2003.
*Rates are based on the estimated number of adult state residents on December 31, 2003.

SOURCE: Adapted from Lauren E. Glaze and Seri Palla, "Table 1. Community Corrections among the States, Yearend 2003," in *Probation and Parole in the United States, 2003*, Bureau of Justice Statistics, July 2004,http://www.ojp.usdoj.gov/bjs/pub/pdf/ppus03.pdf (accessed April 2, 2005)

---

incarceration for the same length of time. The prisoner can shorten his or her sentence only by good behavior—but time off for good behavior is also prohibited in some states. In some jurisdictions parole can only begin after prisoners have served 100% of their minimum sentences.

According to a survey conducted by the National Institute of Corrections, U.S. Department of Justice, *Status Report on Parole, 1995: Results of an NIC Survey* (Washington, DC, November 1995), conflicting policy pressures were changing the manner in which parole was administered in 1995. These pressures came from "legislators seeking ways to be tougher on criminals" by making them serve all or a fixed proportion of their sentences. This had led to changes in some state laws that, in effect, "abolished parole" by taking discretion out of the hands of parole boards. By the early years of the new century, discretionary releases of prisoners by parole boards were decreasing as a percentage of all releases; mandatory parole releases were up; and more prisoners served out their full sentences.

The rise of mandatory paroles over discretionary paroles can be seen in Table 8.13. In 1995 the percentage of discretionary paroles was at 50%; but by 2003 discretionary paroles made up only 39% of the total. In 1995 mandatory parole made up 45% of all paroles; by 2003, 51% of those paroled were under a mandatory parole.

## Characteristics of Parolees

As reported in *Probation and Parole in the United States, 2003*, at the end of 2003 there were 774,588 federal and state parolees in the United States. (See Table 8.14.) Most parolees (688,129) were paroled from state prisons, while 86,459 had been paroled

**TABLE 8.7**

Outcomes of probation supervision, by offense, October 1, 2001–September 30, 2002

| Most serious offense of conviction[a] | Number of probation terminations | Percent of probation supervisions terminating with— | | | | | |
|---|---|---|---|---|---|---|---|
| | | No violation | Technical violations[b] | | | New crime[c] | Administrative case closures |
| | | | Drug use | Fugitive status | Other | | |
| **All offenses** | 15,116 | 79.5% | 3.7% | 2.5% | 5.9% | 6.6% | 1.9% |
| **Felonies** | 7,733 | 80.4% | 3.7% | 2.8% | 5.1% | 6.0% | 2.0% |
| Violent offenses | 266 | 66.9% | 4.5% | 7.5% | 8.3% | 11.7% | 1.1% |
| Murder[d] | 17 | 64.7 | 5.9 | 5.9 | 0.0 | 23.5 | 0.0 |
| Negligent manslaughter | 0 | e | e | e | e | e | e |
| Assault | 98 | 49.0 | 6.1 | 15.3 | 13.3 | 15.3 | 1.0 |
| Robbery | 105 | 85.7 | 3.8 | 1.9 | 1.9 | 5.7 | 1.0 |
| Sexual abuse[d] | 42 | 61.9 | 2.4 | 4.8 | 14.3 | 14.3 | 2.4 |
| Kidnapping | 1 | f | f | f | f | f | f |
| Threats against the President | 3 | f | f | f | f | f | f |
| Property offenses | 4,146 | 81.9% | 3.4% | 2.6% | 5.2% | 5.1% | 1.7% |
| Fraudulent | 3,257 | 84.2% | 3.1% | 2.0% | 4.6% | 4.5% | 1.6% |
| Embezzlement | 299 | 89.3 | 2.3 | 1.3 | 3.3 | 2.0 | 1.7 |
| Fraud[d] | 2,406 | 87.0 | 2.0 | 1.9 | 3.7 | 3.7 | 1.7 |
| Forgery | 119 | 73.1 | 6.7 | 4.2 | 5.9 | 7.6 | 2.5 |
| Counterfeiting | 433 | 67.9 | 8.8 | 2.3 | 10.2 | 10.2 | 0.7 |
| Other | 889 | 73.7% | 4.8% | 4.9% | 7.1% | 7.3% | 2.1% |
| Burglary | 24 | 29.2 | 12.5 | 25.0 | 25.0 | 8.3 | 0.0 |
| Larceny[d] | 704 | 74.4 | 5.1 | 4.7 | 7.1 | 6.5 | 2.1 |
| Motor vehicle theft | 56 | 80.4 | 3.6 | 1.8 | 1.8 | 12.5 | 0.0 |
| Arson and explosives | 32 | 81.3 | 0.0 | 6.3 | 6.3 | 6.3 | 0.0 |
| Transportation and stolen property | 57 | 77.2 | 3.5 | 3.5 | 3.5 | 7.0 | 5.3 |
| Other property offenses[d] | 16 | 56.3 | 0.0 | 0.0 | 12.5 | 25.0 | 6.3 |
| Drug offenses | 1,215 | 75.3% | 6.5% | 2.3% | 5.8% | 7.7% | 2.4% |
| Trafficking | 1,086 | 75.1 | 6.6 | 2.1 | 6.2 | 7.8 | 2.1 |
| Possession and other drug offenses | 129 | 76.7 | 5.4 | 3.9 | 3.1 | 6.2 | 4.7 |
| Public-order offenses | 1,458 | 87.2% | 1.5% | 1.9% | 3.0% | 4.0% | 2.4% |
| Regulatory | 578 | 85.5% | 1.7% | 2.8% | 2.6% | 4.7% | 2.8% |
| Agriculture | 1 | f | f | f | f | f | f |
| Antitrust | 13 | 100.0 | 0.0 | 0.0 | 0.0 | 0.0 | 0.0 |
| Food and drug | 20 | 80.0 | 0.0 | 0.0 | 5.0 | 0.0 | 15.0 |
| Transportation | 17 | 100.0 | 0.0 | 0.0 | 0.0 | 0.0 | 0.0 |
| Civil rights | 15 | 86.7 | 0.0 | 0.0 | 0.0 | 0.0 | 13.3 |
| Communications | 34 | 94.1 | 0.0 | 0.0 | 2.9 | 2.9 | 0.0 |
| Custom laws | 29 | 93.1 | 0.0 | 3.4 | 3.4 | 0.0 | 0.0 |
| Postal laws | 43 | 81.4 | 2.3 | 7.0 | 2.3 | 4.7 | 2.3 |
| Other regulatory offenses | 406 | 83.7 | 2.2 | 3.0 | 2.7 | 5.9 | 2.5 |
| Other | 880 | 88.4% | 1.4% | 1.4% | 3.2% | 3.5% | 2.2% |
| Tax law violations[d] | 289 | 95.5 | 0.3 | 0.3 | 0.7 | 1.4 | 1.7 |
| Bribery | 81 | 88.9 | 1.2 | 2.5 | 1.2 | 3.7 | 2.5 |
| Perjury, contempt, and intimidation | 55 | 85.2 | 0.0 | 3.7 | 0.0 | 5.6 | 5.6 |
| National defense | 6 | f | f | f | f | f | f |
| Escape | 26 | 65.4 | 3.8 | 0.0 | 11.5 | 15.4 | 3.8 |
| Racketeering and extortion | 167 | 87.4 | 1.8 | 1.8 | 3.6 | 3.0 | 2.4 |
| Gambling | 59 | 96.6 | 1.7 | 0.0 | 0.0 | 1.7 | 0.0 |
| Nonviolent sex offenses | 60 | 76.7 | 0.0 | 1.7 | 11.7 | 8.3 | 1.7 |
| Obscene material[d] | 10 | f | f | f | f | f | f |
| Wildlife | 25 | 96.0 | 4.0 | 0.0 | 0.0 | 0.0 | 0.0 |
| Environmental | 14 | 78.6 | 0.0 | 0.0 | 7.1 | 0.0 | 14.3 |
| All other offenses | 88 | 76.1 | 4.5 | 2.3 | 9.1 | 6.8 | 1.1 |
| Weapon offenses | 298 | 67.8% | 5.0% | 2.3% | 8.4% | 13.1% | 3.4% |
| Immigration offenses | 283 | 78.4% | 4.2% | 5.7% | 3.2% | 7.8% | 0.7% |

**TABLE 8.7**

## Outcomes of probation supervision, by offense, October 1, 2001–September 30, 2002 [CONTINUED]

| Most serious offense of conviction[a] | Number of probation terminations | Percent of probation supervisions terminating with— | | | | | |
|---|---|---|---|---|---|---|---|
| | | No violation | Technical violations[b] | | | New crime[c] | Administrative case closures |
| | | | Drug use | Fugitive status | Other | | |
| Misdemeanors[d] | 7,383 | 78.5% | 3.6% | 2.2% | 6.7% | 7.2% | 1.8% |
| Fraudulent property offense | 585 | 88.2 | 1.2 | 1.0 | 4.4 | 2.7 | 2.4 |
| Larceny | 808 | 77.5 | 5.9 | 3.3 | 6.1 | 5.4 | 1.7 |
| Drug possession[d] | 1,207 | 75.0 | 7.6 | 2.7 | 6.5 | 6.6 | 1.6 |
| Immigration misdemeanors | 599 | 53.1 | 1.8 | 3.8 | 9.7 | 30.9 | 0.7 |
| Traffic offenses | 2,288 | 82.0 | 2.3 | 1.4 | 7.1 | 5.3 | 1.8 |
| Other misdemeanors | 1,896 | 81.9 | 2.8 | 2.3 | 6.5 | 4.6 | 2.0 |

Note: Offenses for 67 felony offenders could not be classified. Only records with one or more terminations of active supervision during October 1, 2001, through September 30, 2002, were selected. Each termination was counted separately. Technical violations and terminations for new crimes are shown only if supervision terminated with incarceration or removal from active supervision for reasons of a violation.

[a]The most serious offense was the one with the most severe penalty imposed. If equal prison terms were imposed, or there was no imprisonment, the offense with the highest severity code, as determined by the U.S. Title and Code Criminal Offense Citations Manual, was selected.

[b]Supervision terminated with incarceration or removal to inactive status for violation of supervision conditions other than charges for new offenses.

[c]Supervision terminated with incarceration or removal to inactive status after arrest for a "major" or "minor" offense.

[d]In this table, "Murder" includes nonnegligent manslaughter, "sexual abuse" includes only violent sex offenses; "fraud" excludes tax fraud; "larceny" excludes transportation of stolen property; "other property offenses" excludes fraudulent property offenses, and includes destruction of property and trespassing; "tax law violations" includes tax fraud; "obscene material" denotes the mail or transport thereof; "misdemeanors" includes misdemeanors, petty offenses, and unknown offense levels; and "drug possession" also includes other drug misdemeanors.

[e]No cases of this type occurred in the data.

[f]Too few cases to obtain statistically reliable data.

SOURCE: "Table 7.3. Outcomes of Probation Supervision, by Offense, October 1, 2001–September 30, 2002," in *Compendium of Federal Justice Statistics, 2002*, Bureau of Justice Statistics, September 2004, http://www.ojp.usdoj.gov/bjs/pub/pdf/cfjs0207.pdf (accessed March 26, 2005)

**TABLE 8.8**

## Characteristics of offenders terminating probation supervision, October 1, 2001–September 30, 2002

| Offender characteristic | Number of probation terminations | Percent terminating probation with— | | | | | |
|---|---|---|---|---|---|---|---|
| | | No violation | Technical violations[a] | | | New crime[b] | Administrative case closures |
| | | | Drug use | Fugitive status | Other | | |
| All offenders[c] | 15,116 | 79.5% | 3.7% | 2.5% | 5.9% | 6.6% | 1.9% |
| **Male/female** | | | | | | | |
| Male | 10,836 | 77.8% | 3.8% | 2.5% | 6.3% | 7.6% | 2.0% |
| Female | 4,253 | 83.6 | 3.4 | 2.5 | 4.9 | 4.1 | 1.5 |
| **Race** | | | | | | | |
| White | 9,980 | 81.3% | 3.3% | 2.2% | 4.7% | 6.5% | 1.9% |
| Black | 3,864 | 76.0 | 4.7 | 2.4 | 8.0 | 7.0 | 1.9 |
| Native American | 485 | 53.8 | 5.4 | 10.1 | 18.4 | 10.7 | 1.6 |
| Asian/Pacific Islander | 492 | 90.2 | 1.6 | 1.8 | 2.8 | 2.6 | 0.8 |
| **Ethnicity** | | | | | | | |
| Hispanic | 2,408 | 74.3% | 2.4% | 3.2% | 5.0% | 12.9% | 2.1% |
| Non-Hispanic | 12,556 | 80.4 | 3.9 | 2.3 | 6.1 | 5.4 | 1.8 |
| **Age** | | | | | | | |
| 16–18 years | 157 | 47.1% | 10.2% | 8.3% | 15.9% | 17.2% | 1.3% |
| 19–20 years | 615 | 59.0 | 8.1 | 5.5 | 12.2 | 13.2 | 2.0 |
| 21–30 years | 4,465 | 72.1 | 5.0 | 3.5 | 8.0 | 9.9 | 1.5 |
| 31–40 years | 4,023 | 80.4 | 4.0 | 2.4 | 5.9 | 6.0 | 1.4 |
| Over 40 years | 5,851 | 87.5 | 1.8 | 1.3 | 3.4 | 3.5 | 2.5 |
| **Education** | | | | | | | |
| Less than high school graduate | 3,679 | 69.6% | 5.9% | 4.1% | 9.1% | 9.2% | 2.1% |
| High school graduate | 5,419 | 80.1 | 4.0 | 2.5 | 6.2 | 5.7 | 1.6 |
| Some college | 3,368 | 86.5 | 2.2 | 1.4 | 3.9 | 4.3 | 1.7 |
| College graduate | 1,881 | 90.9 | 1.1 | 0.9 | 2.8 | 2.3 | 2.2 |
| **Drug abuse** | | | | | | | |
| No known abuse | 11,894 | 84.0% | 1.8% | 1.8% | 4.7% | 5.8% | 1.9% |
| Drug history | 3,222 | 62.9 | 10.3 | 5.1 | 10.4 | 9.5 | 1.8 |

[a]Violation of supervision conditions to her than charges for new offenses.

[b]Includes both "major" and "minor" offenses.

[c]Total includes offenders whose characteristics could not be determined.

SOURCE: "Table 7.4. Characteristics of Offenders Terminating Probation Supervision, October 1, 2001–September 30, 2002," in *Compendium of Federal Justice Statistics, 2002*, Bureau of Justice Statistics, September 2004, http://www.ojp.usdoj.gov/bjs/pub/pdf/cfjs0207.pdf (accessed March 26, 2005)

**TABLE 8.9**

**Persons under the supervision of the federal probation system and authorized probation officers, 1975–2003**

| | Number of persons under supervision | Number of probation officers |
|---|---|---|
| 1975 | 64,261 | 1,377 |
| 1976 | 64,246 | 1,452 |
| 1977 | 64,427 | 1,578 |
| 1978 | 66,681 | 1,604 |
| 1979 | 66,087 | 1,604 |
| 1980 | 64,450 | 1,604 |
| 1981 | 59,016 | 1,534 |
| 1982 | 58,373 | 1,637 |
| 1983 | 60,180 | 1,574 |
| 1984 | 63,092 | 1,690 |
| 1985 | 65,999 | 1,758 |
| 1986 | 69,656 | 1,847 |
| 1987 | 73,432 | 1,879 |
| 1988 | 76,366 | 2,046 |
| 1989 | 77,284 | 2,146 |
| 1990 | 80,592 | 2,361 |
| 1991 | 83,012 | 2,802 |
| 1992 | 85,920 | 3,316 |
| 1993 | 86,823 | 3,516* |
| 1994 | 89,103 | NA |
| 1995 | 85,822 | NA |
| 1996 | 88,966 | 3,473 |
| 1997 | 91,434 | 3,603 |
| 1998 | 93,737 | 3,842 |
| 1999 | 97,190 | 3,913 |
| 2000 | 100,395 | 3,981 |
| 2001 | 104,715 | 4,345 |
| 2002 | 108,792 | 4,476 |
| 2003 | 110,621 | 4,560 |

Note: Persons under supervision of the Federal Probation System include persons placed on probation—either by U.S. district courts, U.S. magistrate judges, or at the request of U.S. attorneys (pretrial diversion/deferred prosecution)—and federal offenders released from confinement on parole, supervised release, or mandatory release.
The "number of persons under supervision" data for 1975–87 are reported for the 12-month period ending June 30. Beginning in 1988, these data are reported for the federal fiscal year, which is the 12-month period ending September 30. The "number of probation officers" data for 1975–90 are reported as of June 30. Beginning in 1991, these data are reported as of September 30.
*Approximate.

SOURCE: Kathleen Maguire and Ann L. Pastore, editors, "Table 6.7. Persons under the Supervision of the Federal Probation System and Authorized Probation Officers, 1975–2003," in *Sourcebook of Criminal Justice Statistics*, Bureau of Justice Statistics, August 2004, http://www.albany.edu/sourcebook/pdf/t67.pdf (accessed April 3, 2005)

from federal prisons. The number of parolees grew by 3.1% from 2002 to 2003, almost double the average annual increase of 1.7% since 1995. Since 1995, the number of parolees has increased by 95,167, or 14%. The 23,654 new parolees added to the total number in 2003 was the largest single increase during this period. (See Table 8.3.)

In 2003, 13% of parolees were women, up from 12% in 2000 and 10% in 1995. (See Table 8.13.) In 1995 the percentage of parolees who were white was 34%, while 45% were African-Americans and 21% were Hispanic. Eight years later, whites made up a larger percentage of those on parole, while African-Americans and Hispanics showed a decline. In 2003, 40% of those on parole were white, 41% were African-American, and 18% were Hispanic. Native

Americans and Alaska Natives were 1% of parolees as were Asians, Pacific Islanders, and Native Hawaiians as a group. In general, the gender and racial/ethnic distribution of parolees more closely matched that of the prison population than the distribution of people on probation matched the prison population.

Table 8.13 also shows that 83% of parolees were under the active supervision of parole officers in 2003. Of parolees leaving parole, only 47% had successfully completed the terms of their parole. Parolees, of course, are more serious offenders as a group than are probationers, 95% having been sentenced to one year or more of prison for felonies.

**Parole Geography**

Maine had the fewest parolees in the nation in 2003, a total of thirty-two persons, or three per 100,000 of population. The highest number proportionally to population occurred in the District of Columbia (1,129 per 100,000 adult residents) and in Pennsylvania (1,084 per 100,000 adult residents). (See Table 8.14.) The U.S. average was 357, a value that also includes those on parole from federal institutions. California (110,338), Texas (102,271), and Pennsylvania (102,244) had the largest numbers of parolees. (See Table 8.15.) Several states saw large increases in their numbers of parolees: North Dakota (52.7% increase), Alabama (30.9%), and Kentucky (26.9%). North Dakota's percentage increase, while being the largest of all the states, represented a total of only 226 parolees in that state at the end of 2003. Overall, the Midwest saw the greatest increase in parolees (6.4%) in 2003, while the West saw a decline of 0.3%. (See Table 8.14.)

**Parole Violation and Rearrest Trends**

The overall success rate for parolees has remained fairly stable for several years. As shown in Table 8.13, 45% of individuals on parole completed their sentences successfully in 1995. In 2003, 47% of paroles ended successfully.

The success rate for federal parolees is higher than the national average discussed above. In 2002, 57.5% of federal parolees completed their sentences successfully. (See Table 8.16.) Of those who had committed violent offenses, the success rate was 43.3%. For those who had committed property offenses, the success rate was 62%. Two-thirds of drug offenders (67.7%) completed their parole sentences successfully.

Of those who violated federal parole in the twelve months ending September 30, 2002, most had either violated their parole by committing a new crime or by using drugs. (See Table 8.17.) Male parolees were more than twice as likely to commit a new crime than were female parolees, and they were five times as likely to use drugs than were female parolees. The success rate for white parolees was 63.8%, for Hispanics it was 62.1%, and for African-Americans it was 49.1%. The level of education seemed to make a difference in the success rates of parolees. Those with college degrees had a success rate of 78.7%, but those with less than a high school education had a success rate of only 53.4%. Drug use also had an impact. Those with no known drug abuse problem had a success rate of 66.1%. Those with a known history of drug abuse had a success rate of only 47.6%.

**TABLE 8.10**

**Federal offenders under supervision, by offense, September 30, 2002**

| Most serious offense of conviction[a] | Total offenders under supervision | | Type of supervision | | | | | |
|---|---|---|---|---|---|---|---|---|
| | | | Probation | | Supervised release | | Parole | |
| | Number | Percent | Number | Percent | Number | Percent | Number | Percent |
| All offenses[b] | 107,367 | 100.0% | 30,577 | 100.0% | 73,229 | 100.0% | 3,561 | 100.0% |
| Felonies[c] | 97,518 | 90.8% | 21,290 | 69.5% | 72,673 | 99.2% | 3,555 | 99.8% |
| Violent offenses | 6,281 | 5.9% | 527 | 1.7% | 4,518 | 6.2% | 1,236 | 34.7% |
| Murder[d] | 427 | 0.4 | 21 | 0.1 | 217 | 0.3 | 189 | 5.3 |
| Negligent manslaughter | 9 | e | e | e | 7 | e | 2 | 0.1 |
| Assault | 647 | 0.6 | 138 | 0.5 | 440 | 0.6 | 69 | 1.9 |
| Robbery | 4,490 | 4.2 | 255 | 0.8 | 3,384 | 4.6 | 851 | 23.9 |
| Sexual abuse[d] | 460 | 0.4 | 97 | 0.3 | 324 | 0.4 | 39 | 1.1 |
| Kidnapping | 206 | 0.2 | 11 | e | 109 | 0.1 | 86 | 2.4 |
| Threats against the President | 42 | e | 5 | e | 37 | 0.1 | 0 | 0.0 |
| Property offenses | 29,268 | 27.3% | 11,506 | 37.8% | 17,462 | 23.9% | 300 | 8.4% |
| Fraudulent | 24,439 | 22.8% | 9,310 | 30.6% | 14,983 | 20.5% | 146 | 4.1% |
| Embezzlement | 3,138 | 2.9 | 948 | 3.1 | 2,183 | 3.0 | 7 | 0.2 |
| Fraud[d] | 18,486 | 17.2 | 7,042 | 23.1 | 11,324 | 15.5 | 120 | 3.4 |
| Forgery | 415 | 0.4 | 200 | 0.7 | 203 | 0.3 | 12 | 0.3 |
| Counterfeiting | 2,400 | 2.2 | 1,120 | 3.7 | 1,273 | 1.7 | 7 | 0.2 |
| Other | 4,829 | 4.5% | 2,196 | 7.2% | 2,479 | 3.4% | 154 | 4.3% |
| Burglary | 276 | 0.3 | 54 | 0.2 | 149 | 0.2 | 73 | 2.1 |
| Larceny[d] | 3,367 | 3.1 | 1,803 | 5.9 | 1,524 | 2.1 | 40 | 1.1 |
| Motor vehicle theft | 431 | 0.4 | 110 | 0.4 | 307 | 0.4 | 14 | 0.4 |
| Arson and explosives | 329 | 0.3 | 61 | 0.2 | 254 | 0.3 | 14 | 0.4 |
| Transportation of stolen property | 356 | 0.3 | 133 | 0.4 | 214 | 0.3 | 9 | 0.3 |
| Other property offenses[d] | 70 | 0.1 | 35 | 0.1 | 31 | e | 4 | 0.1 |
| Drug offenses | 44,980 | 42.0% | 3,850 | 12.6% | 39,536 | 54.0% | 1,594 | 44.8% |
| Trafficking | 40,414 | 37.7 | 3,487 | 11.5 | 35,491 | 48.5 | 1,436 | 40.4 |
| Other drug offenses | 4,566 | 4.3 | 363 | 1.2 | 4,045 | 5.5 | 158 | 4.4 |
| Public-order offenses | 9,039 | 8.4% | 3,657 | 12.0% | 5,119 | 7.0% | 263 | 7.4% |
| Regulatory | 2,570 | 2.4% | 1,426 | 4.7% | 1,115 | 1.5% | 29 | 0.8% |
| Agriculture | 4 | e | 2 | e | 2 | e | 0 | 0.0 |
| Antitrust | 27 | e | 17 | 0.1 | 10 | e | 0 | 0.0 |
| Food and drug | 95 | 0.1 | 72 | 0.2 | 23 | e | 0 | 0.0 |
| Transportation | 98 | 0.1 | 62 | 0.2 | 33 | e | 3 | 0.1 |
| Civil rights | 149 | 0.1 | 29 | 0.1 | 116 | 0.2 | 4 | 0.1 |
| Communications | 136 | 0.1 | 92 | 0.3 | 44 | 0.1 | 0 | 0.0 |
| Custom laws | 153 | 0.1 | 69 | 0.2 | 83 | 0.1 | 1 | e |
| Postal laws | 130 | 0.1 | 81 | 0.3 | 48 | 0.1 | 1 | e |
| Other regulatory offenses | 1,778 | 1.7 | 1,002 | 3.3 | 756 | 1.0 | 20 | 0.6 |
| Other | 6,469 | 6.0% | 2,231 | 7.3% | 4,004 | 5.5% | 234 | 6.6% |
| Tax law violations[d] | 1,336 | 1.2 | 735 | 2.4 | 595 | 0.8 | 6 | 0.2 |
| Bribery | 386 | 0.4 | 201 | 0.7 | 182 | 0.2 | 3 | 0.1 |
| Perjury, contempt, and intimidation | 334 | 0.3 | 140 | 0.5 | 185 | 0.3 | 9 | 0.3 |
| National defense | 47 | e | 14 | e | 17 | e | 16 | 0.4 |
| Escape | 282 | 0.3 | 49 | 0.2 | 210 | 0.3 | 23 | 0.6 |
| Racketeering and extortion | 2,246 | 2.1 | 434 | 1.4 | 1,681 | 2.3 | 131 | 3.7 |
| Gambling | 164 | 0.2 | 79 | 0.3 | 85 | 0.1 | 0 | 0.0 |
| Nonviolent sex offenses | 1,006 | 0.9 | 208 | 0.7 | 764 | 1.0 | 34 | 1.0 |
| Obscene material[d] | 66 | 0.1 | 23 | 0.1 | 43 | 0.1 | 0 | 0.0 |
| Wildlife | 99 | 0.1 | 58 | 0.2 | 41 | 0.1 | 0 | 0.0 |
| Environmental | 40 | e | 26 | 0.1 | 14 | e | 0 | 0.0 |
| All other offenses | 463 | 0.4 | 264 | 0.9 | 187 | 0.3 | 12 | 0.3 |
| Weapon offenses | 5,662 | 5.3% | 889 | 2.9% | 4,618 | 6.3% | 155 | 4.4% |
| Immigration offenses | 2,095 | 2.0% | 727 | 2.4% | 1,364 | 1.9% | 4 | 0.1% |

**TABLE 8.10**

**Federal offenders under supervision, by offense, September 30, 2002** [CONTINUED]

| Most serious offense of conviction[a] | Total offenders under supervision | | Type of supervision | | | | | |
| | | | Probation | | Supervised release | | Parole | |
| | Number | Percent | Number | Percent | Number | Percent | Number | Percent |
|---|---|---|---|---|---|---|---|---|
| **Misdemeanors**[d] | 9,849 | 9.2% | 9,287 | 30.5% | 556 | 0.8% | 6 | 0.2% |
| Fraudulent property offenses | 1,104 | 1.0 | 1,042 | 3.4 | 62 | 0.1 | 0 | 0.0 |
| Larceny | 1,187 | 1.1 | 1,090 | 3.6 | 97 | 0.1 | 0 | 0.0 |
| Drug possession[d] | 1,715 | 1.6 | 1,589 | 5.2 | 122 | 0.2 | 4 | 0.1 |
| Immigration misdemeanors | 817 | 0.8 | 805 | 2.6 | 12 | [e] | 0 | 0.0 |
| Traffic offenses | 2,162 | 2.0 | 2,077 | 6.8 | 85 | 0.1 | 0 | 0.0 |
| Other misdemeanors | 2,864 | 2.7 | 2,684 | 8.8 | 178 | 0.2 | 2 | 0.1 |

[a]The most serious offense was the one with the most severe penalty imposed. If equal prison terms were imposed, or there was no imprisonment, the offense with the highest severity code, as determined by the U.S. Title and Code Criminal Offense Citations Manual, was selected.

[b]Total includes offenders whose offense category could not be determined. Year end pending cases (that is, records with offenders who were under active supervision as of the end of the fiscal year, September 30, 2002) were selected. Corporate defendants were excluded.

[c]The are 193 felony offenders for whom an offense category was unknown or indeterminable. These include 134 offenders under probation, 56 under supervised release, and 3 under parole.

[d]In this table, "murder" includes nonnegligent manslaughter; "sexual abuse" includes only violent sex offenses; "fraud" excludes tax fraud; "larceny" excludes transportation of stolen property; "other property offenses" excludes fraudulent property offenses, and includes destruction of property and trespassing; "tax law violations" includes tax fraud; "obscene material" denotes the mail or transport thereof; "misdemeanors" includes misdemeanors, petty offenses, and unknown offense levels; and "drug possession" also includes other drug misdemeanors.

[e]Less than .05%

SOURCE: "Table 7.1. Federal Offenders under Supervision, by Offense, September 30, 2002," in *Compendium of Federal Justice Statistics, 2002*, Bureau of Justice Statistics, September 2004, http://www.ojp.usdoj.gov/bjs/pub/pdf/cfjs0207.pdf (accessed March 26, 2005)

**TABLE 8.11**

**Outcomes of supervised release, by offense, October 1, 2001–September 30, 2002**

| Most serious offense of conviction[a] | Number of supervised release terminations | Percent of supervised releases terminating with— | | | | | |
|---|---|---|---|---|---|---|---|
| | | No violation | Techinical violations[b] | | | New crime[c] | Administrative case closures |
| | | | Drug use | Fugitive status | Other | | |
| **All offenses** | 27,678 | 62.2% | 8.4% | 5.1% | 9.0% | 13.1% | 2.2% |
| **Felonies** | 27,067 | 62.1% | 8.4% | 5.1% | 9.0% | 13.1% | 2.2% |
| Violent offenses | 2,121 | 41.4% | 12.5% | 8.7% | 16.7% | 17.3% | 3.4% |
| Murder[d] | 104 | 40.4 | 7.7 | 22.1 | 15.4 | 13.5 | 1.0 |
| Negligent manslaughter | 5 | f | f | f | f | f | f |
| Assault | 272 | 38.2 | 6.6 | 12.5 | 20.2 | 19.5 | 2.9 |
| Robbery | 1,522 | 42.4 | 14.8 | 7.2 | 15.1 | 17.4 | 3.2 |
| Sexual abuse[d] | 166 | 38.6 | 7.8 | 9.6 | 24.7 | 14.5 | 4.8 |
| Kidnapping | 31 | 54.8 | f | f | 16.1 | 25.8 | 3.2 |
| Threats against the President | 21 | 19.0 | 9.5 | 9.5 | 33.3 | 4.8 | 23.8 |
| Property offenses | 7,195 | 69.2% | 5.5% | 4.7% | 9.0% | 9.8% | 1.8% |
| Fraudulent | 5,898 | 71.7% | 4.9% | 4.0% | 8.4% | 9.1% | 1.9% |
| Embezzlement | 736 | 84.0 | 1.8 | 2.7 | 5.8 | 5.0 | 0.7 |
| Fraud[d] | 4,381 | 72.6 | 4.5 | 3.8 | 8.2 | 8.7 | 2.2 |
| Forgery | 109 | 53.2 | 8.3 | 4.6 | 16.5 | 17.4 | f |
| Counterfeiting | 672 | 55.5 | 10.6 | 7.0 | 11.2 | 14.1 | 1.6 |
| Other | 1,297 | 57.7% | 8.2% | 7.9% | 11.8% | 13.0% | 1.5% |
| Burglary | 99 | 34.3 | 5.1 | 10.1 | 23.2 | 24.2 | 3.0 |
| Larceny[d] | 791 | 56.0 | 9.9 | 8.6 | 12.3 | 12.0 | 1.3 |
| Motor vehicle theft | 152 | 60.5 | 8.6 | 6.6 | 7.9 | 14.5 | 2.0 |
| Arson and explosives | 116 | 67.2 | 3.4 | 6.0 | 12.9 | 8.6 | 1.7 |
| Transportation and stolen property | 119 | 75.6 | 4.2 | 5.0 | 2.5 | 11.8 | 0.8 |
| Other property offenses[d] | 20 | 55.0 | 5.0 | 5.0 | 15.0 | 20.0 | f |
| Drug offenses | 12,320 | 64.1% | 9.6% | 4.5% | 7.5% | 12.3% | 2.1% |
| Trafficking | 11,090 | 63.5 | 9.8 | 4.7 | 7.4 | 12.4 | 2.1 |
| Possession and other drug offenses | 1,230 | 69.3 | 8.0 | 2.1 | 7.6 | 11.0 | 2.0 |
| Public-order offenses | 2,295 | 73.2% | 4.3% | 4.0% | 6.8% | 9.3% | 2.4% |
| Regulatory | 654 | 69.7% | 5.2% | 6.7% | 5.7% | 10.1% | 2.6% |
| Agriculture | 0 | e | e | e | e | e | e |
| Antitrust | 5 | f | f | f | f | f | f |
| Food and drug | 16 | 81.3 | 12.5 | f | f | f | 6.3 |
| Transportation | 19 | 89.5 | f | f | 10.5 | f | f |
| Civil rights | 58 | 77.6 | 5.2 | 3.4 | 1.7 | 10.3 | 1.7 |
| Communications | 23 | 87.0 | 4.3 | 0.0 | 4.3 | 4.3 | f |
| Custom laws | 48 | 58.3 | 4.2 | 10.4 | 6.3 | 8.3 | 12.5 |
| Postal laws | 20 | 55.0 | 5.0 | 10.0 | 30.0 | f | f |
| Other regulatory offenses | 465 | 68.2 | 5.4 | 7.5 | 5.2 | 11.8 | 1.9 |
| Other | 1,641 | 74.6% | 4.0% | 2.9% | 7.3% | 9.0% | 2.3% |
| Tax law violations[d] | 351 | 91.5 | 0.9 | 1.4 | 2.8 | 2.3 | 1.1 |
| Bribery | 60 | 91.7 | 1.7 | f | f | 5.0 | 1.7 |
| Perjury, contempt, and intimidation | 102 | 76.5 | 5.9 | f | 5.9 | 9.8 | 2.0 |
| National defense | 11 | 81.8 | f | f | f | 9.1 | 9.1 |
| Escape | 179 | 39.7 | 10.6 | 10.1 | 13.4 | 23.5 | 2.8 |
| Racketeering and extortion | 564 | 75.7 | 4.8 | 1.8 | 5.7 | 8.5 | 3.5 |
| Gambling | 37 | 91.9 | f | 2.7 | 5.4 | f | f |
| Nonviolent sex offenses | 195 | 69.2 | 1.0 | 4.1 | 14.9 | 9.7 | 1.0 |
| Obscene material[d] | 20 | 70.0 | f | f | 15.0 | 15.0 | f |
| Wildlife | 8 | f | f | f | f | f | f |
| Environmental | 7 | f | f | f | f | f | f |
| All other offenses | 107 | 63.6 | 6.5 | 4.7 | 11.2 | 12.1 | 1.9 |
| Weapon offenses | 2,128 | 49.0% | 11.8% | 6.2% | 11.8% | 18.1% | 3.1% |
| Immigration offenses | 972 | 34.1% | 7.3% | 9.1% | 9.8% | 38.3% | 1.5% |

**TABLE 8.11**

**Outcomes of supervised release, by offense, October 1, 2001–September 30, 2002** [CONTINUED]

| Most serious offense of conviction[a] | Number of supervised release terminations | Percent of supervised releases terminating with— | | | | | |
|---|---|---|---|---|---|---|---|
| | | No violation | Techical violations[b] | | | New crime[c] | Administrative case closures |
| | | | Drug use | Fugitive status | Other | | |
| Misdemeanors[d] | 611 | 63.2% | 8.8% | 4.1% | 10.8% | 10.6% | 2.5% |
| Fraudulent property offense | 66 | 68.2 | 9.1 | 1.5 | 10.6 | 7.6 | 3.0 |
| Larceny | 114 | 64.0 | 8.8 | 3.5 | 10.5 | 11.4 | 1.8 |
| Drug possession[d] | 173 | 56.6 | 12.7 | 5.2 | 11.0 | 14.5 | f |
| Immigration misdemeanors | 12 | 75.0 | f | 8.3 | f | 16.7 | f |
| Traffic offenses | 69 | 68.1 | 7.2 | 1.4 | 13.0 | 8.7 | 1.4 |
| Other misdemeanors | 177 | 64.4 | 6.2 | 5.1 | 10.7 | 7.9 | 5.6 |

Note: Offenses for 36 felony offenders could not be classified. Only records with one or more terminations of active supervision during October 1, 2001, through September 30, 2002, were selected. Each termination was counted separately. Technical violations and terminations for new crimes are shown only if supervision terminated with incarceration or removal from active supervision for reasons of a violation.
[a]The most serious offense was the one with the most severe penalty imposed. If equal prison terms were imposed, or there was no imprisonment, the offense with the highest severity code, as determined by the U.S. Title and Code Criminal Offense Citations Manual, was selected.
[b]Supervision terminated with incarceration or removal to inactive status for violation of supervision conditions other than charges for new offenses.
[c]Supervision terminated with incarceration or removal to inactive status after arrest for a "major" or "minor" offense.
[d]In this table, "murder" includes nonnegligent manslaughter, "sexual abuse" includes only violent sex offenses; "fraud" excludes tax fraud; "larceny" excludes transportation of stolen property; "other property offenses" excludes fraudulent property offenses, and includes destruction of property and trespassing; "tax law violations" includes tax fraud; "obscene material" denotes the mail or transport thereof; "misdemeanors" includes misdemeanors, petty offenses, and unknown offense levels; and "drug possession" also includes other drug misdemeanors.
[e]No cases of this type occurred in the data.
[f]Too few cases to obtain statistically reliable data.

SOURCE: "Table 7.5. Outcomes of Supervised Release, by Offense, October 1, 2001–September 30, 2002," in *Compendium of Federal Justice Statistics, 2002*, Bureau of Justice Statistics, September 2004, http://www.ojp.usdoj.gov/bjs/pub/pdf/cfjs0207.pdf (accessed March 26, 2005)

---

**TABLE 8.12**

**Characteristics of offenders terminating supervised release, October 1, 2001–September 30, 2002**

| Offender characteristic | Number of supervised release terminations | Percent of supervised releases terminating with— | | | | | |
|---|---|---|---|---|---|---|---|
| | | No violation | Technical violations[b] | | | New crime[b] | Administrative case closures |
| | | | Drug use | Fugitive status | Other | | |
| All offenders[c] | 27,678 | 62.2% | 8.4% | 5.1% | 9.0% | 13.1% | 2.2% |
| **Male/female** | | | | | | | |
| Male | 23,103 | 59.9% | 8.7% | 5.3% | 9.5% | 14.3% | 2.4% |
| Female | 4,563 | 73.6 | 7.1 | 4.0 | 6.5 | 7.2 | 1.6 |
| **Race** | | | | | | | |
| White | 17,331 | 64.9% | 7.8% | 5.2% | 7.6% | 12.3% | 2.2% |
| Black | 8,639 | 57.3 | 9.9 | 4.4 | 10.9 | 15.2 | 2.3 |
| Native American | 781 | 36.9 | 8.2 | 14.5 | 22.0 | 16.4 | 2.0 |
| Asian/Pacific Islander | 715 | 78.3 | 6.7 | 2.7 | 7.3 | 3.6 | 1.4 |
| **Ethnicity** | | | | | | | |
| Hispanic | 5,684 | 56.8% | 8.0% | 7.6% | 8.0% | 17.8% | 1.8% |
| Non-Hispanic | 21,824 | 63.5 | 8.6 | 4.5 | 9.3 | 11.9 | 2.3 |
| **Age** | | | | | | | |
| 16–18 years | 1 | d | d | d | d | d | d |
| 19–20 years | 136 | 16.9 | 11.8 | 17.6 | 21.3 | 31.6 | 0.7 |
| 21–30 years | 7,146 | 46.8 | 11.5 | 7.8 | 13.6 | 18.8 | 1.5 |
| 31–40 years | 9,378 | 59.8 | 9.5 | 5.0 | 9.2 | 14.7 | 1.8 |
| Over 40 years | 11,017 | 74.7 | 5.4 | 3.3 | 5.7 | 7.8 | 3.1 |
| **Education** | | | | | | | |
| Less than high school graduate | 10,543 | 53.0% | 10.2% | 6.8% | 11.0% | 16.7% | 2.3% |
| High school graduate | 9,539 | 62.7 | 9.4 | 4.7 | 8.9 | 12.2 | 2.1 |
| Some college | 5,249 | 72.5 | 5.8 | 3.2 | 7.1 | 9.2 | 2.2 |
| College graduate | 1,850 | 87.2 | 1.7 | 1.7 | 3.7 | 3.6 | 2.2 |
| **Drug abuse** | | | | | | | |
| No known abuse | 14,902 | 71.1% | 3.8% | 3.8% | 7.2% | 11.7% | 2.4% |
| Drug history | 12,776 | 51.7 | 13.8 | 6.6 | 11.1 | 14.7 | 2.1 |

[a]Violation of supervision conditions other than charges for new offenses.
[b]Includes both "major" and "minor" offenses.
[c]Total includes offenders whose characteristics could not be determined.
[d]Too few cases to obtain statistically reliable data.

SOURCE: "Table 7.6. Characteristics of Offenders Terminating Supervised Release, October 1, 2001–September 30, 2002," in *Compendium of Federal Justice Statistics, 2002*, Bureau of Justice Statistics, September 2004, http://www.ojp.usdoj.gov/bjs/pub/pdf/cfjs0207.pdf (accessed March 26, 2005)

**TABLE 8.13**

## Characteristics of adults on parole, 1995, 2000, and 2003

| Characteristic | 1995 | 2000 | 2003 |
|---|---|---|---|
| Total | 100% | 100% | 100% |
| **Gender** | | | |
| Male | 90% | 88% | 87% |
| Female | 10 | 12 | 13 |
| **Race** | | | |
| White | 34% | 38% | 40% |
| Black | 45 | 40 | 41 |
| Hispanic | 21 | 21 | 18 |
| American Indian/Alaska Native | 1 | 1 | 1 |
| Asian/Pacific Islander[a] | d | d | 1 |
| **Status of supervision** | | | |
| Active | 78% | 83% | 83% |
| Inactive | 11 | 4 | 4 |
| Absconder | 6 | 7 | 7 |
| Supervised out of state | 4 | 5 | 4 |
| Other | d | 1 | 1 |
| **Sentence length** | | | |
| Less than 1 year | 6% | 3% | 5% |
| 1 year or more | 94 | 97 | 95 |
| **Type of offense** | | | |
| Violent | c | c | 28% |
| Property | c | c | 26 |
| Drug | c | c | 36 |
| Other | c | c | 10 |
| **Adults entering parole** | | | |
| Discretionary parole | 50% | 37% | 39% |
| Mandatory parole | 45 | 54 | 51 |
| Reinstatement | 4 | 6 | 8 |
| Other | 2 | 2 | 2 |
| **Adults leaving parole** | | | |
| Successful completion | 45% | 43% | 47% |
| Returned to incarceration | 41 | 42 | 38 |
|    With new sentence | 12 | 11 | 11 |
|    With revocation pending | 18 | 30 | 26 |
|    Other | 11 | 1 | 1 |
| Absconder[b] | c | 9 | 9 |
| Other unsuccessful[b] | c | 2 | 1 |
| Transferred | 2 | 1 | 1 |
| Death | 1 | 1 | 1 |
| Other | 10 | 2 | 2 |

Note: For every characteristic there were persons of unknown status or type. Detail may not sum to total because of rounding.
[a]Includes Native Hawaiians.
[b]In 1995 "absconder" and "other unsuccessful" statuses were reported among "other."
[c]Not available.
[d]Less than 0.5%.

SOURCE: Lauren E. Glaze and Seri Palla, "Table 7. Characteristics of Adults on Parole, 1995, 2000, and 2003," in *Probation and Parole in the United States, 2003*, Bureau of Justice Statistics, July 2004, http://www.ojp.usdoj .gov/bjs/pub/pdf/ppus03.pdf (accessed April 2, 2005)

TABLE 8.14

## Adults on parole, 2003

| Region and jurisdiction | Parole population, 1/1/03 | 2003 Entries | 2003 Exits | Parole population, 12/31/03 | Percent change, 2003 | Number on parole per 100,000 adult residents, 12/31/03 |
|---|---|---|---|---|---|---|
| **U.S. total** | **750,934** | **492,727** | **470,538** | **774,588** | **3.1%** | **357** |
| Federal | 83,063 | 33,590 | 31,088 | 86,459 | 4.1% | 40 |
| State | 667,871 | 459,137 | 439,450 | 688,129 | 3.0 | 317 |
| **Northeast** | 174,591 | 77,381 | 71,903 | 180,069 | 3.1% | 437 |
| Connecticut | 2,186 | 3,260 | 2,847 | 2,599 | 18.9 | 99 |
| Maine | 32 | 0 | 0 | 32 | 0.0 | 3 |
| Massachusetts | 3,951 | 6,305 | 6,552 | 3,704 | −6.3 | 370 |
| New Hampshire[a] | 963 | 719 | 482 | 1,200 | 24.6 | 124 |
| New Jersey | 12,576 | 10,322 | 9,650 | 13,248 | 5.3 | 203 |
| New York | 55,990 | 25,049 | 25,186 | 55,853 | −0.2 | 386 |
| Pennsylvania[b] | 97,712 | 30,870 | 26,338 | 102,244 | 4.6 | 1,084 |
| Rhode Island | 384 | 456 | 448 | 392 | 2.1 | 48 |
| Vermont | 797 | 400 | 400 | 797 | 0.0 | 170 |
| **Midwest** | 114,173 | 95,242 | 87,882 | 121,533 | 6.4% | 250 |
| Illinois | 35,458 | 32,476 | 32,926 | 35,008 | −1.3 | 374 |
| Indiana | 5,877 | 7,304 | 6,162 | 7,019 | 19.4 | 152 |
| Iowa[c] | 2,787 | 2,787 | 2,475 | 3,099 | 11.2 | 140 |
| Kansas[c] | 3,990 | 4,146 | 3,991 | 4,145 | 3.9 | 207 |
| Michigan | 17,648 | 12,579 | 9,994 | 20,233 | 14.6 | 271 |
| Minnesota | 3,577 | 4,121 | 4,102 | 3,596 | 0.5 | 96 |
| Missouri | 13,533 | 10,407 | 8,720 | 15,220 | 12.5 | 357 |
| Nebraska | 574 | 839 | 763 | 650 | 13.2 | 51 |
| North Dakota | 148 | 585 | 507 | 226 | 52.7 | 48 |
| Ohio | 17,853 | 11,670 | 11,096 | 18,427 | 3.2 | 216 |
| South Dakota | 1,640 | 1,451 | 1,147 | 1,944 | 18.5 | 346 |
| Wisconsin | 11,088 | 6,877 | 5,999 | 11,966 | 7.9 | 293 |
| **South** | 219,849 | 104,142 | 96,351 | 227,668 | 3.6% | 291 |
| Alabama | 5,309 | 4,098 | 2,457 | 6,950 | 30.9 | 206 |
| Arkansas | 12,128 | 7,379 | 5,813 | 13,694 | 12.9 | 672 |
| Delaware | 551 | 217 | 239 | 529 | −4.0 | 85 |
| District of Columbia[a,b] | 5,297 | 3,136 | 3,369 | 5,064 | e | 1,129 |
| Florida | 5,223 | 4,409 | 4,680 | 4,952 | −5.2 | 37 |
| Georgia | 20,822 | 11,738 | 10,391 | 22,135 | 6.3 | 344 |
| Kentucky[c] | 5,968 | 4,719 | 3,115 | 7,572 | 26.9 | 243 |
| Louisiana | 23,049 | 13,468 | 11,452 | 25,065 | 8.7 | 766 |
| Maryland | 13,271 | 8,059 | 7,588 | 13,742 | 3.5 | 334 |
| Mississippi[d] | 1,816 | 1,103 | 963 | 1,816 | 0.0 | 87 |
| North Carolina | 2,805 | 3,214 | 3,342 | 2,677 | −4.6 | 42 |
| Oklahoma[a] | 3,573 | 1,995 | 1,521 | 4,047 | e | 155 |
| South Carolina | 3,491 | 1,025 | 1,306 | 3,210 | −8.0 | 103 |
| Tennessee | 7,949 | 3,130 | 3,314 | 7,967 | 0.2 | 180 |
| Texas[a] | 103,068 | 32,847 | 33,644 | 102,271 | −0.8 | 639 |
| Virginia | 4,530 | 2,779 | 2,475 | 4,834 | 6.7 | 86 |
| West Virginia | 999 | 826 | 682 | 1,143 | 14.4 | 81 |
| **West** | 159,258 | 182,371 | 183,313 | 158,859 | −0.3% | 324 |
| Alaska[c] | 900 | 614 | 587 | 927 | e | 203 |
| Arizona[b] | 4,587 | 8,895 | 8,115 | 5,367 | 17.0 | 129 |
| California[c] | 113,185 | 148,915 | 152,305 | 110,338 | −2.5 | 424 |
| Colorado | 6,215 | 5,298 | 4,954 | 6,559 | 5.5 | 193 |
| Hawaii | 2,525 | 906 | 1,191 | 2,240 | −11.3 | 231 |
| Idaho | 1,961 | 1,486 | 1,118 | 2,329 | 18.8 | 236 |
| Montana[c] | 845 | 601 | 631 | 815 | −3.6 | 119 |
| Nevada | 3,971 | 2,956 | 2,801 | 4,126 | 3.9 | 243 |
| New Mexico | 1,962 | 1,977 | 1,532 | 2,407 | 22.7 | 177 |
| Oregon | 19,090 | 8,059 | 7,380 | 19,769 | 3.6 | 733 |
| Utah | 3,352 | 2,300 | 2,353 | 3,299 | −1.6 | 205 |
| Washington[a] | 95 | 45 | 35 | 105 | 10.5 | 2 |
| Wyoming | 570 | 319 | 311 | 578 | 1.4 | 156 |

Note: Because of incomplete data, the population on December 31, 2003, does not equal the population on January 1, 2003, plus entries, minus exits.
[a]All data were estimated.
[b]Data for entries and exits were estimated for nonreporting agencies.
[c]Excludes parolees in one of the following categories: absconder, out of state, or inactive.
[d]Data are for the year ending December 1, 2003.
[e]Not calculated.

SOURCE: Lauren E. Glaze and Seri Palla, "Table 5. Adults on Parole, 2003," in *Probation and Parole in the United States, 2003*, Bureau of Justice Statistics, July 2004, http://www.ojp.usdoj.gov/bjs/pub/pdf/ppus03.pdf (accessed April 2, 2005)

TABLE 8.15

## Parole population statistics, 2003

| 10 states with the largest 2003 community corrections populations | Number supervised | 10 states with the largest percent increase | Percent increase, 2002–03 | 10 states with the highest rates of supervision, 2003 | Persons supervised per 100,000 adult U.S. residents* | 10 states with the lowest rates of supervision, 2003 | Persons supervised per 100,000 adult U.S. residents* |
|---|---|---|---|---|---|---|---|
| California | 110,338 | North Dakota | 52.7% | Pennsylvania | 1,084 | Washington | 2 |
| Texas | 102,271 | Alabama | 30.9 | Louisiana | 766 | Maine | 3 |
| Pennsylvania | 102,244 | Kentucky | 26.9 | Oregon | 733 | Florida | 37 |
| New York | 55,853 | New Hampshire | 24.6 | Arkansas | 672 | North Carolina | 42 |
| Illinois | 35,008 | New Mexico | 22.7 | Texas | 639 | Rhode Island | 48 |
| Louisiana | 25,065 | Indiana | 19.4 | California | 424 | North Dakota | 48 |
| Georgia | 22,135 | Connecticut | 18.9 | New York | 386 | Nebraska | 51 |
| Michigan | 20,233 | Idaho | 18.8 | Illinois | 374 | West Virginia | 81 |
| Oregon | 19,769 | South Dakota | 18.5 | Massachusetts | 370 | Delaware | 85 |
| Ohio | 18,427 | Arizona | 17.0 | Missouri | 357 | Virginia | 86 |

Note: This table excludes the District of Columbia, a wholly urban jurisdiction, Georgia probation counts, which included probation case-based counts for private agencies, and Idaho in which misdemeanor probation counts were not reported in 2003.
*Rates are based on the estimated number of adult state residents on December 31, 2003.

SOURCE: Adapted from Lauren E. Glaze and Seri Palla, "Table 1. Community Corrections among the States, Yearend 2003," in *Probation and Parole in the United States, 2003*, Bureau of Justice Statistics, July 2004, http://www.ojp.usdoj.gov/bjs/pub/pdf/ppus03.pdf (accessed April 3, 2005)

TABLE 8.16

## Outcomes of parole, by offense, October 1, 2001–September 30, 2002

| Most serious offense of conviction[a] | Number of parole terminations | Percent of paroles terminating with— | | | | | |
|---|---|---|---|---|---|---|---|
| | | No violation | Technical violations[b] | | | New crime[c] | Administrative case closures |
| | | | Drug use | Fugitive status | Other | | |
| **All offenses** | 1,817 | 57.5% | 8.8% | 4.7% | 9.9% | 12.7% | 6.5% |
| **Felonies** | 1,807 | 57.5% | 8.9% | 4.7% | 9.8% | 12.7% | 6.5% |
| Violent offenses | 610 | 43.3% | 14.4% | 6.7% | 11.8% | 16.4% | 7.4% |
| Murder[d] | 46 | 41.3 | 13.0 | 4.3 | 21.7 | 10.9 | 8.7 |
| Assault | 33 | 48.5 | 3.0 | 12.1 | 12.1 | 18.2 | 6.1 |
| Robbery | 470 | 43.8 | 15.5 | 6.0 | 10.9 | 15.5 | 8.3 |
| Sexual abuse[d] | 17 | 47.1 | 5.9 | 23.5 | 11.8 | 11.8 | 0.0 |
| Kidnapping | 42 | 33.3 | 14.3 | 7.1 | 11.9 | 33.3 | 0.0 |
| Property offenses | 179 | 62.0% | 2.8% | 2.8% | 12.3% | 16.2% | 3.9% |
| Fraudulent | 97 | 69.1% | 0.0% | 1.0% | 9.3% | 17.5% | 3.1% |
| Embezzlement | 10 | e | e | e | e | e | e |
| Fraud[d] | 78 | 69.2 | 0.0 | 1.3 | 10.3 | 15.4 | 3.8 |
| Forgery | 6 | e | e | e | e | e | e |
| Counterfeiting | 3 | e | e | e | e | e | e |
| Other | 82 | 53.7% | 6.1% | 4.9% | 15.9% | 14.6% | 4.9% |
| Burglary | 28 | 42.9 | 3.6 | 3.6 | 17.9 | 25.0 | 7.1 |
| Larceny[d] | 27 | 63.0 | 11.1 | 3.7 | 14.8 | 3.7 | 3.7 |
| Motor vehicle theft | 10 | e | e | e | e | e | e |
| Arson and explosives | 7 | e | e | e | e | e | e |
| Transportation and stolen property | 9 | e | e | e | e | e | e |
| Drug offenses | 809 | 67.7% | 6.4% | 2.7% | 6.7% | 10.0% | 6.4% |
| Trafficking | 735 | 68.4 | 6.3 | 2.7 | 6.3 | 9.9 | 6.4 |
| Possession and other drug offenses | 74 | 60.8 | 8.1 | 2.7 | 10.8 | 10.8 | 6.8 |
| Public-order offenses | 125 | 58.4% | 5.6% | 5.6% | 12.8% | 9.6% | 8.0% |
| Regulatory | 15 | 46.7% | 13.3% | 6.7% | 20.0% | 6.7% | 6.7% |
| Other | 110 | 60.0% | 4.5% | 5.5% | 11.8% | 10.0% | 8.2% |
| Escape | 19 | 42.1 | 10.5 | 5.3 | 26.3 | 5.3 | 10.5 |
| Racketeering and extortion | 56 | 66.1 | 0.0 | 7.1 | 1.8 | 17.9 | 7.1 |
| Nonviolent sex offenses | 17 | 47.1 | 11.8 | 5.9 | 29.4 | 0.0 | 5.9 |
| Weapon offenses | 82 | 51.2% | 8.5% | 12.2% | 15.9% | 8.5% | 3.7% |
| Immigration offenses | 1 | e | e | e | e | e | e |
| **Misdemeanors[d]** | 10 | e | e | e | e | e | e |

[a]The most serious offense was the one with the most severe penalty imposed. If equal prison terms were imposed, or there was no imprisonment, the offense with the highest severity code, as determined by the U.S. Title and Code Criminal Offense Citations Manual, was selected.
[b]Supervision terminated with incarceration or removal to inactive status for violation of supervision conditions other than charges for new offenses.
[c]Supervision terminated with incarceration or removal to inactive status after arrest for a "major" or "minor" offense.
[d]In this table, "murder" includes nonnegligent manslaughter; "sexual abuse" includes only violent sex offenses; "fraud" excludes tax fraud; "larceny" excludes transportation of stolen property; "tax law violations" includes tax fraud; "misdemeanors" includes misdemeanors, petty offenses, and unknown offense levels.
[e]Too few cases to obtain statistically reliable data.

SOURCE: "Table 7.7. Outcomes of Parole, by Offense, October 1, 2001–September 30, 2002," in *Compendium of Federal Justice Statistics, 2002*, Bureau of Justice Statistics, September 2004, http://www.ojp.usdoj.gov/bjs/pub/pdf/cfjs0207.pdf (accessed March 26, 2005)

**TABLE 8.17**

## Characteristics of offenders terminating parole, October 1, 2001–September 30, 2002

| Offender characteristic | Number of parole terminations | No violation | Technical violations[a] Drug use | Fugitive status | Other | New crime[b] | Administrative case closures |
|---|---|---|---|---|---|---|---|
| **All offenders[c]** | 1,817 | 57.5% | 8.8% | 4.7% | 9.9% | 12.7% | 6.5% |
| **Male/female** | | | | | | | |
| Male | 1,756 | 57.0% | 9.1% | 4.6% | 9.8% | 12.9% | 6.6% |
| Female | 57 | 71.9 | 1.8 | 8.8 | 8.8 | 5.3 | 3.5 |
| **Race** | | | | | | | |
| White | 1,027 | 63.8% | 7.2% | 3.9% | 6.0% | 12.1% | 7.0% |
| Black | 678 | 49.1 | 11.7 | 5.8 | 13.3 | 14.2 | 6.0 |
| Native American | 31 | 48.4 | 3.2 | 9.7 | 25.8 | 12.9 | 0.0 |
| Asian/Pacific Islander | 10 | d | d | d | d | d | d |
| **Ethnicity** | | | | | | | |
| Hispanic | 227 | 62.1% | 11.5% | 3.5% | 6.2% | 12.8% | 4.0% |
| Non-Hispanic | 1,579 | 56.8 | 8.5 | 4.9 | 10.3 | 12.6 | 6.9 |
| **Age** | | | | | | | |
| 21–30 years | 47 | 53.2% | 8.5% | 8.5% | 10.6% | 14.9% | 4.3% |
| 31–40 years | 271 | 48.7 | 12.9 | 4.1 | 17.3 | 12.9 | 4.1 |
| Over 40 years | 1,499 | 59.2 | 8.1 | 4.7 | 8.5 | 12.5 | 7.0 |
| **Education** | | | | | | | |
| Less than high school graduate | 824 | 53.4% | 10.2% | 5.5% | 10.0% | 13.2% | 7.8% |
| High school graduate | 624 | 56.9 | 9.5 | 4.3 | 10.7 | 13.0 | 5.6 |
| Some college | 236 | 67.8 | 5.5 | 4.7 | 5.5 | 10.6 | 5.9 |
| College graduate | 89 | 78.7 | 0.0 | 0.0 | 7.9 | 9.0 | 4.5 |
| **Drug abuse** | | | | | | | |
| No known abuse | 966 | 66.1% | 4.7% | 3.6% | 8.4% | 11.1% | 6.1% |
| Drug history | 851 | 47.6 | 13.5 | 6.0 | 11.5 | 14.5 | 6.9 |

[a]Violation of supervision conditions other than charges for new offenses.
[b]Includes both "major" and "minor" offenses.
[c]Total includes offenders whose characteristics could not be determined.
[d]Too few cases to obtain statistically reliable data.

SOURCE: "Table 7.8. Characteristics of Offenders Terminating Parole, October 1, 2001–September 30, 2002," in *Compendium of Federal Justice Statistics, 2002*, Bureau of Justice Statistics, September 2004, http://www.ojp.usdoj.gov/bjs/pub/pdf/cfjs0207.pdf (accessed March 26, 2005)

# CHAPTER 9
# SENTENCING

*Sentencing reform policies have paralleled the mood of the country on crime and punishment, shifting between requiring a fixed prison time prior to release or allowing discretionary release of offenders by judges, parole boards, or corrections officials. Over the last two decades, sentencing requirements and release policies have become more restrictive, primarily in response to widespread "get tough on crime" attitudes in the Nation.*

— Paula M. Ditton and Doris James Wilson, *Truth in Sentencing in State Prisons* (Washington, DC: Bureau of Justice Statistics, January 1999)

Sentencing policies have changed since the 1970s. Prison populations began increasing in 1973 from a rate of ninety-six prisoners per 100,000 adult residents in the United States to an estimated 482 per 100,000 in 2003. (See Table 4.3 in Chapter 4.) Between 1925 and 1973 the ninety-six per 100,000 rate was one of the lowest, matched, for instance, by the rate in 1928. The average imprisonment rate during the 1925–73 period was 107 prisoners per 100,000 people. The highest rate in this time period was reached in 1939 when 137 people were incarcerated in state and federal prisons per 100,000 residents. The average in the period 1974–2003 was 279.

The period of expanding incarceration also coincided with emphasis at state and federal levels on controlling the use and distribution of drugs. The first legislation against drugs was the Harrison Act, enacted in 1914, which outlawed opiates and cocaine. Marijuana was outlawed in 1937. The "war on drugs" was declared in the early 1970s when the National Commission on Marihuana and Drug Abuse (also known as the Shafer Commission) published its recommendation that marijuana be legalized (*Marihuana: A Signal of Misunderstanding*, Report of the National Commission on Marihuana and Drug Abuse, March 1972). The commission was appointed by President Richard Nixon, who later rejected the commission's recommendation and declared war on drugs.

As reported in *Key Facts at a Glance* on the Web page of the Bureau of Justice Statistics (BJS) ("Number of Persons in Custody of State Correctional Authorities by Most Serious Offense, 1980–2001," http://www.ojp.usdoj.gov/bjs/glance/tables/corrtyptab.htm), prisoners in state systems incarcerated for drug offenses comprised 6.5% of the prison population in 1980. By 2001 they represented 20.4% of prisoners. Drug prosecutions also have made up a growing proportion of the federal criminal caseload. In 1982, 21% of federal defendants were held on drug charges, while 35% were drug related in 2002. In addition to a sharp growth in drug crimes, crimes of violence also spiked. From 1995 to 2001, half of the increase in the state prison population was due to an increase in the prisoners convicted of violent offenses.

It is against this background that new sentencing policies developed. Paula M. Ditton and Doris James Wilson (*Truth in Sentencing in State Prisons*) summarize the situation beginning with the 1970s as follows:

In the early 1970s, states generally permitted parole boards to determine when an offender would be released from prison. In addition, good-time reductions for satisfactory prison behavior, earned-time incentives for participation in work or educational programs, and other time reductions to control prison crowding resulted in the early release of prisoners. These policies permitted officials to individualize the amount of punishment or leniency an offender received and provided means to manage the prison population.

Such discretion in sentencing and release policies led to criticism that some offenders were punished more harshly than others for similar offenses and to complaints that overall sentencing and release laws were too soft on criminals. By the late 1970s and early 1980s, States began developing sentencing guidelines, enacting mandatory minimum sentences and adopting other sentencing reforms to reduce disparity in sentencing and to toughen penalties for certain offenses, specifically drug offenses (as part of the "war on drugs"), offenses with weapons, and offenses committed by repeat or habitual criminals.

## TRUTH-IN-SENTENCING

Sentence reforms enacted by states came to be known as "truth-in-sentencing" statutes. The first such statute was enacted by the state of Washington in 1984. According to William J. Sabol and colleagues at the Urban Institute (*The Influences of Truth-in-Sentencing Reforms on Changes in States' Sentencing Practices and Prison Populations*, Washington, DC, April 2002), forty-two states and the District of Columbia had enacted some type of truth-in-sentencing statute.

Also in 1984, Congress established the U.S. Sentencing Commission (USSC) in the Sentencing Reform Act. Congress charged this new federal agency with developing sentencing guidelines for federal courts. The Sentencing Reform Act was the federal enactment of truth-in-sentencing.

"Truth-in-sentencing," abbreviated as TIS, is intended to tell the public that a sentence announced by the court will actually be served—rather than the criminal serving only some small fraction of the sentence, the prisoner being released on parole, or the individual having the sentence commuted to probation and serving no time at all. Under TIS statutes, offenders are required to spend substantial portions of their sentences in prison. The federally recommended portion is 85% of the sentence.

With TIS came the distinction between *indeterminate* and *determinate* sentencing. Indeterminate sentencing gives parole boards the authority to release offenders at their option after a process of review. Determinate sentencing takes decision-making power away from parole boards, fixes the term to be served, and provides or denies the means to shorten the sentence by good behavior or other "earned" time. Part of the truth-in-sentencing statues are *mandatory minimum sentences* specified by law for specific offenses and circumstances. Mandatory minima are published in *sentencing guidelines*, which judges are required to use. Guidelines define the range of sentences the judge may apply, again governed by the offense and the prior history of the offender (e.g., first-time or repeat-offender, severity of the offense, etc.).

Setting uniform sentences for offenses and requiring that fixed proportions of them be served by those convicted put pressure on prison and jail capacities. In response, Congress passed the Violent Crime Control and Law Enforcement Act of 1994, known as the 1994 Crime Act. Its grant program provisions set as a requirement for funding that states have in place truth-in-sentencing statutes. Thus, the federal government provided incentives to states for enacting truth-in-sentencing laws or to conform such laws to the federal sentencing guidelines published by the USSC.

Eleven states passed truth-in-sentencing laws in 1995 in response to the federal initiative.

The net effect of federal guidelines, the 1994 Crime Act and its financial incentives, and state actions before and after federal legislation has been to make sentencing more uniform across the nation and, at the state level, to extend the time convicted felons spend in prison.

## FEDERAL SENTENCING GUIDELINES

The Sentencing Reform Act of 1984 is the federal approach to truth-in-sentencing, or determinate sentencing. In the U.S. Sentencing Commission's publication *Fifteen Years of Guidelines Sentencing* (Washington, DC, November 2004) are listed the goals of the Sentencing Reform Act:

1. Elimination of unwarranted disparity

2. Transparency, certainty, and fairness

3. Proportionate punishment; and

4. Crime control through deterrence, incapacitation, and the rehabilitation of offenders

These goals were aimed at eliminating the unregulated power of federal judges to impose sentences of indeterminate length. Such power resulted in persons convicted of the same crime but sentenced by different judges receiving wildly different terms of incarceration. The development of federal guidelines by the USCC was intended to give both a range of sentencing options to federal judges while guaranteeing minimum and maximum sentencing lengths.

The federal guidelines were originally developed by the USSC, which continues to update the guidelines as laws administered by the federal courts are changed or new laws are passed. The latest edition of the guidelines were published in 2004 (*Federal Sentencing Guidelines Manual*, November 2004, http://www.ussc.gov/2004guid/TABCON04.htm). Supplemental volumes are also issued by the USSC.

At the core of the guidelines are offenses as defined by federal statutes. The USSC assigns an "offense level" to each offense, known as the Base Offense Level. Levels are numbered from 1 to 43. The lowest actual offense for which the USSC has a level is Trespass. Trespass is level 4. First degree murder has a Base Offense Level of 43. Based on various circumstances associated with an offense, additional levels may be added or taken away until a particular offense has been precisely defined by level. Levels are abstract numbers. Their purpose is to enable the judge or prosecutor to find a particular sentence, in months of imprisonment, in the federal Sentencing Table.

An illustration is provided for kidnapping, abduction, and unlawful restraint. (See Table 9.1.) The table reproduces the USSC's guideline for this offense. The

**TABLE 9.1**

**Federal sentencing guidelines on kidnapping**

**§2A4.1. Kidnapping, abduction, unlawful restraint**

(a) Base offense level: **32**
(b) Specific offense characteristics
    (1)  If a ransom demand or a demand upon government was made, increase by **6** levels.
    (2)  (A)  If the victim sustained permanent or life-threatening bodily injury, increase by **4** levels;
         (B)  if the victim sustained serious bodily injury, increase by **2** levels; or
         (C)  if the degree of injury is between that specified in subdivisions (A) and (B), increase by **3** levels.
    (3)  If a dangerous weapon was used, increase by **2** levels.
    (4)  (A)  If the victim was not released before thirty days had elapsed, increase by **2** levels.
         (B)  If the victim was not released before seven days had elapsed, increase by **1** level.
    (5)  If the victim was sexually exploited, increase by **6** levels.
    (6)  If the victim is a minor and, in exchange for money or other consideration, was placed in the care or custody of another person who had no legal right to such care or custody of the victim, increase by **3** levels.
    (7)  If the victim was kidnapped, abducted, or unlawfully restrained during the commission of, or in connection with, another offense or escape therefrom; or if another offense was committed during the kidnapping, abduction, or unlawful restraint, increase to —
        (A)  the offense level from the chapter two offense guideline applicable to that other offense if such offense guideline includes an adjustment for kidnapping, abduction, or unlawful restraint, or otherwise takes such conduct into account; or
        (B)  **4** plus the offense level from the offense guideline applicable to that other offense, but in no event greater than level **43**, in any other case,
        if the resulting offense level is greater than that determined above.

SOURCE: "§2A4.1. Kidnapping, Abduction, Unlawful Restraint," in *2004 Federal Sentencing Guidelines Manual*, U.S. Sentencing Commission, November 2004, http://www.ussc.gov/2004guid/2a4_1.htm (accessed March 31, 2005)

offense has a Base Offense Level of 32, but additional levels can be added. For instance, if the victim sustained serious bodily injury, the level is increased by four to 36. If the victim was also sexually exploited, the level is increased by six levels to 38. If the victim was not released before seven days had passed, the level is increased by one to 33.

In the USSC's Sentencing Table, presented as Table 9.2, level 28 points to six columns of sentence ranges indicating a minimum and a maximum sentence in each column. The first column, where the sentence range is seventy-eight to ninety-seven months, the offender either has no prior convictions or has one prior conviction. In the sixth column, where the sentence is 140 to 175 months, the offender has thirteen or more prior convictions. A single level thus provides six different levels of confinement, and, within each level, there is a range from minimum to maximum. Judges are not entirely deprived of discretion by determinate sentencing.

Level 28 falls into the Sentencing Table's Zone D. This means that the individual may not receive any probation and must serve at least the minimum sentence shown in the applicable column. A three-time offender would be minimally sentenced to eighty-seven months in prison and, under the USSC guidelines, could receive, maximally, fifty-four days off per year for good behavior and would therefore serve at least 85% of the minimum sentence. In the case illustrated earlier, where sexual exploitation is involved, the individual would also be charged for criminal sexual abuse (a Base Offense Level of 24) or for sexual abuse of a minor (Level 18 to 24 depending on whether the abuse was

attempted or committed). Parole is not available in any of the guideline cases.

Property crimes are handled in the USSC guidelines in a similar manner. The base level is increased with the amount of property involved. With larceny, embezzlement, and other forms of theft, for instance, the Base Offense Level is 6 in cases where the loss to the victim is $5,000 or less. If the loss is greater than $5,000 but less than $10,000, the level rises to 8 and continues to rise as the amount of the loss rises. If the loss is more than $200,000 but less than $400,000, the level is 18. If the loss is greater than $100 million, the level is 32—which will result in a mandatory sentence of at least ten years in prison for a first-time offender. A person who earned the maximum days for good behavior could expect to be out in eight years and six months if he or she received the minimum sentence. Fines and restitution of stolen money or property would be required in addition.

### "Departures" from the Guidelines

Application of the Federal Sentencing Guidelines has increased the likelihood of imprisonment and the average length of sentences, according to the USSC's *Fifteen Years of Guidelines Sentencing*. In 2002 some 86% of all federal offenders were sentenced to prison, an increase from 69% in 1987. The average sentence in 2002 was almost twice as long as in 1984, but there were yearly variations during this period. Based on data published in the *Sourcebook of Criminal Justice Statistics, 2002* (Bureau of Justice Statistics, 2004), the average sentence imposed in 1990 was 59.2 months, excluding life sentences. The average length peaked at 66.4 months in 1995 and then declined to 46.9 months in 2002. This is

TABLE 9.2

**Federal sentencing table, 2004**

[In months of imprisonment]

| Offense level | Criminal history category (criminal history points) | | | | | |
|---|---|---|---|---|---|---|
| | I (0 or 1) | II (2 or 3) | III (4, 5, 6) | IV (7, 8, 9) | V (10, 11, 12) | VI (13 or more) |
| 1 | 0–6 | 0–6 | 0–6 | 0–6 | 0–6 | 0–6 |
| 2 | 0–6 | 0–6 | 0–6 | 0–6 | 0–6 | 1–7 |
| 3 | 0–6 | 0–6 | 0–6 | 0–6 | 2–8 | 3–9 |
| 4 | 0–6 | 0–6 | 0–6 | 2–8 | 4–10 | 6–12 |
| 5 | 0–6 | 0–6 | 1–7 | 4–10 | 6–12 | 9–15 |
| 6 | 0–6 | 1–7 | 2–8 | 6–12 | 9–15 | 12–18 |
| 7 | 0–6 | 2–8 | 4–10 | 8–14 | 12–18 | 15–21 |
| 8 | 0–6 | 4–10 | 6–12 | 10–16 | 15–21 | 18–24 |
| 9 | 4–10 | 6–12 | 8–14 | 12–18 | 18–24 | 21–27 |
| 10 | 6–12 | 8–14 | 10–16 | 15–21 | 21–27 | 24–30 |
| 11 | 8–14 | 10–16 | 12–18 | 18–24 | 24–30 | 27–33 |
| 12 | 10–16 | 12–18 | 15–21 | 21–27 | 27–33 | 30–37 |
| 13 | 12–18 | 15–21 | 18–24 | 24–30 | 30–37 | 33–41 |
| 14 | 15–21 | 18–24 | 21–27 | 27–33 | 33–41 | 37–46 |
| 15 | 18–24 | 21–27 | 24–30 | 30–37 | 37–46 | 41–51 |
| 16 | 21–27 | 24–30 | 27–33 | 33–41 | 41–51 | 46–57 |
| 17 | 24–30 | 27–33 | 30–37 | 37–46 | 46–57 | 51–63 |
| 18 | 27–33 | 30–37 | 33–41 | 41–51 | 51–63 | 57–71 |
| 19 | 30–37 | 33–41 | 37–46 | 46–57 | 57–71 | 63–78 |
| 20 | 33–41 | 37–46 | 41–51 | 51–63 | 63–78 | 70–87 |
| 21 | 37–46 | 41–51 | 46–57 | 57–71 | 70–87 | 77–96 |
| 22 | 41–51 | 46–57 | 51–63 | 63–78 | 77–96 | 84–105 |
| 23 | 46–57 | 51–63 | 57–71 | 70–87 | 84–105 | 92–115 |
| 24 | 51–63 | 57–71 | 63–78 | 77–96 | 92–115 | 100–125 |
| 25 | 57–71 | 63–78 | 70–87 | 84–105 | 100–125 | 110–137 |
| 26 | 63–78 | 70–87 | 78–97 | 92–115 | 110–137 | 120–150 |
| 27 | 70–87 | 78–97 | 87–108 | 100–125 | 120–150 | 130–162 |
| 28 | 78–97 | 87–108 | 97–121 | 110–137 | 130–162 | 140–175 |
| 29 | 87–108 | 97–121 | 108–135 | 121–151 | 140–175 | 151–188 |
| 30 | 97–121 | 108–135 | 121–151 | 135–168 | 151–188 | 168–210 |
| 31 | 108–135 | 121–151 | 135–168 | 151–188 | 168–210 | 188–235 |
| 32 | 121–151 | 135–168 | 151–188 | 168–210 | 188–235 | 210–262 |
| 33 | 135–168 | 151–188 | 168–210 | 188–235 | 210–262 | 235–293 |
| 34 | 151–188 | 168–210 | 188–235 | 210–262 | 235–293 | 262–327 |
| 35 | 168–210 | 188–235 | 210–262 | 235–293 | 262–327 | 292–365 |
| 36 | 188–235 | 210–262 | 235–293 | 262–327 | 292–365 | 324–405 |
| 37 | 210–262 | 235–293 | 262–327 | 292–365 | 324–405 | 360–life |
| 38 | 235–293 | 262–327 | 292–365 | 324–405 | 360–life | 360–life |
| 39 | 262–327 | 292–365 | 324–405 | 360–life | 360–life | 360–life |
| 40 | 292–365 | 324–405 | 360–life | 360–life | 360–life | 360–life |
| 41 | 324–405 | 360–life | 360–life | 360–life | 360–life | 360–life |
| 42 | 360–life | 360–life | 360–life | 360–life | 360–life | 360–life |
| 43 | life | life | life | life | life | life |

zone A (offense levels 1–8)
zone B (offense levels 9–10)
zone C (offense levels 11–12)
zone D (offense levels 13–43)

Note: Zones indicate whether or not the individual is eligible for probation. Terms that fall into Zone A are eligible for straight probation. Terms that fall into Zone B are eligible for a split sentence in which a portion of the sentence is served in prison, a portion under probation. The person may receive less than the minimum sentence but must serve the remaining time under probation, intermittent confinement, community confinement, or home detention. Terms that fall into Zone C are eligible for probation, but at least half of the guideline sentence must be served in prison. Terms that fall into Zone D require that the minimum term must be served in prison. The criminal history columns refer to prior offenses. Under Category II, for instance, the person to be sentenced has had 2 or 3 prior convictions. This note is not part of the official Sentencing Table; it has been adapted from Lucien B. Cambell and Henry J. Bemporad, *An Introduction to Federal Guideline Sentencing*, United States Sentencing Commission, Washington, DC, March 2003.

SOURCE: "Sentencing Table," in *2004 Federal Sentencing Guidelines Manual*, U.S. Sentencing Commission, November 2004, http://www.ussc.gov/2004guid/5a .htm (accessed March 31, 2005)

due, in part, to stipulations in the guidelines for so-called "departures" from the guidelines' own provisions. Departures may be "upward" for cases where special circumstances merit longer incarceration than the guideline provides for the maximum sentence; "downward" departures authorize lesser than guideline sentences either for extenuating circumstances or because the defendant provided "substantial assistance" to federal authorities, typically in the form of helping a broader investigation or providing testimony against other suspects.

The 2002 *Sourcebook of Federal Sentencing Statistics* (Washington, DC: U.S. Sentencing Commission, 2003) reported that in 2002 only 65% of sentences rendered by federal courts were within the range of the guidelines; 0.8% of sentences were upward departures and 34.2% were downward departures, slightly more than half of those for "substantial assistance." (See Table 9.3.)

Departures mean that the guidelines are applied to a majority but not to all persons charged with federal

**TABLE 9.3**

**Sentences within and departing from U.S. Sentencing Commission guidelines, fiscal year 2002**

[Prior to enactment of the Protect Act]

| Primary offense | Total | Sentenced within range | | Substantial assistance departure | | Other downward departure | | Upward departure | |
|---|---|---|---|---|---|---|---|---|---|
| | | Number | Percent | Number | Percent | Number | Percent | Number | Percent |
| **Total** | **58,423** | **37,968** | **65.0** | **10,170** | **17.4** | **9,828** | **16.8** | **457** | **0.8** |
| Murder | 76 | 50 | 65.8 | 4 | 5.3 | 9 | 11.8 | 13 | 17.1 |
| Manslaughter | 57 | 37 | 64.9 | 1 | 1.8 | 6 | 10.5 | 13 | 22.8 |
| Kidnapping/hostage-taking | 57 | 33 | 57.9 | 4 | 7.0 | 12 | 21.1 | 8 | 14.0 |
| Sexual abuse | 195 | 142 | 72.8 | 2 | 1.0 | 37 | 19.0 | 14 | 7.2 |
| Assault | 445 | 347 | 78.0 | 12 | 2.7 | 70 | 15.7 | 16 | 3.6 |
| Robbery | 1,522 | 1,051 | 69.1 | 227 | 14.9 | 220 | 14.5 | 24 | 1.6 |
| Arson | 59 | 38 | 64.4 | 14 | 23.7 | 4 | 6.8 | 3 | 5.1 |
| Drugs—trafficking | 23,949 | 13,398 | 55.9 | 6,565 | 27.4 | 3,932 | 16.4 | 54 | 0.2 |
| Drugs—communication facility | 421 | 303 | 72.0 | 56 | 13.3 | 61 | 14.5 | 1 | 0.2 |
| Drugs—simple possession | 481 | 458 | 95.2 | 17 | 3.5 | 4 | 0.8 | 2 | 0.4 |
| Firearms | 4,765 | 3,511 | 73.7 | 581 | 12.2 | 602 | 12.6 | 71 | 1.5 |
| Burglary/breaking and entering | 42 | 30 | 71.4 | 5 | 11.9 | 4 | 9.5 | 3 | 7.1 |
| Auto theft | 151 | 93 | 61.6 | 41 | 27.2 | 14 | 9.3 | 3 | 2.0 |
| Larceny | 2,038 | 1,745 | 85.6 | 151 | 7.4 | 126 | 6.2 | 16 | 0.8 |
| Fraud | 6,378 | 4,539 | 71.2 | 1,135 | 17.8 | 633 | 9.9 | 71 | 1.1 |
| Embezzlement | 672 | 588 | 87.5 | 24 | 3.6 | 58 | 8.6 | 2 | 0.3 |
| Forgery/counterfeiting | 1,363 | 1,094 | 80.3 | 159 | 11.7 | 97 | 7.1 | 13 | 1.0 |
| Bribery | 148 | 87 | 58.8 | 41 | 27.7 | 20 | 13.5 | 0 | 0.0 |
| Tax | 557 | 352 | 63.2 | 107 | 19.2 | 95 | 17.1 | 3 | 0.5 |
| Money laundering | 852 | 496 | 58.2 | 245 | 28.8 | 101 | 11.9 | 10 | 1.2 |
| Racketeering/extortion | 744 | 474 | 63.7 | 178 | 23.9 | 75 | 10.1 | 17 | 2.3 |
| Gambling/lottery | 95 | 57 | 60.0 | 27 | 28.4 | 11 | 11.6 | 0 | 0.0 |
| Civil rights | 87 | 60 | 69.0 | 16 | 18.4 | 11 | 12.6 | 0 | 0.0 |
| Immigration | 10,399 | 6,861 | 66.0 | 248 | 2.4 | 3,236 | 31.1 | 54 | 0.5 |
| Pornography/prostitution | 613 | 442 | 72.1 | 34 | 5.5 | 117 | 19.1 | 20 | 3.3 |
| Prison offenses | 297 | 229 | 77.1 | 19 | 6.4 | 46 | 15.5 | 3 | 1.0 |
| Administration of Justice offenses | 1,010 | 719 | 71.2 | 144 | 14.3 | 134 | 13.3 | 13 | 1.3 |
| Environmental/wildlife | 121 | 76 | 62.8 | 25 | 20.7 | 20 | 16.5 | 0 | 0.0 |
| National defense | 9 | 6 | 66.7 | 1 | 11.1 | 2 | 22.2 | 0 | 0.0 |
| Antitrust | 16 | 5 | 31.3 | 9 | 56.3 | 2 | 12.5 | 0 | 0.0 |
| Food & drug | 77 | 55 | 71.4 | 10 | 13.0 | 11 | 14.3 | 1 | 1.3 |
| Other miscellaneous offenses | 727 | 592 | 81.4 | 68 | 9.4 | 58 | 8.0 | 9 | 1.2 |

Note: Of the 64,366 cases, 5,943 were excluded due to one or both of the following reasons: missing primary offense (393) or missing/inapplicable departure information (5,682).

SOURCE: "Table 27. Offenders Receiving Departures in Each Primary Offense Category, Fiscal Year 2002," in *2002 Sourcebook of Federal Sentencing Statistics*, U.S. Sentencing Commission, 2003, http://www.ussc.gov/ANNRPT/2002/table27.pdf (accessed March 31, 2005).

offenses—and also variably by category of offense. In 2002 the two highest categories under guidelines were simple possession of drugs (95.2% under guideline) and embezzlement (87.5%). The lowest category by far was related to antitrust violations (31.3%). Those charged with antitrust violations were most likely to get lower sentences for cooperating with prosecutors; those charged with manslaughter were the most likely to get higher than guideline sentences for unusual violence.

### Blakely v. Washington and United States v. Booker

U.S. Supreme Court decisions in 2004 and 2005 have modified sentencing guidelines. In 2004 the Supreme Court ruled in *Blakely v. Washington* that a state judge cannot impose a longer sentence when the basis for such an enhanced sentence was neither admitted to by the subject nor found by a jury. In the Blakely case the subject admitted to kidnapping his estranged wife. The maximum sentence for the crime was fifty-three months in prison, but the judge imposed a sentence of ninety months after determining that the subject had acted with deliberate cruelty, a factor that under existing statutes allowed a longer sentence. However, the charge of deliberate cruelty had not been part of the subject's plea, and it had not been determined by a jury. The Supreme Court found that the Sixth Amendment right to a trial by jury had thus been violated. The Blakely ruling means that only facts proved to a jury can justify an enhanced sentence.

A related ruling occurred in January 2005 with *United States v. Booker*. In this case the subject had been charged with possession with intent to distribute 50 grams of crack cocaine, a crime for which the federal sentencing guidelines set a twenty-one-year, ten-month sentence. But the judge later determined that the subject had possessed 92 grams of crack cocaine and had obstructed justice as well. Because of these additional offenses, the judge sentenced Booker to thirty years in prison. In language similar to the Blakely ruling, the U.S. Supreme Court ruled that federal judges cannot determine facts that are used to increase a defendant's punishment beyond what is authorized by a jury verdict or the defendant's own admissions. In addition, the court ruled that federal sentencing guidelines should be considered, but judges are not required to follow them. The legal impact of these two decisions is still being worked out in the courts.

## STATE SENTENCES AND TIME SERVED

The adoption of truth-in-sentencing statutes appears to have resulted, at the state level, in a decrease in the *length* of sentences imposed but an increase in the total *time served*, including percent of the sentence imposed actually being spent in prison.

Average sentence lengths can decline while time served can stay the same or increase if mandatory time

**TABLE 9.4**

**Average felony sentence lengths in state courts, by offense and type of sentence, 2002**

| Most serious conviction offense | Maximum sentence length (in months) for felons sentenced to — | | | |
| --- | --- | --- | --- | --- |
| | Incarceration | | | |
| | Total | Prison | Jail | Probation |
| Mean | | | | |
| **All offenses** | 36 mo | 53 mo | 7 mo | 38 mo |
| **Violent offenses** | 62 mo | 84 mo | 8 mo | 43 mo |
| Murder[a] | 217 | 225 | 10 | 76 |
| Sexual assault[b] | 78 | 100 | 8 | 54 |
| Rape | 104 | 132 | 9 | 65 |
| Other sexual assault | 65 | 84 | 8 | 51 |
| Robbery | 79 | 91 | 11 | 52 |
| Aggravated assault | 37 | 54 | 7 | 39 |
| Other violent[c] | 33 | 51 | 8 | 37 |
| **Property offenses** | 28 mo | 41 mo | 7 mo | 37 mo |
| Burglary | 36 | 50 | 7 | 40 |
| Larceny[d] | 22 | 34 | 6 | 36 |
| Motor vehicle theft | 18 | 30 | 6 | 33 |
| Fraud[e] | 24 | 38 | 6 | 36 |
| **Drug offenses** | 32 mo | 48 mo | 6 mo | 36 mo |
| Possession | 22 | 35 | 5 | 33 |
| Trafficking | 38 | 55 | 7 | 39 |
| **Weapon offenses** | 28 mo | 38 mo | 7 mo | 35 mo |
| **Other offenses[f]** | 23 mo | 38 mo | 6 mo | 37 mo |

Note: For persons receiving a combination of sentences, the sentence designation came from the most severe penalty imposed prison being the most severe, followed by jail, then probation. Prison includes death sentences. Felons receiving a sentence other than incarceration or probation are classified under "probation." Means exclude sentences to death or to life in prison. This table is based on an estimated 945,167 cases.
[a]Includes nonnegligent manslaughter.
[b]Includes rape.
[c]Includes offenses such as negligent manslaughter and kidnapping.
[d]Includes motor vehicle theft.
[e]Includes forgery and embezzlement.
[f]Composed of nonviolent offenses such as receiving stolen property and vandalism.

SOURCE: Matthew R. Durose and Patrick A. Langan, Table 3. "Average Felony Sentence Lengths in State Courts, by Offense and Type of Sentence, 2002," in *Felony Sentences in State Courts, 2002*, Bureau of Justice Statistics, December 2004, http://www.ojp.usdoj.gov/bjs/pub/pdf/fssc02.pdf (accessed March 31, 2005)

in prison, as a percent of the sentence, increases. Thus, for instance, a person sentenced to five years serving 60% of his sentence serves as long as a person sentenced to four years who serves 75% of her sentence. In both cases time served will be three years.

Data in Table 9.4, the most recent comprehensive statistical measurement available, show that sentence lengths in 2002 were down almost uniformly from earlier years. Average length of sentence for all offenses was thirty-six months in 2002, down from sixty-nine months in 1990. During the same period, the average sentence for rape dropped from 128 months to 104 months and for robbery from 104 months to seventy-nine months. Only for murder (209 months in 1990 to 217 months in 2002) did the sentence increase in length. The percent of sentence actually served, however, rose during this time. According to *Felony Sentences in State Courts, 2002* (Bureau of Justice Statistics, December 2004), in 2002 convicted persons could expect to serve 51% of their sentences, up from 38% in 1990.

## THREE STRIKES, YOU'RE OUT

Nine years after passing the first truth-in-sentencing law, the State of Washington passed the first of the so-called "three-strikes" laws in December 1993. The measure took effect in the wake of a voter initiative, which passed by a three-to-one margin. Three-strikes laws are the functional equivalent of sentencing guidelines in that they mandate a fixed length of sentence for repeat offenders for specified crimes or a mix of crimes—but their formulation in public debate, using the baseball analogy, is much easier to understand than the complexities of thick books of codes and sentencing tables. Under three-strikes laws, the offender receives a mandatory sentence upon conviction to the third offense—life imprisonment without parole (the case in Washington state), twenty-five years without parole (as in California), or some variant of a long sentence. The purpose behind such laws is to remove the criminal from society for a long period of time or in some instances, for life. Such criminals have been convicted repeatedly of serious offenses or felonies.

The Washington law identifies specific offenses that are "strikable." California, which passed its own (and more famous) three-strikes law just months after Washington passed its measure, specifies the categories of offenses that must precede the third felony conviction. A convicted felon in California has his or her sentence doubled if there is a prior serious or violent felony conviction on his record. The convict receives a 25-year-to-life sentence if convicted of a third felony if the previous two convictions were for serious or

**TABLE 9.5**

**Comparison of Washington and California three-strikes laws**

| Type | Washington | California |
|---|---|---|
| Homicide | Murder 1 or 2<br>Controlled substance homicide<br>Homicide by abuse<br>Manslaughter 1 or 2 | Murder |
| Sexual offenses | Rape 1 or 2<br>Child molestation<br>Incest of child<br><br>Sexual exploitation | Rape<br>Lewd act on child<br>Continual sexual abuse of<br>  child<br>Penetration by foreign object<br>Sexual penetration by force<br>Sodomy by force<br>Oral copulation by force |
| Robbery<br>Felony assault | Robbery 1 or 2<br>Attempt murder<br>Assault 1 or 2 | Robbery<br>Attempt murder<br>Assault with a deadly weapon<br>  on a peace officer<br>Assault with a deadly weapon<br>  by an inmate<br>Assault with intent to rape or<br>  rob |
| Other crimes<br>  against persons | Explosion with threats to<br>  humans<br>Extortion<br>Kidnapping 1 or 2<br>Vehicular assault | Any felony resulting in bodily<br>  harm<br>Arson causing bodily injury<br>Carjacking<br>Exploding device with intent<br>  to injure<br>Exploding device with intent<br>  to murder<br>Kidnapping<br>Mayhem |
| Property crimes | Arson 1<br>Attempt arson1<br>Burglary | Arson<br>Burglary of occupied dwelling<br>Grand theft with firearm |
| **Drug offenses** | | Drug sales to minors |
| Weapons offenses | Any felony with deadly weapon<br>Possession of incendiary device<br>Possession of prohibited<br>  explosive<br>  device | Any felony with deadly weapon<br>Any felony where firearm used |
| Other | Treason<br>Promoting prostitution<br>Leading organized crime | |

SOURCE: John Clark, James Austin, and D. Alan Henry, "Exhibit 1. Comparison of Washington and California Strikes Laws," in *"Three Strikes and You're Out": A Review of State Legislation*, National Institute of Justice, September 1997, http://www.ncjrs.org/pdffiles/165369.pdf (accessed April 3, 2005)

violent felony offenses. All persons convicted under the California Three Strikes law must serve 80% of their sentence before they are eligible for parole. Table 9.5 compares the three-strikes laws in Washington and California.

## Strike Zone

A strike zone refers to the crimes that constitute a strike and under what conditions those crimes become a strike. A strike generally is a serious offense, such as a violent felony, including murder, rape, robbery, arson, aggravated assault, and carjacking. The strike zone is intended to deter offenders convicted repeatedly of such crimes.

## States with Three-Strike Laws

As of 2004, twenty-three states had three-strike laws. California had used the law to jail far more offenders (42,322) than any other state. Georgia was next with 7,631, followed by Florida (1,628) and Maryland (330). (See Table 9.6.)

California's law is unique in that the third offense may be any felony or even a misdemeanor. This is possible because certain classes of offenses are known under California law as "wobblers." Depending on the circumstances of the offense and the history of the offender, some offenses may be prosecuted as misdemeanors or as felonies. In virtually all other states with three-strikes laws, all three offenses must be violent crimes—murder, rape, robbery, arson, aggravated assault, and vehicular assault. In some states other crimes are also specified. These include the sale of drugs (Indiana), drug offenses punishable by five years or more of incarceration (Louisiana), escape from prison (Florida), treason (Washington), and embezzlement and bribery (South Carolina). California includes the sale of drugs to minors as one of the crimes that qualify as strike one or strike two offenses.

The differences between the crime rates for those states with three-strike laws and those without them are listed in Table 9.7. In the period 1993 to 2002, three-strike states overall had a reduction in crime of 26.8%, while those states without three-strike laws had a reduction in crime of 22.3%. California faired best among the three-strike states, with a drop in crime of 38.8%. Among states without three-strike laws, New York saw a drop in crime of 49.6%.

## Tightening Preexisting Statutes

In all but one of the states with three-strikes statutes (Kansas is the exception), legislation was already on the books when the popularity of three-strikes laws caused half the states—and the Federal Government as well (in 1995)—to enact laws pioneered on the West Coast. California, for instance, had a law on its books that was very similar to those that were later passed *as* three-strikes statutes in other states. As reported by the NIJ, California required, pre-three-strikes:

> Life with no parole eligibility before twenty years for third violent felony conviction where separate prison terms were served for the first two convictions; life without parole for fourth violent felony convictions.
> — *'Three Strikes and You're Out': A Review of State Legislation* (Washington, DC: National Institute of Justice, 1997)

California's statute, therefore, represented a *tightening* of existing law and a modification of it so that the triggering offense for life imprisonment was the *third* felony—which did not have to be violent.

**TABLE 9.6**

## States with three-strike laws

| State | Strike zone defined | Strikes needed to "strike out" | Meaning of "striking out" | Number of people in prison under three strikes |
|---|---|---|---|---|
| Arkansas | Murder, kidnapping, robbery, rape, terrorist act. | Two | Not less than 40 years in prison; no parole. | 5 |
| | First degree battery, firing a gun from a vehicle, use of a prohibited weapon, conspiracy to commit: murder; kidnapping; robbery; rape; first degree battery; first degree sexual abuse. | Three | Range of no parole sentences, depending on the offense. | |
| California | Any felony if one prior felony conviction from a list of 'strikeable' offenses' | Two | Mandatory sentence of twice the term for the offense involved. | 42,322 |
| | Any felony if two prior felony convictions from list of 'strikeable' offenses. | Three | Mandatory indeterminate life sentence, with no parole eligibility for 25 years. | 4 |
| Colorado | Any Class 1 or 2 felony, or any Class 3 felony that is violent. | Three | Mandatory life in prison with no parole eligibility for 40 years. | 1 |
| Connecticut | Murder, attempt murder assault with intent to kill, manslaughter, arson, kidnapping aggravated sexual assault, robbery first degree assault. | Three | Up to life in prison. | |
| Florida | Any forcible felony aggravated stalking, aggravated child abuse, lewd or indecent conduct, escape. | Three | Life if third strike involved first degree felony, 30–40 years if second degree felony, 10–15 years if third degree felony. | 1,628 |
| Georgia | Murder, armed robbery, kidnapping, rape, aggravated child molesting, aggravated sodomy, aggravated sexual battery. | Two | Mandatory life without parole. | 7,631 |
| | Any felony. | Four | Mandatory maximum sentence for the charge. | |
| Indiana | Murder, rape, sexual battery with a weapon, child molesting, arson, robbery, burglary with a weapon or resulting in serious injury, drug dealing. | Three | Mandatory life without the possibility of parole. | 38 |
| Louisiana | Murder, attempted murder, manslaughter, rape, armed robbery, kidnapping, any drug offense punishable by more than five years, any felony punishable by more than 12 years. | Three | Mandatory life in prison with no parole eligibility. | N/A |
| | Any four felony convictions if at least one was on the above list. | Four | Mandatory life in prison with no parole eligibility. | |
| Maryland | Murder, rape, robbery, first or second degree sexual offense, arson, burglary, kidnapping, car jacking, manslaughter, use of a firearm in felony, assault with intent to murder, rape, rob, or commit sexual offense. | Four, with separate prison terms served for first three strikes. | Mandatory life in prison with no parole eligibility. | 330 (approximately) |
| Montana | Deliberate homicide, aggravated kidnapping, sexual intercourse without consent, ritual abuse of a minor. | Two | Mandatory life in prison with no parole eligibility. | 0 |
| | Mitigated deliberate homicide, aggravated assault, kidnapping, robbery. | Three | Mandatory life in prison with no parole eligibility. | |
| Nevada | Murder, robbery, kidnapping, battery, abuse of children, arson, home invasion. | Three | Life without parole: with parole possible after 10 years; or 25 years with parole possible after 10 years. | 304 |
| New Jersey | Murder, robbery, carjacking. | Three | Mandatory life in prison with no parole eligibility. | 10 |
| New Mexico | Murder, shooting at or from a vehicle and causing harm, kidnapping, criminal sexual penetration, armed robbery resulting in harm. | Three | Mandatory life in prison with parole eligibility after 30 years. | 0 |
| North Carolina | 47 violent felonies; separate indictment required finding that offender is "violent habitual offender." | Three | Mandatory life in prison with no parole eligibility. | 22 |
| North Dakota | Any Class A, B, or C felony. | Two | If second strike was for Class A felony, court may impose an extended sentence of up to life; if Class B felony, up to 20 years; If Class C felony, up to 10 years. | 10 |
| Pennsylvania | Murder, voluntary manslaughter, rape, involuntary deviate sexual intercourse, arson, kidnapping, robbery, aggravated assault. | Two | Enhanced sentence of up to 10 years. | 50 (approximately) |
| | Same offenses. | Three | Enhanced sentence of up to 25 years. | |
| South Carolina | Murder, voluntary manslaughter, homicide by child abuse, rape, kidnapping, armed robbery, drug trafficking, embezzlement, bribery, certain accessory and attempt offenses. | Two | Mandatory life in prison with no parole eligibility. | 14 |
| Tennessee | Murder, especially aggravated kidnapping, especially aggravated robbery, aggravated rape, rape of a child, aggravated arson. | Two, if prison term served from first strike. | Mandatory life in prison with no parole eligibility. | 14 |
| | Same as above, plus rape, and aggravated sexual battery. | Three, if separate prison terms served. | Mandatory life in prison with no parole eligibility for first two strikes. | |

Much the same pattern, with variations, characterized the introduction of three-strikes laws in other states. In Louisiana before it enacted a "Three Strikes Law," a mandatory life term was required for the *fourth* felony conviction if two previous convictions had been violent or drug offenses. The new law imposed the sentence after the *third* offense. In Tennessee the preexisting law was mandatory life without parole for the third violent felony

**TABLE 9.6**

**States with three-strike laws** [CONTINUED]

| State | Strike zone defined | Strikes needed to "strike out" | Meaning of "striking out" | Number of people in prison under three strikes |
|---|---|---|---|---|
| Utah | N/A | Three | Ranges from additional three years to life without parole, with judicial discretion. | N/A |
| Vermont | Murder, manslaughter, arson causing death, assault and robbery with weapon or causing bodily injury, aggravated assault, kidnapping, maiming, aggravated sexual assault, aggravated domestic assault, lewd conduct with child. | Three | Court may sentence up to life in prison. | 16 |
| Virginia | Murder, kidnapping, robbery, car jacking, sexual assault, conspiracy to commit any of above. | Three | Mandatory life in prison with no parole eligibility. | 328 |
| Washington | Charges listed in source detail. | Three | | 209 |
| Wisconsin | Murder, manslaughter, vehicular homicide, aggravated battery, abuse of children, robbery, sexual assault, taking hostages, kidnapping, arson, burglary. | Three | Mandatory life in prison with no parole eligibility. Mandatory life in prison with no parole eligibility. | 9 |

SOURCE: Vincent Schiraldi, Jason Colburn, and Eric Lotke, "Appendix A, Table 1. States with Three-Strike Laws," in *Three Strikes and You're Out: An Examination of the Impact of 3-Strike Laws Ten Years after Their Enactment*, Justice Policy Institute, 2004, http://www.justicepolicy.org/downloads/JPIOUTOFSTEPREPORTFNL.doc (accessed March 31, 2005)

conviction. Tennessee's new law imposed the same requirement for the *second* violent felony. In Vermont, also, a "four-strikes" law was modified and made into a three-strikes law as in Louisiana. In some states the tightening was more stringent. Thus in New Mexico, the preexisting law imposed an increased sentence of one year for the second, an increase of four years for the third, and an add-on of eight years for the fourth felony. The new law imposed a life sentence after the third violent felony but permitted parole after thirty years.

## Impact and Effectiveness

In *Impacts of Three Strikes and Truth in Sentencing on the Volume and Composition of Correctional Populations* (Rockville, MD: National Institute of Justice, 2000), E. Chen states: "This study of Three Strikes and You're Out ... and Truth in Sentencing ... laws found in general [that] they had only a few short term impacts on the dynamics of prison populations in all States except Washington and for one variable in California." The impact of three strikes in Washington indicates "some reductions in the growth of parole entries and exits associated with three strikes laws." In California, three-strikes laws and truth-in-sentencing combined to increase the percentage of prisoners older than fifty years. The author attributes the absence of effects for three-strikes laws elsewhere to their minimal use in other states.

More significant effects were reported for California in the U.S. Supreme Court's judgment in the case of *Ewing v. California*, authored by Justice Sandra Day O'Connor (538 U.S., 2003). Citing a statement issued by the Office of the Attorney General, California Department of Justice, *"Three Strikes and You're Out"—Its Impact on the California Criminal Justice System after Four Years*, 1998, the Justice wrote: "Four years after the passage of California's three strikes law, the recidivism rate of parolees returned to prison for the commission of a new crime dropped by nearly 25%." She continued to cite from the statement as follows:

> [a]n unintended but positive consequence of "Three Strikes" has been the impact on parolees leaving the state. More California parolees are now leaving the state than parolees from other jurisdictions entering California. This striking turnaround started in 1994. It was the first time more parolees left the state than entered since 1976. This trend has continued and in 1997 more than 1,000 net parolees left California.

The statement suggests that a three-strikes law with severe penalties, energetically enforced, appears at least to cause the net export of offenders to other jurisdictions.

Another examination of three-strikes laws, written by Eric Lotke, Jason Colburn, and Vincent Schiraldi, was published in 2004 by the Justice Policy Institute. *Three Strikes and You're Out: An Examination of the Impact of Three-Strike Laws Ten Years after Their Enactment* (Washington, DC: Justice Policy Institute, 2004) judged the decrease in crime in three-strike states (down 26.8%) to be not significantly different from that found in states without three-strike laws (down 22.3%). In the areas of violent crime and homicide, states without three-strikes laws performed marginally better than did those with such laws. "Considering that Three Strikes was a movement largely targeted at violent recalcitrant criminals, with promises of great impact," the Justice Policy Institute report pointed out, "these findings are disappointing ten years after most strikes laws were enacted."

TABLE 9.7

**Change in crime rate per population in strike and nonstrike states, by state, 1993–2002**

| States | Crime index | Violent crime | Property crime | Homicide |
|---|---|---|---|---|
| Arkansas | −13.5% | −28.4% | −11.4% | −48.5% |
| California | −38.8% | −44.9% | −37.6% | −48.0% |
| Colorado | −21.3% | −37.9% | −19.5% | −31.3% |
| Connecticut | −35.6% | −31.9% | −36.0% | −63.3% |
| Florida | −34.8% | −35.9% | −34.7% | −38.9% |
| Georgia | −27.3% | −36.6% | −26.1% | −38.0% |
| Indiana | −16.1% | −27.1% | −14.8% | −22.0% |
| Louisiana | −25.6% | −37.7% | −23.4% | −35.1% |
| Maryland | −22.5% | −23.1% | −22.4% | −26.0% |
| Montana | −26.7% | −98.1% | −31.5% | −41.0% |
| Nevada | −27.5% | −27.4% | −27.5% | −20.0% |
| New Jersey | −36.9% | −40.2% | −36.4% | −26.4% |
| New Mexico | −18.9% | −20.4% | −18.6% | 2.0% |
| North Carolina | −16.3% | −30.6% | −14.3% | −41.6% |
| North Dakota | −14.4% | −4.5% | −14.7% | −54.3% |
| Pennsylvania | −13.3% | −3.9% | −14.7% | −26.1% |
| South Carolina | −10.4% | −19.8% | −8.4% | −30.0% |
| Tennessee | −4.3% | −6.5% | −4.0% | −29.2% |
| Utah | −14.4% | −20.7% | −14.0% | −34.4% |
| Vermont | −36.5% | −6.9% | −37.4% | −42.4% |
| Virginia | −23.9% | −22.0% | −24.1% | −36.1% |
| Washington | −14.3% | −32.9% | −12.5% | −41.3% |
| Wisconsin | −19.5% | −14.6% | −19.8% | −35.5% |
| **Three-strikes total** | **−26.8%** | **−33.0%** | **−25.9%** | **−38.2%** |
| **Non-strike states** | | | | |
| Alabama | −8.2% | −42.9% | −1.6% | −41.4% |
| Alaska | −22.6% | −25.9% | −22.1% | −43.1% |
| Arizona | −12.6% | −21.3% | −11.6% | −16.2% |
| Delaware | −19.1% | −12.6% | −20.1% | −35.5% |
| Hawaii | −4.3% | −0.2% | −4.4% | −50.1% |
| Idaho | −17.5% | −9.5% | −18.1% | −7.8% |
| Illinois | −28.3% | −35.1% | −26.8% | −33.6% |
| Iowa | −15.3% | −21.8% | −14.6% | −53.5% |
| Kansas | −12.1% | −14.0% | −11.9% | −37.4% |
| Kentucky | −10.8% | −39.6% | −6.0% | −31.5% |
| Maine | −15.9% | −14.3% | −15.9% | −33.1% |
| Massachusetts | −36.7% | −39.8% | −36.1% | −30.5% |
| Michigan | −28.5% | −31.3% | −28.0% | −31.1% |
| Minnesota | −19.4% | −18.2% | −19.5% | −35.0% |
| Mississippi | −6.0% | −21.0% | −4.3% | −32.0% |
| Missouri | −9.6% | −27.5% | −6.5% | −48.2% |
| Nebraska | 3.8% | −7.1% | 4.8% | −28.9% |
| New Hampshire | −23.7% | 16.8% | −25.8% | −54.1% |
| New York | −49.6% | −53.9% | −48.6% | −64.4% |
| Ohio | −8.5% | −30.4% | −5.7% | −23.5% |
| Oklahoma | −10.4% | −20.7% | −9.0% | −44.8% |
| Oregon | −15.5% | −41.8% | −12.9% | −55.7% |
| Rhode Island | −20.3% | −29.1% | −19.4% | −1.8% |
| South Dakota | −22.8% | −14.7% | −23.4% | −56.8% |
| Texas | −19.4% | −24.1% | −18.8% | −49.8% |
| West Virginia | −1.1% | 12.0% | −2.2% | −54.5% |
| Wyoming | −14.2% | −4.6% | −14.9% | −11.9% |
| **Non Strike Total** | **−22.3%** | **−34.3%** | **−20.4%** | **−43.9%** |

SOURCE: Vincent Schiraldi, Jason Colburn, and Eric Lotke, "Appendix B, Table II. Change in Crime Rate per Population in Strike and Nonstrike States, by State, 1993–2002," in *Three Strikes and You're Out: An Examination of the Impact of 3-Strike Laws Ten Years after Their Enactment*, Justice Policy Institute, 2004, http://www.justicepolicy.org/downloads/JPIOUTOFSTEPREPORTFNL.doc (accessed March 31, 2005).

## Constitutional Test

California's statute, the most stringent, was upheld by the U.S. Supreme Court in *Ewing v. California* on March 5, 2003. The case involved Gary Ewing, who was on parole from a nine-year prison term when he stole three golf clubs from a pro shop in El Segundo, California. He had hidden the clubs in his trousers and consequently walked a little strangely as he left. An employee of the shop called the police after seeing Ewing limp out. The police arrested Ewing in the parking lot outside. Each of the stolen clubs was worth $399. Ewing had a long record of offenses going back to 1982. He had been sentenced for theft and given a suspended sentence. A series of offenses followed: grand theft auto (1988), petty theft (1990), battery and theft on separate occasions (1992), burglary (January 1993), possession of drug paraphernalia (February 1993), appropriating lost property (July 1993), unlawful firearms possession and trespassing (September 1993), and three burglaries and one robbery (October and November 1993). During the last of these episodes, he threatened a victim, claiming to have a gun. When the victim resisted, Ewing pulled a knife, forced the victim into an apartment, and rifled through the victim's bedroom. The victim managed to escape, raised the alarm, and Ewing fled with the victim's money and credit cards. He was arrested in December 1993 and sentenced to prison. He was released in 1999 on parole. Ten months after his release came his arrest for stealing the golf clubs. Ewing was sentenced under the three-strikes statute to twenty-five years to life. After the California Court of Appeals upheld his conviction, Ewing appealed to the U.S. Supreme Court claiming grossly disproportionate punishment under the Eighth Amendment's protection against cruel and unusual punishment.

The Supreme Court upheld Ewing's conviction, basing its ruling on an earlier case, *Harmelin v. Michigan* (501 U.S. 957, 996–997), which states in part that the "Eighth Amendment does not require strict proportionality between crime and sentence [but] forbids only extreme sentences that are 'grossly disproportionate' to the crime." The Court also affirmed the right of the state legislature to set policy for the purposes of protecting public safety, and, quoting from *Harmelin*, stated that "The Constitution 'does not mandate adoption of any one penological theory.'" The Court recognized that among the justifications for a sentence, alongside deterrence, retribution, and rehabilitation, incapacitation—making the offender incapable of preying on the public—could also be used.

Justice Stephen Breyer, joined by Justices John Paul Stevens, David Souter, and Ruth Bader Ginsburg, dissented. Justice Breyer, author of the dissenting opinion, held that Ewing's sentence had been disproportionate to the offense. Justice Breyer based himself on a similar 1983 case (*Solem v. Helm*, 463 U.S. 277) in which the Court ruled in the petitioner's favor. In *Solem* a recidivist offender (Jerry Helm) received a longer sentence (a life sentence) for a lesser crime (passing a bad check for $100). All of Helm's offenses were committed in South Carolina under laws that predated South Carolina's three-strikes law but nevertheless mandated life without parole for third offenses.

The Court's five to four decision in *Ewing* leaves open the possibility that, in some future case, the Supreme Court may look at California's three-strikes law again and reach a different decision. For the present, however, three-strikes laws have been upheld by the highest court in the United States.

## ALTERNATIVE SENTENCING

Forms of sentencing other than probation, prison, or a combination of the two (split sentences) also exist and are widely used in virtually every state. The most recent compilation of such approaches was published by the Bureau of Justice Statistics in 2000 in cooperation with the Conference of State Court Administrators (David B. Rottman, et al., *State Court Organization 1998*, Bureau of Justice Statistics, June 2000).

The BJS identified eleven forms of distinct alternative sentences, although some of these are functionally similar. With the exception of boot camps for young or adult offenders, they all provide offenders more freedom than incarceration but less freedom than ordinary probation. Alternative sentencing is, in part, a response to calls by penal reformers for, as suggested in *Americans behind Bars*, a "continuum of punishments with probation at one end, more severe community-based sanctions in the middle, and incarceration at the most restrictive end" (New York: Edna McConnell Clark Foundation, 1993) and in part a response to crowding in prisons. Thus, for instance, according to the Bureau of Justice Statistics, many states use halfway houses as a way of relieving crowding. Alternative sentencing is, of course, applied to offenders whose absence of prior criminal history or general characteristics indicate that they can be trusted not to abuse their greater freedom. Opponents, however, see prison sentencing as the only "real punishment" for criminals.

State departments of correction, the District of Columbia, and the Federal Bureau of Prisons offer a range of alternative sentencing options for criminal offenders. Although programs can vary among regions, those options include work release and weekend sentencing, shock incarceration (sometimes called boot camp), community service programs, day fines, day reporting centers, electronic monitoring and house arrest, residential community corrections, and diversionary treatment programs. There is also more variation in the availability of other types of alternative sentencing options, such as mediation and restitution.

In the article "The Effectiveness of Community-Based Sanctions in Reducing Recidivism" (*Corrections Today Magazine*, February 2003), Ginger Martin surveyed existing data from the state of Oregon concerning the recidivism rates for alternative forms of sentencing. Some 13,219 prisoners released from January 1999 to December 2001 were included in the study. Martin found that such options as community service programs, work release, and electronic monitoring were cheaper than incarceration and showed lower levels of recidivism after twelve months. The addition of a treatment component to the community-based option, such as a drug treatment program, produced a further 10% reduction in recidivism.

## Mediation and Restitution

Mediation began in Canada in 1974 and was later adopted in the United States, where more than twenty states were using mediation by the beginning of the twenty-first century. In mediation the victim and the offender meet under the auspices of a community worker and work out a "reconciliation" between them, usually involving some type of restitution and requiring offenders to take responsibility for their actions. This technique is used mainly for minor crimes and often involves private organizations; therefore, the judiciary does not always accept its resolution. Most often restitution is not considered the complete punishment but part of a wider punishment, such as probation or working off the restitution dollar amount while in prison.

## Work Release and Weekend Sentencing

Work-release programs permit selected prisoners nearing the end of their terms to work in the community, returning to prison facilities or community residential facilities during nonworking hours. Such programs are designed to prepare inmates to return to the community in a relatively controlled environment while they are learning how to work productively. Work release also allows inmates to earn income, reimburse the state for part of their confinement costs, build up savings for their eventual full release, and acquire more positive living habits. Those on weekend sentencing programs spend certain days in prison, usually weekends, but are free the remainder of the time. Both of these types of sentences are known as "intermittent incarceration." Violent offenders and those convicted of drug offenses are usually excluded from such programs by the courts. In Ohio and North Carolina, inmates can work in apprentice programs arranged with private industry to earn certification in such skilled trades as printing and construction.

Work-release programs seem to help prisoners once they return to society. In the study *Baltimore Prisoners' Experiences Returning Home* (Washington, DC: Urban Institute, March 2004), it was found that "those who found jobs after release were more likely to have participated in work release jobs while incarcerated than those who did not find jobs." A related Urban Institute publication, *Chicago Prisoners' Experiences Returning Home* (December 2004), revealed the same advantage of work release participation.

## Shock Incarceration (Boot Camps)

Shock incarceration is another name for reformatories or "boot camps" operated under military discipline for juveniles and adults. The name comes from William Whitelaw, British Home Secretary (1979–83), who called for a "short, sharp shock" that would end teenagers' criminal careers. Boot camps established in Great Britain attracted youths who liked the challenge, but the facilities did not lower the recidivism rate according to testimony presented to the British Parliament by corrections officials in February 2002 (http://www.parliament.the-stationery-office.co.uk/pa/cm200102/cmselect/cmpubacc/619/2021110.htm).

According to Alexander W. Pisciotta in *Benevolent Repression* (New York: New York University Press, 1994), the prototype of such a facility in the United States was established at the Elmira Reformatory in New York as far back as 1876. The first modern, correctional boot camp was established in Georgia in 1983. Faced with unprecedented overcrowding in its prisons and jails, Georgia was looking for alternatives to incarceration for adult offenders. Oklahoma began its program in 1984 and, by the end of 1988, fifteen programs were operating in nine states. The majority of programs started in the 1990s. By 1998, thirty-three correctional agencies (state and federal) operated forty-nine camps for adult inmates. Sentences are usually short (three to five months) and intended to be rehabilitative by instilling self-respect and discipline in the offender.

Boot camps are intended to be both punitive in their rigid discipline and rehabilitative in the self-esteem they claim to confer upon successful completion of the program. Shock incarceration is intended to motivate prisoners, teach respect for oneself and others, and break destructive cycles of behavior. Virtually all work on the assumption that a military regimen is beneficial.

The major selling points for boot camps have been saving money and reducing prison crowding. However, the major factor contributing to reduced costs and less overcrowding is that the boot camp programs are shorter in duration than traditional sentences, and thus participants are released earlier. In addition, studies of boot camps have indicated that the facilities have not had a major effect on recidivism.

Many adult boot camps claim to be oriented toward developing programs aimed at offender rehabilitation. Typically, boot camp programs include physical training and regular drill-type exercise, housekeeping and maintenance of the facility, and often hard labor. Some programs include vocational, educational, or treatment programs. Drug and alcohol counseling, reality therapy, relaxation therapy, individual counseling, and recreation therapy are often incorporated into such programs. Because some offenders in boot camps have drug problems, many programs devote time to drug treatment each week. Programs closely regulate dress, talking, movement, eating, hygiene, etc. Obedience to rules reinforces submission to authority and forces the prisoners to handle a challenge that is both tedious and demanding.

## Community Service Programs

Begun in the United States in Alameda County, California, in 1966 as a penalty for traffic offenses, community service has spread throughout the United States. The penalty is most often a supplement to other penalties and mainly given to "white-collar" criminals, juvenile delinquents, and those who commit nonserious crimes. Offenders are usually required to work for government or private nonprofit agencies cleaning parks, collecting roadside trash, setting up chairs for community events, painting community projects, and helping out at nursing homes. Examples of such civic programs include a California Department of Forestry and Fire Protection project that uses over 1,500 prison inmates as wildland firefighters and the Washington State Corrections Center for Women program in which inmates are taught how to train, groom, and board dogs that can assist people with disabilities.

The BJS in *State Court Organization 1998* (June 2000) labeled community service "an exception to unconstitutional servitude," indirectly referring to the Thirteenth Amendment to the Constitution, which states, in Section 1: "Neither slavery nor involuntary servitude, except as a punishment for crime whereof the party shall have been duly convicted, shall exist within the United States, or any place subject to their jurisdiction." By exempting the involuntary servitude of convicted criminals, the Constitution makes both community service and chain gangs possible.

## Day Fines

Under this type of alternative sentence, the offender pays out a monetary sum rather than spending time in jail or prison. Most judges assess fixed, flat-fee fines sparingly. The fees are tied to the seriousness of the crimes and the criminal records of the offenders, and they bear no relationship to the wealth of the offender. As a result, judges often think the fixed fines are too lenient on wealthy offenders and too harsh on poor ones. Using the day fine alternative, however, permits judges to first determine how much punishment an offender deserves, which is defined in some unit other than money.

For example, a judge decides that the gravity of the offense is worth fifteen, sixty, or 120 punishment units, without regard to income. Then the value of each unit is set at a percentage of the offender's daily income, and the total fine amount is determined by simple multiplication. The fine is paid into the jurisdiction's treasury. Day fines are also used in Europe.

## Day Reporting Centers

These centers, known as DRCs, were developed in Great Britain and first instituted in the United States during the 1980s. Intended to allow offenders to reside in the community, such programs require participants to report daily or less frequently.

These programs, designed for persons on pretrial release, probation, or parole, require participants to appear at day reporting centers on a frequent and regular basis in order to partake in services or activities provided by the center or other community agencies. Those sentenced to report to DRCs are often in need of treatment or counseling for drug or alcohol abuse, and most centers provide a wide array of onsite treatment and services. Failure to adhere to program requirements or to report at stated intervals can lead to commitment in prison or jail. Participation at the DRC can also be terminated if the subject is charged with a new crime.

DRCs monitor offenders on the road to rehabilitation. They are also intended to relieve jail or prison overcrowding. Many DRCs operate in distinct phases in which offenders move from higher to lower levels of control based on their progress in treatment and compliance with supervisory guidelines. Most programs run five or six months. DRCs do not generally exclude serious offenders, although many programs appear to select nonserious drug- and alcohol-using offenders. Some DRCs require offenders to perform community service, but the level and type of community service performed varies from jurisdiction to jurisdiction.

## Intensive Probation Supervision (IPS)

IPS is another implementation of close supervision of offenders while they reside in the community. Offenders on probation are increasingly people convicted of felonies (rather than misdemeanors), who are sentenced to intensively supervised probation because prisons are crowded, but the offenders require close monitoring. Routine probation, however, was neither intended nor structured to handle this type of high-risk probationer. Therefore, IPS was developed as an alternative to prison or routine probation, with the additional aim of reducing the risk to public safety.

Caseloads of officers assigned to IPS offenders are kept low. In typical programs, the offender must make frequent contacts with a supervising officer, pay restitution to victims, participate in community service, have and keep a job, and, if appropriate, undergo random and unannounced drug testing. Offenders are often required to pay a probation fee. All states had IPS programs in 2005.

## House Arrest and Electronic Monitoring Program (EMP)

Some nonviolent offenders are sentenced to house arrest (or home confinement) in which they are legally ordered to remain confined in their own homes. They are allowed to leave only for medical purposes or to go to work, although some curfew programs permit offenders to work during the day and have a few hours of free time before returning home at a specified time. The idea began as a way to keep drunk drivers off the street, but quickly expanded to include other nonviolent offenders.

The most severe type of house arrest is home incarceration, where the offender's home is actually a prison that he or she cannot leave except for very special reasons, such as medical emergencies. Home-detention programs require the offender to be at home when he or she is not working. Some offenders are required to perform a certain number of hours of community service and, if they are employed, to repay the cost of probation and/or restitution.

Electronic monitoring works in tandem with house arrest. Electronic monitoring can consist of a small radio transmitter attached to the offender in a nonremovable bracelet or anklet. Some systems send a signal to a small monitoring box, which is programmed to phone a Department of Corrections computer if the signal is broken; other systems randomly call probationers, and the computer makes a voice verification of the prisoner. In some cases, a special device in the electronic monitor sends a confirmation to the computer. More advanced technologies are being applied to electronic monitoring of probationers and parolees, including Global Positioning Systems (GPS) technologies, which uses satellites to keep track of subjects. GPS can help corrections officers ensure that the subject is not violating any territorial restrictions.

Electronic monitoring is often used to monitor the whereabouts of those under house arrest and permitted to be only at home or at work. EMP is sometimes used to ensure that child molesters stay a specified distance from schools. Electronic monitoring costs much less than building new prison cells or housing more inmates. However, close supervision by officers is crucial to the success of any home confinement or electronic monitoring program. Officers must insure that the participants are indeed working when they leave the house and that they are not using illegal drugs. Periodic checks of any electronic monitoring equipment must also be done to see if there have been any attempts to disable the equipment.

According to the National Law Enforcement Corrections Technology Center (*Keeping Track of Electronic Monitoring*, October 1999), "a properly run electronic monitoring program (EMP) can be a cost-effective, community-friendly program to harbor 'low-risk' offenders."

### Residential Community Corrections

These facilities are known less formally as "halfway houses" because they are intended to serve as places where prisoners spend their pre-release time becoming reintegrated into community life. Offenders may also be sentenced to halfway houses directly in lieu of incarceration if their offenses and general profile indicate that they will benefit from the structure and counseling available in such facilities. According to the Bureau of Justice Statistics, halfway houses are frequently used in many states to relieve prison overcrowding.

Residential programs house offenders in a structured environment. Offenders work full time, maintain the residence center, perform community service, and can attend educational or counseling programs. They may leave the centers only for work or approved programs such as substance-abuse treatment. One type of residential program, called the restitution center, allows the offender to work to pay restitution and child-support payments. Centers also regularly test the residents for drugs.

### Diversionary Treatment Programs

Probation combined with mandatory treatment programs is an alternative sentence for nonviolent offenders convicted of drug offenses, alcohol abuse, or sex offenses. Sentenced individuals are free on probation but typically are required to attend sessions of group therapy and supervised professional treatment.

# CHAPTER 10
# SPECIAL FACILITIES AND POPULATIONS

Most prisons and jails are associated with federal, state, and local government, and adhere to the same general sets of laws and regulations. There are some exceptions, however. A few organizations and areas within the United States have specialized prison facilities of their own. There are also some types of prisoners, such as immigrants and death row inmates, that are handled differently from most other prisoners in the American correctional system.

## MILITARY INCARCERATION

The U.S. military has always operated under laws of its own. Today, that is the Uniform Code of Military Justice (UCMJ), enacted by Congress on May 5, 1950 (U.S. Court of Appeals for the Armed Forces, "History," http://www.armfor.uscourts.gov/Establis.htm). Congress created the U.S. Court of Appeals for the Armed Forces as the final appellate court under the UCMJ, but an amendment of the code on August 1, 1984, provided for U.S. Supreme Court review of judgments in a limited number of cases. Before UCMJ, a military Board of Review adjudicated, with the president having final authority to decide conflicts. The UCMJ's Articles 77 through 134 define offenses equivalent to felonies. Article 118, for instance, deals with murder. Offenses are tried in general courts-martial and may result in the imprisonment of offenders. The most serious cases are incarcerated at the military's Fort Leavenworth Penitentiary in Kansas, established in 1875 as a military prison.

In 2003 about 2.1 million men and women served in the U.S. military. That same year, according to Paige M. Harrison and Allen J. Beck in *Prisoners in 2003* (Bureau of Justice Statistics, November 2004), 2,165 military personnel were held in military prisons, an 8.9% drop from the 2,377 prisoners in 2002. (See Table 10.1.)

All four of the combat services maintain correctional facilities. In 2003 the Army's six facilities, including the Disciplinary Barracks in Fort Leavenworth, Kansas, housed 45% of all military prisoners. Nearly 30% of all inmates were held in the Navy's eleven facilities, another 20% were in the six Marine Corps facilities, and the Air Force's thirty-four facilities held 5% of all inmates. According to *Prisoners in 2003*, 58% of military prisoners in 2003 were sentenced to terms of one year or more. The nation's fifty-seven military confinement facilities were operating in 2003 at only 65% of capacity.

Data for 2003 are a snapshot. Levels can shift over time, as shown in Table 10.2. The table tracks military incarceration rates from 1996 to 2003. Total prisoners were down by 582 prisoners during this time. For the Army, the number dropped from 1,106 in 1996 to 840 in 2003, a decrease of 24%. Most other branches of the service showed similar decreases: the Air Force was down 19.7%, the Marines were down 21.3%, and the Navy was down 17.1%. Only the Coast Guard showed a slight increase in the number of personnel in prison, increasing from fourteen prisoners in 1996 to eighteen prisoners in 2003.

## U.S. TERRITORIES AND COMMONWEALTHS

The reach of crime and of corrections is worldwide, extending even to tiny islands in the Caribbean or in the Pacific Ocean—two regions where U.S. territories and commonwealths are located. In the Pacific are American Samoa, Guam, and the Northern Mariana Islands; in the Caribbean are Puerto Rico and the U.S. Virgin Islands.

The largest of the U.S. possessions, the Commonwealth of Puerto Rico, is an island approximately three times the size of Rhode Island in land area. According to the Central Intelligence Agency's *World Factbook* (http://www.cia.gov/cia/publications/factbook/), Puerto Rico had a population of

TABLE 10.1

## Prisoners under military jurisdiction, by branch of service, yearend 2002 and 2003

| Branch of service | Total | | Percent change, 2002–03 | Sentenced to more than 1 year | | Percent change, 2002–03 |
|---|---|---|---|---|---|---|
| | 2003 | 2002 | | 2003 | 2002 | |
| **To which prisoners belonged** | | | | | | |
| **Total** | **2,165** | **2,377** | **−8.9%** | **1,258** | **1,361** | **−7.6%** |
| Air Force | 391 | 450 | −13.1 | 251 | 264 | −4.9 |
| Army | 840 | 860 | −2.3 | 572 | 610 | −6.2 |
| Marine Corps | 539 | 565 | −4.6 | 229 | 265 | −13.6 |
| Navy | 377 | 489 | −22.9 | 199 | 219 | −9.1 |
| Coast Guard | 18 | 13 | 38.5 | 7 | 3 | * |
| **Holding prisoners** | | | | | | |
| **Total** | **2,165** | **2,377** | **−8.9%** | **1,258** | **1,361** | **−7.6%** |
| Air Force | 105 | 128 | −18.0 | 17 | 14 | 21.4 |
| Army | 967 | 966 | 0.1 | 763 | 767 | −0.5 |
| Marine Corps | 441 | 478 | −7.7 | 134 | 171 | −21.6 |
| Navy | 652 | 805 | −19.0 | 344 | 409 | −15.9 |

*Not calculated.

SOURCE: Paige M. Harrison and Allen J. Beck, "Prisoners under Military Jurisdiction, by Branch of Service, Yearend 2002 and 2003," in *Prisoners in 2003*, Bureau of Justice Statistics, November 2004, http://www.ojp.usdoj .gov/bjs/pub/pdf/p03.pdf (accessed March 30, 2005)

their judicial officials are named by the Secretary of the Interior.

Nearly 16,500 people were in the custody of correctional authorities in the territories/commonwealths in 2003. (See Table 10.3.) Out of this number, 12,532 had been sentenced to serve more than one year, more than 75%. The incarceration rate in the territories/commonwealths for 2003 was 292 per 100,000 persons in the resident population, compared to 482 per 100,000 in the United States. The lowest incarceration rate was experienced by the Northern Mariana Islands, 101 per 100,000; some fourteen small islands provide this commonwealth with a territory about 2.5 times the size of Washington, D.C. The highest rate was experienced by the U.S. Virgin Islands, 338 per 100,000. Puerto Rico's experience, at 301 per 100,000, dominated results for all U.S. possessions in 2003 because of its large population; the 15,046 prisoners in custody of correctional authorities in Puerto Rico in 2003 represented more than 91% of all prisoners in U.S. territories and commonwealths.

3.9 million people in 2005. The smallest territory is American Samoa, two islands inhabited by about 57,900 people. U.S. territories and associated commonwealths had a combined total population in 2004 of 4.31 million. The commonwealths are self-governing entities. The territories are administered by the U.S. Department of the Interior, but these territories also have self-governing political bodies;

## JAILS IN INDIAN COUNTRY
### Tribal Jurisdiction

In its management of Native American nations, Congress reserved for federal jurisdiction fourteen crimes committed by or against Native Americans in Indian Country (tribal lands and reservations; for the U.S. Code, see http://uscode.house.gov/). The relevant provisions of the Major Crimes Act of 1885, codified as 18 USC 1153, read as follows:

TABLE 10.2

## Prisoners under military jurisdiction, by branch of service, yearend 1996–2003

| Branch of service | Number | | | | | | | | Percent change 2002 to 2003 |
|---|---|---|---|---|---|---|---|---|---|
| | 1996 | 1997 | 1998 | 1999 | 2000 | 2001 | 2002 | 2003 | |
| **To which prisoners belonged** | | | | | | | | | |
| **Total** | **2,747** | **2,772** | **2,426** | **2,279** | **2,420** | **2,436** | **2,377** | **2,165** | **−8.9%** |
| Air Force | 487 | 575 | 484 | 409 | 413 | 480 | 450 | 391 | −13.1 |
| Army | 1,106 | 1,063 | 862 | 761 | 789 | 804 | 860 | 840 | −2.3 |
| Marine Corps | 685 | 628 | 682 | 565 | 730 | 628 | 565 | 539 | −4.6 |
| Navy | 455 | 490 | 389 | 523 | 474 | 516 | 489 | 377 | −22.9 |
| Coast Guard | 14 | 16 | 9 | 21 | 14 | 8 | 13 | 18 | 38.5 |
| **Holding prisoners** | | | | | | | | | |
| **Total** | **2,747** | **2,772** | **2,426** | **2,279** | **2,420** | **2,436** | **2,377** | **2,165** | **−8.9** |
| Air Force* | NA | 103 | 128 | 92 | 102 | 126 | 128 | 105 | −18.0 |
| Army | 1,486 | 1,494 | 1,115 | 1,026 | 994 | 981 | 966 | 967 | 0.1 |
| Marine Corps | 650 | 571 | 617 | 480 | 563 | 428 | 478 | 441 | −7.7 |
| Navy | 611 | 604 | 526 | 681 | 761 | 901 | 805 | 652 | −19.0 |

Note: Detail may not add to total because of rounding.
*Data for 1996 exclude prisoners confined in Air Force facilities.

SOURCE: Kathleen Maguire and Ann L. Pastore, editors, Table 6.61. "Prisoners under Jurisdiction of U.S. Military Authorities by Branch of Service, Dec. 31, 1996–2003," in *Sourcebook of Criminal Justice Statistics*, Bureau of Justice Statistics, August 2004, http://www.albany.edu/sourcebook/pdf/t661.pdf (accessed March 30, 2005)

TABLE 10.3

**Prisoners in custody of correctional authorities in U.S. territories and commonwealths, yearend 2002 and 2003**

| Jurisdiction | Total | | | Sentenced to more than 1 year | | | |
|---|---|---|---|---|---|---|---|
| | 2003 | 2002 | Percent change 2002–03 | 2003 | 2002 | Percent change 2002–03 | Incarceration rate, 2003* |
| Total | 16,494 | 16,200 | 1.8% | 12,532 | 12,211 | 2.6% | 292 |
| American Samoa | 174 | 169 | 3.0 | 143 | 143 | 0.0 | 247 |
| Guam | 579 | 546 | 6.0 | 277 | 219 | 26.5 | 169 |
| Commonwealth of the Northern Mariana Islands | 136 | 123 | 10.6 | 77 | 76 | 1.3 | 101 |
| Commonwealth of Puerto Rico | 15,046 | 14,705 | 2.3 | 11,667 | 11,351 | 2.8 | 301 |
| U.S. Virgin Islands | 559 | 657 | −14.9 | 368 | 422 | −12.8 | 338 |

*The number of prisoners with a sentence of more than 1 year per 100,000 persons in the resident population

SOURCE: Paige M. Harrison and Allen J. Beck, "Prisoners in Custody of Correctional Authorities in the U.S. Territories and Commonwealths, Yearend 2002 and 2003," in *Prisoners in 2003*, Bureau of Justice Statistics, November 2004, http://www.ojp.usdoj.gov/bjs/pub/pdf/p03.pdf (accessed March 30, 2005)

(a) Any Indian who commits against the person or property of another Indian or other person any of the following offenses, namely, murder, manslaughter, kidnapping, maiming, a felony under chapter 109A, incest, assault with intent to commit murder, assault with a dangerous weapon, assault resulting in serious bodily injury (as defined in section 1365 of this title), an assault against an individual who has not attained the age of 16 years, arson, burglary, robbery, and a felony under section 661 of this title within the Indian country, shall be subject to the same law and penalties as all other persons committing any of the above offenses, within the exclusive jurisdiction of the United States.

(b) Any offense referred to in subsection (a) of this section that is not defined and punished by Federal law in force within the exclusive jurisdiction of the United States shall be defined and punished in accordance with the laws of the State in which such offense was committed as are in force at the time of such offense.

In other words, under 18 USC 1153 serious crimes must be tried in federal court if federal criminal code can be brought to apply—and if not, it falls to the states to try such crimes.

In Public Law 280, passed in 1953 and codified as 18 USC 1162, Congress made the state responsibility clearer:

(a) Each of the States or Territories listed in the following table [table lists Native American jurisdictions within Alaska, California, Minnesota, Nebraska, Oregon, and Wisconsin] shall have jurisdiction over offenses committed by or against Indians in the areas of Indian country listed opposite the name of the State or Territory to the same extent that such State or Territory has jurisdiction over offenses committed elsewhere within the State or Territory, and the criminal laws of such State or Territory shall have the same force and effect within such Indian country as they have elsewhere within the State or Territory.

This provision of U.S. Code gives states authority over criminal prosecutions taking place on reservations. Offenses left over for tribal jurisdiction are, in effect, petty offenses and misdemeanors. In the Indian Civil Rights Act of 1968 (ICRA), Congress spelled out the limitation under which tribal courts could operate. The relevant provision was codified as 25 USC 1302 (7):

No Indian tribe in exercising powers of self-government shall (7) require excessive bail, impose excessive fines, inflict cruel and unusual punishments, and in no event impose for conviction of any one offense any penalty or punishment greater than imprisonment for a term of one year and a fine of $5,000, or both.

### Native American Offenders under Tribal Jurisdiction

In 2002, 47,724 Native Americans and Alaska Natives were under correctional supervision, 22,245 of whom were in custody and 25,479 under community supervision, either on parole or probation. (See Table 10.4.)

Of the 22,245 in custody in 2002, 2,006 (9%) were held in jails in Indian Country. Most (58%) were in state prisons; 6,000 (27%) were held in local jails in cities, towns, and counties; and 1,315 (5.9%) were in federal prisons. (See Table 10.4.) Similarly, virtually all of those under community supervision were under state or federal control, most on probation (80.7%), the rest on parole (18.9%).

Of the 2,006 inmates held in Indian Country jails in 2002, 1,399 were adult males (69.7%). Most inmates had been convicted of a misdemeanor (86%) rather than a felony (5.3%). Some 35% (699) had committed a violent offense. (See Table 10.5.)

Based on U.S. Census Bureau definitions, Native Americans lived either inside or outside of "identified areas," these being reservations, trust lands, tribal designated statistical areas, tribal jurisdiction statistical areas,

## TABLE 10.4

### Native Americans under correctional supervision, 2001–02

| | Native Americans (includes Alaska Natives) |
|---|---|
| Total | 47,724 |
| **In custody, midyear 2002** | 22,245 |
| Local jails[a] | 6,000 |
| Jails in Indian country[b] | 2,006 |
| State prisons | 12,924 |
| Federal prisons | 1,315 |
| **Under community supervision** | |
| State/federal, 12/31/01 | 25,479 |
| Probation | 20,577 |
| Parole | 4,828 |
| Indian country, midyear 2002 | 74 |

[a]Estimated from the Annual Survey of Jails, 2002
[b]"Indian country" is a statutory term that includes the following: all lands within an Indian reservation, dependent Indian communities, and Indian trust allotments. The Bureau of Justice Statistics (BJS) conducted the Survey of Jails in Indian Country (SJIC) to describe all adult and juvenile jail facilities and detention centers in Indian country. For purposes of this report, Indian country includes reservations, pueblos, rancherias, and other appropriate areas. The reference date for the most recent survey is June 28, 2002.

SOURCE: Todd D. Minton, "American Indians and Alaska Natives under Correctional Supervision, 2001–02," in *Jails in Indian Country 2002*, Bureau of Justice Statistics, November 2003, http://www.ojp.usdoj.gov/bjs/pub/pdf/jic02.pdf (accessed March 30, 2005)

## TABLE 10.5

### Indian country jail inmate characteristics, midyear 2001–02

| | Number of persons | |
|---|---|---|
| | 2002 | 2001 |
| Total | 2,080 | 2,030 |
| In custody | 2,006 | 1,912 |
| Adult | 1,699 | 1,600 |
| Male | 1,399 | 1,366 |
| Female | 300 | 234 |
| Juvenile | 307 | 312 |
| Male | 219 | 212 |
| Female | 88 | 100 |
| Convicted | 120 | 1,062 |
| Unconvicted | 857 | 836 |
| Felony | 107 | 113 |
| Misdemeanor | 1,725 | 1,738 |
| Other | 174 | 61 |
| Violent offense | 699 | * |
| DWI/DUI | 226 | 181 |
| Drug law violation | 126 | 130 |
| Under community supervision | 74 | 118 |

Note: Omaha Tribal Police Department did not report conviction status in 2002. "Indian country" is a statutory term that includes the following: all lands within an Indian reservation, dependent Indian communities, and Indian trust allotments. The Bureau of Justice Statistics (BJS) conducted the Survey of Jails in Indian Country (SJIC) to describe all adult and juvenile jail facilities and detention centers in Indian country. For purposes of this report, Indian country includes reservations, pueblos, rancherias, and other appropriate areas. The reference date for the most recent survey is June 28, 2002.
*Not collected in 2001.

SOURCE: Todd D. Minton, "Table 1. Indian Country Jail Inmate Characteristics, Midyear 2001–2002," in *Jails in Indian Country 2002*, Bureau of Justice Statistics, November 2003, http://www.ojp.usdoj.gov/bjs/pub/pdf/jic02.pdf (accessed March 30, 2005)

## TABLE 10.6

### Indian country inmates and facility capacity, 1998–2002

| | 2002 | 2001 | 2000 | 1998 |
|---|---|---|---|---|
| **Number of inmates** | | | | |
| Midyear | 2,006 | 1,912 | 1,775 | 1,479 |
| Average daily population[a] | 1,653 | d | d | d |
| Peak day in June | 2,737 | 2,656 | 2,441 | 2,306 |
| Rated capacity | 2,177 | 2,101 | 2,076 | 1,945 |
| **Percent of capacity occupied[b]** | | | | |
| Midyear | 92% | 91% | 86% | 76% |
| Average daily population[c] | 79 | d | d | d |
| Peak day in June | 126 | 126 | 118 | 119 |

[a]Average daily population is the number of inmates confined in June, divided by 30.
[b]Number of inmates in custody divided by rated capacity.
[c]2002 percent occupied excludes 2 facilities that did not report their average daily population.
[d]Not collected.
Note: "Indian country" is a statutory term that includes the following: all lands within an Indian reservation, dependent Indian communities, and Indian trust allotments. The Bureau of Justice Statistics (BJS) conducted the Survey of Jails in Indian Country (SJIC) to describe all adult and juvenile jail facilities and detention centers in Indian country. For purposes of this report, Indian country includes reservations, pueblos, rancherias, and other appropriate areas. The reference date for the most recent survey is June 28, 2002.

SOURCE: Todd D. Minton, "70 Facilities Were Operating in Indian Country, with the Capacity to Hold 2,177 Persons on June 28, 2002," in *Jails in Indian Country 2002*, Bureau of Justice Statistics, November 2003, http://www.ojp.usdoj.gov/bjs/pub/pdf/jic02.pdf (accessed March 30, 2005)

and Alaska Native village statistical areas. According to the Statistical Abstract of the United States 2004–05 (Washington, DC: Census Bureau, 2005), the 2000 Census of the U.S. population included 4,119,301 Native Americans and Alaska Natives.

Following the 1990 Census, the bureau published data showing that, as of April 1990, 37.7% of Native Americans, Eskimos, and Aleuts lived "inside" these areas; the majority lived "off the reservation" (*Statistical Abstract of the United States 1993*, Washington, DC, 1993). Similar data for the 2000 Census have not as yet been tabulated. Proportionally more Native Americans live in Indian Country than are tried and held in tribal facilities when they commit offenses because the legal structure governing offenses favors federal and state jurisdictions.

Tribal jails are crowded much like state and federal facilities—and appear to be growing slightly more crowded. (See Table 10.6.) In 1998, 76% of jail beds were in use in midyear, and 119% of capacity was used on the peak day, in June. Capacity increased more slowly than incarcerations so that by 2002 some 92% of capacity was in use in midyear and jails in Indian Country operated at 126% of capacity on the peak day in June.

## IMMIGRANTS IN CONFINEMENT

Since the passage of the Immigration and Nationality Act of 1965, which eliminated a quota system based on country of origin, immigration has risen in the United

FIGURE 10.1

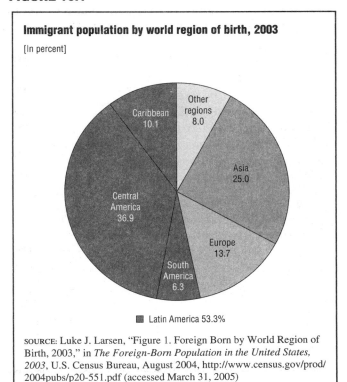

**Immigrant population by world region of birth, 2003**

[In percent]

- Other regions 8.0
- Caribbean 10.1
- Asia 25.0
- Central America 36.9
- Europe 13.7
- South America 6.3
- Latin America 53.3%

SOURCE: Luke J. Larsen, "Figure 1. Foreign Born by World Region of Birth, 2003," in *The Foreign-Born Population in the United States, 2003*, U.S. Census Bureau, August 2004, http://www.census.gov/prod/2004pubs/p20-551.pdf (accessed March 31, 2005)

States. In 1960 the foreign-born population of the United States stood at 9.7 million, and the foreign-born comprised 5.4% of the U.S. population. By 2003, according to Luke J. Larsen in *The Foreign-Born Population in the United States: 2003* (Census Bureau, August 2004), the foreign-born numbered 33.5 million and represented 11.7% of the population. In 1960, 75% of the foreign born were of European origin, with another 9.8% from Canada. By 2003 people born in Latin America represented 53.3% of the foreign-born and Asians 25%; those of European origin had slipped to 13.7% of all foreign-born. (See Figure 10.1.)

As legal immigration increased, so did illegal entry, mostly from Latin America. In 2000 about 4.8 million illegal aliens, 68.7% of the total, were from Mexico (*Estimates of the Unauthorized Immigrant Population Residing in the United States: 1990 to 2000*, U.S. Citizenship and Immigration Services, http://uscis.gov/graphics/shared/aboutus/statistics/Ill_Report_1211.pdf). One response to this problem was the Immigration Reform and Control Act of 1986, which enabled some illegal aliens to obtain lawful permanent residence. The Immigration Act of 1990 increased the overall number of legal immigrants admitted. Midway through the 1990s, opposition to immigration, particularly to the presence of illegal aliens, began to focus around the issues of jobs taken by illegal aliens and tax dollars expended on the education, health care, and maintenance (through welfare expenditures) of illegal

aliens. Some activists also pointed to the strain on the environment of so many additional people entering the country every year. Since 1996 Congress has generally pursued a policy of immigration reform ranging from beefing up border controls to strengthening court authority over illegal aliens. The Illegal Immigration Reform and Immigration Responsibility Act of 1996 signaled the turn in policy. According to John Scalia and Marika F. X. Litras in *Immigration Offenders in the Federal Criminal Justice System, 2000* (Bureau of Justice Statistics, August 2002), the law authorized an increase in the number of law enforcement officers from 12,403 to 17,654. Two-thirds of the new positions were assigned to border patrol, and states that received these new officers noted a 75% increase in the number of cases referred to U.S. attorneys for immigration offenses.

One of the aims of Congress in the 1996 act was to remove illegal immigrants from the country rapidly and without long processes of judicial review—a policy that would later be reaffirmed in the USA Patriot Act of 2001. The 1996 act's chief focus was on the entry of illegal aliens, not terrorism, and also on U.S. citizens engaged in smuggling aliens into the country.

Responsibility for the security of the nation's borders was handed over to the newly created Department of Homeland Security in November 2002. Subsequently, the U.S. Immigration and Naturalization Service became part of the U.S. Bureau of Immigration and Customs Enforcement (ICE). A shift in emphasis occurred after the terrorist attacks of September 11, 2001. The new policy was announced by Attorney General John Ashcroft in a September 18 press briefing. Ashcroft announced that the twenty-four-hour detention rule, in place before the policy changed, would be doubled to forty-eight hours, "or to an additional reasonable time if necessary under an emergency or in other extraordinary circumstances" (quoted by CNN.com, "Rules for Aliens Changed, Anti-Terrorism Task Forces Established"). This policy, later formalized as part of the USA Patriot Act, was signed into law on October 26, 2001, giving the government the power to hold immigrant terror suspects or those immigrants suspected of aiding terrorists for longer periods.

The policy change is evident in data that record persons detained under ICE auspices (rather than referred to U.S. attorneys, although these numbers overlap). In the category of detained persons, numbers have increased dramatically. In 1995, 8,177 persons were detained. By yearend 2003 the number had increased to 23,514. (See Table 10.7.) Of these detainees, according to *Prisoners in 2003*, 12,603 had been convicted of criminal offenses. Violent offenses accounted for 31.7% of the convictions and drug offenses another 29.5%. Federal and state

TABLE 10.7

**Bureau of Immigration and Customs Enforcement (ICE) detainees, by type of facility, yearend 1995, 2002, and 2003**

| Facility type | Number of detainees | | | Percent change, 2002–03 |
|---|---|---|---|---|
| | 2003 | 2002 | 1995 | |
| Total | 23,514 | 21,065 | 8,177 | 11.6% |
| ICE*-operated facilities | 5,109 | 5,087 | 3,776 | 0.4 |
| Private facilities under exclusive contract to ICE | 1,935 | 1,936 | 652 | −0.1 |
| Federal Bureau of Prisons | 1,338 | 1,100 | 1,282 | 21.6 |
| Other federal facilities | 88 | 130 | 181 | −32.3 |
| Intergovernmental agreements | 15,044 | 12,812 | 2,286 | 17.4 |
| State prisons | 477 | 453 | 8 | 5.3 |
| Local jails | 11,376 | 9,764 | 1,984 | 16.5 |
| Other facilities | 3,191 | 1,595 | 294 | 23.0 |

*ICE=Bureau of Immigration and Customs Enforcement

SOURCE: Paige M. Harrison and Allen J. Beck, "Detainees under the Jurisdiction of the Bureau of Immigration and Customs Enforcement (ICE), by Type of Facility, Yearend 1995, 2002, and 2003," in *Prisoners in 2003*, Bureau of Justice Statistics, November 2004, http://www.ojp.usdoj.gov/bjs/pub/pdf/p03.pdf (accessed March 31, 2005)

prisons and local jails housed 15,044 of the detainees and 5,109 were held in ICE-operated facilities.

The Patriot Act is controversial because it gives the government powers of surveillance that some people believe violate their right of privacy. In the context of prisons and jails, the act's Section 412 concerns mandatory detention of suspected terrorists. (A copy of the act is available on the U.S. Citizenship and Immigration Services Web site at http://uscis.gov/graphics/lawsregs/patriot.pdf.) Section 412 gives the Attorney General the power to "certify" that an alien is engaged in an activity that endangers the national security of the United States. The intent of the legislation is that a certified person be held until removed from the United States. The Attorney General must either charge the person with a crime or place the person "in removal procedures." But if removal is "unlikely in the reasonably foreseeable future, [the person] may be detained for additional periods of up to six months only if the release of the alien will threaten the national security of the United States or the safety of the community or any person." The act provides for judicial review of the Attorney General's actions by the U.S. Supreme Court or federal district courts. Unless courts overrule the Attorney General's judgment, circumstances can arise under which an alien can be held indefinitely, always for successive six-month periods.

### Other Foreigners under Detention

A related issue of detention is the federal government's confinement of persons at the U.S. military base in Guantanamo Bay, Cuba, as "unlawful combatants." These persons, captured during the conflict in Afghanistan, are held under a presidential order issued November 13, 2001 ("President Issues Military Order," The White House, http://www.whitehouse.gov/news/releases/2001/11/20011113-27.html). According to the order, such individuals are in the custody of the Department of Defense and are to be tried, when tried, by military commissions rather than in U.S. district courts. This order has been controversial because some see it as an attempt to circumvent the legal protections offered to prisoners by the conventional U.S. legal system and by international treaties regulating prisoners of war.

The lengthy detention of such prisoners has also been the subject of much controversy. In April 2004 the Department of Defense acknowledged that there were approximately six hundred such individuals still being held at Guantanamo. In a public statement addressed to the UN Commission on Human Rights on April 20, 2004, Amnesty International charged:

> International law has been flouted from the outset. None of the detainees was granted prisoner of war status nor brought before a competent tribunal to determine his status, as required by the Third Geneva Convention. None has been granted access to a court to be able to challenge the lawfulness of his detention, as required by the International Covenant on Civil and Political Rights (Article 9) to which the United States is a party. Detainees have been denied access to legal counsel and their families.

According to the U.S. government, as unlawful combatants, these detainees are not guaranteed legal assistance and do not have to be charged with a crime. They may be held indefinitely for interrogation.

### DEATH ROW INMATES

In 1972 the U.S. Supreme Court ruled that the death penalty was "cruel and unusual punishment" in three cases the Court agreed to hear—two for rape and one for murder, each involving a African-American offender. The Court's ruling was based on the manner in which the death penalty was then administered by the states. The states left sentencing to juries with little or no guidance; juries could impose the death penalty or a lesser sentence. The Court reasoned that this left open the possibility that minorities might be more severely punished than members of the white majority. The Court discussed but did not rule, in the abstract, on the constitutionality of the death penalty per se. The case is known as *Furman v. Georgia* (408 US 238, 1972) in which the Court also decided *Jackson v. Georgia* and *Branch v. Texas*, two similar cases.

Between 1972 and 1976, states passed new legislation implementing sentencing guidelines and provided procedural safeguards for defendants in response to the Supreme Court's guidance contained in *Furman v. Georgia*. In *Gregg v. Georgia* (428 US 453, 1976), the

Court held that as implemented under revised laws in Georgia, the death sentence was legal. The Court went further and stated that it was not cruel and unusual punishment per se and argued that the Eighth Amendment's prohibition of such punishment did not outlaw the death penalty. It was widely used at the time when the amendment passed; the Constitution also mentioned capital punishment in other contexts.

Executions reached a peak of 199 in 1935 and then began declining. When *Furman v. Georgia* was decided, the last execution had occurred six years before, in 1966, the only execution in that year. No person was executed between 1967 and 1976. One execution occurred in 1977, a year after the Supreme Court in effect reinstated the death penalty in *Gregg v. Georgia*. After that, executions began to grow year by year and reached a new peak of ninety-eight executions in 1999. (See Figure 10.2.)

The number of prisoners on death row has grown dramatically since the 1970s in part because the Supreme Court's 1972 and 1976 rulings set new boundaries for the administration of capital punishment. Since that time, states have been engaged in a process of modifying their laws. According to Thomas P. Bonczar and Tracy L. Snell in *Capital Punishment 2003* (Bureau of Justice Statistics, December 2002), in 2003 alone, eleven states revised their statutes regarding capital punishment. The most common revision was to prohibit the use of the death penalty in cases involving mentally retarded persons; Illinois, Louisiana, Nevada, Utah, and Virginia changed their laws to that effect. The Missouri State Supreme Court ruled that the minimum age for a capital sentence be raised from sixteen years old to eighteen years old.

In 1973 prisoners on death row numbered 134, the lowest number in the 1968–2001 period. The highest number was reached in 2000—3,601. The most recently available count, for 2003, was 3,374. African-Americans on death row exceeded whites in 1968, 271 to 243, showing why the Supreme Court, in its 1972 decision, believed that discrimination may have been present in the administration of the death penalty. (See Figure 10.3.) Beginning in 1976, whites began to outnumber blacks on death row consistently. In 2003, 1,878 death row inmates were white, while 1,418 were African-American, and seventy-eight were of all other races. Proportionally whites (56% of death row inmates) were under-represented, and African-Americans (42%) were over-represented relative to their share of the population.

### Death Row Demographics

During 2003, 144 new prisoners were put on death row while 332 were removed. (See Table 10.8.) Among those removed, sixty-five were executed, ten died (six of natural causes, four by suicide), and 224

**FIGURE 10.2**

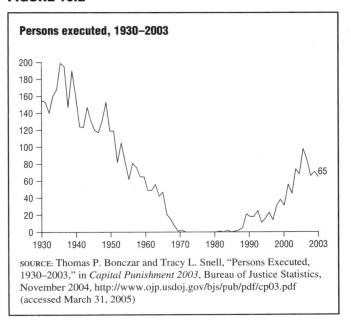

**Persons executed, 1930–2003**

SOURCE: Thomas P. Bonczar and Tracy L. Snell, "Persons Executed, 1930–2003," in *Capital Punishment 2003*, Bureau of Justice Statistics, November 2004, http://www.ojp.usdoj.gov/bjs/pub/pdf/cp03.pdf (accessed March 31, 2005)

**FIGURE 10.3**

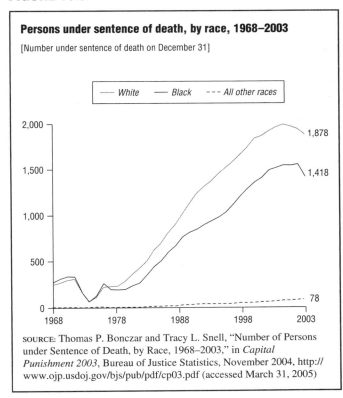

**Persons under sentence of death, by race, 1968–2003**

[Number under sentence of death on December 31]

SOURCE: Thomas P. Bonczar and Tracy L. Snell, "Number of Persons under Sentence of Death, by Race, 1968–2003," in *Capital Punishment 2003*, Bureau of Justice Statistics, November 2004, http://www.ojp.usdoj.gov/bjs/pub/pdf/cp03.pdf (accessed March 31, 2005)

were now serving a reduced sentence. Illinois accounted for 84% of those inmates removed from death row. In January 2003 Illinois Governor George Ryan commuted the sentence of every prisoner on that state's death row—164 inmates in all—citing what he called the "arbitrary and capricious" nature of the Illinois justice system (*Chicago Tribune*, January 12,

## TABLE 10.8

**Demographic characteristics of prisoners under sentence of death, 2003**

| Characteristic | Prisoners under sentence of death, 2003 | | |
| --- | --- | --- | --- |
| | Yearend | Admissions | Removals |
| Total number under sentence of death | 3,374 | 144 | 332 |
| **Gender** | | | |
| Male | 98.6% | 98.6% | 98.2% |
| Female | 1.4 | 1.4 | 1.8 |
| **Race** | | | |
| White | 55.7% | 63.9% | 46.1% |
| Black | 42.0 | 30.6 | 53.3 |
| All other races* | 2.3 | 5.5 | 0.6 |
| **Hispanic origin** | | | |
| Hispanic | 12.5% | 27.0% | 6.2% |
| Non-Hispanic | 87.5 | 73.0 | 93.8 |
| **Education** | | | |
| 8th grade or less | 15.2% | 18.3% | 11.6% |
| 9th–11th grade | 37.1 | 41.7 | 40.4 |
| High school graduate/ general equivalency diploma | 38.3 | 35.0 | 37.2 |
| Any college | 9.3 | 5.0 | 10.8 |
| Median | 11th | 11th | 11th |
| **Marital status** | | | |
| Married | 22.5% | 29.1% | 21.9% |
| Divorced/separated | 20.7 | 17.1 | 20.2 |
| Widowed | 2.8 | 4.3 | 3.1 |
| Never married | 54.0 | 49.6 | 54.8 |

Note: Calculations are based on those cases for which data were reported. Missing data by category were as follows:

| | Yearend | Admissions | Removals |
| --- | --- | --- | --- |
| Hispanic origin | 416 | 55 | 44 |
| Education | 483 | 24 | 55 |
| Marital status | 333 | 27 | 40 |

*At yearend 2002, other races consisted of 29 American Indians, 35 Asians, and 14 self-identified Hispanics. During 2003, 3 American Indians, 3 Asians, and 2 self-identified Hispanics were admitted; 1 Asian was removed; and 1 American Indian was executed.

SOURCE: Thomas P. Bonczar and Tracy L. Snell, "Table 5. Demographic Characteristics of Prisoners under Sentence of Death, 2003," in *Capital Punishment 2003*, Bureau of Justice Statistics, November 2004, http://www.ojp.usdoj.gov/bjs/pub/pdf/cp03.pdf (accessed March 31, 2005)

## TABLE 10.9

**Executions and other dispositions of inmates sentenced to death, by race and Hispanic origin, 1977–2003**

| Race/Hispanic origin | Total under sentence of death, 1977–2003[b] | Prisoners executed | | Prisoners who received other dispositions[a] | |
| --- | --- | --- | --- | --- | --- |
| | | Number | Percent of total | Number | Percent of total |
| Total | 7,061 | 885 | 12.5% | 2,802 | 39.7% |
| White[c] | 3,451 | 510 | 14.8% | 1,400 | 40.6% |
| Black[c] | 2,903 | 301 | 10.4 | 1,198 | 41.3 |
| Hispanic | 597 | 61 | 10.2 | 167 | 28.0 |
| All other races[d] | 110 | 13 | 11.8 | 37 | 33.6 |

[a]Includes persons removed from a sentence of death because of statutes struck down on appeal, sentences or convictions vacated, commutations, or death by other than execution.
[b]Includes 7 persons sentenced to death prior to 1977 who were still under sentence of death on 12/31/03; 373 persons sentenced to death prior to 1977 whose death sentence was removed between 1977 and 12/31/03; and 6,681 persons sentenced to death between 1977 and 12/31/03.
[c]Excludes persons of Hispanic origin.
[d]Includes Native Americans and Asians.

SOURCE: Thomas P. Bonczar and Tracy L. Snell, "Table 10. Executions and Other Dispositions of Inmates Sentenced to Death, by Race and Hispanic Origin, 1977–2003," in *Capital Punishment 2003*, Bureau of Justice Statistics, November 2004, http://www.ojp.usdoj.gov/bjs/pub/pdf/cp03.pdf (accessed March 31, 2005)

2003). The action meant that those Illinois prisoners formerly awaiting execution would now serve life in prison without parole.

Between 1977 and 2003 a total of 7,061 persons were in prison under a death sentence. However, during this period, only 885 inmates (12.5%) were executed; 2,802 others (39.7%) had their sentences commuted or otherwise had their death sentence removed due to a court ruling. (See Table 10.9.) Since the late 1990s, the number of persons admitted to prison under a sentence of death fell from about three hundred a year to about 150 a year. At the same time, those prisoners on death row who had their death sentences removed rose from under 200 a year to over 300 a year. (See Figure 10.4.)

At the end of 2003, 3,374 persons were on death row, down from 3,562 in 2002. According to *Capital Punish-ment 2003*, forty-seven of the death row inmates at the end of 2003 were women. Of these, twenty-nine were white, fifteen were black, and three were of other races. California had the largest number (fourteen) followed by Texas (eight) and Pennsylvania (five).

The overwhelming majority of prisoners on death row were men (98.6%). Among men, 1,849 were white, 1,403 were African-American, and seventy-five were of other races. Among all prisoners sentenced to death, 87.5% were non-Hispanic, and 12.5% were of Hispanic origin. (See Table 10.8.)

By educational attainment, more than half of inmates (52.3%) had less than a high school education, 38.3% had a high school diploma or equivalent certification, 9.3% had attended or had graduated from college.

The majority of inmates at the end of 2003 had never been married (54%), 22.5% were married, 20.7% were divorced, and 2.8% were widowed.

### Age of Inmates and Time on Death Row

In 2003 nearly half of death row inmates, 49%, had been between twenty and twenty-nine years of age at the time of arrest. (See Table 10.10.) As of December 31, 2003, the two age groups with the largest population under sentence of death were thirty-five to thirty-nine and forty to forty-four. The youngest inmate was nineteen years of age, the oldest eighty-six. The average age

**FIGURE 10.4**

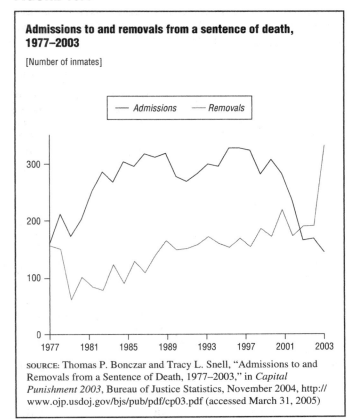

**Admissions to and removals from a sentence of death, 1977–2003**

[Number of inmates]

— Admissions    — Removals

300

200

100

0

1977  1981  1985  1989  1993  1997  2001  2003

SOURCE: Thomas P. Bonczar and Tracy L. Snell, "Admissions to and Removals from a Sentence of Death, 1977–2003," in *Capital Punishment 2003*, Bureau of Justice Statistics, November 2004, http://www.ojp.usdoj.gov/bjs/pub/pdf/cp03.pdf (accessed March 31, 2005)

**TABLE 10.10**

**Age at time of arrest for capital offense and age of prisoners under sentence of death at yearend 2003**

| | Prisoners under sentence of death | | | |
| | At time of arrest | | On December 31, 2003 | |
| Age | Number[a] | Percent | Number | Percent |
|---|---|---|---|---|
| Total number under sentence of death on 12/31/03 | 3,117 | 100% | 3,374 | 100% |
| 17 or younger | 67 | 2.1 | 0 | |
| 18–19 | 341 | 10.9 | 1 | [b] |
| 20–24 | 843 | 27.0 | 133 | 3.9 |
| 25–29 | 687 | 22.0 | 400 | 11.9 |
| 30–34 | 512 | 16.4 | 565 | 16.7 |
| 35–39 | 333 | 10.7 | 582 | 17.2 |
| 40–44 | 177 | 5.7 | 613 | 18.2 |
| 45–49 | 97 | 3.1 | 477 | 14.1 |
| 50–54 | 38 | 1.2 | 297 | 8.8 |
| 55–59 | 16 | 0.5 | 196 | 5.8 |
| 60–64 | 3 | 0.1 | 67 | 2.0 |
| 65 or older | 3 | 0.1 | 43 | 1.3 |
| Mean age | 28 years | | 40 years | |
| Median age | 27 years | | 40 years | |

Note: The youngest person under sentence of death was a white male in Texas, born in April 1984 and sentenced to death in August 2002. The oldest person under sentence of death was a white male in Arizona, born in September 1915 and sentenced to death in June 1983. Detail may not add to total due to rounding.
[a]Less than 0.05%.
[b]Excludes 257 inmates for whom the date of arrest for capital offense was not available.

SOURCE: Thomas P. Bonczar and Tracy L. Snell, "Table 7. Age at Time of Arrest for Capital Offense and Age of Prisoners under Sentence of Death at Yearend 2003," in *Capital Punishment 2003*, Bureau of Justice Statistics, November 2004, http://www.ojp.usdoj.gov/bjs/pub/pdf/cp03.pdf (accessed March 31, 2005)

of those at sentencing was twenty-eight. The average age of all death row inmates in 2003 was forty.

Substantial time elapses between sentencing and the resolution of cases on death row, be it by execution or other forms of "removal." Those executed in 2003 had been in prison an average of ten years and eleven months. The time between sentencing and execution has been lengthening. It was four years and three months between 1977 and 1983 and six years and two months in 1984. For this reason, the age of prisoners at sentencing is about ten years lower than the average age of the population on death row.

**Executed Prisoners**

As reported in *Capital Punishment, 2003*, eleven states executed sixty-four prisoners in 2003; the federal government executed one. Of the sixty-five executed prisoners, all were men. In terms of race, forty-one were white, twenty were black, three were white Hispanics, and one was a Native American. Sixty-four executions were by lethal injection; one was by electrocution.

Preliminary data reported by BJS in *Capital Punishment 2003* for 2004 (January 1 through December 11) indicate that twelve states executed fifty-nine prisoners,

all of whom were men. Within this group, thirty-nine were white, nineteen were African-American, and one was Asian. Fifty-eight were executed by lethal injection; one prisoner was electrocuted.

Thirty-eight states provide capital punishment for murder and, in some instances, for other offenses. California, for example, authorizes capital punishment for train wrecking, treason, and perjury that leads to someone else's execution. Florida and New Jersey have capital punishment for drug trafficking. Louisiana provides for capital punishment for rape of a person under twelve and also punishes treason by death. Mississippi includes aircraft piracy. Twelve states and the District of Columbia do not have the death penalty. States with no death penalty provisions in their laws as of December 31, 2003, were Alaska, Hawaii, Iowa, Maine, Massachusetts, Michigan, Minnesota, North Dakota, Rhode Island, Vermont, West Virginia, and Wisconsin.

The federal government has forty-one laws imposing the death penalty, including espionage, genocide, terrorist murder of a U.S. national in another country, and treason.

# CHAPTER 11
# PRISONERS' RIGHTS UNDER LAW

In 1871 a Virginia court, in *Ruffin v. Commonwealth* (62, Va. 790, 1871), commented that a prisoner "has, as a consequence of his crime, not only forfeited his liberty, but all his personal rights except those which the law in its humanity accords to him. He is for the time being the slave of the state." Eighty years later, in *Stroud v. Swope* (187 F. 2d. 850, 9th Circuit, 1951), a federal circuit judge asserted: "We think it well settled that it is not the function of the courts to superintend the treatment and discipline of persons in penitentiaries, but only to deliver from imprisonment those who are illegally confined." Correctional administrators held that prisoners lost all of their constitutional rights after conviction. Prisoners had privileges, not rights, and privileges could be taken away arbitrarily (William C. Collins, *Legal Responsibility and Authority of Correctional Officers*, American Correctional Association, Laurel, Maryland, 1982).

A significant change in the legal view came in the 1960s. In *Cooper v. Pate* (378 U.S. 546, 1964) the U.S. Supreme Court held that the Civil Rights Act of 1871 (42 USC 1983) granted protection to prisoners. The code states that:

> Every person who, under color of any statute, ordinance, regulation, custom, or usage, of any State or Territory or the District of Columbia, subjects, or causes to be subjected, any citizen of the United States or other person within the jurisdiction thereof to the deprivation of any rights, privileges, or immunities secured by the Constitution and laws, shall be liable to the party injured in an action at law, suit in equity, or other proper proceeding for redress.

With the *Cooper* decision, the Supreme Court announced that prisoners had rights guaranteed by the U.S. Constitution and could ask the judicial system for help in challenging the conditions of their imprisonment. Cases brought later came to be known as Section 1983 lawsuits because the Court had based itself on Section 1983 of Title 42 of the U.S. Code. Prisoners' suits in

federal courts skyrocketed from 218 in 1966 to 26,824 in 1992. After 1992 new laws made it more difficult for prisoners to sue.

Observers differ about the nature of the lawsuits, how the federal courts process them, and the manner in which they are resolved. Many consider some of the lawsuits to be frivolous and undeserving of the limited resources of the federal courts. Others assert that some lawsuits have merit, but that the federal courts tend to treat all Section 1983 lawsuits in an assembly line fashion with little or no individual attention.

## PRODUCE THE BODY

In *Cooper v. Pate* the Supreme Court relied upon civil rights. Another source of prisoners' rights arose from the Court's reliance on habeas corpus. The Latin phrase is an imperative meaning "Have the body . . ." with the rest of the phrase, "brought before me," implied. A writ of habeas corpus is therefore the command issued by one court to another court (or lesser authority) to produce a person and to explain why that person is being detained. Habeas corpus dates back to an act of the British Parliament passed in 1679. The U.S. Congress enacted the Judiciary Act of 1789 and gave federal prisoners the right to habeas corpus review. The Habeas Act of 1867 later protected the rights of newly freed slaves and also extended habeas corpus protection to state prisoners. The effective meaning of habeas corpus for prisoners is that it enables them to petition federal courts to review any aspect of their cases.

The Court also revisited habeas corpus in the 1960s. In *Smith v. Bennett* (365 U.S. 708, 1961), the Court ruled that states could not deny a writ of habeas corpus to prisoners who could not pay a filing fee. In *Long v. District Court* (385 U.S. 192, 1966), the Court ruled that a state must furnish prisoners, not otherwise able to obtain them, with transcripts of prior hearings. In

*Johnson v. Avery* (393 U.S. 483, 1969) the Court emphasized the basic purpose of the writ of habeas corpus in enabling those unlawfully imprisoned to obtain their freedom. The case concerned whether the state could prevent inmates from helping each other file petitions. The Justices held that "it is fundamental that access of prisoners to the courts for the purpose of presenting their complaints may not be denied or obstructed." They ruled that until the state provides some reasonable alternative to assist inmates in the preparation of petitions for postconviction relief, it "may not validly enforce a regulation which absolutely bars inmates from furnishing such assistance to other prisoners." In *Bounds v. Smith* (430 U.S. 817, 1977) the Court further asserted that prison authorities must "assist inmates in the preparation and filing of meaningful legal papers by providing prisoners with adequate law libraries or adequate assistance from persons trained in the law."

*Bounds* did not create an abstract, freestanding right to a law library or legal assistance; rather it acknowledged the right of access to the courts. Inmates have to prove that the alleged shortcomings in the prison library or legal assistance program hindered their efforts to pursue a nonfrivolous legal claim. In addition, the Court relied on a constitutional principle that:

> prevents courts of law from undertaking tasks assigned to the political branches. . . . It is the role of courts to provide relief to claimants, in individual or class actions, who have suffered, or will imminently suffer, actual harm; it is not the role of courts, but that of the political branches to shape the institutions of government in such fashion as to comply with the laws and the Constitution. . . . If—to take another example from prison life—a healthy inmate who had suffered no deprivation of needed medical treatment were able to claim violation of his constitutional right to medical care. . . , simply on the ground that prison medical facilities were inadequate, the essential distinction between judge and executive would have disappeared: it would have become the function of the courts to assure adequate medical care in prisons.

*Bounds* did not guarantee prison law libraries and legal assistance programs. They are only "one constitutionally acceptable method to assure meaningful access to the courts." There can be "alternative means to achieve that goal." An inmate has to show that access to the courts was so "stymied by inadequacies of the law library that he or she was unable even to file a complaint."

Some twenty-four years after *Bounds*, in *Shaw v. Murphy* (532 U.S. 223, 2001), a more conservative Court ruled that Kevin Murphy, incarcerated in a Montana state prison, did not "possess a special First Amendment right to provide legal assistance to fellow inmates." Murphy was punished after he attempted to intervene in a process in which a fellow prisoner was charged with assaulting a guard. Much had changed since the 1970s. Murphy was employed as an "inmate law clerk," and he provided legal assistance to other inmates. Murphy had applied to assist another prisoner, Pat Tracy, but the prison had denied the request because Murphy, a high-security inmate, could not meet with Tracy, a maximum-security inmate. Murphy persisted nonetheless, investigated the case on his own, and wrote a letter to Tracy offering his help. Murphy's punishment arose from this action.

## FIRST AMENDMENT CASES

The First Amendment of the U.S. Constitution guarantees that:

> Congress shall make no law respecting an establishment of religion, or prohibiting the free exercise thereof; or abridging the freedom of speech, or of the press; or the right of the people peaceably to assemble; and to petition the government for a redress of grievances.

### Censorship

In *Procunier v. Martinez* (416 U.S. 396, 1973) the Supreme Court ruled that prison officials cannot censor inmate correspondence unless they:

> show that a regulation authorizing mail censorship furthers one or more of the substantial governmental interests of security, order, and rehabilitation. Second, the limitation of First Amendment freedom must be no greater than is necessary or essential to the protection of the particular governmental interest involved.

Prison officials can refuse to send letters that detail escape plans or encoded messages but cannot censor inmate correspondence simply to "eliminate unflattering or unwelcome opinions or factually inaccurate statements." Because prisoners retain rights, when "a prison regulation or practice offends a fundamental constitutional guarantee, federal courts will discharge their duty to protect constitutional rights."

However, the Court recognized that it was "ill-equipped to deal with the increasingly urgent problems of prison administration." Running a prison takes expertise and planning, all of which, said the Court, is part of the responsibility of the legislative and executive branches. The task of the judiciary, however, is to establish a standard of review for prisoners' constitutional claims that is responsive to both the need to protect inmates' rights and the policy of judicial restraint.

The Court ruled in 1974 (*Pell v. Procunier*, 417 U.S. 817) that federal prison officials could prohibit inmates from having face-to-face media interviews. The Court reasoned that judgments regarding prison security "are peculiarly within the province and professional expertise of corrections officials, and in the absence of substantial evidence in the record to indicate that the officials have exaggerated their response to these considerations, courts should ordinarily defer to their expert judgement in such matters." Prisoners had other means by which to communicate with the media.

In 1985, in *Nolan v. Fitzpatrick* (451 F. 2d 545), the First Circuit Court ruled that inmates had the right to correspond with newspapers. The prisoners were limited only in that they could not write about escape plans or include contraband material in their letters.

The Missouri Division of Corrections permitted correspondence between immediate family members who were inmates at different institutions and between inmates writing about legal matters, but allowed other inmate correspondence only if each prisoner's "classification/treatment team" thought it was in the best interests of the parties. Another Missouri regulation permitted an inmate to marry only with the superintendent's permission, which can be given only when there were "compelling reasons" to do so, such as a pregnancy. In *Turner v. Safley* (482 U.S. 78, 1987) the Supreme Court found the first regulation constitutional and the second one unconstitutional.

The Court held that the "constitutional right of prisoners to marry is impermissibly burdened by the Missouri marriage regulation." The Supreme Court had ruled earlier that prisoners had a constitutionally protected right to marry (*Zablocki v. Redhail*, 434 U.S. 374, 1977), subject to restrictions due to incarceration such as time and place and prior approval of a warden. However, the Missouri regulation practically banned all marriages.

The findings in *Turner v. Safley* have become a guide for prison regulations in the United States. The High Court observed that:

> When a prison regulation impinges on inmates' constitutional rights, the regulation is valid if it is reasonably related to legitimate penological interests. . . . First, there must be a "valid, rational connection" between the prison regulation and the legitimate government interest put forward to justify it. . . . Moreover, the government objective must be a legitimate and neutral one. . . . A second factor relevant in determining the reasonableness of a prison restriction . . . is whether there are alternative means of exercising the right that remain open to prison inmates. A third consideration is the impact accommodation of the asserted constitutional right will have on guards and other inmates, and on the allocation of prison resources generally.

## Religious Beliefs

While inmates retain their First Amendment freedom to practice their religions, the courts have upheld restrictions on religious freedom when corrections departments need to maintain security, when economic considerations are involved, and when the regulation is reasonable.

The District of Columbia jail allowed, at public expense, interdenominational services, as well as services by Catholics, Jews, Protestants, Unitarians, the Salvation Army, and other religious groups. Public funds paid for Protestant and Catholic chaplains and for religious medals. An honorarium was paid to a rabbi when needed.

Several times in 1959 a group of Muslims requested permission to hold religious services. The Director of Corrections of the District of Columbia, Donald Clemmer, refused the requests because he believed that "Muslims teach racial hatred." The director also confiscated a religious medal from the petitioner, William Fulwood, because Clemmer deemed the medal was symbolic of a doctrine of hate and wearing it would promote racial tension in the prison. The jail administration also did not allow Fulwood to correspond with Elijah Muhammad, the leader of the Black Muslims, or subscribe to the Los Angeles *Herald Dispatch* because it carried a column by Muhammad.

In 1962 the U.S. District Court of the District of Columbia in *Fulwood v. Clemmer* (206 F. Supp 370) ruled that, by allowing some religious groups to hold religious services and by conducting such services at public expense while denying that right to Muslims, the jail officials had discriminated against the Muslim inmates. These acts violated the "Order of the Commissioners of the District of Columbia No. 6514-B, dated Nov. 25, 1953, which requires prison officials to make facilities available without regard to race or religion."

The court held the same opinion on the distribution and wearing of religious medals. However, on the issue of correspondence and the newspaper subscription, the court stated that the judiciary "lacked general supervisory powers over prisons, and in absence of . . . abuse of discretion by prison officials, courts should not interfere."

In 1972 in *Cruz v. Beto* (405 U.S. 319), Fred A. Cruz, a Buddhist serving in a Texas prison, claimed that while other prisoners were allowed use of the prison chapel, officials refused Buddhists the right to hold religious services. Cruz was placed in solitary confinement on a diet of bread and water for two weeks for sharing religious materials with other prisoners.

The Supreme Court stated that prison officials are "accorded latitude in the administration of prison affairs, and prisoners necessarily are subject to appropriate rules and regulations." However, prisoners have the right to petition the government for "redress of grievances," and the federal courts, while they do not sit to supervise prisons, must "enforce constitutional rights of all 'persons,' including prisoners." The Court concluded that "reasonable opportunities must be afforded to all prisoners to exercise the religious freedom guaranteed by the First and Fourteenth Amendments without fear of penalty."

A five-to-four split Supreme Court in *O'Lone v. Shabazz* (482 U.S. 340, 1987) declared that "state prison officials acted in a reasonable manner" and were not violating First Amendment freedoms when they did not allow inmates who were members of the Islamic faith to attend religious services held on Friday afternoons. "Prison policies were related to legitimate security and rehabilitative concerns, alternative means of exercising religious faith with respect to other practices were available, and placing Islamic prisoners into work groups so as to permit them to exercise religious rights would have adverse impact" on the running of the prison.

In the opinion of the four dissenters, however, when:

> exercise of the asserted right is not presumptively dangerous . . . and where the prison has completely deprived an inmate of that right, then prison officials must show that "a particular restriction is necessary to further an important governmental interest." The prison in this case has completely prevented respondent inmates from attending the central religious service of their Moslem faith.

> The State has neither demonstrated that the restriction is necessary to further an important objective nor proved that less extreme measures may not serve its purpose. . . . If a Catholic prisoner were prevented from attending Mass on Sunday, few would regard that deprivation as anything but absolute, even if the prisoner were afforded other opportunities to pray, to discuss the Catholic faith with others, and even to avoid eating meat on Friday if there were a preference.

Cases in lower courts have also dealt with religious food preferences, the wearing of religious jewelry, religious hairstyles and dress, and compulsory attendance in programs that use religious thematics. For instance, courts have ordered pork-free diets for groups whose religion forbids them from eating pork, although they must make up a significant portion of the inmate population. There are also limits to what a prison administrator is reasonably expected to do. In New York the federal court upheld the prison's refusal to meet the food requirements of Rastafarians, a religion of Jamaican origin (*Benjamin v. Coughlin*, 708 F. Suppl. 570, 1989) because the complex requirements would have burdened the prison administratively and financially. Depending on the sect of the religion, the group wanted no meats, no canned foods or dairy products, no foods grown with inorganic pesticides or fertilizers, and foods cooked in natural materials, such as clay pots.

In 1996 the U.S. 7th Circuit Court of Appeals held that Wisconsin could not prohibit the wearing of religious jewelry (*Sasnett v. Sullivan*, 91 F.3d 1018), according to

the Religious Freedom Restoration Act. Prison officials had claimed that such jewels could be used as weapons but had permitted the use of rosary beads, which, the Circuit held, could be used in strangling others. The state was held to be inconsistent.

The courts themselves can be inconsistent, as well. Michael G. Gallahan, a Cherokee, practiced his religious beliefs, including having worn long hair since the age of five. Tenets of his religion recognize hair as a "sense organ" and taught that loss of hair was equated to losing part of the body. Prison officials had established hair-length regulations because of the belief that long hair was a convenient place for hiding weapons, could obscure facial identification, and could cause sanitary problems.

In *Gallahan v. Hollyfield* (516 F. 2d 1004, 1981) a U.S. District Court in Virginia ruled that "a prisoner is not stripped of all rights on incarceration; specifically he retains those First Amendment rights that are not inconsistent with his status as a prisoner or with the legitimate penological objectives of the corrections system." The judges found that Gallahan "established a sincere belief in his religion" and that the state's reasons were "insufficient" to enforce the hair-length regulation, especially since Gallahan had agreed to wear his hair tied back in a ponytail.

However, in 1992 the appellate court upheld haircut rules in a case involving a Rastafarian hairstyle (*Scott v. Mississippi Department of Corrections*, 961 F. 2d 77) arguing that the "loss of absolute freedom of religious expression is but one sacrifice required by incarceration."

The Sixth Circuit Court of Appeals, in *Abdullah v. Kinnison* (769 F. 2d 345, 1985), ruled that a prison directive requiring practicing Muslims to keep white prayer robes in the institutional chapel rather than in cells was justified by security reasons and did not violate the First Amendment.

In *Rust v. Clarke*, prisoners in the Nebraska prison system who practiced Asatru, an ancient religion of Northern Europe that is sometimes called Wotanism, charged that it was necessary for each of them to have certain items—including a small stone altar, a cauldron, and a drinking horn—in order to practice their religion in prison. They also requested the right to build sacred fires during ceremonial occasions. In 1995 the Eighth Circuit Court ruled against the plaintiffs. According to the National Prison Kindred Alliance, an organization formed to assist Asatru members in prison or recently released, seventeen states have rewritten their policies to accommodate the practice of Asatru in prison.

In 1996 the New York Court of Appeals ruled on *Griffin v. Coughlin* (NY CtApp, No 73), a case involving twelve-step programs. As a precondition to his continued participation in a family reunion program, David Griffin had been required to participate in a substance abuse program modeled after Alcoholics Anonymous (AA), which makes references to "God" and a "Higher Power." He claimed that the requirement to participate in such a program violated his right to practice atheism under the First Amendment. The court ruled that the prison could not compel an inmate to attend a substance abuse program in which references to "God" and a "Higher Power" were made. The court concluded that the program violated the Establishment clause of the Constitution and "the state has exercised coercive power to advance religion by denying benefits of eligibility for the family reunion problem to atheist and agnostic inmates who object and refuse to participate in religious activity."

The dissenters thought that, although the twelve-step program may be perceived as:

> somewhat religious, [it] remains overwhelmingly secular in philosophy, objective, and operation. . . . The inmate was not compelled to participate in the . . . program. He voluntarily chose the course of action that placed his agnosticism and nonbeliefs at risk because he wished to receive something he is not unqualifiably entitled to from the state.

In September 2000 the Religious Land Use and Institutionalized Persons Act was signed into law by President Bill Clinton. The act primarily limits the ability of local governments to use zoning laws against religious institutions. It also asserts the right of prisoners to practice their religion and restricts prison authorities from denying them whatever items they may reasonably need to do so. In October 2004 the U.S. Supreme Court agreed to rule on the constitutionality of the law and to render a decision in the summer of 2005.

## FOURTH AMENDMENT

The Fourth Amendment guarantees the "right of the people to be secure . . . against unreasonable searches and seizures . . . and no warrants shall issue, but upon probable cause." The courts have not been as active in protecting prisoners under the Fourth Amendment as under the First and Eighth Amendments. In *Bell v. Wolfish* (441 U.S. 520, 1979) the U.S. Supreme Court asserted that:

> simply because prison inmates retain certain constitutional rights does not mean that these rights are not subject to restrictions and limitations. . . . Maintaining institutional security and preserving internal order and discipline are essential goals that may require limiting or retraction of the retained constitutional rights of both convicted prisoners and pretrial detainees. Since problems that arise in the day-to-day operation of a corrections facility are not susceptible to easy solutions, prison administrators should be accorded wide-ranging deference in the adoption and execution of policies and

practices that, in their judgment, are needed to preserve internal order and discipline and to maintain institutional security.

Based on this reasoning the Court ruled that body searches did not violate the Fourth Amendment. "Balancing the significant and legitimate security interest of the institution against the inmates' privacy interest, such searches can be conducted on less than probable cause and are not unreasonable."

In another Fourth Amendment case (*Hudson v. Palmer*, 46 U.S. 517, 1984), the Supreme Court upheld the right of prison officials to search a prisoner's cell and seize property.

> The recognition of privacy rights for prisoners in their individual cells simply cannot be reconciled with the concept of incarceration and the needs and objectives of penal institutions. . . . [However, the fact that a prisoner does not have a reasonable expectation of privacy] does not mean he is without a remedy for calculated harassment unrelated to prison needs. Nor does it mean that prison attendants can ride roughshod over inmates' property rights with impunity. The Eighth Amendment always stands as a protection against "cruel and unusual punishments."

### Sexual Misconduct

Sexual misconduct by corrections personnel refers to any type of improper conduct of a sexual nature directed at prisoners. Given the control and power imbalance inherent between a corrections officer and a prison inmate, there is widespread consensus within society that this sort of misconduct should not be tolerated.

In a paper prepared by the General Accounting Office (GAO) (*Women in Prison, Sexual Misconduct by Correctional Staff*, June 1999), a summary of sexual misconduct allegations in the three largest prison jurisdictions—Federal Bureau of Prisons, California, and Texas—is presented. The allegations summarized were those made by female inmates during the period 1995–98. There were 506 such allegations of which 18% (92 cases) were sustained resulting in staff resignations or employment terminations. Officials in these jurisdictions cited lack of evidence as the primary reason why more allegations were not sustained. They reported that most of the allegations involved verbal harassment, improper visual surveillance, improper touching, and/or consensual sex. Allegations involving rape and other forms of forced sexual assault were relatively rare. Generally, however, the jurisdictions studies did not have readily available, comprehensive data on the number, nature, and outcomes of sexual misconduct allegations. As a result, the GAO report highlighted the need for more formalized systems of monitoring, analyzing, and reporting allegations of staff-on-inmate sexual misconduct.

## TABLE 11.1

**Number of facilities covered under the Prison Rape Elimination Act of 2003**

| Facility type | Number of facilities | Sampled for collection in 2004 |
|---|---|---|
| **Total** | 8,727 | 3,269 |
| **Prisons** | | |
| Public—federal | 84 | all[a] |
| Public—state | 1,320 | all[a] |
| Private | 264 | 30 |
| **Local jails** | | |
| Public | 3,318 | 390 |
| Private | 47 | 10 |
| **Juvenile facilities** | | |
| Public | 1,211 | All[a] |
| Private | 2,323 | 194 |
| **Other facilities** | | |
| Indian country jails | 70 | 10 |
| Military-operated | 59 | 10 |
| Bureau of Immigration and Customs Enforcement (ICE)-operated[b] | 31 | 10 |

[a]The administrative records collection will cover all 50 state prison and juvenile systems and the Federal Bureau of Prisons.
[b]Includes facilities operated by or exclusively for the Bureau of Immigration and Customs Enforcement, formerly the U.S. Immigration and Naturalization Service.

SOURCE: "Number of Facilities Covered under the Prison Rape Elimination Act of 2003," in *Data Collections for the Prison Rape Elimination Act of 2003*, Bureau of Justice Statistics, June 30, 2004, http://www.ojp.usdoj.gov/bjs/pub/pdf/dcprea03.pdf (accessed March 30, 2005)

Due to the incidence of sexual misconduct involving correctional staff and inmates, forty-four states, the District of Columbia, and the federal government have passed legislation criminalizing such behavior in a correctional setting. Of the forty-four states that have custodial sexual misconduct laws, thirty-seven have made such behavior a felony. Legal protections also vary from state to state, with nineteen state laws not covering all forms of sexual abuse. In Colorado, Missouri, and Wyoming, correctional staff can still claim inmate consent to avoid prosecution. In *Abuse of Women in Custody: Sexual Misconduct and Shackling of Pregnant Women: A State-by-State Survey of Policies and Practices in the USA* (New York: Amnesty International–USA, 2001), Amnesty International criticized "the continuing lack of laws prohibiting custodial sexual misconduct in some states; the failure of existing laws to provide adequate protection; and the widespread lack of legislation and uniform standards, in policy and practice, to protect incarcerated women in labor from being shackled during child birth."

In response to continuing concerns about sexual misconduct in prisons, President George W. Bush signed into law the Prison Rape Elimination Act in September 2003. As part of this legislation, the Bureau of Justice Statistics is charged with developing a national data collection on the incidence and prevalence of sexual assault within correctional facilities. Few studies have been conducted on the subject, and most of those focused on only a limited number of prisons and prisoners. The new study to be conducted by the Bureau of Justice Statistics will cover all federal and state prisons, all juvenile facilities, and a large sampling of local jails, jails in Indian Country, and military jails. (See Table 11.1.) After this initial survey is conducted and reliable data have been collected, the Department of Justice will create a Review Panel on Prison Rape. This panel will conduct yearly public hearings concerning the operation of the three prisons with the highest incidence of prison rape and the two prisons with the lowest incidence of prison rape within each category of facilities. From the data collected and the annual hearings, policies to address and eliminate prison rape can be developed.

## EIGHTH AMENDMENT

The Eighth Amendment guarantees that "cruel and unusual punishment [not be] inflicted." The Eighth Amendment has been used to challenge the death penalty, three-strikes laws, crowded prisons, lack of health or safety in prisons, and excessive violence by the guards. The Supreme Court has established several tests to determine whether conditions or actions violate the Eighth Amendment:

- Did the actions or conditions offend concepts of "decency and human dignity and precepts of civilization which Americans profess to possess"?

- Was it "disproportionate to the offense"?

- Did it violate "fundamental standards of good conscience and fairness"?

- Was the punishment unnecessarily cruel?

- Did the punishment go beyond legitimate penal purposes?

### Isolation

Several landmark cases changed the way prisoners can be held in isolation. In *Holt v. Sarver* (300 F. Supp 82, 1969) a U.S. District Court in Arkansas found "solitary confinement or close confinement in isolation units of prisons not unconstitutional per se, but, depending on circumstances, it may violate the Eighth and Fourteenth Amendments." Isolation cells in an Arkansas prison were used for prisoners who broke rules, those who needed protective custody to separate them from other inmates, and those who were:

> general escape or security risks or who were awaiting trial on additional charges. . . . Confinement in isolation cells was not "solitary confinement" in the conventional sense of the term. On the contrary, the cells are substantially

overcrowded.... The average number of men confined in a single cell seems to be four, but at times the number has been much higher (up to ten and eleven).

While the judges agreed that "if confinement of that type is to serve any useful purpose, it must be rigorous, uncomfortable, and unpleasant. However, there are limits to the rigor and discomfort of close confinement which a state may not constitutionally exceed."

The court found that the confinement of inmates in these isolation cells, which were "overcrowded, dirty, unsanitary, and pervaded by bad odors from toilets, constituted cruel and unusual punishment." The court also asserted that "prolonged confinement" of numbers of men in the same cell under unsanitary, dangerous conditions was "mentally and emotionally traumatic as well as physically uncomfortable. It is hazardous to health. It is degrading and debasing; it offends modern sensibilities, and, in the Court's estimation, amounts to cruel and unusual punishment."

In addition, those inmates who were not in isolation slept together in barracks where many of the inmates had weapons and attacked each other. While the court recognized that assaults, fights, and killings occurred in all penal institutions, the Arkansas Farm had not taken reasonable precautions. Prisoners should at least be "able to fall asleep at night without fear of having their throats cut before morning, and the state has failed to discharge a constitutional duty in failing to take steps to enable them to do so."

Another landmark case involving isolation occurred in the late 1970s, again in Arkansas. The state sentenced inmates to punitive isolation in extremely small cells for an indeterminate period, with their status being reviewed at the end of each fourteen-day period. While most were released within fourteen days, many remained in that status for weeks or months, depending on their attitudes as appraised by prison personnel. Usually the inmates shared a cell with one other inmate, and at times three or four were together, causing them to sleep on the floor. Considering that these were violent men filled with "frustration and hostility," and that some were "dangerous and psychopaths," confining them together caused threatening situations that produced "a forcible response from prison personnel."

The lower courts found that the force used by the guards was excessive and declared that "confinement of prisoners in punitive isolation for more than thirty days constituted cruel and unusual punishment and was impermissible." In *Finney v. Hutto* (548 F. 2d. 740, 1977) the U.S. Court of Appeals agreed.

## The Death Penalty

Three Supreme Court cases, all decided in the 1970s, have produced the current interpretation of the Eighth Amendment relative to the death penalty. In *Furman v. Georgia* (408 U.S. 238, 1972), the Court held that the death penalty in three cases under review was "cruel and unusual" because under the then prevailing statutes juries had "untrammeled discretion to impose or withhold the death penalty." Due process required procedural fairness, including consideration of the severity of the crime and the circumstances. In the three cases decided in *Furman*, three individuals were condemned to die, two for rape and one for murder. All three of the offenders were black.

In response to *Furman*, states modified their statutes. North Carolina imposed a mandatory death sentence for first-degree murder. This law was tested in the Supreme Court as *Woodson v. North Carolina* (428 U.S. 980, 1976). The Court held that while the death penalty was not cruel and unusual punishment in every circumstance, it ruled that a mandatory death sentence did not satisfy the requirements laid down in *Furman*. The Court said: "North Carolina's mandatory death penalty statute for first-degree murder departs markedly from contemporary standards respecting the imposition of the punishment of death and thus cannot be applied consistently with the Eighth and Fourteenth Amendments' requirement that the State's power to punish 'be exercised within the limits of civilized standards.'" The Court overturned the North Carolina law.

*Woodson* was decided on July 2, 1976. On the same day the Court rendered its judgment in the case of *Gregg v. Georgia*, the case of a man sentenced to death for murder and robbery committed under new legislation passed in Georgia following *Furman*. In this case the Court upheld the death penalty saying, in part:

> The Georgia statutory system under which petitioner was sentenced to death is constitutional. The new procedures on their face satisfy the concerns of *Furman*, since before the death penalty can be imposed there must be specific jury findings as to the circumstances of the crime or the character of the defendant, and the State Supreme Court thereafter reviews the comparability of each death sentence with the sentences imposed on similarly situated defendants to ensure that the sentence of death in a particular case is not disproportionate. Petitioner's contentions that the changes in Georgia's sentencing procedures have not removed the elements of arbitrariness and capriciousness condemned by *Furman* are without merit.

## Death Penalty for Juveniles

In March 2005 the U.S. Supreme Court ruled that the death penalty for minors is cruel and unusual punishment. In a five to four ruling, the court found it unconstitutional to sentence someone to death for a crime they committed under the age of eighteen. The ruling took seventy-three prisoners off death row.

As part of its argument for outlawing the death penalty for minors, the court cited scientific opinion that teenagers are too immature to be held accountable for the crimes they commit in the same way that adults are. Justice Anthony M. Kennedy, speaking for the majority, explained: "From a moral standpoint, it would be misguided to equate the failings of a minor with those of an adult, for a greater possibility exists that a minor's character deficiencies will be reformed."

## Three-Strikes

In 2003 the Supreme Court ruled on the constitutionality of the California three-strikes law, the nation's most severe. The case involved a defendant, Gary Albert Ewing, who had been sentenced to twenty-five years to life for a third offense, the theft of three golf clubs each valued at $399. His previous offenses included (among others) a burglary and a robbery while threatening his victim with a knife. *Ewing v. California* (538 U.S., 2003) was a good test of the California statute because neither one of Ewing's first two offenses were of a seriously violent character and the third, the triggering offense, was what under California law is known as a "wobbler," namely an offense that can be tried, at the prosecutor's option, as either a felony or a misdemeanor.

The petition in *Ewing* argued that the punishment was "cruel and unusual" and disproportionate to the offense committed. In effect Ewing had the profile of a habitual but petty criminal whose theft of golf clubs should have been tried as a misdemeanor. In this case the Court dismissed the proportionality argument and, instead, affirmed the state's right to set policy for the protection of the public. Quoting from another case, the Court said that "The Eighth Amendment does not require strict proportionality between crime and sentence [but] forbids only extreme sentences that are 'grossly disproportionate' to the crime." California had the right to incapacitate repeat offenders by incarcerating them. According to the Court, the Constitution did not mandate that the states apply any one penological theory.

## Prison Conditions and Medical Care

In *Rhodes v. Chapman* (452 U.S. 337, 1981) the Supreme Court ruled that housing prisoners in double cells was not cruel and unusual punishment. The justices maintained that:

> conditions of confinement, as constituting the punishment at issue, must not involve the wanton and unnecessary infliction of pain, nor may they be grossly disproportionate to the severity of the crime warranting imprisonment. But conditions that cannot be said to be cruel and unusual under contemporary standards are not unconstitutional. To the extent such conditions are restrictive and even harsh, they are part of the penalty that criminals pay for their offenses against society.

The Court concluded that the Constitution "does not mandate comfortable prisons," and only those "deprivations denying the 'minimal civilized measure of life's necessities'" violate the Eighth Amendment.

In two later cases as well, the Supreme Court held that unpleasant or inadequate prison conditions and poor medical care did not constitute cruel and unusual punishment unless deliberate indifference by the authorities could be established. The Court established this principle in *Wilson v. Seiter* (501 U.S. 294, 1991) when it upheld the judgment of a lower court that prisoners "claiming that conditions of confinement constituted cruel and unusual punishment were required to show deliberate indifference on the part of prison officials." Wilson "alleged overcrowding, excessive noise, insufficient locker storage space, inadequate heating and cooling, improper ventilation, unclean and inadequate restrooms, unsanitary dining facilities and food preparation, and housing with mentally and physically ill inmates" proved "at best" that the authorities were negligent. However, the Court found that Wilson had insufficient grounds for claiming Eighth Amendment protection.

An earlier case, *Estelle v. Gamble* (429 U.S. 97, 1976) had paved the way for *Wilson*. On November 9, 1973, J. W. Gamble, an inmate of the Texas Department of Corrections, injured his back while performing a prison work assignment. Although he complained numerous times about his injury and received some pills, the guards accused him of malingering. In January the disciplinary committee placed Gamble in solitary confinement for refusing to work. On February 4 he asked to see a doctor for chest pains and blackouts. Almost twelve hours later a medical assistant saw him and had him hospitalized.

The next morning, after an electrocardiogram, he was placed on Quinidine for treatment of irregular cardiac rhythm and moved to administrative segregation. On February 7, after experiencing pain in his chest, left arm, and back, Gamble asked to see a doctor and was refused. The next day he was refused again. After finally seeing the doctor again on February 9 and being given Quinidine, Gamble swore out a complaint that the staff had "subjected him to cruel and unusual punishment in violation of the Eighth Amendment."

In *Estelle v. Gamble*, the Court concluded that deliberate indifference to serious medical needs of prisoners constitutes "unnecessary and wanton infliction of pain," whether the indifference is displayed by prison doctors in their response to the prisoner's need or by prison guards who deny or delay access to treatment or interfere with the treatment. The Court, however, ruled that "every claim by a prisoner that he has not received adequate medical treatment" does not mean a violation of the Eighth Amendment. An "inadvertent failure to provide adequate medical care" is not "an unnecessary and wanton infliction of pain" or "repugnant to the conscience of mankind. . . . Medical malpractice does not become a constitutional violation merely because the victim is a prisoner." Only deliberate indifference "can offend 'evolving standards of decency' in violation of the Eighth Amendment." Because Gamble saw medical personnel seventeen times over three months, the court did not find this a violation of the Eighth Amendment. "A medical decision not to order an X ray or like measures does not represent cruel and unusual punishment."

In another case, *Helling v. McKinney* (509 U.S. 25, 1993), the Court ruled that a Nevada inmate had the right to bring a court action because he had been assigned to a cell with another prisoner who smoked five packs of cigarettes daily, and he had not been informed of the health hazards that he could incur from second-hand smoke. Quoting its earlier decision in *DeShaney v. Winnebago County Dept. of Social Services* (489 U.S. 189, 1989), the Court declared:

> [W]hen the state takes a person into its custody and holds him there against his will, the Constitution imposes upon it a corresponding duty to assume some responsibility for his safety and general well-being. . . . The rationale for this principle is simple enough: when the state by the affirmative exercise of its power so restrains an individual's liberty that it renders him unable to care for himself, and, at the same time fails to provide for his basic human needs—e.g., food, clothing, shelter, medical care, and reasonable safety—it transgresses the substantive limits on state action set by the Eighth Amendment.

The justices asserted that prison administrators could not:

> ignore a condition of confinement that is sure or very likely to cause serious illness and needless suffering the next week or month or year. In *Hutto v. Finney* (437 U.S. 678, 1978) we noted that inmates in punitive isolation were crowded into cells and that some of them had infectious maladies such as hepatitis and venereal disease. This was one of the prison conditions for which the Eighth Amendment required a remedy, even though it was not alleged that the likely harm would occur immediately and even though the possible infection might not affect all of those exposed. . . . Nor can we hold that prison officials may be deliberately indifferent to the exposure of inmates to a serious, communicable disease on the ground that the complaining inmate shows no serious current symptoms.

The Supreme Court sent the case back to the district court for retrial, where McKinney had to prove his allegations to show that the Eighth Amendment was violated and that "society considers the risk that the prisoner complains of to be so grave that it violates contemporary standards of decency to expose anyone unwillingly to such a risk." However, in 1992, the director of the Nevada State Prisons had adopted a smoking policy restricting smoking to specified areas, which made McKinney's case virtually moot (a hypothetical case—only cases involving real injury can be considered by the courts).

## Guards Using Force

In *Whitney v. Albers* (475 U.S. 372, 1986) the Supreme Court ruled that guards, during prison disturbances or riots, must balance the need "to maintain or restore discipline" through force against the risk of injury to inmates. Those situations require prison officials "to act quickly and decisively" and allow guards and administrators leeway in their actions. In *Whitney* a prisoner was shot in the knee during an attempt to rescue a hostage. The Court found that the injury suffered by the prisoner was not cruel and unusual punishment under the circumstances.

In 1983 Keith Hudson, an inmate at the state penitentiary in Angola, Louisiana, argued with Jack McMillian, a guard. McMillian placed the inmate in handcuffs and shackles to take him to the administrative lockdown area. On the way, according to Hudson, McMillian punched him in the mouth, eyes, chest, and stomach. Another guard held him while the supervisor on duty watched. Hudson sued, accusing the guards of cruel and unusual punishment.

A magistrate found that the guards used "force when there was no need to do so," and the supervisor allowed their conduct, thus violating the Eighth Amendment. The Court of Appeals for the Fifth Circuit, however, reversed the decision, ruling that:

> inmates alleging use of excessive force in violation of the Eighth Amendment must prove: (1) significant injury; (2) resulting "directly and only from the use of force that was clearly excessive to the need"; (3) the excessiveness of which was objectively unreasonable; and (4) that the action constituted an unnecessary and wanton infliction of pain.

The court agreed that the use of force was unreasonable and was a clearly excessive and unnecessary infliction of pain. However, the Court of Appeals found against Hudson because his injuries were "minor" and "required no medical attention."

The Supreme Court heard this case in 1992 (*Hudson v. McMillian* (503 U.S. 1)) and disagreed that the inmate had to suffer serious injury before the Eighth Amendment could be invoked. In *Whitney*, the Court argued, the "extent of injury suffered by an inmate is one factor" considered to determine whether the use of force was unnecessary. However, the absence of serious injury, while "relevant . . . does not end" the Eighth Amendment inquiry. The question must be asked whether the force applied was a "good faith effort to maintain or restore discipline, or maliciously and sadistically [applied] to cause harm." Although the Circuit Court termed the blows "minor," the Supreme Court viewed the extent of Hudson's injuries as no basis to dismiss his claims and ruled in Hudson's favor by reversing the Court of Appeals.

## DUE PROCESS COMPLAINTS

The Fifth Amendment provides that no person should be deprived of life, liberty, or property by the federal government "without due process of the law." The Fourteenth Amendment reaffirmed this right and explicitly applied it to the states. Due process complaints brought by prisoners under the Fourteenth and the Fifth Amendments are generally centered on questions of procedural fairness. Most of the time disciplinary action in prison is taken on the word of the guard or the administrator, and the inmate has little opportunity to challenge the charges. Rules are often vague or not formally written out. Disrespect toward a guard tends to be defined by the guards themselves.

The Supreme Court, however, has affirmed that procedural fairness should be used in some institutional decisions. In *Wolff v. McDonnell* (418 U.S. 539, 1974), the Supreme Court declared that a Nebraska law providing for sentences to be shortened for good behavior created a "liberty interest." Thus, if an inmate met the requirements, prison officials could not deprive him of the shortened sentence without due process, according to the Fourteenth Amendment. The Court asserted

> that due process required that prisoners in procedure resulting in loss of good-time or in imposition of solitary confinement be afforded advance written notice of claimed violation, written statement of fact findings, and the right to call witnesses and present documentary evidence where such would not be unduly hazardous to institutional safety or correctional goals. . . .

> A prisoner is not wholly stripped of constitutional protections and though prison disciplinary proceedings do not imply the full panoply of rights due a defendant, such proceedings must be governed by a mutual accommodation between institutional needs and generally applicable constitutional requirements.

> However, the inmate at a procedural hearing does not have a right to have counsel (lawyer, advisor) in the proceedings. Silence at a hearing can be used against the inmate because it is a disciplinary hearing, not a criminal proceeding. If incriminating testimony by an inmate could be used in later criminal proceedings, then he must be offered immunity if forced to testify (*Baxter v. Palmigiano*, 425 U.S. 208, 1975).

At the Metropolitan Correctional Center (MCC), a federally operated short-term custodial facility in New York City designed mainly for pretrial detainees, inmates challenged the constitutionality of the facility's conditions. As this was a pretrial detention center, the challenge was brought under the due process clause of the Fifth Amendment. The District Court and the Court of Appeals found for the inmates, but the Supreme Court disagreed in *Bell v. Wolfish* (441 U.S. 520, 1979). Justice William Rehnquist argued that:

> While confining a given number of people in a given amount of space in such a manner as to cause them to endure genuine deprivations and hardship over an extended period of time might raise serious questions under the Due Process Clause as to whether those conditions amounted to punishment, nothing even approaching such hardship is shown by this record.

> Detainees are required to spend only seven or eight hours in their room, during most or all of which they presumably are sleeping. The rooms provide more than adequate space for sleeping. . . . While "double bunking" may have taxed some of the equipment or particular facilities in certain of the common areas, . . . this does not mean that the conditions at the MCC failed to meet the standards required by the Constitution. Our conclusion in this regard is further buttressed by the detainees' length of stay (most are released in sixty days).

The Court also ruled in *Bell* that the administrator could constitutionally prohibit inmates from receiving books that were not mailed directly from publishers, book clubs, or bookstores, and stop the delivery of packages of food and personal items from outside the institution. The administrator could also have body-cavity searches of inmates following contact visits with persons from the outside and require the detainees to remain outside their rooms during inspection.

## EARLY RELEASE

Two cases decided in the late 1990s pertained to prisons releasing inmates early to relieve overcrowding and then later revoking their release status. Beginning in 1983 the Florida legislature enacted a series of laws authorizing the awarding of early release credits to prison inmates when the state prison population exceeded predetermined levels. In 1986 Kenneth Lynce received a twenty-two-year prison sentence on a charge of attempted murder. In 1992 he was released based on the determination that he had accumulated five different types of early release credits totaling 5,668 days, including 1,860 days of "provisional credits" awarded as a result of prison overcrowding.

Shortly thereafter the state attorney general issued an opinion interpreting a 1992 statute as having retroactively canceled all provisional credits awarded to inmates convicted of murder and attempted murder. Lynce was rearrested and returned to custody. He filed a habeas corpus petition alleging that the retroactive cancellation of provisional credits violated the *ex post facto* ("from a thing done afterward") clause of the Constitution.

The Supreme Court agreed with Lynce. In *Lynce v. Mathis* (65 LW 4131, 1997) the Court ruled that to fall within the *ex post facto* prohibition a law must be "retrospective" and "disadvantage the offender affected by it" (*Weaver v. Graham*, 450 U.S. 24, 29, 1981). The 1992 statute was clearly retrospective and disadvantaged Lynce by increasing his punishment.

The second case concerned Oklahoma's Pre-parole Conditional Supervision Program, which took effect whenever the state prisons became overcrowded and could authorize the conditional release of prisoners before their sentences expired. The Pardon and Parole Board determined who could participate in the program. An inmate was eligible for pre-parole after serving only 15% of a sentence, and was eligible for parole after one-third of the sentence had elapsed.

Ernest Harper was released under the pre-parole program. After he spent five apparently uneventful months outside prison, the governor denied him pre-parole. He was returned to prison without a hearing and on less than five hours' notice.

Despite Harper's claim that his reincarceration deprived him of liberty without due process in violation of the Fourteenth Amendment, the Oklahoma Court of Criminal Appeals and the Federal District Court denied him habeas corpus relief. The corrections department argued that the court had ruled that a hearing was not necessary to transfer a prisoner from a low-security prison to a higher-security one and that was what they were doing in this case.

The Tenth Circuit Court of Appeals, however, held that the pre-parole program was sufficiently like parole and a program participant was entitled to procedural protections. In *Leroy L. Young v. Ernest Eugene Harper* (65 LW 4197, 1997), the Supreme Court upheld the decision of the Tenth Circuit Court. It ruled that Oklahoma had violated Harper's due process rights by sending him back to prison without giving him a hearing to show that he had not met the conditions of the program.

## THE COURT GOES BACK TO BASICS

In 1995 the Supreme Court made it harder for prisoners to bring constitutional suits to challenge due process rights. In a five to four decision in the case of *Sandin v. Conner* (515 U.S. 472), the majority asserted that it was frustrated with the number of due process cases, some of which, it felt, clogged the judiciary with unwarranted complaints such as claiming a "liberty interest" in not being transferred to a cell with an electrical outlet for a TV set.

*Sandin* concerned an inmate in Hawaii who was not allowed to call witnesses at a disciplinary hearing for misconduct that had placed him in solitary for thirty days. The Court of Appeals of the Ninth Circuit had held in 1993 that the inmate, Demont Conner, had a "liberty interest," allowing him a range of procedural protections in remaining free from solitary confinement. The Supreme Court overruled the Court of Appeals, stating that the inmate had no "liberty interest." Due process protections play a role only if the state's action has infringed on some separate, substantive right that the inmate possesses. For example, Wolff's loss of good-time credit was a substantive right that he possessed. The punishment Conner had received "was within the range of confinement to be normally expected" since he was serving thirty years-to-life for a number of crimes, including murder.

"States may create liberty interests which are protected by the due process clause," but these will be limited to actions that "impose atypical and significant hardship on the inmate in relation to the ordinary incidents of prison life." Being put in solitary confinement in a prison where most inmates are limited to their cells most of the day anyway is not a liberty-interest issue. Because there was no liberty interest involved, how the hearing was handled was irrelevant.

Based on this ruling, the Court held that a federal court should consider a complaint to be a potential violation of a prisoner's due process rights only when prison staff imposed "atypical and significant hardship on the inmate." Mismanaged disciplinary hearings or temporary placement in solitary were just "ordinary incidents of prison and life and should not be considered violations of the Constitution."

Chief Justice Rehnquist asserted that past Supreme Court decisions have "led to the involvement of Federal courts in the day-to-day management of prisons, often squandering judicial resources with little offsetting benefit to anyone." Judges should allow prison administrators the flexibility to fine tune the ordinary incidents of prison life.

This decision continues the more conservative trend of the Supreme Court. Before the 1960s prisoners had few rights. A climate of reform beginning in the 1960s brought about a rash of cases that extended prisoners' rights over time. The pendulum has swung back since the 1980s. A more conservative approach has led to more judicial restraint as the courts sought to balance the constitutional rights of the prisoners with the security interests of the correctional administrators.

## THE INNOCENCE PROTECTION ACT

DNA testing has emerged as a powerful tool capable of establishing the innocence of a person in cases where organic matter from the perpetrator of a crime (blood, skin, semen, etc.) has been obtained by law-enforcement officials. This organic matter can be tested against DNA samples taken from an accused, or indeed from a convicted, person. If the two samples do not match then they came from different people and the person being tested is innocent.

The Innocence Protection Act became law in 2004 as part of the Justice for All Act. Introduced in Congress by Senators Patrick Leahy (D-VT), Dorothy Smith (R-OR), and Susan Collins (R-ME) early in 2000 as Senate Bill 486, the Innocence Protection Act represents a potentially important step in the protection of prisoners' rights because it would provide prisoners convicted in capital cases access to post-conviction DNA testing. According to Senator Leahy (Hearing on "Protecting the Innocent: Proposals to Reform the Death Penalty," Senate Judiciary Committee, June 18, 2002) as of mid-2002, 101 persons had been exonerated of a capital crime by the use of post-conviction DNA testing.

# IMPORTANT NAMES
# AND ADDRESSES

**American Bar Association**
321 North Clark St.
Chicago, IL 60610
(312) 988-5000
E-mail: askaba@abanet.org
URL: http://www.abanet.org

**American Civil Liberties Union (ACLU)**
National Prison Project
915 15th St. NW, Suite 620
7th Floor
Washington, DC 20005
(202) 393-4930
FAX: (202) 393-4931
http://www.aclu.org/Prisons/
PrisonsMain.cfm

**American Correctional Association**
4380 Forbes Blvd.
Lanham, MD 20706-4322
(301) 918-1800
FAX: (301) 918-1900
1-800-ACA-JOIN
E-mail: jeffw@aca.org
URL: http://www.aca.org

**American Jail Association**
1135 Professional Court
Hagerstown, MD 21740-5853
(301) 790-3930
E-mail: dorothyd@aja.org
URL: http://www.corrections.com/aja/
index.shtml

**Amnesty International USA**
National Office
5 Penn Plaza, 14th Floor
New York, NY 10001
(212) 807-8400
FAX: (212) 627-1451
E-mail: aimember@aiusa.org
URL: http://www.amnestyusa.org

**Becket Fund for Religious Liberty**
1350 Connecticut Ave. NW
Suite 605

Washington, DC 20036
(202) 955-0095
FAX: (202) 955-0090
E-mail: mail@becketfund.org
URL: http://www.becketfund.org/

**Bureau of Justice Statistics**
810 Seventh St. NW
Washington, DC 20531
(202) 307-0765
E-mail: askbjs@ojp.usboj.gov
URL: http://www.ojp.usdoj.gov/bjs

**Criminal Justice Institute, Inc.**
213 Court St., Suite 606
Middletown, CT 06457
(860) 704-6400
FAX: (860) 704-6420
E-mail: cji@cji-inc.com
URL: http://www.cji-inc.com

**Families Against Mandatory Minimums**
1612 K St. NW, Suite 700
Washington, DC 20006
(202) 822-6700
FAX: (202) 822-6704
E-mail: famm@famm.org
URL: http://www.famm.org/index2.htm

**Federal Bureau of Investigation**
J. Edgar Hoover Bldg.
935 Pennsylvania Ave. NW
Washington, DC 20535-0001
(202) 324-3000
URL: http://www.fbi.gov

**Federal Bureau of Prisons**
320 First St., NW
Washington, DC 20534
(202) 307-3198
E-mail: info@bop.gov
URL: http://www.bop.gov/

**Federal Judicial Center**
Thurgood Marshall Federal Judiciary
Building
1 Columbus Circle NE
Washington, DC 20002-8003
(202) 502-4000
FAX: (202) 502-4099
URL: http://www.fjc.gov/

**Justice Research and Statistics Association**
777 North Capitol St. NE, Suite 801
Washington, DC 20002
(202) 842-9330
FAX: (202) 842-9329
E-mail: cjinfo@jrsa.org
URL: http://www.jrsa.org

**Manhattan Institute for Policy Research**
52 Vanderbilt Ave.
New York, NY 10017
(212) 599-7000
FAX: (212) 599-3494
E-mail: mi@manhattan-institute.org
URL: http://www.manhattan-institute.org/

**NAACP Legal Defense and Educational Fund, Inc.**
99 Hudson St., Suite 1600
New York, NY 10013
(212) 965-2200
E-mail: kshaw@naacpldf.org
URL: http://www.naacpldf.org/

**National Center on Institutions and Alternatives**
7222 Ambassador Rd.
Baltimore, MD 21244
(410) 265-1490
FAX: (410) 597-9656
URL: http://www.ncianet.org

**National Conference of State Legislatures**
7700 East First Pl.
Denver, CO 80230
(303) 364-7700

FAX: (303) 364-7800
URL: http://www.ncsl.org/

**National Correctional Industries Association**
1202 North Charles St.
Baltimore, MD 21201
(410) 230-3972
FAX: (410) 230-3981
info@nationalcia.org
URL: http://www.nationalcia.org/
index2.html

**National Council on Crime and Delinquency**
1970 Broadway, Suite 500
Oakland, CA 94612
(510) 208-0500
FAX: (510) 208-0511
URL: http://www.nccd-crc.org/

**National Criminal Justice Association**
720 Seventh St. NW, Third Floor
Washington, DC 20001-3716
(202) 628-8550
FAX: (202) 628-0080
E-mail: info@ncja.org
URL: http://www.ncja.org/

**National Criminal Justice Reference Service**
P.O. Box 6000
Rockville, MD 20849-6000
(301) 519-5500
FAX: (301) 519-5212
1-800-851-3420
URL: http://www.ncjrs.org/

**National Institute of Corrections**
320 First St. NW
Washington, DC 20534
(202) 307-3106
1-800-995-6423
URL: http://nicic.org/

**National Institute of Justice**
810 Seventh St. NW
Washington, DC 20531
(202) 307-2942
E-mail: asknij@ncjrs.org
URL: http://www.ojp.usdoj.gov/nij/

**National Legal Aid and Defender Association**
1140 Connecticut Ave. NW, Suite 900
Washington, DC 20036
(202) 452-0620
FAX: (202) 872-1031
E-mail: info@nlada.org
URL: http://www.nlada.org/

**National Prison Kindred Alliance**
P.O. Box 6493
Napa, CA 94581
(707) 251-9526
E-mail: coordinator@natpka.org
URL: http://www.natpka.org/

**Office of Juvenile Justice and Delinquency Prevention**
810 Seventh St. NW
Washington, DC 20531

(202) 307-5911
E-mail: askjj@ncjrs.org
URL: http://www.ojjdp.ncjrs.org/

**The Sentencing Project**
514 Tenth St. NW, Suite 1000
Washington, DC 20004
(202) 628-0871
FAX: (202) 628-1091
E-mail: staff@sentencingproject.org
URL: http://www.sentencingproject.org/

**U.S. Parole Commission**
5550 Friendship Blvd., Suite 420
Chevy Chase, MD 20815-7286
(301) 492-5990
FAX: (301) 492-6694
URL: http://www.usdoj.gov/uspc/

**U.S. Sentencing Commission**
1 Columbus Circle NE
Washington, DC 20002-8002
(202) 502-4500
E-mail: pubaffairs@ussc.gov
URL: http://www.ussc.gov/

**Urban Institute**
2100 M St. NW
Washington, DC 20037
(202) 833-7200
E-mail: paffairs@ui.urban.org
URL: http://www.urban.org/

# RESOURCES

The Bureau of Justice Statistics (BJS) of the U.S. Department of Justice is a major source of data and information concerning crime, sentencing, and inmates. *Correctional Populations in the United States, 1998* (2002) summarizes information on inmates in the nation's jails and prisons. Other valuable BJS publications include: *Capital Punishment, 2003* (2004); *Compendium of Federal Justice Statistics, 2002* (2004); *Education and Correctional Population* (2003); *Felony Sentences in State Courts 2002* (2004); *Hepatitis Testing and Treatment in State Prisons* (2004); *HIV in Prisons and Jails 2002* (2004); *Jails in Indian Country, 2002* (2003); *Juveniles in Adult Prisons and Jails: A National Assessment* (2000); *Prison and Jail Inmates at Midyear 2003* (2004); *Prisoners in 2003* (2004); *Probation and Parole in the United States, 2003* (2004); and *Recidivism of Sex Offenders Released from Prison in 1994* (2003). The BJS also produced the *Sourcebook of Criminal Justice Statistics 2002* (2004), with the Hindelang Criminal Justice Research Center, State University of New York, Albany.

The National Institute of Justice (NIJ) researches criminal issues and publishes the *National Institute of Justice Journal,* whose article "Can Telemedicine Reduce Spending and Improve Prisoner Health Care?" (April 1999) was cited in this publication. The NIJ publication *Correctional Boot Camps: Lessons from a Decade of Research* (2003) was also valuable.

The Federal Bureau of Investigation's *Crime in the United States—2003* (2004) provides the latest arrest statistics and crime rates and is an essential resource for those interested in studying crime across the country.

The U.S. government's Office of Juvenile Justice and Delinquency Prevention (OJJDP), an excellent resource on juvenile justice, produced *Juvenile Arrests 2002* (2004); *Juvenile Offenders and Victims: 1999 National Report* (1999); *Juvenile Offenders in Residential Placement: 1997–1999* (2002); *Juvenile Residential Facility Census, 2000: Selected Findings* (2002); and *OJJDP Statistical Briefing Book* (2002).

Information Plus thanks the U.S. Census Bureau for numerous population studies, including *Profile of the Foreign-Born Population in the United States: 2000* (2001) as well as information contained in the *Statistical Abstract of the United States: 2004–05* (2005).

Other sources include: *Emerging Issues on Privatized Prisons*, Bureau of Justice Assistance (2001); *Recidivism Report: Inmates Released from Florida Prisons, July 1995 to June 2001*, Florida Department of Corrections (2003); and *Disease Profile of Texas Prison Inmates*, University of Texas Health Science Center at San Antonio (2002). Information Plus is also thankful for the valuable data presented in the United States Sentencing Commission's publication *2004 Federal Sentencing Guideline Manual* (2004). Also very useful were the data from the Central Intelligence Agency's *World Factbook 2004* published in 2004.

# INDEX

*Page references in italics refer to photographs. References with the letter t following them indicate the presence of a table. The letter f indicates a figure. If more than one table or figure appears on a particular page, the exact item number for the table or figure being referenced is provided.*

## A

*Abdullah v. Kinnison*, 116

Abuse
  past abuse of prisoners, 45
  prior physical or sexual abuse of jail inmates, 46 (*t*5.6)
  sexual misconduct, 117–118

*Abuse of Women in Custody: Sexual Misconduct and Shackling of Pregnant Women: A State-by-State Survey of Policies and Practices in the USA* (Amnesty International), 118

ACA. *See* American Correctional Association

Accreditation, of correctional facilities, 4

Acquired Immune Deficiency Syndrome. *See* Human Immunodeficiency Virus and Acquired Immune Deficiency Syndrome

Adults, prosecution of juveniles as, 59, 63–64

African-Americans
  death penalty, persons under sentence of death, by race, 109 (*f*10.3)
  death penalty rulings and, 108–109, 119
  death row inmates, 109, 110
  death sentence, demographic characteristics of prisoners under sentence of death, 110 (*t*10.8)
  education of prisoners, 44
  executed prisoners, 111
  HIV/AIDS, prisoners with, 52
  jail inmates, 24
  jail inmates, gender, race, Hispanic origin, conviction status of local jail inmates, 24 (*t*3.6)

jail inmates, gender, race of, 24 (*t*3.7)
jail inmates/staff, 28
juvenile arrest rates by offense and race, 65*f*–66*f*
juvenile arrests, 62
juvenile arrests of African-American youths as percentage of all juvenile arrests, 64*t*
juveniles in jail or prison, 65
mental illness, prisoners with, 54
parole violations/rearrest trends, 80
parolees, 79
prisoner characteristics, 41
prisoners, number of sentenced state, federal prisoners per 100,000 residents, by gender, race, Hispanic origin, and age, 42 (*t*5.2)
prisoners, number of state and federal prisoners, by gender, race, Hispanic origin, and age, 42 (*t*5.1)
probationers, 73

Age
  capital punishment, minimum age authorized for, 70*t*
  capital punishment, minimum age for, 109
  death penalty and, 70
  death row inmates, 110–111
  death sentence, age at time of arrest for capital offense, age of prisoners under sentence of death, 111*t*
  HIV/AIDS, prisoners with, 52
  jail population by age/gender, 26 (*t*3.11)
  juvenile court jurisdiction and, 59
  juvenile court jurisdiction in delinquency matters, oldest age for original, 60*t*
  of prisoners, 41
  prisoners, number of sentenced state, federal prisoners per 100,000 residents, by gender, race, Hispanic origin, and age, 42 (*t*5.2)

prisoners, number of state/federal prisoners, by gender, race, Hispanic origin, and age, 42 (*t*5.1)
probation violation by, 74
supervised release violations by, 75

Age of Reason (Enlightenment), 2

Aggravated assault, 65*f*–66*f*

AIDS/HIV. *See* Human Immunodeficiency Virus and Acquired Immune Deficiency Syndrome

Alameda County (CA), 101

Alaska Natives. *See* Native Americans

*Albers, Whitney v.*, 121

Alcohol use
  convicted jail inmates using drugs or alcohol, at time of offense, by characteristics of inmates, 26 (*t*3.10)
  day reporting centers and, 101
  jail inmates, 25
  juvenile arrests for substance abuse, 62
  prior alcohol use of jail inmates, 25 (*t*3.8)
  by prisoners' families, 45–46

Alternative sentencing, 99–102

American Correctional Association (ACA)
  accreditation standards, 4
  *Legal Responsibility and Authority of Correctional Officers*, 113
  *Standards for Adult Correctional Facilities*, 32
  suicide prevention standards, 56

American Indians and Alaska Natives. *See* Native Americans

American Samoa, incarceration in, 104

*Americans Behind Bars* (Edna McConnell Clark Foundation), 99

Amnesty International–USA, 118

Ancient times, punishment in, 1

*Annual Survey of Jails* (Bureau of Justice Statistics), 26–27

Apprentice programs, 100

rated capacity of local jails, percent of capacity occupied, 23 (*t*3.4)

Capital punishment
  death penalty rulings, 108–109
  Innocence Protection Act and, 124
  juveniles and, 70
  minimum age authorized for, 2003, 70*t*
  *See also* Death penalty; Death row

*Capital Punishment 2003* (Bureau of Justice Statistics)
  death row inmates, 110
  executed prisoners, 111
  revision of statutes on, 109

Carlson, Kenneth, 58

CCJ (College of Criminal Justice), 5

Cells, 32

Censorship, 114–115

*Census of Jails, 1999* (Bureau of Justice Statistics), 27–28

*Census of State and Federal Adult Correctional Facilities, 2000* (Bureau of Justice Statistics), 49

*Census of State and Federal Correctional Facilities, 2000* (Bureau of Justice Statistics)
  increase of correctional facilities, 13–14
  prison capacities, 31–32
  private prisons, 37

Central Intelligence Agency (CIA), 103–104

*Chapman, Rhodes v.*, 120

Chen, E., 97

*Chicago Prisoners' Experiences Returning Home* (Urban Institute), 100

*Chicago Tribune*, 109

Child molestation
  recidivism rate for sex offenders, 6
  recidivism rate of child molesters, statutory rapists released from prison in 1994, by type of recidivism measure, time after release, 6 (*t*1.4)

Children
  estimated number of state, federal prisoners with minor children, by gender, 47*t*
  of prisoners, 47
  *See also* Juvenile confinement; Juveniles

CIA (Central Intelligence Agency), 103–104

Cincinnati (OH), 3

Civil Rights Act of 1871, 113

Clark County (WA), 29

*Clarke, Rust v.*, 116

Clemmer, Donald, 115

*Clemmer, Fulwood v.*, 115

Clinton, Bill, 117

CNN.com, 107

Code of Hammurabi, 1

Colburn, Jason, 97

College education, 44

College of Criminal Justice (CCJ), 5

Collins, Susan, 124

Collins, William C., 113

Colonial period, corrections in, 2

Colonies, 2

Columbine High School shooting (Littleton, CO), 59

Commission on Law Enforcement and Administration of Justice, 4

*Commonwealth, Ruffin v.*, 113

Commonwealths, U.S., 103–104, 105*t*

Community-based programs
  alternative sentencing, 99–102
  for juveniles, 7, 60

Community corrections, 4

Community service
  in alternative sentencing programs, 102
  description of, 101
  persons sentenced to, 26

Community supervision
  Native Americans and Alaska Natives under, 105
  number of offenders under, 26
  supervised release, 74–75

*Compendium of Federal Justice Statistics, 2002* (Bureau of Justice Statistics), 74

Conditional release, 123

Conference of State Court Administrators, 99

Confinement
  in medieval times, 1–2
  as punishment, 1
  status of offenders, 26–27
  status of persons under jail supervision, by confinement status, type of program, 27*t*
  *See also* Juvenile confinement

Conner, Demont, 123

*Conner, Sandin v.*, 123

Constitution. *See* U.S. Constitution

Conviction
  characteristics of jail inmates, by conviction status, 45*t*
  felony convictions in state courts, number of, 35 (*t*4.5)
  percent of convicted felons who received prison sentence, 36*f*
  status of adult inmates, 26

Conviction rates, 32

*Cooper v. Pate*, 113

*Correctional Boot Camps: Lessons from a Decade of Research* (U.S. Department of Justice), 70

Correctional staff
  due process complaints and, 122
  guards using force, court cases on, 121–122
  persons under supervision of the federal probation system and authorized probation officers, 79*t*

Prison Rape Elimination Act of 2003, number of facilities covered under, 118*t*
  probation officers, 74
  sexual misconduct by, 117–118

Correctional supervision
  adult correctional populations, 73*f*
  adults on parole, 85*t*
  adults under correctional supervision, by region and jurisdiction, 72*t*
  federal offenders under supervision, by offense, 80*t*–81*t*
  Native Americans and Alaska Natives under, 105–106
  Native Americans under correctional supervision, 106 (*t*10.4)
  parole, 75–77, 79–80
  parole, change in number of adults on, 73 (*t*8.3)
  parole, characteristics of adults on, 84*t*
  parole, characteristics of offenders terminating parole, 87*t*
  parole, outcomes of, by offense, 86 (*t*8.16)
  parole population statistics, 86 (*t*8.15)
  probation, 71, 73–74
  probation, adults on, by region and jurisdiction, 75*t*–76*t*
  probation, change in number of adults on, 73 (*t*8.2)
  probation, characteristics of adults on, 74*t*
  probation, characteristics of offenders terminating probation supervision, 78 (*t*8.8)
  probation/parole, number of persons on, 71
  probation, persons under supervision of federal probation system, authorized probation officers, 79*t*
  probation population statistics, 76 (*t*8.6)
  probation supervision, outcomes of, by offense, 77*t*–78*t*
  supervised release, 74–75
  supervised release, characteristics of offenders terminating, 83 (*t*8.12)
  supervised release, outcomes of, by offense, 82*t*–83*t*

Corrections, 21
  *See also* Expenditures; Jails; Prisons

Corrections Corporation of America, 36–37

Corrections, history of
  ancient times, 1
  colonial/post-revolutionary periods, 2
  community corrections, 4
  justice model, 4–5
  juveniles, 7–8
  medieval times, 1–2
  prison reform in early twentieth century, 3–4

expenditures, state prison expenditures for medical care, food service, and utilities, 17t

incarceration rates of, 9

parole, adults on, 85t

probation, adults on, by region, jurisdiction, 75t–76t

sentenced prisoners under jurisdiction of state or federal correctional authorities, 12t

state, federal prisoners held in private facilities, local jails, by jurisdiction, 19t

Northern Mariana Islands, 104

"Number of Persons in Custody of State Correctional Authorities by Most Serious Offense, 1980–2001" (Bureau of Justice Statistics), 89

# O

O'Connor, Sandra Day, 97

*Offenders Returning to Federal Prison, 1986–97* (Sabol), 6–7, 7t

Offenses

    federal offenders under supervision, by offense, 80t–81t

    federal prisoners by type of offense, 43 (t5.4)

    felony sentence lengths, average, in state courts, by offense, type of sentence, 2002, 94t

    juvenile arrest rate for property crimes, 61 (f7.1)

    juvenile arrest rate for violent crimes, 61 (f7.2)

    juvenile arrest rates by offense and race, 65f–66f

    juvenile arrest rates for assault, weapons, and drug offenses, by gender, 63f–64f

    juveniles in jail or prison and, 64

    parole outcomes, by offense, 86 (t8.16)

    prisoners, by types of crime, 42–43

    probation supervision, outcomes of, by offense, 77t–78t

    sentencing guidelines and, 90–94

    state prison population by offense type, 43f

    supervised release, characteristics of offenders terminating, 83 (t8.12)

    supervised release, outcomes of, by offense, 82t–83t

    three-strikes laws and, 95

Office of Justice Programs

    juvenile boot camps, 70

    *Juveniles in Adult Prisons and Jails*, 64–65

Office of Juvenile Justice and Delinquency Prevention (OJJDP)

    juvenile arrests, 62

    juvenile boot camps study, 68–69

    juvenile court jurisdiction, 59

    juvenile laws, changes to, 60

    juveniles in residential facilities, 65–67

    laws for juvenile offenders, 7–8

Office of Management and Budget, 10

Office of the Attorney General, California Department of Justice, 97

Ohio, apprentice programs in, 100

OJJDP. *See* Office of Juvenile Justice and Delinquency Prevention

*OJJDP Statistical Briefing Book* (Office of Juvenile Justice and Delinquency Prevention)

    juvenile arrests, 62

    juvenile court jurisdiction, 59

Oklahoma, boot camp in, 100

Oklahoma Court of Criminal Appeals, 123

Oklahoma Pre-parole Conditional Supervision Program, 123

*O'Lone v. Shabazz*, 116

"Order of the Commissioners of the District of Columbia No. 6514-B," 115

# P

Pacific Islander Americans. *See* Asian and Pacific Islander Americans

Palla, Seri, 71

*Palmer, Hudson v.*, 117

Parole

    adult correctional populations, 73f

    adults on, 85t

    adults under correctional supervision, by region and jurisdiction, 72t

    change in number of adults on, 73 (t8.3)

    characteristics of adults on, 84t

    characteristics of offenders terminating parole, 87t

    federal offenders under supervision, by offense, 80t–81t

    geographical distribution, 79

    justice model and, 4

    Native Americans and Alaska Natives on, 105

    number of persons on, 71

    outcomes of, by offense, 86 (t8.16)

    parole population statistics, 86 (t8.15)

    parolees, characteristics of, 77, 79

    pre-parole program, 123

    three-strikes laws and, 97

    trends in, 75–77

    truth-in-sentencing and, 90

    violation/rearrest trends, 79–80

Parole board

    discretion of, 89

    discretionary parole and, 75, 77

    truth-in-sentencing and, 90

Parole officers, 79

Parolees

    adults on parole, 85t

    characteristics of, 77, 79

characteristics of offenders terminating parole, 87t

definition of, 71

geographical distribution of, 79

parole population statistics, 86 (t8.15)

parole violation, prison population growth and, 35

three-strikes laws and, 97

violation/rearrest trends, 79–80

*Pate, Cooper v.*, 113

Payroll, justice system, 18 (t2.10)

*Pell v. Procunier*, 114–115

Penitentiaries, 2

Penitentiary Act of 1779, 2

Penn, William, 2

Pennsylvania

    criminal code of, 2

    death row inmates in, 110

    system of, 3

Pentonville Penitentiary (London, England), 2

Petersilia, Joan, 4–5

Philadelphia (PA), 3

Philadelphia Society for Alleviating the Miseries of Public Prisons, 3

Physical abuse

    prior physical or sexual abuse of jail inmates, 46 (t5.6)

    of prisoners, 45

PIECP (Prison Industry Enhancement Certification Program), 38, 39

Pisciotta, Alexander W., 100

Police protection

    expenditure for justice activities, by level of government, justice activity, 10(t2.2)

    expenditure, total and per capita justice expenditure across government and by function, 10(t2.1)

    expenditures on, 9, 11

    juveniles taken into police custody, percent distribution of, 67t

Population. *See* Prison population; Special facilities/populations

Post-revolutionary period, corrections in, 2

Pre-parole program, 123

"President Issues Military Order" (The White House), 108

*Prior Abuse Reported by Inmates and Probationers* (Bureau of Justice Statistics), 45

*Prison and Jail Inmates at Midyear 2003* (Bureau of Justice Statistics)

    findings of, 11

    jail inmate characteristics, 24

    jail jurisdictions, 23

    jail occupancy as percent of capacity, 24 (t3.5)

    juveniles in jail, 26